S0-CGR-601

SAN FRANCISCO LIBRARY

3 1223 014 178

CONDITION NOTED

DATE DUE			
JUL 1 7 1997			
APR 2 3 1998			
FEB 1 0 2000			
FEB 2 2 2000			

HIGHSMITH #45230

Printed in USA

THE
CONQUEST
OF MICHOACÁN

THE
CONQUEST
OF MICHOACÁN

THE SPANISH DOMINATION OF THE
TARASCAN KINGDOM IN WESTERN MEXICO, 1521-1530

By J. Benedict Warren

UNIVERSITY OF OKLAHOMA PRESS : NORMAN

By J. Benedict Warren

Vasco de Quiroga and His Pueblo-Hospitals of Santa Fe (Washington, D.C., 1963; Spanish version, Morelia, Michoacán, 1977).
La conquista de Michoacán (Morelia, Michoacán, 1977)
Hans P. Kraus Collection of Hispanic American Manuscripts: A Guide (Washington, D.C., 1974).
La administración de los negocios de un encomendero en Michoacán (Morelia, Michoacán 1984).

972.02,W253c
Warren, J. Benedict.
The conquest of
Michoac_an.

Library of Congress Cataloging in Publication Data

Warren, J. Benedict.
    The conquest of Michoacán.

    Bibliography: p. 327
    Includes index.
    1. Michoacán de Ocampo (Mexico)—History. 2. Mexico—History—Conquest, 1519-1540. 3. Tarasco Indians—History. 4. Indians of Mexico—Michoacán de Ocampo—History. I. Title. II. Title: Tarascan Kingdom in Western Mexico, 1521-1530.
F1306.W37 1984   972'.02'0924   84-40280
ISBN 0-8061-1858-X

The paper in this book meets the guidelines for permanence and durability of the Committee on Production Guidelines for Book Longevity of the Council on Library Resources, Inc.

Copyright © 1985 by the University of Oklahoma Press, Norman, Publishing Division of the University. Manufactured in the U.S.A. First edition.

S.F. PUBLIC LIBRARY

3 1223 01477 9178

To

*the late
Dr. France V. Scholes,
who supplied the idea*

and

*Patricia, my wife,
who contributed the continuing encouragement
and inspiration*

Contents

Illustrations

Preface

THE Spanish conquest and domination of Michoacán, in western Mexico, brought a rich, powerful, and independent Indian kingdom into the realm of Spanish control. It was also an important initial step in the expansion of Spain's control west and north of the regions that had been dominated by the Aztecs. Nuño de Guzmán used Michoacán as a forward provisioning base for his expedition of conquest into New Galicia, and from this latter outpost Francisco Vázquez de Coronado led his great exploratory expedition into Arizona, New Mexico, and the western plains in the early 1540s.

In pre-Spanish times the region of Michoacán constituted a separate Indian kingdom, second in importance among Indian realms of Mesoamerica only to the Aztec empire dominated by the Triple Alliance of Tenochtitlan, Texcoco, and Tlacopan (or Tacuba). The dominant people of Michoacán, later designated by the name Tarascans, spoke a language that was unrelated to the other linguistic groups of Mesoamerica. They migrated into central Michoacán at various times before the Spanish conquest and spread through the mountains, valleys, and lake districts that characterize the region, settling in towns and villages. During the fifteenth century they were brought under a united political control by a line of aggressive chieftains, who established their capital on the eastern shores of Lake Pátzcuaro, first in Pátzcuaro and later in Tzintzuntzan (the city of Michoacán). The native title for the rulers or kings of this united realm of Michoacán, as recorded in the Spanish sources of the early sixteenth century, was Cazonci.

During the decades immediately preceding the Spanish conquest, the rulers of the Aztec empire launched attacks on the eastern frontier of Michoacán, which the Tarascans successfully repelled. But the crushing defeat of the Aztecs by the combined Spanish and Indian forces under command of Fernando Cortés, followed soon afterward by the arrival of the first few Spanish soldiers in Michoacán, constituted an increasingly serious threat to the Tarascan state. In the face of this crisis the ruling Cazonci, young, newly invested, and unsteady on the throne, accepted Spanish suzerainty rather than risk sharing the fate of Tenochtitlan and its monarch. Later, as further evidence of his submission, he accepted Christian baptism and brought Franciscan missionaries into Michoacán.

The Cazonci's actions were inspired not only by recognition of the superior military power of the Spaniards and some superstitions regarding their supposed supernatural origin but also by the thought that he would retain for himself and his kingdom some measure of autonomy within the framework of the new empire that he could see Cortés and his captains forging in Mesoamerica. Yet the subsequent history of Michoacán during the 1520s, which saw the introduction of the encomienda, the ruthless exploitation of the human and natural resources of the province by Spanish colonists and fortune hunters, and the repeated demands for treasure made on the Cazonci by Spanish officials, proved that his hope was ill-founded. In the late 1520s many Spanish lives were lost in Michoacán, and severe repressive measures were taken against the natives. In this rapidly worsening situation, one mitigating factor was the presence of the Franciscan friars, who brought to Michoacán the uplifting force of the Christian Gospel.

The position of the Cazonci during these years has generally been described by historians as that of a pitiable object of cruel oppression, finally sacrificed to the greed of Nuño de Guzmán. But the colonial sources that are now available give some evidence that the native king did not honestly fulfill the obligations that he had assumed by his acceptance of Spanish sovereignty and the Christian faith.

There can be little doubt that the coming of the Spaniards wrought havoc with the traditional norms of life and society in the Tarascan kingdom and that social stability was reestablished only during the forceful episcopacy of Vasco de Quiroga, often described as the true founder of colonial Michoacán. The humanitarian policies of this prelate, who was the dominant paternal figure in the Spanish province for a period of nearly thirty years (1538-65), left an imprint on Michoacán that perdures to the present time.

The period covered by the body of this work falls between two very significant dates in the early history of Spanish influence in Michoacán: February 23, 1521, when the first Spanish soldier appeared on the borders of Michoacán, and February 14, 1530, when the Cazonci Tzintzicha Tangaxoan, the last native king of the Tarascans, was executed. The dates signify, respectively, the birth of the new era and the death of the old. They mark off a period of transition during which the new Spanish culture and its representatives became dominant over the native way of life. I use the word "Conquest" in the title of the book in a broad sense, indicating not a strictly military conquest but rather the whole process of Spanish domination.

The introductory chapter presents the pre-Spanish ethnological picture in Michoacán. It depends largely on secondary sources with some gleanings from manuscript materials, and makes no claim at being a complete treatment. It is intended merely to set the scene for later developments and to serve as an explanation for some of the post-Conquest occurrences.

Chapters 2 to 4 discuss the first exploratory contacts between the Spaniards and the Tarascans, the aborted military occupation under Cristóbal de Olid, and the census of towns made by Antonio de Caravajal in preparation for the distribution of the encomiendas.

The book then proceeds in three directions, as we study the religious, political, and economic domination of the area. Chapter 5 traces the efforts of the Spanish clergy and laymen to eliminate the native religion and substitute Christianity for it. Chapters 6 to 8 follow the course of the turbulent Spanish politics in New Spain from 1524 through 1529 and the effects of that turmoil upon the Cazonci and his kingdom in Michoacán. Chapters 9 and 10 treat of the economic exploitation of the region by means of the encomiendas and the mines.

The final drama, in which all the forces of the conquest conspired to destroy the Cazonci, is presented in chapter 11.

This work has been in preparation for a long time. I wish to acknowledge the debts of gratitude that I owe to many individuals and institutions for their help along the way.

First, I owe the greatest debt to the late France V. Scholes, Professor Emeritus of the University of New Mexico, who first suggested the idea, supplied copies of many basic documents, and gave guidance for locating many other documentary sources.

To the Fathers of the Academy of American Franciscan History, near Washington, D.C., I wish to express my indebtedness for enabling me to travel to Spain for research in 1961, while I was a member of that institute.

A postdoctoral fellowship at the John Carter Brown Library, Providence, Rhode Island, enabled me to spend two months researching in that fine collection. Two grants for summer research from the General Research Board of the University of Maryland and a year's sabbatical leave from the same university gave me opportunities to complete my research in Mexico and to finish writing the book.

The directors and staffs of various archives and libraries have been very helpful to me, notably those of the Archivo General de Indias, Seville; the Archivo General de la Nación, Mexico City; the Hispanic Division (formerly the Hispanic Foundation) and the Manuscript Division of the Library of Congress, Washington, D.C.; and the John Carter Brown Library, Providence, Rhode Island.

I wish also to thank Vicenta Cortés Alonso, Inspector General of Archives in Spain, who has helped me at many stages of the work; the Reverend Francisco Miranda Godínez, of the Colegio de Michoacán, for sharing his ideas regarding the *Relación de Michoacán* and for assistance regarding the place-names; Richard Greenleaf, of Tulane University, for supplying me with a transcript of the Inquisition trial of Gonzalo Gómez; Donald E. Chipman, of North Texas State University, for very helpful information regarding the career of Nuño de Guzmán; Rosemary Mudd, who found important published materials for me; and Fidel Ramírez Aguirre and Salvador Ramírez Lara, of Fímax publicistas, Morelia, Michoacán, who demonstrated their continuing support for the study of the history of Michoacán by publishing an earlier version of this work in Spanish and who kindly gave permission for the publication of this English-language version.

Special thanks are due Agustín García Álcaraz, who was pastor of San Andrés Ziróndaro when this book was in its final phase of preparation and who drew upon his training as a linguist and anthropologist to provide me with many valuable insights; and to my wife, Patricia, whose long-term knowledge of Michoacán and love for its people has been the source of invaluable advice and encouragement.

The Spanish version of this work was published in Morelia, Michoacán, in 1977. In preparing the English version, I have introduced a number of changes. In the first chapter, on pre-Spanish Tarascan culture, I have tried to incorporate the results of more recent anthropological studies, and I want to thank Helen Perlstein Pollard, of the

State University of New York at Plattsburgh, for her advice in regard to these revisions. I have moved the summary of the data from the Caravajal visitation from chapter 4 to appendix A, and, since that left the chapter very abbreviated, I have incorporated into it the material on the initial distribution of encomiendas that appeared at the beginning of chapter 6 in the Spanish version. Similarly, I have transferred the listings of encomenderos and encomiendas and most of the supporting material from chapter 9 to appendix B and have combined the remainder of chapter 9 with chapter 10. I have also brought together some material on the *estancia* into a new section in chapter 10, to bring out more clearly some evidence of a relationship with the origins of the hacienda. There did not seem to be any need to include here the fairly long documentary appendices that appeared in the Spanish version. I hope that these revisions result in a book that is both useful and interesting to English-language readers.

J. BENEDICT WARREN

College Park, Maryland

THE
CONQUEST
OF MICHOACÁN

Michoacán at the time of the Spanish conquest.

MEXICO

Guadalajara
Mexico City
MICHOACAN
Guadalajara

Gulf of Mexico

Pacific Ocean

- - - Tarascan kingdom at the time of the Spanish conquest (estimated)
——— Present state of Michoacán

0   25   50 miles

N

20°
19°

101°

Lerma River

Maravatío
Acámbaro
Ucareo
Taimeo
Zinapécuaro
Tarímbaro
Indaparapeo
Tajimaroa
LAKE YURIRIA
Yuriapúndaro
Cuitzeo
LAKE CUITZEO
Araro
Charo
Guayangareo (Morelia)
Chucándiro
Chiquimitio
Undameo
Tzintzuntzan
Tiripetío
LAKE PATZCUARO
Erongaricuaro
Pátzcuaro
Tacámbaro

Tuzantla
Cutzio
Cutzamala R.
Cutzamala
Balsas R.
Ajuchitlan
Coyuca
Pungarabato
Guayameo
Guayameo

Puruándiro
Huaniqueo
Zacapu
Naranja
Teremendo
Comanja
Capula
Tlazazalca
Chilchota
Jacona
Tarecuato
Tinguindin
Peribán
Uruapan
Tancítaro
Apatzingán
Arimao
Tepalcatepec
Tepalcatepec River
Sinagua
La Huacana
Urapa
Turicato
Churumuco
Balsas River
Zacatula

MICHOACAN
MOTIN

Sahuayo
Guaracha
Jiquilpan
LAKE CHAPALA
Cuitzeo
Cocula
Zacoalco
Techaluta
Teocuitatlán
Amacueca
Tepec
Atoyac
Mazamitla
LAKE SAYULA
Sayula
Zapotlán
Tamazula
Tuxpan
Jilotlán
Coalcomán
Coalcoman R.
Nexpa River
Coahuayana River
Colima
Armería River

PACIFIC
OCEAN
PACIFIC Ocean

103°   102°   101°   100°

20°
19°
18°

104°   103°   102°

•••

Michoacán on the Eve of the Spanish Conquest

TARASCAN government and life at the time of the first Spanish contacts would have a lasting impact on the relationships between the two cultures. We will look at salient aspects here, not to provide an exhaustive ethnological study but to form for ourselves a basic picture of the Tarascan empire and its culture, especially emphasizing those elements that played an important part in the post-Conquest adjustment.

At the time of the Spanish conquest the Tarascan empire had roughly the same extent as the present Mexican state of Michoacán. Its eastern limit, bordering the realm of the Aztecs, was practically the same as the modern boundary between the states of Michoacán and México. Don Antonio Huitziméngari, the son of the last king of Michoacán, claimed that his father had maintained a garrison near Toluca, but there is little evidence to support his contention, beyond the rather noncommittal answers of his witnesses.[1] To the south the Tarascans controlled both sides of the Río Balsas as far east as Ajuchitlán, where the Tarascan king maintained a strong garrison against the Mexicans.[2] The mouth of the Río Balsas was controlled by the lord of Zacatula and constituted part of the Mexican empire.[3] The Tarascans apparently had only a small colony on the Pacific Coast of the present state. The "Relaciones de los Motines" (1580) speak of an immigrant colony at Epatlán, on the coast, who had come from the Tarascan area and warred with the people of the Tlatica Valley. It is not certain, however, whether they could be considered part of the Tarascan empire.[4] Of the provinces that were certainly subject to the Tarascan monarch, the one closest to the Pacific Coast was Coalcomán.[5]

To the west the Tarascan realm included a large corner of the present

3

state of Jalisco. Tamazula, Tuxpan, and Zapotlán (present-day Ciudad Guzmán) were tributaries to the Tarascans, and Zapotitlán was for at least a time subject to them.[6] The inclusion of the Pueblos de Ávalos— Sayula, Atoyac, Teocuitatlán, Techaluta, Zacoalco, and Cocula—as part of Michocacán in Juan de Ortega's tribute assessment of 1528 suggests that they were also Tarascan dominions.[7]

On the north the Tarascans controlled the southeastern portion of the present state of Guanajuato. Yuriria and Acámbaro were subject to them, and Acámbaro included in its jurisdiction an area extending as far north as Apaseo and as far east as Coronèo.[8] This control effectively blocked the advance of the Aztecs along the valley of the Río Lerma. Also subject to Acámbaro were colonies of Otomis and Chichimecas, who were ruled by their own lords and gave service on the frontier as their tribute to the Tarascan king. They carried on warfare with the Indians of Jocotitlán, who faced them along the frontier.[9]

Pablo de Beaumont, an eighteenth-century Franciscan historian, depending ultimately upon a document drawn up by Don Constantino Huitziméngari in 1594, indicated that the boundaries of the Tarascan empire extended northwest to include the present states of Jalisco and Nayarit and the southern end of Sinaloa. He also projected an arm of the empire into Querétaro and Guanajuato as far north as Xichu.[10] The anthropologist José Corona Núñez cites the *Codex Plancarte* to support his contention that at one time the Tarascan kingdom included a large part of northwestern Mexico and even extended as far as Zuñi, in New Mexico. He bases his argument on the similarity between the place-name Zibulan, which appears in the codex, and Cíbola, another name for Zuñi.[11] It is interesting to note in this context that there appears to be some linguistic connection between the Tarascan and Zuñian languages.[12] Whatever may be the validity of these estimates of the earlier extent of the Tarascan empire of Michoacán, its bounds at the time of the Conquest seem to have exceeded only slightly those of the present-day state.

The name Michoacán is probably Nahuatl in origin, signifying "the place of the fish." It refers to the great number of fish found in the lakes of the Michoacán plateau.[13] Other ideas regarding its derivation have been presented but have not won widespread acceptance. Eduard Seler, for example, proposed that it might have come from the Nahuatl word *chalchimmichuacan*, which in Aztec mythology was associated with the west.[14] There is also a possibility that it may be derived from the Tarascan word *michamacuan,* meaning "to be near the water," but this derivation also has attracted little support.[15]

At the time of the Conquest the capital city of Michoacán was Tzintzuntzan, situated on the south shore of the northern arm of Lake Pátzcuaro. To the Aztecs it was known as Uitzitzilan, and the latter name is commonly found in the Spanish documents of the early sixteenth century, generally spelled Uchichila or some variant of that form. Both the Tarascan and the Nahuatl names mean "the place of the hummingbird." The name came from the hummingbirds of the region, prized for their feathers, which were used in making pictures.[16] As the sixteenth-century Franciscan linguist Juan Baptista de Lagunas puts it in his grammar of the Tarascan language:

But Cintzuntza, which the natives call and consider the court and capital of the province, signifies the place of some tiny birds, from the feathers of which they make rich images. And in Mexico they call them Vitzitzilin. And thus all of the natives do not call the province and language anything but the province and language of Cintzuntza.[17]

Apparently Tzintzuntzan had been the capital of Michoacán for a relatively short time before the arrival of the Spaniards, though it is not clear just when the center of government was established there. In 1538, when Vasco de Quiroga was requesting permission to move the seat of his bishopric from Tzintzuntzan to Pátzcuaro, he had testimony taken to the effect that Tzintzuntzan had been made the Tarascan capital only during the reign of Zuangua, the father of the king who was in power at the time of the Conquest, Tzintzicha Tangaxoan. Previously, according to the document, the seat of government had been Pátzcuaro, where the king and many of the prominent nobles continued to maintain their principal dwellings and to carry on many of their important religious ceremonies.[18] Helen Perlstein Pollard's studies of the archaeology of Tzintzuntzan suggest, however, that such a short period of preeminence of the city would compress the archeological evidence into too short a period and that it would be more realistic to think that the city probably became the capital of the empire under Tzitzispandácuare, the expansionist grandfather of the king who was ruling when the Spaniards arrived.[19] Perhaps the difference in time is more apparent than real. Quiroga stated that the king forced the nobility to move to Tzintzuntzan because the valley belonged to him and it was his barrio.[20] We can assume, then, that it had belonged to his father, Tzitzispandácuare, who had probably concentrated the wealth and population there. Zuangua may later have compelled the civil and religious nobility of Pátzcuaro to move there also.

By the time of the Conquest, Tzintzuntzan had developed into a true urban center with a diversified population of 25,000 to 35,000.[21] The population of the Lake Pátzcuaro basin had probably outgrown the basin's capacity to produce adequate food to support it and was forced to import food from surrounding areas to meet its needs.[22]

The ruling tribe in Michoacán at the time of the Conquest was a rather mysterious group; we know neither their origin nor their name for themselves. The name that we apply to them, Tarascans, is derived from their word *tarascue*, which means "son-in-law" or "father-in-law"; this, at least, is the most commonly accepted derivation. The *Relación de Michoacán* and the "Relación de Pátzcuaro" assert that use of this name began when the Spaniards first came to Michoacán and were given the daughters of some caciques.[23]

Lagunas and the "Relación de Cuitzeo" indicate that the name was first used during the heat of a battle of the Conquest. Lagunas gives the following explanation in his definition of the Tarascan word:

Tarhascue. My father-in-law, or mother-in-law, or son-in-law, or daughter-in-law. And from this it came about that the province of Michoacán was called Tarascan, because when the Spaniards entered the province, the first person whom they met among the natives, seeking his son-in-law (fearing lest perhaps they had killed him), was shouting in this way, calling him and saying, "Tarhascue, tarhascue." Then the Spaniards, not understanding the language, said that they were called Tarascos.[24]

Father Bernardino de Sahagún, the famed sixteenth-century Franciscan writer on Aztec life and customs, suggested that the name Tarascan was derived from the name of a native god called Taras.[25] A sixteenth-century dictionary of the Tarascan language (the last part of which is preserved in the John Carter Brown Library, Providence, Rhode Island) lends some support to Sahagún's statement, with the following sequence of words:

Thares. Idol.
Tharesquatani, tucupacha arirahpeni. To adore idols.

Thares vandatzequareni.   To make prayer to the idols.
Thares vandatzequaretehpeni.   To cause a prayer to be made to the idols.[26]

Thus there may be some validity to Sahagún's theory of the derivation of the name. Nevertheless, the derivation given in the *Relación de Michoacán*, which is Tarascan in origin and dates from less than twenty years after the Conquest, seems to be more trustworthy.

The nearest approach that we have to a native name for this people is Purépecha. The "Relación de Cuitzeo" maintains that this was their name for themselves and their language and that it signified "working men."[27] This meaning suggests that the name referred only to the lower class, though it seems to be a fairly common practice among tribal groups to refer to themselves by a word that means "the people."

The art historian Manuel Toussaint found in the *Relación de Michoacán* four names that he considered possible native names for the tribe: Eneami, Tzacapurhireti, Vacuxecha, and Vanacaze, or Vacanaze. He suggested that Vacanaze, more correctly written Huacanace, was the most adequate of them.[28]

The origin of the Tarascans is even more difficult to determine than is their true name. Their own tradition, as preserved in the *Relación de Michoacán*, does not take them back even to the era of their arrival in Michoacán. Several theories about their racial origins have been proposed by early as well as modern writers; most of them present the Tarascans as having a common origin with the Aztecs. Typical of the early explanations is the following, which Juan de Tovar, a sixteenth-century Jesuit, gave in his *Historia de la venida de los indios a poblar a México de las partes remotas de Occidente . . . (History of the Arrival of the Indians to Settle in Mexico from Remote Parts of the West . . .).* In this passage he is telling of the progress of the Aztecs in their wanderings before they reached the Valley of Mexico:

The second thing that they did was plant grain and other seeds that they use for their sustenance, whether grown by irrigation or by rain; and they did this with such indifference that, if their god considered it good that they should harvest it, they harvested it; and if he did not, when he commanded them to break camp, it all remained there for seed and for the support of the sick, the old men and women, and the people who grew tired, whom they left as they went along wherever they settled, so that the whole land might be populated by them, for this was their principal purpose. Pursuing their journey in this manner, they finally came out in the province called Michoacán, that is, "the land of those who have fish," because of the great amount of fish there. They found there beautiful lakes and a pleasant climate. Since this place pleased them very much, the priests consulted the god Vitzilopochtli about whether this was not the land that he had promised them, or whether he would at least be pleased that it should be populated by them. The idol answered them in dreams that the matter that they were asking would be pleasing to him and that the manner of doing it would be that as soon as everyone, both men and women, who would go in to bathe in a lake which is in a place there called Pátzcuaro, had entered the water, notice should be given to those who remained on shore that they should steal the clothing of the others, and, without the others knowing of it, they should break camp. And thus it was done. Those who were bathing did not notice the deceit because of the pleasure of the bathing, and when they came out and found themselves despoiled of their clothing, and thus deceived and abandoned by others, they were very deeply offended. And in order to disown the others in everything, they purposely changed their dress and language, and in this way they made themselves different from their Mexican nation.[29]

Explanations such as Tovar's, however, founder against the nature of the Tarascan language, which is in no way affiliated with Nahuatl, the language of the Aztecs, and is generally placed in a family by itself among Mexican languages. It has phonetic resemblances to some South American languages, but the establishment of a clear relationship has been difficult. A similarity has also been found between some of the implements used in Michoacán and those used in Peru, although in general the ethnographic characteristics of the Tarascans are closer to those of the Chichimec peoples of the north.[30]

The possibility of an immigration of Indians from the south by way of the sea is supported by a statement of the royal accountant, Rodrigo de Albornoz, in a letter that he wrote to the king of Spain in 1525. He said that, according to the Indians of Zacatula, at the mouth of the Río Balsas, their fathers and grandfathers had told them that from time to time Indians had come to that coast from certain islands on the south in large dugout canoes, bringing excellent things to trade and taking other things from the land. Sometimes, when the sea was running high, those who came stayed for five or six months until good weather returned, the seas became calm, and they could go back.[31]

The archaeology of the Tarascan area has not been adequately explored to show what light it may eventually throw on the question of Tarascan immigration into Michoacán. At present, then, we can say little about the background of the Tarascans other than that they constituted a linguistic island among the Mexican Indians but had absorbed much of the Mesoamerican cultural pattern.

The Tarascans were not the only Indian group in Michoacán at the time of the Spanish conquest. The Matlatzincas, or Pirindas, were an Otomian group who had come from the Valley of Toluca during the late 1400s and had been settled in various places in Michoacán by Tzitzispandácuare. They were excellent warriors and contributed greatly to the power of the Tarascan king. At the time of the Conquest they still formed a frontier guard for the kingdom.[32]

There was also a group of Nahua-speaking Indians in the central area of Michoacán around Lake Pátzcuaro. In 1556, Don Andrés, *principal* of the barrio of Ihuatzio, testified that five of the twenty-three barrios that had been subject to Tzintzuntzan were "of *naguatatos* of the Mexican language."[33] In 1573 several witnesses referred to these Nahua speakers of the Pátzcuaro area as *naguales* or *tecos*.[34] There is some evidence that the Tecos were the original inhabitants of the region and that the late-coming Tarascans fused with them.[35] It appears to have been from among them that the Tarascan king drew his interpreters for his dealings with the Aztecs and later with the Spaniards. Some of these *naguatatos* became very influential during the early period of Spanish colonization.[36]

When the Spaniards arrived, the head of the Tarascan state was a monarch known by the title Cazonci or, to use the Nahuatlized spelling, Caltzontzin.[37] Again we encounter disagreement in regard to the interpretation of the origin and meaning of the term. Nearly all sources maintain that it is of Nahuatl origin. There is an old tradition, found even in the "Relación de Pátzcuaro" (1581), which gives the derivation of the title as coming from the Nahuatl word *caccoli*, meaning "old cactle" ("sandal"). The title is said to have been given to the Tarascan ruler by the Aztecs in derision when he first came to visit Cortés in Mexico dressed in humble clothes to show his respect for the Conqueror.[38] But it seems contrary to good sense that the Tarascans would have adopted a name of derision for their king to the extent that it appears throughout the pages of the *Relación de Michoacán*, written less than twenty years after the Conquest. Moreover, the *Relación* uses the title Cazonci in the speech of an embassy of Mexicans who were speaking to Zuangua, the father of the monarch who went to Mexico to submit to Cortés.[39]

Alonso de la Rea, a seventeenth-century Franciscan chronicler of Michoacán, states that the name arose from the fact that only the king of Michoacán could wear sandals in the presence of the Mexican monarch whereas all the tributary kings had to remove their sandals in his presence.[40]

Corona Núñez interprets the name from an entirely different point of view, though still from a Nahuatl base. Rejecting the "old-sandal" interpretations, he breaks the title into three Nahuatl elements: *calli*, meaning "house"; *tzontli*, meaning "four hundred," or "innumerable"; and *tzin*, a reverential diminutive suffix somewhat equivalent to "lord." According to his interpretation, then, the title means "lord of innumerable houses or towns."[41]

Another interpretation of the title, based on a Tarascan derivation, was proposed by Maurice Swadish. He took it from the Tarascan word *kats-o-n-tsi*, meaning "shaven," from which he interpreted the title to mean "he with the shaven head." Shagún indicated that in ancient times the Tarascans shaved their heads and that they had been known by a name that meant "people with the shaven heads." Swadish's derivation of the title Cazonci would apply this designation to the monarch in a preeminent manner.[42] This interpretation not only has the advantage of being derived from a Tarascan root but also is closer to the way the title was generally written during the first years after the Conquest: Cazonci.

There is some disagreement about whether the Cazonci was the king by inheritance or by election. Don Antonio Huitziméngari, son of the last Cazonci, claimed that the kingship had come down by inheritance through the eldest sons of the family for more than seven hundred years.[43] Yet the *Relación de Michoacán* says that Tangaxoan was elected as his father's successor.[44] Perhaps the solution to this seeming contradiction is given elsewhere in the *Relación*, where it indicates that an aging Cazonci would choose one of his sons as his heir and would gradually induct him into the affairs of government. After the death of the old Cazonci the choice of his successor would be formally approved by a council of nobles and officials.[45] This suggests that the office was hereditary within the family of the king but did not always fall to the eldest son.

At the time of the Conquest the Cazonci was an absolute monarch, aided by a group of appointed officials who were always subject to his will. His office, however, was fundamentally a religious one. The religion of the Tarascans centered around the adoration of the god Curi-caueri, whose name is interpreted as meaning Great Bonfire and who was identified with the sun.[46] The principal service rendered to this god was the burning of a perpetual fire in the temples, especially in that of Tzintzuntzan. The Cazonci was considered to be a representative of Curicaueri. His principal duties were to conquer land in the name of Curicaueri and see to it that the fires in the temples were supplied with wood. In the words of the *Relación*:

It has been said in the first part, in speaking of the history of the god Curi-caueri, how the gods of heaven told him that he had to be king and that he had to conquer the whole earth and that there would have to be one who would be in his place, whose duty it would be to command that wood be brought for the temples, and so forth. So, this people said that he who was Cazonci was in the place of Curicaueri.[47]

The Cazonci was also one of the *axamencha*, members of the priestly hierarchy whose function it was to extract the hearts of the human sacrificial victims and offer them to the gods.[48]

At the time when the Spaniards arrived in Michoacán, the Cazonci was the head of a united empire that had been forged from several chieftainships by his grandfather Tzitzispandácuare. During the latter's reign both the Aztecs and the Tarascans were in a period of expansion. The Aztecs became aware of the strong nation to their west and sent a powerful force to overcome them and capture prisoners for sacrifice. The force was disastrously defeated, and Tzitzispandácuare pushed the war into the Valley of Toluca but was himself defeated there. The Mexicans attacked Michoacán again during the reign of Zuangua, son of Tzitzispandácuare, but their forces, under the Tlaxcaltecan Tlahuicole, were soundly beaten. The Mexicans made one more determined effort to destroy Tarascan independence, but they were again driven back with great loss of life.[49] Father la Rea noted that still at his time (1639) the bones of the dead from one of these battles could be seen in the old frontier region between Maravatío and Zitácuaro.[50]

Thus by the time of the Conquest a tradition of enmity and warfare had developed between the Mexican and Tarascan states, and the Tarascan empire remained the strongest area of resistance against Mexican domination. The Cazonci carried a bow and arrow as the symbols of his leadership and authority over this warlike nation.[51]

The structure of the Tarascan government is well described in the *Relación de Michoacán*:

[The Cazonci] had his governor and a captain general in the wars, and [the latter] was outfitted like the Cazonci himself. He had four very outstanding lords placed on the four frontiers of the province. And his kingdom was divided into four parts. In all the towns he had caciques whom he placed there by his own authority, and they were in charge of having the wood brought for the *cúes* (temples) with the people whom each had in his town and of going to the conquests with his warriors. There were others called *achaecha*, who were chiefs, who accompanied the Cazonci continually and formed his retinue; likewise, most of the time, the caciques of the province were with the Cazonci. They called these caciques *caracha-capacha*. There are others, called *ocanbecha*, who have charge of counting the people and of making them gather together for the public works and the collecting of the tributes. Each of them has a barrio entrusted to him.[52]

The *Relación* lists many other minor officials who extended the civil and military administration of the Cazonci throughout the empire or who oversaw the various guilds of workers, such as the builders, the hunters, the fishermen, and the messengers. The offices were hereditary in the family that held them and were passed on to either a son or a brother as the Cazonci decreed.[53]

The duties of the Cazonci's household were taken care of by a special group of women:

All the service of his household was by women, and he did not employ anyone in his house except women, and he had one who was set over all the others, called *yreri*, and she was more familiar to him than were the others and was like the mistress over the others and like his natural wife. He had within his house many ladies, daughters of the chief nobles, in an enclosure, who did not go out except on feasts to dance with the Cazonci. These made the offerings of blankets and bread for their god Curicaueri. The people said that these were the wives of Curicaueri. From them the Cazonci had many children, and many of these women were his relatives; and afterward he married some of these women to some of his chief nobles. All of these women had the duties of his household divided among themselves.[54]

The *Relación* lists the household offices in detail. The "women of the Cazonci" appear a number of times in the historical documents, and

Clay pipe and other ceramic vessels. Torres Collection, Casa de Cultura, Morelia.

perhaps it was from among them that Tarascan girls were selected to be given to the first Spanish visitors.

The principal religious duty of the Tarascans, as has been mentioned, was the burning of a perpetual fire in the temples in honor of Curicaueri. The god was served by five priests, the chief of whom was known as *curi-htsit-acha*, or "the lord who is in charge of the fire."[55] Smoke was considered to have special religious significance, since it was viewed as the only contact between man on earth and the gods of heaven. Pellets of tobacco were thrown into the sacred fire to give the smoke a pleasant fragrance for the divinity. But only the lords and priests, as representatives of the divinity, were allowed to smoke this herb of the gods, for which rite they used long-stemmed clay pipes.

One office of the women who belonged to Curicaueri was to weave

Anthropomorphic pipe. Torres Collection,
Casa de Cultura, Morelia.

rich blankets and make bread, which were burned in honor of the god. Another offering to the fire was blood, especially human blood. The Tarascans, like the Aztecs, followed the practice of drawing blood from some part of the body, particularly the ears, to offer to the diety.

Because of their great veneration for fire the Tarascans considered that one who was struck by lightning was deified. And the body of the dead Cazonci, the representative of the god of fire, was committed to the flames rather than buried in the earth.[56] That may be the reason why all fire was extinguished in the city for five days after the burning of the Cazonci's body.[57]

The Tarascans also practiced human sacrifice, though it does not seem to have been as extensive as it was among the Aztecs. Death by such means was thought to be as glorious as death in battle, or more so. Most of the victims were prisoners of war. They were considered to have taken on the personality of Curita-caheri, the messenger of the

Ceramic incense burners. Torres Collection, Casa de Cultura, Morelia.

gods, and were reverenced as such. Before the sacrifice the victims were made drunk almost to a state of insensibility and were then led to the temple. There they were held on the stone of sacrifice, while their hearts were cut out and offered to the sun. The office of cutting out the heart was reserved to the Cazonci and certain higher nobles. The head of the victim was put in a place set aside for this purpose, and the rest of the body was given over to ceremonial cannibalism.[58] In time of war, when a town was captured, the old people, the wounded, and the children were sacrificed at the place of capture, while the other prisoners were taken back with the army to be sacrificed or enslaved.[59]

In conjunction with the feast called Sicuindiro the priests danced in the flayed skins of the sacrificial victims. At this feast the hearts of the victims were thrown into the thermal springs at Araró, near Zina pécuaro, from which the goddess Cuerauáperi was said to produce the clouds.[60] Her cult shows similarities to that of two Aztec gods, Tlaloc and Xipe Totec. Like Tlaloc she was venerated as the source of the clouds and rain; like Xipe Totec she was an agricultural goddess, the source of seeds and harvests, who was honored with human sacrifices and dances of priests dressed in the skins of the sacrificial victims. Apparently she was regarded as a kind of earth mother, or fertility goddess, since her name signifies "she who causes to be born."[61]

Besides Curicaueri and Cuerauáperi the Tarascans venerated a great number of other deities—gods of heaven, gods of earth, and gods of the underworld. A special cult was directed to Xaratanga, an agricultural goddess. Her cult seems to have been very ancient on the island of Jarácuaro, in Lake Pátzcuaro. Cuerauáperi and Xaratanga were identified with the old and the new moon, respectively.[62]

The temples of the Tarascans were known as *yácatas*. At the time of the Conquest the great fivefold *yácata* at Tzintzuntzan was the center of the cult of Curicaueri. This structure consisted of a rectangular platform, measuring 425 meters by 250 meters, on top of which were five pyramids, each consisting of a rectangular section with a round section jutting out from the front. The rectangular sections were joined to one another at the base of their sides.[63]

Another important center of religious cult was Zacapu, where Curicaueri was revered under the name Querenda-Angapeti, signifying "the stone that is in the temple."[64] The Cazonci and the lords of Michoacán carried the first fruits there to offer them to the idol. The priest of the temple was shown the greatest reverence by the Cazonci and his lords.[65]

The hierarchy of the priesthood was independent from that of the civil government, though closely allied to it. The high priest, known as the Petámuti, lived in Tzintzuntzan and had authority over all the priests. He also exercised the office of judge in the name of Cazonci. To quote the *Relación* once more:

There was a high priest over all the priests, called Petámuti, whom they held in great reverence. It has already been said how this priest was accoutered, that is, that he put on a gourd set with turquoises [on his back], and he had a lance with a flint point and other finery; and there were many other priests who had this duty, called *curitiecha*, who were like preachers, and they performed the ceremonies, and they all had their gourds on their backs, and

Platform of the yácatas, Tzintzuntzan, looking southwest.

they said that they had all of the people on their back. These went through the province to see to it that wood was brought, as has already been said. In each *cu*, or temple, there was its high priest, like a bishop, set up over the other priests. They called all of these priests *cura*, which means "grandfather"; and they were all married; and these offices came to them by reason of their lineage. And they knew the history of their gods and their feasts.[66]

Besides these priests of the higher rank, the *Relación* also tells of several other ranks of priests who had specific offices to perform in the religious ceremonies. They are depicted in one of the illustrations of the *Relación*.[67]

A number of social customs of the Tarascans later proved to be very troublesome to the friars in their missionary work. Polygyny was the common practice of kings and nobles, and probably of all other men

Burros grazing where hearts were offered. The yácatas, Tzintzuntzan, looking north-east.

who could afford to support several wives. Marriages within close degrees of consanguinity and affinity were also allowed by custom. Marriage of a man with his sisters-in-law was common, and a man could also marry his mother-in-law or stepdaughter.[68] Father Juan Focher, a sixteenth-century Franciscan missionary, reported that marriage was forbidden within the first degree of blood relationship, that is, father to daughter, mother to son, or brother to sister, although it seemed that half brothers and half sisters could sometimes marry. It was not allowed for a man to marry his maternal aunt, but apparently a niece could marry an uncle on either side of the family. Focher indicated that it was difficult to arrive at a conclusive opinion regarding these matters because of the contradictory statements made

The yácatas, Tzintzuntzan, looking southwest.

by the Indians and because they sometimes violated their own social customs.[69]

Homosexuality was not uncommon among them. Antón Caicedo, who was Cortés' *mayordomo* in Michoacán during most of the 1520s, made the following statement about the traffic in homosexual prostitution (all testimony in judicial cases in the Spanish system at this time was recorded by a notary [*escribano*] and was presented in the third person; for example "The witness said that he . . ."):

This witness has been in many markets and *tianguez* [marketplaces] of that province, and before this sin of sodomy was punished, this witness knew many times that, when he asked the Indians why they made sacrifices and idolotries and sodomies, they told him that in the markets there were sodomitic Indians who were accustomed to do this and who carried it on as a business and for

Obsidian mask. Torres Collection, Casa de Cultura, Morelia.

profit and who had it as their trade to be sodomites and to be in the aforesaid marketplaces and to do that sin and abomination with the Indians who paid them for it; and frequently a Spanish interpreter pointed out to this witness in the marketplaces some of the Indians who it was said carried on and practiced this sodomy; this Spaniard was named Juan, and later the Indians of Michoacán killed him.[70]

They frequently indulged in drunkenness, especially at times of ceremonies and festivals. The principal inebriants were pulque, a wine fermented from the sap of the maguey plant, and a beer made from maize. A special royal official, the *atari*, was in charge of the maguey wine used in the feasts.[71] The Tarascans also made use of a fairly extensive list of hallucinogenic plants. Besides hallucinogenic mushrooms, datura, and peyote, which were widely used in Mesoamerica, they also utilized some local plants, *etzcuaiutzcua, thiumeezcua,* and *umbacucua.*[72] This may be the explanation for some of the visionary experiences related in the *Relación.*

In regard to the material expressions of their culture, the Tarascans did not develop as elaborate an architecture as did the Aztecs and the Mayas, but their sculpture and ceramics were among the most interesting in Mesoamerica.[73] They had evolved a kind of guild system in the

Alabaster bowl. Torres Collection, Casa de Cultura, Morelia.

crafts, each craft being under the authority of an overseer subject to the Cazonci.[74] They were particularly able in the decorative arts. Their paintings and figures made from feathers were valued as trade items even in Tenochtitlán. In this regard Bartolomé de las Casas commented: "The artisans who exceed all others of New Spain in this art are those of the province of Michoacán."[75] The lacquering of wooden vessels and gourds, which has continued as a folk art into modern times, had its beginnings in the pre-Conquest period, as is seen in the decoration of the symbolic gourds of the high priests and in some painted gourds that were sent as a gift to Cortés. The extent of their development of physical ornamentation can be judged from the paintings in the *Relación de Michoacán*, the fine lip plugs and ear plugs that can be seen in the museums in Morelia, and the list of items that the Cazonci sent as his first gifts to the Spanish king.[76]

The treasures of gold and silver taken from the Tarascans by the Spanish conquerors were the accumulation of generations, mainly offerings made to the gods by the kings. The plateau of Michoacán proper, a young volcanic region, was not rich in precious metals. The sources of metallic wealth lay principally west and south of the central area of Michoacán. There, where the edge of the plateau was broken by deep-cut gorges, the veins of ore were revealed in the older rocks.

Shaping a copper pot in Santa Clara del Cobre.

The metals were also deposited in the subsoil and stream beds, where they could be obtained by panning.[77]

Copper was an important metal for the Tarascans, who used it to make their metal tools. In Spanish times they mined copper at Guaraxo, in the area of La Guacana; at Cholomoco in the jurisdiction of Sinagua; and at Cocian, a subject town of Turicato. Their method of smelting was to put the ore and charcoal together in a large bowl and blow on the lighted charcoal through hollow canes until they developed enough heat to melt the copper. This method of smelting is shown pictorially in the *Relación de Michoacán*.[78]

This brief, selective introduction to the Tarascans and their way of life should be of help in understanding the account that follows.

CHAPTER 2

The Coming of the First Spaniards, 1521-1522

AMONG the Tarascans, as among the Aztecs, there were recorded a number of omens that presaged the Spanish conquest. Several of them were reported in the *Relación de Michoacán*: during the four years before the Conquest the temples had seemed to be mysteriously falling apart; two great comets had appeared in the heavens; a priest had dreamed that he saw the Spaniards coming on their horses; and a concubine of the lord of Ucareo had reportedly witnessed a great meeting of the gods in which they told her that the time of their reign was nearly at an end and that they would soon be driven out.[1] A Jesuit writer of a later period told the story of an aged pagan priest in Erongarícuaro, on Lake Pátzcuaro, who had predicted that someone would soon come to teach the people the truth about what they should believe and adore. He had exhorted them to be on the watch for these messengers of the truth, and he had even instituted certain feasts that were similar to Christmas and Easter. The Jesuit had heard this story from some elderly men who claimed to have assisted the native priest in his sacrifices.[2]

The first notification of the arrival of the Spaniards in Mexico came with the appearance of an Aztec embassy in Michoacán seeking the aid of the Tarascan king in a common effort against the invaders. For this event, as for many others in the early history of Michoacán, the colonial sources record conflicting versions.

The Franciscan historian Jerónimo de Mendieta, writing in the last quarter of the sixteenth century, stated that Moctezuma sent messengers to the Cazonci when the Spaniards were first insisting on coming to Tenochtitlan.[3] This would imply that the Aztec embassy was dispatched to Michoacán as early as October, 1519. Pablo de Beaumont,

Ominous signs and visions forewarning of the coming of the Spaniards, as depicted in the Relación de Michoacán, Codice del Escorial. *Reproduced from* The Chronicles of Michoacán, *trans. and ed. Eugene R. Craine and Reginald C. Reindorp (Norman: University of Oklahoma Press, 1970).*

who compiled his *Crónica de Michoacán* in the eighteenth century, also related that, before the arrival of Cortés in Tenochtitlan, Moctezuma proposed that the Tarascans should unite forces with the Aztecs against the invaders and their Tlaxcalan allies. To this appeal the Tarascan king made a favorable response, but he apparently did so only after the Spaniards had entered the Aztec capital. Subsequently he received reports about the military prowess of the invaders with their horses and firearms. This seemed to confirm the portents as well as native traditions that had predicted the coming of men from the east who would establish dominion over Mexico. He decided that it would be futile to offer resistance to the Spaniards, and he found excuses for withholding the aid that he had promised to the Aztecs. Beaumont states, probably with justice, that the Cazonci was also inspired by a secret desire to see his Aztec enemies destroyed and that he hoped a policy of neutrality would be rewarded by the conquerors.[4]

Diego Muñoz, a Franciscan chronicler of Michoacán who was writing at about the time of Mendieta, tells us that in 1520 Moctezuma sent an embassy to the Tarascan king Sihuanga (Zuangua) of Michoacán, asking for peace and an alliance against the Spaniards. Instead of complying, the Tarascan king ordered the ambassadors killed. A few days later the king himself died, as we shall see below.[5]

The earliest, and also the most detailed, version of the proposals for an Aztec-Tarascan alliance against the Spaniards is found in the *Relación de Michoacán*, compiled in 1540–41, but this account presents some problems of interpretation. The text records the appearance of an Aztec embassy on the borders of Michoacán, where the men were detained and held in the fortress town of Tajimaroa until King Zuangua ordered them to be conducted safely to his presence. They brought gifts: turquoise and jade, ornaments of green feathers, shields of precious metals, and beautiful clothing.[6] The ambassadors spoke with wonder of the strange new men who had come riding on "deer" which wore shoes of a harder metal than any the Indians had seen before. The new arrivals also had something that sounded like thunder and killed anything that it struck. The Aztecs had fought a battle with the strangers, killing two hundred mounted men and two hundred foot soldiers. Now, however, the invaders, with the aid of Tlaxcalans, had the city surrounded and isolated. The ambassadors asked the Tarascan king to send one of his sons with warriors to help them drive off the Spaniards.[7]

The description that the *Relación* gives of the situation in Tenochtitlan, surrounded and isolated after a great battle in which many Spaniards had lost their lives, could refer only to the period of siege of the city during the summer of 1521. This conclusion is supported by the statement that after the Aztec embassy returned to Mexico the Tarascans captured three Otomis, who reported that the Mexicans were destroyed and that the entire city was stinking with dead bodies.[8]

Aztec ambassadors requesting the Cazonci Zuangua's support against the Spanish invaders, painting from the Relación de Michoacán. *Note the Spanish shield, crossbow, and sword that they brought as gifts. From* Códice del Escorial. *Reproduced from* The Chronicles of Michoacán, *trans. and ed. Craine and Reindorp.*

On the other hand, a date in the summer of 1520 is suggested by a statement of the Aztec ambassadors that the Spaniards were in Tlaxcala at that time.[9] A fact to keep in mind in this confusion is that the *Relación* sometimes telescopes a series of similar events and presents them as one incident; it is possible that in this narrative the history of several embassies has been consolidated into one.

The *Relación* goes on to say that King Zuangua was deeply suspicious of possible trickery by these traditional enemies of Michoacán, especially since he had not previously heard of the new people. He was disturbed by the report, however, and sent four of his Nahuatl-speaking interpreters back with the Aztecs to learn whether they were telling the truth.[10] Don Juan, later Tarascan governor of Erongarícuaro, was present at the interview. In 1553 he testified that on this occasion the king had commanded his messengers to tell the Aztec ruler to do whatever he wished in his own realm, since the Aztecs considered themselves strong, but that if the Spaniards should come to Michoacán the king of Michoacán would know what to do about it.[11]

After a time the Tarascan messengers returned. They told of having been taken to Tenochtitlan, where Moctezuma tried to convince them that they should join him in annihilating the Spaniards. They had been taken to a hill near Texcoco from which they were given a view of the Spanish forces, and the Aztec leaders had mapped out a plan by which the Spaniards could be caught between their two forces. The messengers returned to Zuangua with many gifts from the Mexicans and gave their report. But the old king was still suspicious of his traditional enemies, fearing that his men might be sold to the invaders and killed. He attributed the misfortunes of the Aztecs to the fact that they merely sang songs to their gods, instead of carrying wood to their temples to keep the fires burning.[12]

But the Spaniards had brought with them a more deadly killer than their military weapons: smallpox. In the late spring of 1520, Pánfilo de Narváez arrived on the coast of Mexico with a large force of Spaniards, intending to take over the leadership of the Conquest from Cortés. The latter was able to dominate Narváez and incorporate most of the men into his own army. Nevertheless, even with these reinforcements the Spaniards were soon disastrously expelled from Tenochtitlan on the famous "Noche Triste" (June 30, 1520), with the loss of many men. But a black slave who came with the army of Narváez was sick with smallpox, and the disease spread rapidly among the natives, who had no resistance to it and did not know how to treat it.[13]

The plague appeared in Michoacán soon after Zuangua's messengers returned, probably carried by them, and it soon killed off not only the chief priest and many of the nobles but also the king himself.[14] The *Codex Plancarte* places the death of King "Tziuangua" (Zuangua) in the year 1519.[15] But since he died of smallpox, his death must have occurred during or after the smallpox epidemic in Mexico in the summer and fall of 1520.

The Cazonci Zuangua was survived by four sons, Tzintzicha Tangaxoan, Tirimarasco, Azinche, and Cuini. The elders of the realm chose the oldest, Tzintzicha, to succeed his father. Not long after his selection his brothers were accused before him of being too free with his women and of plotting to take over the kingdom. On the advice of a war chief named Timas, Tzintzicha had them all killed.[16]

At some time during this period of upheaval a new embassy of ten Aztecs appeared on the scene to beg for Tarascan aid. The new king would not listen to them but ordered them to be sacrificed so that they might carry their message to his father, to whom they had been sent.[17] Father La Rea wrote that a defense agreement was actually reached between the Aztecs and the Tarascans during Tzintzicha's reign, but none of the earlier sources lends any support to his statement.[18]

The first actual contact between the Spaniards and the Tarascans occurred in the Tarascan frontier fortress of Tajimaroa on February 23, 1521. As the *Relación* tells it, "And news arrived that a Spaniard had come and that he had gotten as far as Tajimaroa, on a white horse, and it was the feast of Purecoraqua on the twenty-third of February, and he was in Tajimaroa for two days and returned to Mexico."[19] Although Sauer dates this visit in 1522,[20] it must have taken place in 1521. As we shall see shortly, some of Cortés' men had already visited the Cazonci and returned by November 18, 1521.

The Spanish sources tell of two visits to the frontier towns of Michoacán by Spanish soldiers soon after the conquest of Tenochtitlan, which fell to the Spaniards in mid-August, 1521. The chronicler Cervantes de Salazar describes the adventure of a soldier named Porrillas, who had gained the favor of the Indians and was sent out by Cortés to obtain turkeys to feed the army. When Antonio de Herrera copied this section from Cervantes de Salazar, he changed the soldier's name to Parrillas, and it is by this name that he has come to be known in the literature.[21] The soldier was accompanied by some friendly Indians of Matalcingo, who took him little by little toward the borders of Michoacán, within which were many people of their own tribe. The town of Matalcingo in Michoacán (now known by its Tarascan name, Charo) was composed of Indians of this group, and they also formed a number of other towns in the area of present-day Morelia. They were an Otomian people, known as Matlatzincas or Perindas, who had sought refuge in Michoacán from the Aztecs.[22]

The Spaniard was much admired by these frontier people of Michoacán, who inspected him very carefully, even feeling him with their hands, as something unlike anything they had ever seen before. They came to the conclusion that many men like him would be able to conquer even greater cities than Mexico City. By signs and interpreters they asked him many things, and he on his part inquired about the land of Michoacán, its people, and its gold and silver. When he returned to Mexico, he took with him some pieces of worked silver and two of the natives. Cortés was happy to receive the information about the new area, and he had the Indians treated well. To impress them with Spanish power, he had his men take them to see the army, with its horses, arms, and artillery. The horsemen staged a mock battle, and the soldiers shot off their firearms, all of which caused great admiration among the Indians. Finally Cortés sent them back to Michoacán with some gifts and a message for their king. His message to the Cazonci was, in brief, that the Spaniards were as strong in defending their friends as in fighting their enemies and that he wished to come to their nation to show them their errors, especially in their adoration of false gods and their human sacrifices. He offered to send along some Aztecs as an escort for the Tarascans' return journey, but the Tarascans, still distrustful of their ancient enemies, asked for an escort of Tlaxcalans. Upon reaching their homeland, they gave the Cazonci a report of all that they had seen and heard, and because of this the Cazonci decided to send ambassadors to Cortés.[23]

Another, or perhaps the same, visit to the frontier towns of Michoacán is recorded by the brothers Juan de Herrera and Pedro Hernández in their *probanza de méritos y servicios*, made in 1541. The *probanza* was a kind of judicial inquiry which many of the conquerors initiated to prove their services to the crown in hopes of getting some form of recompense. It began with the presentation of an interrogatory in which the interested party stated his services to the crown in a series of formal questions; he then brought forward witnesses, who gave sworn testimony before a justice regarding what they knew about the questions. From the third question of the interrogatory of Herrera and Hernández and from the depositions of Juan de Nájara, Andrés de Trozas, and Diego Hernández, we gather that Juan de Herrera, together with Juan Francés and a certain Porras, all of whom were soldiers in the camp of Pedro de Alvarado in Tacuba, left the camp soon after the surrender of Tenochtitlan. Although they had no previous knowledge of Michoacán, they went in that direction and entered the Tarascan kingdom. After a few days, when their friends had already given them up for dead, they returned to camp, bringing along some Indian *principales* and some provisions for the army. They took the Indians to Coyoacán, where Cortés, the captain-general, was residing, and the Indians rendered obedience to him as the representative of the Spanish king.[24]

The many similarities between this narrative and the previous one suggest that they may be reports of the same incident. There is the similarity between the names Porras and Porrillas, as well as the absence of a Christian name in either story. Each episode was supposedly the first Spanish entry into Michoacán, the Spaniards brought back provisions for the army, and a group of Tarascan *principales* accompanied them to render obedience to Cortés. On the other hand, to identify them with the first contact mentioned in the *Relación* would be more difficult, since that occurred in February, while these events took place after the fall of Tenochtitlan on August 13. Neither incident is mentioned in the letters of Cortés, perhaps because he did not consider them very significant or perhaps because the men were from the camp of Pedro de Alvarado.

It is probably at this juncture, however, that we must place Cortés' first mention of contact with Michoacán, which he included in his "Third Letter of Relation." He wrote that, when knowledge of the conquest of Tenochtitlan and of the destruction of the city had reached the lord of a great province known as Michoacán, the lord, either from fear or because it pleased him, sent messengers to Cortés. They carried the message that their lord wished him well and proposed to live in friendship with him. Cortés answered that, provided they would become vassals of the emperor, he did not wish to make war on them and that they had done well in coming to him.[25] Diego Hernández Nieto, one of the conquerors who testified in favor of the Cazonci's son in 1553, asserted that the embassy went to visit Cortés only a few days after the fall of Tenochtitlan.[26] They stayed with Cortés for four days and were given a military show calculated to impress them with the Spaniards' strength.[27]

During their stay Cortés asked them whether the Spaniards could reach the South Sea (Pacific Ocean) by passing through their country. They answered that it was possible, and Cortés proposed to send two Spaniards with them to report on their province and the sea. The Indians, however, told him that, although they would be glad to take the Spaniards with them, they could not go to the sea because the route passed through the land of a great lord with whom they were at war.[28]

Cortés sent some of his men to Michoacán with the native embassy on the return trip, but there is some disagreement about their number. Both Cortés and his biographer Francisco López de Gómara state that there were two Spaniards but do not give the names of either of them.[29] In 1553, Hernández Nieto testified that Antonio Caicedo, with two other Spaniards, was sent into Michoacán by Cortés before Cristóbal de Olid went there; the rest of his statement fits very well with Cortés' description of the outcome of his first embassy to the Cazonci.[30] The *Relación de Michoacán* also indicates that there were three Spaniards in the first group who actually reached the capital city of Michoacán.[31] Perhaps the solution is that only two Spaniards went by command of Cortés and that another joined the party unofficially. A number of authors who follow Cervantes de Salazar's rather fanciful account, as copied by Herrera, identify this first expedition to Tzintzuntzan with that of Francisco Montaño, but that does not appear to be correct. The Montaño question will be considered later.

During the autumn of 1521, Caicedo and his companions made their way with the Tarascans across the mountains to Tzintzuntzan. To greet these new arrivals on their great four-footed beasts, the Cazonci now apparently determined to put on a military show of his own to make clear to the Spaniards that he also had military strength. He sent out an impressive group of warriors, painted up for the hunt, to inspire fear in the Spaniards. The hunters killed a great number of deer with their bows and arrows and gave five of them to the Spaniards. In return the Spaniards gave the Cazonci and his lords some green plumage, probably quetzal feathers, which the Tarascans valued highly.

The Cazonci, who looked upon the Spaniards as gods, had them outfitted like gods, with golden garlands on their heads and golden shields at their necks. Saying, "These are gods from heaven," he had offerings made to them of wine, wild amaranth bread, and fruit. The Spaniards expressed a desire to trade with the merchants, offering some feathers and other items that they had brought from Mexico. The Cazonci gave them permission to do so, but secretly he commanded that none of the merchants or lords were to buy the feathers. The sacristans and guards of the gods took the blankets that were set

The arrival of the first Spaniards at Tzintzuntzan and the flight of the native people at their approach (painting from the Relación de Michoacán, Códice del Escorial. Reproduced from The Chronicles of Michoacán, trans. and ed. Craine and Reindorp.

aside for buying ornaments for the gods and bought everything that
the Spaniards offered.

The Spaniards also gave the Cazonci ten pigs and a dog, telling
him that the dog could guard his wife, but the native king was not
convinced of the value of the new animals. After the Spaniards had
left, he looked at the pigs and said, "What kind of a thing are these?
Are they rats that these people are bringing?" He took it as an omen
and ordered them killed along with the dog, and then they were
dragged away and thrown into the open fields.[32]

When the *Relación* mentions that the Cazonci regarded this incident as an omen, it is possibly referring to the fact that before his
death central Michoacán would be invaded by Spanish swineherds
and their droves of pigs. It is interesting to note also that the Tarascans came to use the word *hayaqui* for both rats and pigs.[33]

When the Spaniards were ready to return to Cortés in Coyoacán,
the Cazonci proposed to go with them, his curiosity having been
aroused by the reports of his ambassadors and by these first personal
contacts. His advisers, however, dissuaded him from going. Instead,
he sent along one of his adopted brothers, some Tarascan nobles, and
a large number of bearers with gifts, totaling more than a thousand
persons.[34]

The adopted brother of the Cazonci who went with the Spaniards
must have been Huitzitziltzi, whose Tarascan name was Tashuaco. He
was an outstanding war captain among the Tarascans and, with his
brother Cuinierángari, was among the most prominent of the Cazonci's advisers. He and Cuinierángari, who is better known by his
Spanish name, Don Pedro Panza, were considered brothers of the Cazonci by both the Spaniards and the Indians, as is evident from the
wording of many documents. But the *Relación de Michoacán,* in a section that derives from statements of Don Pedro Panza himself, makes
it clear that they were actually sons of a Tarascan priest and had been
adopted as brothers by the Cazonci after he had executed his blood
brothers.[35]

There is no actual mention of Huitzitziltzi's trip to Mexico in the
Tarascan narrative, but the journey is implied. The *Relación* later indicates that Don Pedro went to Mexico City in 1522, where Cortés
asked him about Huitzitziltzi, whom the Conqueror apparently considered to be a brother of the Cazonci.[36] This acquaintance with the

Tarascan nobleman must have been a result of his having accompanied Caicedo.

On their return trip the Spanish soldiers also took along two Indian girls, and on their way back to Mexico they slept with them; in the words of the *Relación:* "Por el camino juntábanse con ellas." Because of this, the Indians who accompanied them, who were apparently members of the girls' immediate families, began to consider the Spaniards as in-laws and to use the word *tarascue* in regard to them, encouraging the Spaniards to do likewise. The *Relación* indicates that this was the occasion when the Spaniards began using the word *tarascue*, hispanicized into *tarasco*, to refer to the tribe, as mentioned above.[37]

At this time the Cazonci sent many gifts to Cortés to be forwarded to the Emperor. (King Charles I of Spain was also Emperor Charles V of the Holy Roman Empire, and is generally referred to in the documents simply as the Emperor.) The gifts were delivered over to the royal treasurer, Julián de Alderete, in Mexico City on November 18, 1521, and his listing of them has survived. Besides some silver shields, which Cortés mentioned to the king in his "Third Letter,"[38] there were many other items of native craftsmanship: diadems, one of silver and another of copper; ear pieces; leather collars and shoes; leather armguards for shooting with bow and arrow; ornaments of white and blue plumage; cotton blankets; and large and small gourd vessels painted in various colors.[39]

If we compare these items with those mentioned or depicted in the *Relación*, they seem to have constituted important elements of an imperial wardrobe by Tarascan standards, probably the kind of accouterments destined for deities. They were sent on to the king in 1522, part of an ill-fated shipment of Mexican treasure that was captured by the French. They have long been known from the published list of the shipment, although they were considered Aztec items, since there was no indication of their Tarascan origin.[40]

After the members of the Tarascan embassy had delivered their presents to Cortés in his camp at Coyoacán, the Conqueror decided to put on another military show to impress his guests, undoubtedly in the hope that some saber rattling would lessen their will to resist the Spanish advance. He called out the cavalry to stage a show of military horsemanship in one of the plazas. The infantrymen also marched out in military formation, while those who had muskets assaulted the senses of the Indians with the usual noisy, smoky, and smelly exhibition of firearms. An impressive finale to the show came with the appearance of the artillery pieces, which were used to bombard a tower, once more assaulting the senses of the natives from the quiet hills of Michoacán.

The Cazonci's men were duly astounded by all of this, but they were perhaps even more profoundly shocked when the Spaniards took their leaders on a tour of the desolated city of Tenochtitlan to show them the destruction and ruin that had been inflicted on it in spite of its fortifications and the strength of its location, on an island in a lake. Trying in every way to deepen their impressions of Spanish military power, Cortés kept the ambassadors with him for four or five days. Then he sent them home with gifts for their lord and for themselves, with which they were very well pleased.[41]

When they returned to Michoacán, the Cazonci heard their impressions regarding the Spaniards. Then he called a conference of the elders of the tribe to discuss the situation with them. They advised him to strengthen himself against future Spanish incursions.[42]

Another Spanish expedition was not long in coming. The *Relación* tells us that a group of four Spaniards soon appeared in the Tarascan capital. They asked the Cazonci to give them the support of twenty *principales* and a large contingent of warriors. After they had been in the city for only two days, they marched out toward Colima with their Tarascan allies. They went as far as a town called Hazquaran, where the Spaniards stopped, sending their new allies ahead to demand that the lords of Colima come to the Spaniards and submit peacefully. The result was a disaster. The lords of Colima captured the Tarascans and sacrificed all of them. The Spaniards waited day after day for their reappearance, but when they did not return, the Spaniards lost confidence and returned to Tzintzuntzan. After staying there for only two days, they returned to Mexico.[43]

This account appears to correspond to an expedition of four Spaniards led by Francisco Montaño. He gave his own brief description of it in the following question from his relation of merits and services, composed in 1531:

Further [let them be asked] whether they know, etc., that after the city [of Tenochtitlan] had been conquered, the aforesaid Don Hernando [Cortés], being in Coyoacán, sent me, the aforesaid Francisco Montaño, and one Diego

de Peñalosa and Gaspar de Tarifa and Bartolomé López to the city of Michoacán, so that we might go from there in search of the Amazons, and while
we were on the said search, the natives of the land resisted us so that we
could not pass further on, and on this account they wanted to kill us many
times; and from this journey we brought back great reports of the lands that
we had seen. Let the witnesses say and declare what it is that they know.[44]

Montaño's witnesses added very little information to his basic statement. Francisco de la Milla said that he had seen Montaño and his
companions bring back some fine cloth, silver, pots, and other items,
which he had shared. Vasco Porcallo testified merely that he had seen
them go to Michoacán and later had seen them return *"escandalizados"*
("scandalized"), a term that seems to indicate that they were upset and
unhappy when they came back.[45]

Montaño was apparently a very hardy individual. During the conquest of Tenochtitlan, when Cortés' force was running out of gun-
powder, Montaño had led a group of soldiers to the nearly 5,500-
meter summit of Popocatépetl to obtain sulfur for making the needed
explosives.[46] In later years he reared a clan of children: in an undated
petition to the king he asserted that he had eighteen children, ten of
them male and six of them female (he does not tell us what sex the
other two were).[47] He was still living in Mexico when the classicist
scholar Francisco Cervantes de Salazar was writing his *Crónica de la
conquista de la Nueva España,* between 1554 and 1566. In Montaño's
retelling of his story to Cervantes de Salazar and in the classicist's re-
styling of it, the story seems to have grown a great deal. It takes up
nearly forty pages in the printed version of Cervantes de Salazar's work.
In summary it goes as follows:

Montaño and his three companions, accompanied by 20 Mexican
lords, were sent by Cortés to visit the Cazonci, to find out about
the land and its people, and to tell the Cazonci about the pope and
the king and about the Christian God. After four days' journey they
came to the fortress of Tajimaroa, where they were greeted by the
governor of the town and were well treated. The next day they sent
a report back to Cortés and continued onward. The governor of Tajimaroa sent paintings of the Spaniards ahead to the governors of the
cities through which they would pass and to the king. After six days
they arrived in Tzintzuntzan, where they were greeted by 800 lords,

each accompanied by 10,000 or 12,000 vassals. The leaders of the army welcomed them and expressed the wish of their king to be a friend of Cortés and a vassal of the Spanish king. The Spaniards and their Mexican companions were taken to a spacious dwelling, where the Cazonci greeted them and gave them something to eat. About two hours later he spoke to them with great severity, demanding to know who they were and why they had come. The Spaniards answered that they had come out of friendship and that they wanted to bring the true teachings of Christianity, emphasizing that they had destroyed the Mexicans with the help of God. The Cazonci deferred his answer, and for the meantime he had a limit drawn around the place where the Spaniards were staying, marking a boundary beyond which they were not allowed to pass. He set a strong guard around them without making it apparent.

Montaño and his men were confined in this way for eighteen days, while the natives celebrated a feast with many human sacrifices. The Cazonci considered using the Spaniards also as sacrificial victims, but his advisers counseled him not to do so. At the end of the feast he sent for four of the Mexicans, who told him about the effectiveness of Spanish warfare and the advantages of making peace with them. The Cazonci and his council, frightened by what the Mexicans had told them, kept them in the palace for a day and a half. The Spaniards were worried by this, and they prepared themselves for a fight to the death if necessary. Finally, however, the Mexicans returned.

Three hours later the Cazonci appeared in great pomp, with a retinue of 40 or 50 lords, 10 or 12 pages, and more than 20,000 armed warriors. He carried his symbol of authority, a bow set with many emeralds. He appeared friendly and presented the Spaniards with many different kinds of wild game. He excused his long delay by saying that he had been detained by an annual feast. He informed them that he could not let them go on to Cihuatlán ("the land of women") because he could not be responsible for their safety. Instead he would send them back to Cortés with gifts and ambassadors, and later he would visit Cortés in person. The Spaniards, much relieved, expressed their thanks to him. He later sent them enough food for 400 men and told them that they might leave the next day.

Before their departure he brought many gifts for the four Spaniards and for Cortés. He sent 8 lords with them as an embassy to Cortés and 800 bearers to carry the gifts and food. Just as they were about

to leave, he sent to ask them to leave a dog that belonged to Peñalosa, who gave it up with considerable reluctance. The Spaniards later
heard that it had been sacrificed to the gods to placate them for not
sacrificing the Christians.

The Spaniards went on their way, constantly vigilant against treachery
by the Tarascans who were accompanying them. When they were four
leagues from Cortés' camp, he sent out horsemen to welcome them,
happy to learn that they were not dead. He received the Tarascan
ambassadors very formally and accepted their gifts and expressions of
submission. Then he staged a military show for them and afterward
sent them home with gifts of Castilian goods.

When the ambassadors returned to Michoacán, they told the Cazonci such remarkable stories about the Spaniards that he too wanted
to visit Cortés, but his advisers persuaded him to send his brother
Huitzitziltzi in his stead. The latter took gifts of gold, silver, cotton,
and featherwork to Cortés. At the request of this Tarascan war captain Cortés put on an especially good show of arms. The Spaniards
also took Huitzitziltzi by canoe to see the ruins of Tenochtitlan and
showed him the operation of one of the brigantines that Cortés had
used in maintaining the final siege of the city. Immediately afterward
the Tarascan leader left for home, satisfied with the presents, honor,
and good treatment that had been accorded him.

The Cazonci, stirred by his brother's report, now determined to
visit Cortés in person to ally himself with these new conquerors and to
rejoice over the downfall of Mexico. He proceeded with great majesty
until he came to Cortés' camp. There, dressed in humble and common garb, he made a speech of submission to Cortés. Because of his
unpretentious appearance the Aztecs were said to have given him the
title Cazoncin, signifying an "old hemp sandal." Cortés graciously received the Tarascan king's submission, wined and dined him and his
nobles, and again staged an impressive show of arms. Before the Cazonci returned home, he told Cortés that he might send Spaniards into
Michoacán whenever he wished and they would be well received.[48]

That is the story of Montaño's expedition and its aftermath, as
told by Francisco Cervantes de Salazar, who claimed to have based
it on information supplied by Montaño himself. Cervantes as a classicist wrote it in the lofty style of the Latin and Greek historians,
including grandiloquent speeches by both Spaniards and Indians that

could not possibly have been recalled with such precision at the time he was writing, more than thirty years after the event. It takes on something of the tone of dramatic historical fiction.

The account also contains some obvious exaggerations, such as the statement that the four Spaniards and their allies were met by 800 Tarascan lords, each with 10,000 to 12,000 vassals. That would constitute a grand army of 8,000,000 to 9,800,000 warriors, far beyond the resources of the Tarascan empire.

More seriously, the account presents some difficulties when compared with earlier documentation. For example, if Montaño had played such a major role in achieving the peaceful submission of Michoacán, it is hardly thinkable that he would have devoted to it only one rather brief question in his relation of merits and services, which he presented in 1531, only ten years after the event. Further, it is to be noted that in his question Montaño said that his problems with the Indians occurred during his *search* for the Amazons, not in the city of Michoacán itself. This agrees more closely with the narrative of the expedition of the four Spaniards as given in the *Relación*.

Cervantes' statement that the Cazonci himself went to Mexico City to visit Cortés soon after Montaño's return there seems to run contrary to Cortés' letters of 1522 and 1524. In both letters Cortés mentioned only the visit of the Cazonci's brother and messengers and pointed to the visit as a motive for his sending an expedition into Michoacán under Cristóbal de Olid.[49] If the Cazonci himself had come, there would have been no reason for Cortés to lay such emphasis on the visit of his brother. It is true that in 1527 Luis de Cárdenas stated in a letter to the king that the Cazonci had come to Mexico with forty-five loads of gold and silver and that this was the reason why Cortés sent Olid into Michoacán.[50] Cárdenas, however, whose letter shows him to have been no friend of Cortés, was probably not included in the inner councils of the Conqueror and could very well have confused the Tarascan king's brother for the king himself.

Cervantes' narrative of the Montaño expedition seems to include elements of all the early expeditions to Michoacán, and there are further indications that Cervantes intended to credit Montaño with the major role in subjugating Michoacán. Unfortunately, the unfinished character of his book does not allow us to be sure of this. The only known manuscript copy of his work breaks off short with the title of an unwritten chapter a few pages after the end of the Montaño narrative. The title itself, however, is significant. It speaks of Cortés' dispatch of Juan Rodríguez de Villafuerte to the seacoast and of Gonzalo de Sandoval's expedition up the coast from the south to Zacatula.[51] The significance of this is that Juan Rodríguez de Villafuerte went to the seacoast and joined Sandoval's expedition at Zacatula only after he had gone to Michoacán with Cristóbal de Olid, as we shall see below. It appears possible, therefore, that Cervantes had no intention of treating the Olid expedition but was going to give Montaño the credit for attaching the Tarascan kingdom to the Spanish crown. By the time of his writing, Olid was long dead in Honduras and forgotten. But Montaño was on the scene, with an eye to presenting a good story of his exploits, hoping to gain a larger pension for himself and to benefit his multitude of children, for whom he must already have embellished his story many times.

Montaño's story, however, became an important element in the historical literature of the conquest of Michoacán. When Antonio de Herrera y Tordesillas was preparing his *Historia general de los hechos de los castellanos en las islas y tierra firme del Mar Océano* in the early seventeenth century, he lifted the story bodily from Cervantes' book, changing only an occasional word, to include it in his own work.[52]

Although we may not be willing to accept the whole of Montaño's story as presented by Cervantes, there is no doubt that his expedition provided one more steppingstone toward Spanish domination of Michoacán. Through these early visits between the Spaniards and Tarascans the natives had become acquainted with the strengths of the newcomers, and the Spaniards had seen enough evidence of wealth in Michoacán to whet their appetites for occupying the region. Whether the Spanish advance into Michoacán would be a relatively peaceful movement or would encounter native resistance would depend in large measure on the attitude of the Cazonci and his advisers, who must have realized by now that the coming of the Spaniards in force was inevitable.

•••

CHAPTER 3

The Expedition of Cristóbal de Olid, 1522

IN the summer of 1522, less than a year after the fall of Tenochtitlan, Cortés decided to send a fairly large contingent of soldiers into
Michoacán to establish a Spanish colony in the Tarascan kingdom.
Bernal Díaz asserted that Cortés made this decision to rid himself of
discontented soldiers who were complaining that he was taking all
the spoils of the Conquest for himself.[1] Cortés gave as his reasons for
the expedition the large size of the province, its proximity to Mexico
City, and the reported evidence of great riches there.[2]

At the head of the expedition Cortés placed one of his outstanding
captains, Cristóbal de Olid. The captain had accompanied Cortés
throughout the trying experiences of the Conquest, having joined the
expedition at Trinidad, in Cuba. He was the owner of one of the few
precious horses that had come to Mexico with the original expedition.
Bernal Díaz portrays him as almost inseparable from Cortés during the
important phases of the two-year struggle for control of the Aztec empire. He served as quartermaster of the army, and for a time during
Montezuma's captivity he was in charge of the guard over the emperor. He rode side by side with his commander during the "Noche
Triste" and shared the horrors of that defeat, when the Spaniards
were sent reeling back to their allies in Tlaxcala. During the final
siege of Tenochtitlan, Cortés appointed him captain-general over one
of the three divisions of the army; Olid's division operated from Cortés'
headquarters in Coyoacán. Shortly before leading the expedition into
Michoacán, he married a Portuguese lady, Doña Felipa de Arauz (or
Araujo). Bernal Díaz described him as tall, robust, and strong, a man
of openhanded generosity, but one who needed to have a commander
over him rather than to be in command.[3]

42

Various estimates have been given of the size of the Olid expedition. Cortés later claimed to have sent out 70 horsemen and 200 foot soldiers.[4] Gómara, followed by Herrera and Fernando de Alva Ixtlilxochitl, wrote that 40 horsemen and 100 foot soldiers made up the expedition, but Gómara arrived at these numbers by confusing the Olid expedition with the later expedition of Juan Rodríguez de Villafuerte to Zacatula, for which Cortés gave these numbers.[5] The *Relación de Michoacán* merely states that Olid came with 200 Spaniards.[6] Ixtlilxochitl added that his Texcocan ancestor of the same name accompanied Olid at the head of a force of more than 5,000 Indian allies.[7] We have no idea how many other Indian allies may have accompanied Olid besides those at the command of the Texcocan leader. The *Relación* gives the impression that there was a very large force, led by many princes.[8]

In an unpublished section of the judgment of *residencia* of Cortés, there is a listing of 174 Spaniards who went on the expedition. The list was made for the purpose of distributing money obtained from the auction of the gold and silver that the army had brought back from Michoacán. Thus it does not contain the names of any soldiers who may have died during the course of the expedition. Also missing are the names of some men who later consistently claimed that they had gone with the expedition. Nevertheless, it does give us a fairly authoritative view of the structure of the army: there were 13 officials of various degrees; 28 other horsemen; 20 crossbowmen, among whom were 2 musketeers; and 113 foot soldiers.[9] The army was organized in the early summer of 1522 and set out for Michoacán in July.[10]

The Cazonci's had been preparing for just such an eventuality. We have seen that after Caicedo's visit the Cazonci and his advisers reached a decision to strengthen the defenses of the kingdom against future Spanish incursions.[11] In a meeting of all the important men of the kingdom they determined to fortify the area around Tzintzuntzan with trenches and pits to enable them to put up a good defense against the Spaniards.[12] Later, however, the Tarascan determination to resist seems to have softened. Perhaps the kind reception given to his embassy in Mexico had lessened the Cazonci's opposition to the Spaniards, and the stories of Spanish military strength had undoubtedly dampened his enthusiasm to meet them in the field.

The only extensive relation of the Olid expedition that we have is the one presented in the *Relación de Michoacán*, which gives us the story as told to the author of the *Relación* by the Tarascan nobleman Don Pedro.[13] It contains some historical weaknesses when compared with other sixteenth-century sources, but it has a special charm of its own, and first let us see what it says.[14]

The Cazonci's messengers brought a report to him as soon as the Spanish forces under Olid, with their many Indian allies, arrived at the frontier fortress of Tajimaroa. All this happened at the time of the Tarascan feast Cahera-cosquaro, which was observed on July 17. It was in the middle of the season of heavy rains. The Cazonci, fearful that the soldiers were coming to kill him and all of his people, summoned an assembly of elders and lords and asked them what should be done. In the assembly were the powerful lord Timas, to whom the Cazonci accorded the honorary title of "uncle," as well as the brothers Huitzitziltzi and Cuinierángari (Don Pedro). Don Pedro anachronistically uses his Christian name throughout the narrative, and for the sake of clarity I shall do the same.

When the Cazonci asked the assembled leaders to give their individual opinions about what should be done, they told him that he was the king and that he should make the decision. He then sent runners throughout the kingdom to summon the warriors so that they might be ready to die in opposing the Spaniards as the Mexicans had died. He believed that there would be no dearth of men to support the cause of their god Curicaueri with their arrows. As his supporting tribes he named the Matlatzincas, Otomis, Huetama, Cuitlatecas, Escamoecha, and Chichimecas and asked what they were for if not to support Curicaueri. The runners went through the whole kingdom, calling on lords and priests to assemble their warriors.

The Cazonci called Don Pedro to his side and confided to him that he felt great melancholy because of the loss of his older relatives who had died in the epidemic, and he expressed a desire to die quickly and follow them. Then he sent Don Pedro to see to the organization of the troops at Tajimaroa and other towns. When Don Pedro arrived in Tajimaroa a day and a half later, he learned that the warriors from the towns of the eastern frontier, Ucareo, Acámbaro, Araró, and Tuzantla, were not in the town but were in the wild country nearby with their bows and arrows.

On the road Don Pedro met a *principal* named Quezequampare, who was coming from Tajimaroa, where the Spaniards were. He appeared very frightened and at first refused even to greet Don Pedro.

When the latter explained his mission, the *principal* informed him that everyone in Tajimaroa was dead. When Don Pedro entered the town, he found no one; all the people had fled.

That evening he was captured by the Spaniards and Mexicans, and the next morning they took him before Olid. The expedition had brought along a Tarascan named Xanaqua, who had been captured by the Mexicans and now served as their interpreter. Through him Olid carried on the following conversation with Don Pedro, as reported by the Tarascan leader eighteen years later:

Olid: "Where do you come from?"
Don Pedro: "The Cazonci has sent me."
Olid: "What did he say to you?"
Don Pedro: "He called me and said to me: 'Go and receive the gods and see if it is true that they are coming. Perhaps it is a lie. Perhaps they came only as far as the river and turned back because it is the rainy season. Go and see, and let me know whether they have come; and let them come from afar to the city.' That is what he told me."
Olid: "What you have just told me is a lie. It is not so, but you want to kill us. You are already all assembled to carry on war against us. Let them come quickly if they are going to kill us, or perhaps I will kill them with my people" (For he had brought many soldiers from México.)
Don Pedro: "That is not so. Why wouldn't I have told you that?"
Olid: "It is good, if it is as you say. Go back to the city. And let the Cazonci come with some present. Let him come out to receive me at a place called Quangaceo, which is near Matalcingo. And let him bring rich blankets of the kinds that are called *catangari, curice, zizupu,* and *echere atacata* and other light blankets, and chickens [i.e., turkeys], and eggs and fish of the kinds called *cuerepu, acumarani, urapeti,* and *thiru,* and ducks. He should bring everything to that place and not refuse to fulfill it nor go against my word." [We can safely assume that the Tarascan interpreter somewhat embellished Olid's words. The Spanish captain would hardly have known the various distinctions in Tarascan blankets and fish.]
Don Pedro: "It is good. I will go and tell him that."
Apparently as a sign of good will toward the Tarascans, the Spaniards hanged two Mexicans because they had burned some wooden fences in the religious centers of Tajimaroa.

Then Olid told Don Pedro, "Tell the Cazonci that he should not be afraid, and that we will not harm him."

Afterward the Spaniards attended Mass, and Don Pedro went with them. When he saw the priest take the chalice and speak words into it, he said to himself, "These people must all be medicine men like our medicine men who look into the water to see what is going to happen, and there they know that we want to make war on them." And he was afraid.

When the Mass was finished, Olid summoned five Mexicans and five Otomis and commanded them to go to Michoacán with Don Pedro. Xanaqua, the interpreter, told Don Pedro as he was leaving: "Go, sir, it is well. Tell the Cazonci that he should not make war and that the Spaniards are liberal and will do no harm. But tell him that he should quickly take away his gold and silver and blankets and corn and hide them, because how will he keep it from the Spaniards once they have seen it? This is the way they acted in Mexico, where they hid it all."

"What you have told me is sufficient," Don Pedro replied. "You speak very kindly in what you have told me. I will go and tell it to the Cazonci."

After this Don Pedro left with the Mexicans and Otomis, but at a place called Uzumao, about three leagues before they reached Matal-cingo, he told them to wait for him while he went on ahead, because he was afraid that they might see the warriors who were in readi-ness. Hurrying ahead, he came upon 8,000 warriors at the town of Indaparapeo, under command of a captain named Xamando. Don Pedro commanded them: "Disperse yourselves and go away from here, for the Spaniards are not coming in anger but in joy. The Cazonci must come out to receive them in Quangaceo. They told me that I should tell him this, and that is why I am coming. Go to your homes."

Further on, at a place called Hetuquaro, he met his older brother Huitzitziltzi, who had another 8,000 men stationed in ambush. Don Pedro gave them much the same message that he had given the pre-vious group. His brother wanted to know why Quezequampare had come through spreading so much fear. Don Pedro said that he did not know what the reason was and told his brother that Quezequam-pare had not even wanted to greet him when they met. Huitzitziltzi then told him: "Go quickly, brother. We are causing pain to the Cazonci, who is only awaiting the news that you are bringing him. At daybreak I will go to the city with the men."

When Don Pedro arrived in the capital, he found it in turmoil. Apparently the hysterical report of Quezequampare was having a destructive effect. The Cazonci was on the verge of going to the lake and drowning himself, and his soldiers and servants were preparing to follow him. He had been induced to do so by a group of *principales* who wanted to kill him and usurp his power. Their leader was the powerful warlord Timas, the one who had previously influenced the Cazonci to execute his blood brothers and whom the Cazonci called "uncle."

When Don Pedro was able to gain admittance to the presence of the Cazonci, the king asked him: "What news is there? In what mood are the Spaniards coming?"

Don Pedro replied, "My lord, they do not come in anger but in peace." Then he told the Cazonci about seeing the Spaniards in their armor and about the conversation that he had held with their captain, and he relayed the command of Olid that the Cazonci should go out to receive them, taking along blankets and fish.

But Timas interrupted him: "What are you saying, sniveling boy? Did you say something to them? My lord, let us go. We are already bedecked. Perchance were your grandfathers and ancestors slaves of anyone, that you should want to be a slave? Let Huitzitziltzi and this one who brings this news stay behind."

Don Pedro asked: "I? What could I have said to them? But their interpreter Xanaqua was from here, from this city, and when I took leave of them he told me how it should be and that we should not make war on them."

Timas said to the Cazonci: "My lord, have copper brought, and let us put it on our backs and drown ourselves in the lake. In that way we will arrive more quickly and catch up with those who are dead."

Don Pedro spoke to the Cazonci and those who were advising him: "What are you saying? Why do you want to drown yourselves? Go up to the mountain in the meantime, and we will go out to receive them. Let them kill us first, and afterward you can drown yourselves in the lake." Then, speaking to the Cazonci alone, he said: "My lord, look how they are lying to you and how they want to kill you. They are taking all their blankets and adornments and fleeing. If it were true that they wanted to die, why should they take their possessions and flee? My lord, don't believe them."

The Cazonci answered, "You have spoken well to me."

Timas and the other *principales* who were encouraging the Cazonci to drown himself got drunk and sang chants in order to go drown themselves, as they said.

Don Pedro took much copper on his back and made the rather mysterious statement: "I am doing it so as not to die. Let us go now. Let us all drown ourselves."

The *principales* once more said to the Cazonci: "Lord, drown yourself, so that you will not go about as a beggar. Will you perhaps be a commoner and a person of the lower class? Were your ancestors by chance ever slaves? Kill yourself as we do. We will not show you mercy, and we will follow you and go with you."

The Cazonci answered: "That is the truth, uncles. Wait a little while." Then he adorned himself, putting little gold bells on his legs, turquoises at his neck, and green feathers on his head. And the *principales* did the same.

They said to him, "Have the plumes brought out that belonged to your grandfather, and we will put them on for a while. We do not know who will be king and who will wear them." The Cazonci commanded the plumes to be brought, as well as golden bracelets and shields. The *principales* took them all from him, and they all danced.

Don Pedro watched it all with great pain and said to himself: "Why are they taking the Cazonci's adornments from him? Why do they want them? What is this? Aren't they going to drown themselves and die? How they are deceiving him, and they speak to him with lies and in deceit and treachery! They want to kill him. How is it? Did they hear what I heard from the Spaniards? I who went to them, I heard it very well. They do not come in anger. And I saw the lords of Mexico who come with them. If they had enslaved them, how could they wear turquoise collars and rich blankets and green plumes, as they are wearing? How is it? The Spaniards do not harm them. What is it that these people are saying?"

The ladies of the Cazonci's household then came out and asked Don Pedro what news he had for the Cazonci. He told them: "Ladies, I brought him very good news—that the Spaniards are not wrathful or angry. I do not know what these *principales* are telling him."

The ladies were astonished, and, wringing their hands and weeping, they said, "It saddens us that you should not have brought him this pleasant news sooner." Don Pedro was also very sad because he was there by himself, and even his brother Huitzitziltzi had not yet come.

But the Cazonci was able to elude the *principales*. While they were calling out to him, "Lord, let us go, come here," he went into a room of his house. Then he secretly made an opening in a wall of the house that opened out onto the road. Because it was night, he had all the lights extinguished, and, taking his women, he fled up a mountain nearby. The *principales*, drunken and adorned as they were, went after him, with their little bells tinkling along the way. But apparently most of the people, including Don Pedro, did not know of his escape.

The Cazonci fled across the mountains to the town of Uruapan. But the *principales* found out about it, and they went there, inquiring after him. When they found him, he said to them: "Welcome, uncles. How is it that you come over here?"

"Lord," they said, "we came asking after you. Where shall we go? Lord, let us go to some very distant place."

But the Cazonci would not go with them. "Let us stay here," he said, "to see what news comes and what the Spaniards will do when they arrive. Huitzitziltzi and his brother Cuinierángari [Don Pedro] are there prepared. Let us wait to see what news they bring us, and to see whether the Spaniards mistreat them."

Meanwhile, in the city of Tzintzuntzan the caciques and lords who remained there were saddened by the departure of the Cazonci, and they began saying: "How is it that he went away? Did he not have compassion for us? Whom did we wish to favor but him? Those who took him away are very evil."

The ten Indian *principales* whom Olid had sent arrived in the city, and when they saw the distress of the people, they asked, "Why are you sad?"

"Our lord the Cazonci has drowned in the lake," they answered.

"Well, what shall we do?" the Mexicans asked one another. "Let us go back to receive those who sent us. This is a matter of importance."

When they went back to Olid and informed him that the Cazonci had drowned, Olid responded: "That's all right, that's all right. Let's go. We must reach the city."

Before the arrival of the Spaniards the Tarascans in Tzintzuntzan sacrificed 800 imprisoned slaves, so that they would not flee and join the Spaniards.

Huitzitziltzi and Don Pedro and all the lords and leaders of the kingdom went out with their warriors in battle formation to receive the Spaniards at a place called Apío, about half a league from the city on the road to Mexico. There they drew a line and told the Spaniards that they could come no farther until they said why they had come and whether they intended to kill them.

The captain replied: "We do not want to kill you. We have come from afar to this place where we are now. Perhaps it is you who want to make war on us."

"We do not wish to do so," they said.

"Well, then," said Olid, "leave your bows and arrows there and come over here to where we are."

They laid down their arms, and all the lords and caciques went over to where the Spaniards were waiting in the road. The Spaniards received and embraced them warmly, and then they all went together to Tzintzuntzan and entered into the courtyard of the great *yácatas*. There the Spaniards discharged their firearms, and the Indians fell to the ground in fear. The Spaniards also performed a skirmish with their horses in the courtyard, which was very large.

Later they went to the Cazonci's houses and looked at them, then they came back to the courtyard of the *yácatas* and set up their quarters in the houses of the priests and in the *yácatas* themselves, even though the steps and entrances of the *yácatas* were still wet with the blood of the slaves who had been sacrificed.

Many of the bodies of the sacrificial victims were lying about, and the Spaniards looked at them all to see whether any of them were bearded Spaniards. Then they went up to the *yácatas* and overturned the stone of sacrifice and the statue of the messenger of the gods, Curita-caheri, and rolled them down the steps. The people looked on and asked: "Why don't our gods become angry? Why don't they curse them?"

This narrative of the entry of Olid and his expedition into Michoacán gives us a realistic view of the internal weakness of the Tarascan empire, with a new young king trying to find his way among traitorous and loyal advisers. It also shows the religious factors that entered into the picture: fear of the Spaniards as some kind of gods and fear that the Spaniards would enslave and possibly sacrifice the Tarascans if they capitulated. If the part of Don Pedro in the story seems very large, we must remember that the narrative was his story, as told to the compiler of the *Relación de Michoacán* about eighteen years after the fact.

Other sources give us limited additional information. Pedro de Vargas, who was a member of the expedition, supplies us with a date for the entry into Tzintzuntzan. In 1544 he testified that the expedition entered the Tarascan capital on the Feast of Santiago de Compostela, that is, on July 25, 1522. He corroborated Don Pedro's statement that the Tarascans came out prepared for war but received the Spaniards in peace.[15]

Two estimates of the size of the Tarascan force that met the Spaniards have come down to us. Jorge Carrillo, a member of the expedition, stated in 1553 that the force consisted of more than 200,000 armed men under the leadership of Huchecilce (Huitzitziltzi).[16] An anonymous Jesuit chronicler, who wrote his work late in the sixteenth century but seems to have depended on some native traditions, gave the number of Tarascan warriors as 80,000.[17] Spanish estimates of large groups of people were notoriously inaccurate and frequently exaggerated, but a statement like Carrillo's indicates certainly that there was a massive gathering of Tarascan soldiers, large enough to make a long-lasting impression.

One point on which there is little outside support for Don Pedro's story is the part about the flight of the Cazonci. In fact, it is contradicted by a series of depositions made for the Cazonci's son, Don Antonio Huitziméngari, in 1553 and 1554. In the testimony by Carrillo cited above, he asserted that the Cazonci and his men received the Spaniards in peace. Diego Hernández Nieto, also a member of the expedition, testified that they arrived at the city of Huchichila (Tzintzuntzan), where the Cazonci was, and he came out to receive Olid in peace. Several aged *principales* also testified in December, 1553, and January, 1554. Don Marcos Quaniguata, *principal* of Pátzcuaro, and Don Francisco Quirongari, governor of Tiripetío, said that they had been with the Cazonci when the Spaniards arrived and had accompanied him when he went to receive the Spaniards.[18]

The only suggestion of support for Don Pedro's story of the Cazonci's flight is found in a statement made by Pedro Moreno in 1538

in which he asserted that he was present when the Spaniards occu-
pied Tzintzuntzan and that the Cazonci was in his residence in Pátzcuaro when the Spaniards arrived.[19] Moreno's name, however, does
not appear among those who received shares in the loot from Olid's
expedition. There is a long-standing tradition in Michoacán that the
Cazonci made his submission to the Spaniards at a spot on the out-
skirts of Pátzcuaro where the chapel known as the Humilladero now
stands and that the chapel takes its name from this submission.

It is difficult to resolve this contradiction in the sources. In telling
his narrative of the Conquest, Don Pedro could have invented the
story of the flight of the Cazonci to make his own part seem more
significant and that of the Cazonci inglorious. But it is hard to close
one's eyes to the consistency of Don Pedro's story and to the many
realistic human elements that appear in it. On the other hand, it is also
possible that the witnesses for the Cazonci's son wanted to make the
dead Tarascan king's contribution appear more important in the eyes
of the Spanish monarch and that they therefore overlooked the initial
absence of the Cazonci, though the explicitness of the statements by
both Spanish and Indian witnesses seems to argue against this.

Continuing with the story as Don Pedro tells it, we find that a
major immediate problem for the Tarascans was the provisioning of
their crowd of self-invited guests. According to Don Pedro, all the
women had fled from the city to Pátzcuaro and other towns, and the
men had to work at the metates to prepare corn flour for bread for
the Spaniards, the lords, and the elders.[20] The Indian women must
have come back later, because Jorge Carrillo stated that the Cazonci
gave the Spaniards Indian women to serve them and make bread for
them.[21] The Spaniards stayed on for six Indian months (of twenty
days each) with all of their army and their Mexican allies, and during
the whole time the Tarascans supplied them with bread, turkeys, eggs,
and fish.[22]

About four days after their arrival the Spaniards began asking about
idols, but the lords denied that they had any (probably having hidden
them away after observing the destruction of Curita-caheri). The Spaniards then demanded the accouterments of the idols, and when the
lords brought out articles of featherwork, shields, and masks, the Spaniards burned all the items in the courtyard of the temples.

Then they turned their interest to gold. The kings of Michoacán had
built up considerable wealth over the course of time, most of which

Island of Janitzio, Lake Pátzcuaro (dominated now by a statue of José María Morelos, hero of Mexican independence).

was dedicated to their gods. It consisted primarily of articles of personal adornment, such as shields (or ornamental breastplates), bracelets, half-moons, lip plugs, and ear plugs, which they used for their festivals and dances. The compiler of the *Relación* noted that he had inquired about the quantity of such articles from some of the former guards of the treasure, and although some of them would not answer him, he was able to assemble an impressive list of gold, silver, and featherwork stored in the royal houses in Tzintzuntzan and Ichechenirenba and on the islands of Apupato, Xanecho (or Janitzio), Pacanda, and Urandén in Lake Pátzcuaro. These treasure troves were watched over by guards who passed on their duties from father to son.

The first treasure that the Spaniards found was in the house of the Cazonci in Tzintzuntzan. In the turmoil of his departure he had obviously not been able to carry out Xanaqua's admonition to hide from the Spaniards anything of value. There some of the soldiers found twenty chests of golden shields and began carrying some of the pieces out under their cloaks. Some of the Cazonci's women, who saw this taking place, went out after them with stout clubs and began beating them, even though the Spaniards were carrying swords. The soldiers did not dare harm the women, and so they covered their

Lip plugs of obsidian, gold, and turquoise; cylindrical obsidian ear plugs. Torres Collection, Casa de Cultura, Morelia.

heads with their arms and fled, some losing their booty but others managing to keep it. Some *principales* were standing nearby, and the women began to berate them, asking why they wore the lip plugs of valiant men.[23] Were they not there to protect the gold and silver that these people were taking? And were they not ashamed to wear their lip plugs? The *principales* told the women not to harm the Spaniards, because these gods were merely taking what belonged to them.

When Olid found out about the chests, he had them brought out and taken to the houses of the priests, where the Spaniards were staying. There they separated the shields of better quality from the others, placing them in separate piles. Then they cut them in two with their swords and tied them up in blankets, making two hundred packs of them. These shields, or breastplates, were thin pieces, intended for purely ornamental purposes rather than for defense, as is evident from the ease with which the Spaniards were able to cut them up. This conclusion is borne out by the descriptions of some shields that were looted by Pedro de Arellano in 1531.[24]

After Olid had assembled the gold and silver, he summoned Don Pedro and commanded him to conduct it to Mexico to Cortés. The bearers were to go in groups of twenty, carrying small banners on their packs so as not to lose sight of one another along the way. Accompanied by some Spaniards, Don Pedro and his convoy of bearers made their way across the mountains to the Valley of Mexico and Cortés' camp at Coyoacán, where they counted the packs and then presented the loot to Cortés.

The Conqueror soon began to question Don Pedro concerning the whereabouts of the Cazonci. Don Pedro answered, "My lord, he drowned in the lake when he was crossing it quickly in order to come out to receive you."

"Well, then," said Cortés, "since he is dead, who will be lord? Doesn't he have any brothers?"

"My lord," Don Pedro replied, "he doesn't have any brothers."

"Well, what has happened to Huzizilci?" Cortés asked. "What relationship does he have with him?"

"He is not related to him," Don Pedro responded. "He and I are sons of the same mother."

"He will be the lord," Cortés decided. "Now make yourself welcome."

Then, according to Don Pedro, Cortés gave him some turquoise collars and told him that he had kept them to give to the Cazonci but that, since the Cazonci had drowned, Don Pedro should take them and throw them where his lord had drowned so that he might take them with him. Such a typically Indian concept does not sound very authentic in the mouth of the Spanish conqueror; perhaps the interpreter or interpreters through whom they were speaking Indianized the Conqueror's expressions.

Cortes then commanded that Don Pedro be fed and told him, "Go to Mexico (Tenochtitlan), and you will see how we destroyed it."

Some *principales* took Don Pedro to Mexico City, which he had never seen before. The lords came out to receive him and his companions, offering them flowers and saying: "Welcome, Chichimecas of Michoacán. Just recently we have seen one another [probably referring to the previous embassies to Cortés]. We do not know who these gods are who have destroyed us and conquered us. Look at this city of Mexico, renowned for our god Tzintzu-uiquixo [Tarascan for the principal Aztec god, Huitzilopochtli]. How completely it is laid waste! They have put women's skirts on all of us. How they have attired us! Have they also conquered you, renowned though you were? Let it be thus as the gods have willed. Have strength in your hearts. We have seen and known this, we who are children. I do not know what our ancestors saw and knew. They knew very little. We have seen and known it, though we are children."

Don Pedro answered them: "My lords, now you have consoled me in what you have said. Now you have seen us. How would we have seen and visited one another, if they did not treat us in this way? Let us be brothers for many years, since it has pleased the gods that we should remain and escape from their hands. Let us serve them and plant fields for them. We do not know what people will come, but let us obey them. Enough of this! Let us go back to Coyoacán to the Marqués. We have seen Mexico." (The use of the title "Marqués" in this context is an obvious anachronism, since Cortés did not receive the title until several years later.) Then they exchanged rich blankets and other precious items.

As Don Pedro was returning to Coyoacán with his people, Cortés sent someone to meet them and bring them into his presence. Some letters had arrived from Tzintzuntzan notifying him that the Spaniards had found the Cazonci.

"Come here," Cortés commanded Don Pedro. "Why did you tell me that the Cazonci had drowned? They say that he is hidden in the wilds and that they intimidated two *principales*, and they revealed where he was."

"Perhaps it is as they say," Don Pedro answered. "Perhaps he went out to some part of the lake to some small island and fled away, and we did not see him when he left." And Don Pedro began weeping for fear the Spaniards would have him killed.

Cortés comforted him with the words: "Do not weep. Go to your land. Tomorrow I will give you a letter, and you will leave here three days from now."

"Let it be thus, my lord," Don Pedro replied. "What you say is good."

On the following day the Spaniards gave him a letter and many turquoises and *charchuis* [chalchihuitl, or Chalchuite—another semi-precious green stone], and Cortés said to him: "Tell the Cazonci that he should come to where I am, that he should not be afraid, that he should come to his houses in Michoacán. The Spaniards will not harm him, and he shall come to visit me."

Don Pedro took his leave and returned to Michoacán, where he told the assembled nobles how matters had gone with him and his companions and what Cortés had said. They were greatly relieved.

Huitzitziltzi and two Spaniards then went to get the Cazonci, but Huitzitziltzi went ahead of the Spaniards and arrived first at Uruapan, where the Cazonci was staying. He told the Cazonci, "My lord, let us go to the city. Two Spaniards are coming for you, but I came on ahead. Do not be afraid. Have strength."

"Let us go, brother," the Cazonci answered. "I do not know where they have made me come to, these people who have treated me in this way because of their animosity toward me. Truly they are not my relatives."

When he was preparing to leave, the *principales* who had wanted to kill him asked, "Lord, what shall we do?"

"I am going over there to Tzintzuntzan," he told them. But they stayed there.

As the Cazonci and Huitzitziltzi were going on their way, they met the two Spaniards. They embraced the Cazonci and said, "Don't be afraid. They will not harm you. We have come for you."

"Let's go, sirs," the Cazonci answered.

When they arrived at Pátzcuaro, Don Pedro came out to meet them and welcomed the Cazonci. The Cazonci returned the salutation and asked him, "How did it go for you there where you went?"

"It went well for me," Don Pedro replied, "and there is no danger. All the Spaniards are happy. The Captain says that you should go to see him there in Mexico."

"Let's go then," said the Cazonci, "since they are already bringing me."

They arrived in Tzintzuntzan, and the Spaniards placed a guard on the Cazonci so that he would not go into hiding again. Then they began to ask him for more gold. The Cazonci summoned the *principales*: "Brothers, come here. Where have they taken the gold that was here?"

They replied, "Lord, they have already taken it all to Mexico."

"Where shall we go for more?" he asked them. He undoubtedly hesitated to hand over the various sacred caches that his ancestors had dedicated to the gods on various islands and in other spots around the lake. But then he decided: "Let us show them what is on the islands of Pacanda and Urandén."

Statue of the Cazonci, Pátzcuaro (work of sculptors Juan Cruz and Francisco Zúñiga and founder Moisés del Aguila).

Meeting of the Cazonci and Cristóbal de Olid. Modern relief in bronze (work of sculptors Juan Cruz and Francisco Zúñiga and founder Moisés del Aguila).

Chapel called the Humilladero, Pátzcuaro, built at the place where, according to a local tradition, the Cazonci submitted to the Spaniards.

Some of the *principales* showed it to the Spaniards, and at night the Spaniards came and tied the caches of shields and "miters" into eighty packs and took them by night to Tzintzuntzan. When Olid saw them, he chided the Cazonci: "Why do you bring so little? Bring more. You have a lot of gold. Why do you want it?"

The Cazonci remarked in an aside to his *principales*: "Why do they want this gold? These gods must eat gold, and that is why they want it so much."[25]

He then commanded that the Spaniards be shown the treasures on the islands of Apupato and Utuyo, from which they took a total of 360 pack loads. Then he asked, "What shall we do now that they have taken it all away from us?" Having informed the Spaniards that there was no more, he told them, "What was here was not ours, but it belonged to you who are gods, and now you are taking it for yourselves because it was yours." The element of divine cult in the attitude toward the Spaniards contained in this statement did not bother their consciences enough to cause them to hesitate for a moment to accept the offering.

Olid answered: "Good. Perhaps you are telling me the truth when you say that you do not have any more. But you must go to Mexico with these loads."

"It pleases me, lords," the Cazonci replied. "I will go."

In actuality, the Cazonci's supply of gold had not run out, and the Spaniards would continue to extort it from him for the rest of his life. After his death Pedro de Arellano would loot yet another cache that the Cazonci had left for his sons.

The Cazonci started out for Mexico with the lords, caciques, and *principales* of the province. Tearfully he said to Don Pedro and Huitzitziltzi: "Perhaps you did not tell me the truth when you said that the Spaniards in Mexico were happy. I escaped from the hands of those *principales* who wanted to kill me, and now you want to have me killed there in Mexico, and you have lied to me."

"Lord, we have not lied to you," they said. "We have told you the truth. Certainly! You will go there and see. They will rejoice greatly at your coming. Say what you are saying there, after you have arrived, not here. And there you will see whether we are lying, and you will believe what we are saying to you."

When he reached Coyoacán, where Cortés was staying, the Conqueror received him with great joy and said to him: "Welcome. You will not be punished. Go and see what a son of Montezuma did. We have imprisoned him there because he sacrificed many of us." (Cortés' reported reference here to a son of Moctezuma was apparently intended to indicate Cuauhtémoc, the last of the supreme Aztec war leaders, though he was not actually a son of Moctezuma.)

Cortés summoned all the lords of Mexico and informed them that the lord of Michoacán had come and that they should make merry and hold feasts for him and that they should be very fond of one another.

After showing the Cazonci some houses where he would stay, they took him to see the "son of Montezuma," whose feet had been burned in torture. They told the Cazonci, "Now you have seen him and what has happened to him for what he did. Do not be bad as he was."

The Cazonci stayed in Mexico for four days, and the Mexicans made him happy with the celebration of many feasts. "Certainly the Spaniards are liberal," he remarked. "I did not believe you."

The *principales* said to him, "Now, lord, you have seen that we were not lying to you. We will not leave you. We will see to the fulfillment of what the Spaniards and their interpreters command us. Eat and be merry. You will not be punished. Let us see what they say and command us."

Later Cortés summoned the Cazonci and told him: "Go to your land. I now consider you as a brother. Have your people carry these anchors [for ships that Cortés was having built at Zacatula, on the Pacific Coast]. You shall not harm the Spaniards who are there in your domain, so that they will not kill you. Give them food. And do not ask tribute from the towns, because I must give them out as encomiendas to the Spaniards."

The Cazonci replied that he would do as commanded and that, now having met Cortés, he would come back again to visit him. He left with his *principales,* and as he went along the way back to Michoacán, he was relaxed and even played a game called *patol.*[26] When he arrived in Tzintzuntzan, Olid told him, "Relax and rest in your house." Olid commanded that no one but the Cazonci's *principales* should enter his house.

This visit of the Cazonci to Cortés at this time is not recorded in any of the sources of Spanish origin, not even in the letters of Cortés himself, but there is no strong argument against it. Perhaps, once the region had been subjected to control by Spanish arms, the visit of the native king was no longer considered of primary importance.

Bernal Díaz mentions that a son of the Cazonci went back to Mexico with Olid but does not speak of any visit by the Cazonci himself.[27] But Bernal Díaz is surely mistaken. Nine years after Olid's expedition in November, 1531, the age of the older son of the Cazonci was given as only about ten years.[28] It is possible that, because of the youth of the reigning Cazonci at the time of the Olid expedition, Díaz thought that he was the son of the Cazonci rather than the reigning monarch himself. Díaz, who did not participate in the Olid expedition, seems to have been rather poorly informed about it.

The treasury records give support to the idea that someone did take some precious metal to Cortés from Michoacán before Olid's return. They speak of the silver that "Cristóbal de Olid, captain of the province of Michoacán, sent and brought back." But there is no indication of when these shipments of precious metal occurred.[29]

Regarding the anchors for Zacatula, Don Pedro related that the Cazonci put him in charge of seeing to it that they reached their destination. On November 14, 1522, accompanied by two Spaniards, he set off at the head of 1,600 men. On the road his men encouraged him to dress himself up so as to impress the lords of Zacatula, and he put on many turquoise collars for that purpose. In Zacatula the Tarascans had their first view of the primitive Spanish shipyard, where Cortés was having four ships built so that he could push his explorations out into the Pacific.[30]

We do not have much information about the activities of Olid's soldiers in Michoacán beyond their idol breaking and treasure hunting. Nearly all the *relaciones geograficas* for the region name Olid as their conqueror,[31] but we cannot be sure whether this indicates that he actually went around to all the towns or merely that they submitted to him in a general way as parts of the Tarascan kingdom.

The original intention of Cortés was that the Spaniards should colonize the area and establish a Spanish municipality there. With this purpose in mind he appointed a list of municipal officials. He named Andrés de Tapia as the alcalde (local judge) and Alonso Canpucano, Antonio de Villaroel, Bachiller Sotomayor, and Alvarado Maldonado as *regidores* (aldermen). Alonso Canpucano also had the office of *alférez* (ensign) of the military operation, and Antonio de Villaroel was also treasurer. Rodrigo Morejón de Lobrera and Cristóbal Martín de Gamboa were also listed among the officials, but their positions were not specified.[32] In later statements Cristóbal Martín de Gamboa claimed that he had been appointed alcalde for the town, and Andrés de Tapia said that his own position was that of *justicia mayor* (*alcalde mayor*, or judge-administrator over the whole region).[33]

The plan to establish a Spanish municipality in Michoacán was unsuccessful at this time. The reasons for its failure are a subject of dispute. Domingo Niño, one of Olid's horsemen, who later showed himself unfriendly toward Cortés, stated in Cortés' *residencia* that Olid had already laid out a town in a good place but that when Cortés found out that the land was rich he commanded Olid to return to Mexico and sent on to Zacatula those who wanted to settle in Michoacán. Then he took Michoacán for himself and did not distribute any of the towns as encomiendas for two years.[34] It is true that Cortés waited for nearly two years before distributing the towns, but we shall see that in the meantime he sent Spaniards into the area to make a general survey and census, and his reason for not distributing the towns earlier was probably his desire for more exact knowledge of the land and its population.

The reason Cortés gave to the king of Spain for withdrawing the colony was that the Spaniards were not satisfied with the land and some of them were causing trouble:

And since the land was not very satisfying to them for colonizing, they showed ill will toward it, and even caused some little disturbances for which some of them were punished; and for this reason I ordered those who wished to return to do so, and I commanded the rest to go with a captain to the South Sea, where I have settled a town called Zacatula.[35]

Juan Rodríguez de Villafuerte, who was appointed captain of the expedition to Zacatula, indicated in 1525 that some problems had also arisen within the Spanish camp:

Between some of the Spaniards and Cristóbal de Olid, while they were on the said conquest, there arose certain differences and discords; and the said lord governor [Cortés] knew about it, and he recalled the said Cristóbal de Olid, and I remained as captain of all the men who were there.[36]

We do not have an exact date for the departure of either contingent of the Spanish-Mexican force from Michoacán. The *Relación* states somewhat querulously that the Tarascans had to feed the occupying force for six of their months (120 days).[37] This would place their departure sometime in November, 1522. But are we to take this as the date of the departure of Olid's contingent, presumably with the Mexican allies, or does it indicate the time of Villafuerte's departure with the second group? The latter's statement of 1525 indicates that he stayed on in Michoacán for a while after Olid left. That is supported by a statement made by Jerónimo Flores in 1560:

After the conquest and pacification of the said province of Michoacán and other neighboring provinces was completed, the said Cristóbal de Olid came away to this said city of Mexico to give an account to the said Marqués

[Cortés] concerning what he had done in the said conquest, and Juan Rodríguez de Villafuerte stayed on in his place as captain.[38]

There is an indication in the *Relación* that Olid was still in Michoacán in late November: when Don Pedro tells of taking the anchors to Zacatula in November, he says that the Spaniards there sent back cacao for Olid.[39]

Juan Rodríguez de Villafuerte was not universally considered a good choice to replace Olid in the position of leader. Critics of Cortés attacked him in his *residencia* for putting Villafuerte in a position of authority, referring to the latter as "a man who knew very little for holding the office of justice," "one very lacking in authority for holding the said office because he was very young," and "an incapable, foolish young man who had greater need to be given a guardian than to be given an office of justice or a captaincy."[40]

Although we could ascribe such general criticisms merely to envy, one of the men who was in Michoacán under Villafuerte, Ruy González, testified more specifically regarding activities of the kind that may have motivated the antipathy toward Villafuerte:

[Cortés] gave the office of his lieutenant in the province of Michoacán to Villafuerte, who is an undependable man of little knowledge. When a certain man came from this said city [Mexico City] to the said Michoacán and stated that those who were living in this said city were richer and better off, Villafuerte took him and had him stripped naked and exposed him to public shame from morning to midday. This witness and others went to ask him to free the man because it appeared bad, but the said Villafuerte was not willing to do so until such a time as he did it of his own will. Also, while he was lieutenant in the said province, he would go through the streets giving jabs [*picotadas*] to people indiscriminately.[41]

Villafuerte's inexperience, coupled with a desire to gain some added esteem, showed itself in a disastrous way upon his departure from Michoacán. Instead of following Cortés' orders to go directly to Zacatula, he tried to achieve special glory by conquering Colima. He was badly defeated, however, and had to fall back quickly to Zacatula.[42] Antonio de Herrera records that in the attempted conquest of Colima some of Villafuerte's Tarascan allies looted a great deal from the areas along the way, even though some of the territory was subject to the Cazonci. The Tarascan king then went to Cortés to seek redress, and,

having received satisfaction, he always remained a loyal friend of
Cortés.[43]

There is no doubt that Cortés was quite displeased by the unauthorized activity of his captain, as we can judge from his report to the king:

> While this said captain and his men were going to the said city of Zacatula,
> they were informed of a province called Colima, which lies about fifty leagues
> off the road which they should have taken, to the right, that is, to the west.
> With the men whom he was leading and with many of the allies of that
> province of Michoacán, he went there without my permission. He entered into
> it for several days' journey and there he had some encounters with the natives.
> Although his force consisted of more than forty horsemen and a hundred
> foot soldiers, crossbowmen and shield bearers, the natives defeated them and
> cast them out of the land, killing three Spaniards and many of the allies. And
> then they went on to the said city of Zacatula. When this came to my knowl-
> edge, I commanded that captain to be brought to me as a prisoner, and I
> punished him for his disobedience.[44]

Gómara named Olid as the captain of this unauthorized expedition
into Colima, but the testimony of the participants contradicts this.[45]
Bernal Díaz tells us that after Olid's return to Mexico he went back
down to the west coast to relieve Villafuerte, who was surrounded by
hostile Indians in Zacatula. Then he went on to Colima and conquered
it, though it rebelled again as soon as he had left.[46] Díaz, however,
was not well informed about what was happening in the western
provinces at this time, since he had gone off with Gonzalo de Sandoval
on an expedition to the southeast and had settled in Coatzacoalcos.[47]

Those who were present do not mention any intervention by Olid
in the conquest of western Mexico after his departure from Michoacán. What they do indicate is that only seven or eight days after
Villafuerte arrived in Zacatula he led a successful campaign against
the Impilcingas. Then he and his little army returned once more to
Zacatula, where Gonzalo de Sandoval soon arrived with additional
forces and orders from Cortés to incorporate Villafuerte's men into his
own army and proceed against Colima. On that occasion they were
successful in subjugating the province.[48]

We know very little in detail about this expedition into Colima
under Sandoval. Cortés devoted only a paragraph to it in his "Fourth
Letter," without naming the captain who led it. He reported that he
sent a captain from Mexico City with 25 horsemen and 70 or 80 foot

soldiers to pacify Impilcingo and then to go on to Zacatula. There the captain was to gather as many more men as possible and proceed to Colima. In Zacatula he added enough men to his force to make a total of about 50 horsemen and 150 foot soldiers. Then they moved north-westward toward Colima. Cortés seems to imply that they made their way to Colima by struggling through the extremely difficult terrain along the Pacific coast. This inference is supported by a statement of Jerónimo Flores, a participant in the campaign, who stated that he had accompanied Sandoval in the conquest of Colima and Motín. Motín lay along the Pacific coast between Zacatula and Colima.[49]

When they arrived at the site of Villafuerte's defeat, they found a native army waiting for them. In a hard-fought hand-to-hand battle the victory went to the Spaniards, not a single one of whom was killed, although many men and horses were wounded. Cortés indicates that the Spaniards inflicted severe punishment on the natives, probably meaning that they enslaved many of them. Several other provinces of the area also then submitted to the Spaniards.[50]

Another aspect of this conquest is shown in the *Relación de Michoacán*. Forces of Tarascan auxiliaries were led by Huitzitziltzi, and even the women came along bearing burdens for the Spaniards. The Tarascans, who went into battle as in former times carrying their cloth-covered idols, sacrificed many of the Indian captives, and the Spaniards did nothing to prevent it. Like Cortés, Don Pedro noted that not one Spaniard was killed but that the Spaniards killed many of the natives of Colima.[51]

Cortés ordered Sandoval to find a good site for a town and to establish a colony there which was to be called Colimán. He also sent along a list of officials appointed for the new municipality. Further, at Cortés' command, Sandoval visited the native towns of the province and made up a list of them, and Cortés apportioned them out as encomiendas for the 25 horsemen and 120 foot soldiers who decided to settle there.[52] This series of events explains why many of the men who originally entered Michoacán with Olid appeared later as *vecinos* (freeholders) of Colima.[53]

In the meantime Olid had returned to Mexico, where the loot was distributed. There is some disagreement about the amount that was involved. Cortés wrote to the king that it totaled as much as 3,000 marks of silver alloyed with copper and 5,000 pesos of gold alloyed with silver.[54] Gómara likewise mentioned 5,000 pesos of mixed gold and silver, but reported only 1,000 marks of silver-copper alloy. He added that the treasure was all in pieces of adornment for the body.[55] Luis de Cárdenas asserted that Olid sent to Mexico 122 cargas of silver and 5 cargas of gold that he had taken from the temples in Michoacán, but the amounts give us very little idea of their value.[56]

In Mexico the pile of Tarascan artifacts was offered at public auction, and the treasury records indicate that the price for which the "white and gilded silver" was sold at auction was 9,601 pesos, 4 tomines, 6 granos. The same accounts mention that in Michoacán itself there had been held an auction of certain articles of clothing, given to Olid at the same time as the silver, which had brought 159 pesos, 4 tomines of gold.[57]

The money obtained from the auction in Mexico City was distributed to the members of the expedition, after one-fifth had been deducted for the king (1,920 pesos, 11 granos) and one-fifth of the remainder had been set aside for Captain-General Cortés (1,536 pesos, 2 tomines). From the total that remained, 6,145 pesos, 1 tomín, 4 granos, each of the two captains, Olid and Villafuerte, received 160 pesos; Andrés de Tapia, alcalde and captain of the foot soldiers, 120 pesos; each of the city officials who had been appointed for Michoacán and Zacatula, 80 pesos; each horseman, 60 pesos; each crossbowman, 30 pesos; and each foot soldier, 20 pesos. In an act of special largesse Cortés commanded that each of the crossbowmen and the foot soldiers was to be given an additional 10 pesos from the fifth part that had been set aside for him. He gave the remainder of his fifth (166 pesos) to Cristóbal Martín de Gamboa and Miguel Díaz de Aux in compensation for injuries to their horses during the campaign.[58] Unfortunately the record gives no date for either the auction of the artifacts or the distribution of the money.

The principal bidder at the auction of precious metals from Michoacán was Cortés himself, who was collecting silver to be cast into a gift for the king, a silver cannon, which he would call "El Fénix." Both Bernal Díaz and Gómara mention that the cannon was made of the adulterated silver from Michoacán.[59] Antonio de Oliver, who was present when it was cast, stated that it was made from *part* of the gold and silver that the Cazonci had given to Cortés.[60] Cortés, however, placed the value of "El Fénix" at 24,500 pesos of gold, evaluating the silver at 5 pesos per mark.[61] That comes to 4,900 marks of silver, which is greater than all the other estimates of the silver that Olid sent and brought back from Michoacán. This discrepancy may indicate one or a combination, of several possibilities: that Cortés overestimated the value of the cannon when he wrote about it to the king, that the auction price of the silver did not represent its full value, that more silver was received from Michoacán than was officially registered, or that not all of the silver for the cannon came from Michoacán. Cortés sent "El Fénix" off to the king in 1524 in the care of Francisco de Montejo, Diego de Soto, and Juan Velázquez de Salazar.[62] He had a verse inscribed on it that he had composed for the purpose:

> This was born without equal;
> I in serving you am without second;
> You are without equal in the world.

The verse, which seemed a bit grandiose to some of the Spanish courtiers, aroused considerable jealousy among them toward Cortés.[63]

In Michoacán, meanwhile, after the departure of the Spaniards the Cazonci took his vengeance on the warlord Timas and the other *principales* who had tried to kill him. Again Don Pedro tells the story in a very dramatic fashion, with himself as the central figure.[64]

He narrates that soon after he returned from taking the anchors to Zacatula the Cazonci summoned him and said: "Come here. What shall we do about those *principales* who wanted to kill me because of their pride? I escaped from their hands, but they will not escape from mine. Go and kill them, and you will be a valiant man." (Apparently the expression "valiant man" was used by the Tarascans to describe one who had achieved prominence by disposing of the king's enemies, in battle or otherwise.)

Don Pedro answered simply, "My lord, let it be as you command."

Taking with him forty men armed with clubs, he crossed the lake at dawn. Timas, who knew that the Cazonci wanted to have him executed, had fled to Capacuero, west of the lake; he had set spies along the road and was waiting for whoever was sent to kill him. When Don Pedro and his men reached Capacuero, they found Timas decked out in all of his finery, with turquoise collars around his neck, golden plugs in his earlobes, little golden bells on his legs, and a garland of trefoil on his head; and he was drunk.

Don Pedro was carrying a letter in his hand, possibly as an excuse for getting past the warlord's spies. When Timas saw him, he asked, "Where are you going?"

"We are going to Colima," Don Pedro replied. "The Spaniards sent us there." Then, coming close to Timas, he said, "The Cazonci has issued a sentence of death against you."

"Why? What have I done?" Timas asked.

"I don't know," replied Don Pedro. "I am merely his emissary."

The warlord, resentful that this untried young man had been sent against him, challenged Don Pedro: "Why are you the one who has come? Are you a valiant man? Let us fight with one another. What should we fight with? With bows and arrows, or with clubs?"

"We shall fight with clubs," Don Pedro told him.

Timas belittled him: "What? Are you a very valiant man? Where have you been in the danger of battle, where enemies fight against enemies? Where have you killed anyone there? For what purpose did you come? But, welcome, and since my nephew the Cazonci commands it, let it be so. I missed killing him by only a little. All of you, go away. You are not going to kill me. Tomorrow or the next day I will hang myself. You are all very avaricious and covetous, you who come to kill me."

Don Pedro replied: "Where have you sent me that I have robbed anyone? You are the one who robbed the Cazonci and his brothers and killed the lords. Why are you ashamed to die?"

Timas then went into the house and told his wives what was happening. They burned large amounts of cloth (literally, "thread") and some of his adornments, and he killed one of his wives so that he could take it all with him in death. Then he returned to Don Pedro, who was awaiting him with his men, and he offered them a drink. But Don Pedro took the wine and threw it on the ground.

Timas asked: "Why did you pour it out? What was wrong with it?"

Don Pedro replied: "Did I come just to pay you a visit? Why should you offer me a drink? I am hungry, not thirsty." (The reference to hunger here is hard to interpret. Is Don Pedro perhaps speaking in terms of cannibalism, which the Tarascans practiced in conjunction with human sacrifice?)

The warlord then ridiculed him, saying, "Who does not know that you are a valiant man and that you conquered Zacatula?"

"You are making fun of me when you say that I conquered Zacatula," Don Pedro replied. "Did not the Spaniards conquer it?"

Then Don Pedro and his men went up to Timas and grabbed him as he cried out: "Let me pass! Let me pass!" They hit him with their clubs and broke open his skull and then dragged him around on the ground before he died. All his supporters fled away out of fear. His wives did not know about his death, because they did not think that it would come so quickly. But some of the Indians who were with Don Pedro went into Timas's house and began taking his wives' blankets away from them, because it was a custom among the Tarascans that whenever they killed anyone they would rob his house of everything that was in it.

But Don Pedro demanded of them, "Why are you taking their blankets away from them?"

"This is our custom, sir," they replied.

But he commanded them to give the blankets back to the women.

The women began to weep over the slain *principal*. "Oh, our lord, wait for us," they wailed. "We want to go with you."

"Don't weep, but stay here," Don Pedro told them. "Him alone are we going to kill. Don't go anywhere else, but stay here with his children, and don't be afraid."

They buried Timas in Capacuero, and then Don Pedro returned to Tzintzuntzan. Later the Cazonci sent him out to execute other *principales* who had wanted to kill him, and he took away all their possessions.

In this way Don Pedro tells us how he was gradually rising to an ever-higher position in the surviving native power structure of Michoacán, serving, literally, as the Cazonci's hatchet man. At the same time, however, two other important participants in the action of this period were taking a common route to their final end. During 1523, Cristóbal de Olid was preparing to lead an expedition by sea to Honduras, but the departure of the expedition had to be delayed because of the arrival of a strong force of Spaniards under Francisco de Garay at Pánuco, on the Gulf near present-day Tampico.[65] A rebellion of Indians erupted in Pánuco in late 1523, as a result of criminal activities by Garay's men, and Cortés sent in an expedition under Gonzalo de Sandoval to pacify the area once again.[66] Two of the leaders of Olid's expedition to Michoacán, Andrés de Tapia and Cristóbal Martín Millán de Gamboa, stated that they went to Pánuco after leaving Michoacán.[67] Don Pedro also noted in the *Relación* that his brother Huitzitziltzi went to Pánuco with Olid.[68] Apparently, then, Huitzitziltzi, who had assisted Sandoval in the conquest of Colima and was waiting to depart for Honduras with Olid, led his group of warriors into Pánuco.

Olid's expedition was finally able to depart for Honduras on January 11, 1524.[69] Huitzitziltzi also accompanied Olid on this expedition.[70] On the way to Honduras, Olid stopped in Cuba to take on supplies, and there he was persuaded by the governor, Cortés' archenemy Diego Velásquez, to set himself up in Honduras independent of Cortés. Cortés sent his kinsman Francisco de las Casas to bring Olid back into submission. Although Olid was able to capture Las Casas, the latter soon turned the tables and made Olid his captive. Immediately he had Olid executed by beheading in the Plaza of Naco, in Honduras.[71] Don Pedro said that Huitzitziltzi also died in Honduras,[72] but the Spanish chroniclers do not give any information regarding the circumstances of his death.

∴

CHAPTER 4

The Caravajal Survey of Michoacán
and the Granting of Encomiendas

CRISTÓBAL de Olid's attempt to colonize Michoacán ended in fail-ure. Fernando Cortés, however, did not lose interest in the Tarascan kingdom but determined to distribute the towns to his followers as encomiendas. In preparation for this he sent out a small expedition under Antonio de Caravajal to survey the region thoroughly and bring back an adequate description of the main towns and the districts sub-ject to them.[1] Very little has been known about this early survey—so little, in fact, that the chroniclers of Michoacán do not even mention it. Only slight references to it are found in the published documenta-tion of the period. For instance, Cortés, in a letter to his father in 1526, mentioned a visitation of Michoacán that Caravajal had made at some previous time.[2] In 1530, during the trial of the Cazonci, Nuño de Guzmán asked the Tarascan king whether he knew that the towns had been distributed among the Spaniards. The Cazonci answered that Caravajal and Tomás had made a visitation to distribute them.[3]

It is evident that this visitation was of fundamental importance for the early history of the Spanish occupation of Michoacán, since it formed the basis for the distribution of the encomiendas. Because of this fact the visitation record became a document of primary impor-tance for proving the geographical extent of the encomiendas. The five fragments of the record that I have been able to find were all pre-served in lawsuits over encomiendas. Each of the five fragments com-prises the complete visitation of a major town, a *cabecera*, with all of its subject towns and estancias. The towns represented are Comanja (Espopuyuta), Uruapan, Turicato, Huaniqueo (Guaniqueo), and Eron-garícuaro.[4]

The researcher faces an immediate problem with the fragments, in that none of them gives the year in which the visitation was made. This lacuna, however, can be filled because in each case both the day of the week and the date of the month are given. Since the visitation occurred between mid-1521, when Mexico City was conquered, and 1526, when Cortés wrote about the visitation as a completed work, the span of years is small enough that the year of the visitation can be determined exactly through the concurrence of dates. Thus, for example, the survey of Comanja was made on Friday, October 9; Saturday, October 10; and Monday, October 12. By a comparison with other known dates of the period, such as those given in Cortés' letters, we can determine that this concurrence of dates and days of the week took place in October, 1523, less than a year after Olid abandoned Michoacán.[5]

At the time he was sent out to make the visitation, Antonio de Caravajal already had considerable experience in the New World. According to his own relation of his activities, made in 1559, he had gone to Española with Diego Columbus in 1509 and had later taken part in the conquest of San Juan Boriquén (Puerto Rico) and Cuba. Early in 1521 he left Española for New Spain on one of four ships carrying four hundred men to reinforce Cortés after his defeat in his first attempt to conquer Mexico. In the final battles for the conquest of Tenochtitlan he was captain of one of the brigantines on the lake and helped maintain the siege of the city. In Coyoacán after the victory he was chosen as a captain of the foot soldiers. He helped in the pacification of the provinces of the Huasteca and Pánuco and went with soldiers to aid Pedro de Alvarado in Tututepec. Later he had some experience in the kind of work that he was to do in Michoacán, going as judge visitor to the provinces that lay between Mexico City and the Huasteca, where he tried to draw the Indians away from idolatry and human sacrifice by admonitions and good treatment.

Cortés sent Caravajal on his mission to Michoacán sometime in mid-1523. Caravajal stated that he spent a year in the visitation and returned to Mexico at the time when Cortés was preparing to leave for Honduras. As we shall see later, Cortés left for Honduras in October, 1524; Caravajal seems to have been back in Mexico by the middle of July of that year. In Michoacán, as in his previous area of visitation, he tried to draw the natives away from idolatry and sacrifices. In 1561, Jerónimo Ruiz de la Mota, one of the witnesses in Caravajal's *probanza*, stated that he had seen the commission of Cortés to

Caravajal, commanding him to see to it that the Indians did not have idols or make sacrifices. Another witness, Alonso Ortiz de Zúñiga, expressed surprise that Caravajal had not been killed while carrying out his commission, considering the rebellious spirit of the Indians at the time, but, as far as we know, Caravajal did not have any trouble in his campaign against native religion. Gonzalo Gómez testified that he had heard Cortés state that the judge visitor had done a great deal of good toward the conversion of the natives.[6] The visitation preceded by a year or two the first entry of missionary friars into the area.

The group with whom Caravajal ventured into Michoacán was very small. The *relación geográfica* of Zirándaro, written in 1579, states that Caravajal arrived there accompanied by three Spaniards and a black man named Juan Garrido. They were the first Spaniards to enter this town on the Río Balsas.[7] One of the three Spaniards was Francisco Morcillo, who went with Caravajal as the official notary of the visitation.[8] Another was Tomás de Rijoles, interpreter for the expedition, who must have been the Tomás mentioned by the Cazonci.[9] Possibly the third Spaniard was Juan de la Torre, who is mentioned with Caravajal as *visitador* of Erongarícuaro.[10]

We know comparatively little about Caravajal's itinerary, except for the information actually recorded in the visitations. From these we find that he was surveying the district of Comanja on October 9, 10, and 12, 1523; Uruapan, December 22 to 24, 1523; Turicato, January 21 to 23, 1524; Huaniqueo, March 25, 26, 30, and 31, 1524; and Erongarícuaro, April 19 to 21, 1524.[11]

An Indian witness in a lawsuit between Diego Hernández Nieto and Antonio Oliver over Turicato indicated that Caravajal had been in Tacámbaro before coming to Turicato.[12] We do not know when he was in Zirándaro, but the *relación geográfica* for that area indicates that he was in the town for three days and from there went to Zacatula.[13] To judge from the dates that we have, he seems to have covered the outlying regions first and saved the more heavily populated towns of central Michoacán until last. The first *cédulas de encomienda* by which Cortés distributed the towns of Michoacán as tributaries to the Spaniards are dated in late July, 1524, indicating that Caravajal had returned to Mexico by that time.[14]

Caravajal's census of Michoacán appears to have been a relatively complete listing of all major towns of the region together with the smaller settlements subject to each town. The fragments that have survived are of great interest to the student of the Tarascan area, since they give an indication of the population density at the time of the Conquest, which is very difficult to estimate in the absence of tribute rolls for the area. The listing for each town or estancia gives two statements regarding the number of houses contained in it, the first given by the native headman, the second recorded by the visitor after he had gone through the settlement. In nearly every instance the number recorded by the Spanish official is greater than that given by the Indian, though occasionally the two agree. It is difficult to judge which number is the more trustworthy, since both were given by interested parties. The cacique would probably have given a lower number than the true one to lessen the assessment of tribute; the visitor, on the other hand, could very easily have counted unoccupied houses and would have tended to exaggerate the number of potential tributaries. The difference may also be explained by a statement in the *Relación de Michoacán* regarding the work of the *ocambecha*, whose duty it was to count the population: "They do not count these houses by hearths or *vecinos* [here meaning adult male residents] but by how many belong to one family, for it is customary that in some houses there are two or three *vecinos* with their relatives. And there are other houses in which there is no one but a man and wife, and in others a mother and son."[15]

The contrast between the two counts is most remarkable in the totals for each jurisdiction. For Comanja and its subject area the Indians gave a total of 341 houses, while the Spaniards counted 782 houses. For Uruapan the two counts are 185 and 497 (or 462), respectively; for Turicato, 99 and 246; for Huaniqueo, 323 (or 326) and 827; and for Erongarícuaro, 289 and 863.

A further idea of population density can be gained by considering the number of settlements subject to a *cabecera* and their distance from it. For instance, twelve settlements were listed as subjects of Uruapan, but only six of them were within one league of the main town. By contrast, within the jurisdiction of Huaniqueo (Guaniqueo in the original) there were forty-five settlements, and twenty-one of them were no more than a league from the *cabecera*.

There is clear evidence, however, that Caravajal missed some of the smaller settlements in his survey. In the lawsuit between Hernández Nieto and Oliver an Indian witness named Juan Catao, who had been present during the original visitation, mentioned four places in the district of Turicato which the Cazonci had commanded not to be shown to the Spaniards. Since Caravajal listed only eighteen settlements in his visitation of Turicato, he missed 18 percent of the places subject to the town. These settlements continued to give service to the native monarch until his death.[16] If this happened in the one town about which we have an explicit statement, we may well suspect that it occurred in other areas also, although in Turicato, where the terrain is very rugged and difficult, it would have been easier to mislead the Spaniards to protect the Cazonci's interests than it would have been in many other districts. Such tactics, however, would eventually contribute to the Cazonci's undoing. As we shall see, one of the charges brought against him before his execution by Guzmán in 1530 was that he had continued to take tribute from areas within the jurisdiction of the encomiendas of the Spaniards.[17] In spite of deficiencies in Caravajal's survey, it met with approval. Hernández Nieto testified in Caravajal's behalf in 1561 that the visitation was "the best and most accurate and important visitation that has been made in this New Spain by any of the *visitadores* who were so appointed."[18]

Besides the listing of towns, the visitation record also gives other geographical information. For each place visited it provides a concise statement regarding its geographic setting, preserving the native names for the mountains, rivers, springs, and lakes and other outstanding features (see appendix A). Thus, for example, it describes Erongarícuaro as situated on the slope of a mountain called Uchataro and says that at the other end of the town was Lake Apunda de Uchichila (Lake Pátzcuaro).[19] Huaniqueo lay in a lush plain at the foot of a high, bald mountain called Tucapachirato, and through the town ran a river called Uripitio.[20] One notices the frequency of the use of the term "Apunda" for lakes and of various forms of "Yurequa" for river. These words mean "lake" and "river" respectively, in the Tarascan language, and probably were not intended as proper names.[21]

For the region of Comanja the record shows evidence of linguistic diversity. The name of the *cabecera* is given in a Nahuatl form (Espopuyutla), and some of the other names show the Nahuatl endings *-tlan* for "place" and *-tepec (tepetl)* for "hill" or "mountain," rather than the corresponding Tarascan endings of *-ro* and *-ato*.[22]

The surveying party was to be on the watch for evidences of mineral wealth, as indicated in the entry for Comanja. The men noted that in the gizzards of the "chickens" (turkeys) they had found grains that appeared to be gold or copper and had sent them to Cortés.[23]

When Caravajal completed his survey and returned to Mexico City, the period of basic exploration of Michoacán by the Spaniards was completed. By means of the Olid expedition and the Caravajal survey the way was prepared for the division of the Tarascan kingdom into encomiendas and the gradual Spanish occupation of the region.

The beginning of the systematic Spanish exploitation of Michoacán occurred in the summer of 1524, when Caravajal returned from Michoacán and Cortés distributed the towns of the Tarascan kingdom among his followers. Only a few of the grant records have come down to us. No official register of grants for this period has come to light, and indeed, as far as we know, none was kept. This omission would fuel a great amount of litigation in later years, since the individual encomendero's cedula was the only full record of the grant.

An instance of this is seen in the case of Diego Hernández Nieto, who claimed to have received a cedula granting him one-half of Turicato. His contention was supported by Francisco Morcillo, notary of the Caravajal visitation. But while Hernández Nieto was in Honduras with Cortés, the cedula of encomienda was lost, and he lacked the best proof of his case in the long lawsuit that he carried on with Antonio de Oliver regarding the town.[24]

The documents of a few grants, however, have been preserved in lawsuits that the parties appealed to the Council of the Indies. One of the earliest of these documents records that Matalcingo (Charo) and its subject towns were granted to Rodrigo de Albornoz on July 24, 1524. The document reads as follows:

By this present cedula there is deposited in you Rodrigo de Albornoz, accountant of their Majesties for this New Spain, the lord and natives of the town of Matalcingo which is in the province of Michoacán, with the towns of Uritla, Irapeo, Moquenzan, Totula, Coyzula, Necotan, Maratuhaco, Vichitepeque, and Maritaro, all subject to the aforementioned head town of Matalcingo, so that you may use them and they may help you on your farms and enterprises, in conformity with the ordinances that have been and will be made concerning this matter, with the duty that you shall have of instructing them in the matters of our holy Catholic faith, applying to it all possible and necessary vigilance and solicitude. Dated in Tenochtitlan on the twenty-fourth of July of the year one thousand five hundred and twenty-four. Fernando Cortés. By command of the governor my lord. Rodrigo de Paz.[25]

By similar documents Cortés granted Tajimaroa (called Taxinda)

and its subject towns to Gonzalo de Salazar on July 24, 1524; half of
Tancítaro to Domingo de Medina on August 24, 1524; Jacona and its
district to Juan de Albornoz on August 24, 1524; and Uruapan with
its jurisdiction to Francisco de Villegas on August 25, 1524.[26]

It becomes evident from these grants that Cortés was taking care of
the interests of the royal-treasury officials in this distribution of encomiendas. Two of them, Accountant Rodrigo de Albornoz and Factor
Gonzalo de Salazar, received grants, as did two of their relatives, Juan
de Albornoz and Juan Velázquez de Salazar. (The latter claimed that
Pungarabato was given to him in 1524, although he did not give the
precise date of his cedula.)[27] The treasury officials had arrived only
recently from Spain and were giving Cortés some cause for concern
by their close scrutiny of fiscal affairs in the colony.[28]

It was also at this time that Cortés took for himself some of the
choicest holdings in Michoacán. In 1531 he brought suit against Peralmíndez Chirino for income of which he had been deprived owing
to the confiscation of his towns at the time of his supposed death in
Honduras in 1525. Cortés claimed that in Michoacán he had held the
capital city, Uchichila (Tzintzuntzan), as well as Huaniqueo, and the
important mineral-producing towns of Tamazula, Tuxpan, Amula,
and Zapotlán.[29] Since he had assumed control of these towns before
his departure for Honduras in October, 1524, he must have learned
of their wealth from the Caravajal visitation and immediately skimmed
them off for himself.

In the course of Cortés' *residencia* two witnesses, Juan de Burgos
and Andrés de Monjaraz, testified that Cortés had first placed Tzintzuntzan directly under the authority of the crown but afterwards had
taken it for himself.[30] Perhaps these statements refer to the abortive
effort to found a Spanish town there under Olid, after which Cortés
took the Tarascan capital as one of his own encomiendas.

The method of distributing encomiendas that Cortés employed in
Michoacán—that is, making the distribution only after an adequate
survey—was much more satisfactory to him than the precipitous way
in which he had felt compelled to make the distribution of other areas.
In later testimony Andrés de Tapia recalled that during a visit to
Colima he had commented to Cortés about the poor encomienda
(Tecozitlán) that Cortés had given to Jorge Carrillo, one of the soldiers
who had passed through Michoacán with Olid and had later gone on
to Colima. Cortés' answer was: "Now you see how it has turned out

for many — for the person of whom it was thought that we were giving him something, it turned out not to be good, but quite the contrary, as in this case. The harm that was done was not my fault but yours, since you hurried me so much to distribute the land to you that I could do nothing else but do it almost blindly."[31]

With the distribution of the encomiendas in Michoacán the Spaniards had achieved what the Aztecs had failed to do: they had made Tenoch-titlan-Mexico the capital and had reduced the kingdom of Michoacán to a tributary province. The compelling decisions regarding Michoacán would henceforth be made in Mexico City, and the wealth of the province would make its way to the new Spanish capital of New Spain and across the ocean to a monarch whom the natives would never see. Within Michoacán Spanish influence of two kinds would soon begin to make itself felt, that of the zealous missionary and that of the enterprising colonist.

•••

CHAPTER 5

Christian Beginnings in Michoacán

FROM the very first contacts between the Spaniards and the Indians there was an element of proselytizing. Cortés' intentions in this regard are apparent from the first paragraph of his Ordinances of December 22, 1520:

First, in view of the fact that by experience we have seen and see every day how much solicitude and vigilance the natives of these regions show in the cult and veneration of their idols, from which great disservice is done to God Our Lord; and the devil, by the cunning and deceit in which he holds them, is much venerated by them; and in separating them from such great error and idolatry and converting them to the knowledge of our holy Catholic faith Our Lord would be greatly served; and besides gaining glory for our souls by being the cause that [*henceforth*] so many souls should [*not*] be lost and condemned, in the [*future*] God would always be our help and support: therefore, with every insistance with which I can and must do so, I exhort and entreat all the Spaniards who may go in my company to this war to which we are going at the present, and to all other wars and conquests to which in the name of His Majesty they may have to go at my command, that their principal motive and intention should be to separate and root out the said idolatries from the natives of these regions and to convert them or at least to desire their salvation and their conversion to the knowledge of God and of His holy Catholic faith, because if the said war were waged with any other intention it would be unjust, and everything that might be taken during it would be subject to obligatory restitution, and His Majesty would not have any reason to command that those who serve in it should be rewarded; and concerning this matter I burden the consciences of the said Spaniards, and from this moment I protest in the name of His Catholic Majesty that my principal intention and motive is to wage the said war, and the others that I may wage, in order to draw and lead the said natives to the said knowledge of our faith and belief, and afterward to subject and subdue them under the imperial and royal yoke and dominion of His Sacred Majesty, to whom the lordship over all of these regions juridically belongs.[1]

We have seen that Cortés commanded his first emissaries to instruct the Cazonci regarding the service to God as well as to the Spanish king. One of the first activities of Olid's men after entering Tzintzuntzan was to destroy the idols. Antonio de Caravajal also destroyed idols and idol offerings during his visitation. All these conquerors shared in the crusading spirit that had been built up in Spain during the eight previous centuries of conflict with the Mohammedans. They reacted strongly against the elements of the native material culture that were opposed to Christianity, and their whole background taught them to destroy these symbols of native religion. As far as we know, however, these beginnings were almost entirely negative and destructive.

The first Catholic priest or priests who entered Michoacán arrived in the company of Cristóbal de Olid. We have seen the reaction of the Tarascan lord Don Pedro Cuinierángari when he was captured by the Olid expedition and attended one of the first Masses celebrated in Michoacán. For him the most logical interpretation of the liturgical ceremony was that it was a form of divination, since that was the use that Tarascan priests made of vessels containing water.

It is difficult to determine the identity of the priest who celebrated the Mass that Don Pedro attended. Among Olid's horsemen we find the name of a Francisco Martín, followed by a word that might be interpreted as clérigo or chigo.[2] It seems possible that this was the secular priest who was later pastor of Zacatula, whom Gonzalo Gómez in one place called Francisco Martín[3] but who was generally known as Francisco Martínez. He was pastor of Zacatula as early as November 3, 1525, and as late as 1529.[4] He may have gone there with Villafuerte. Another of Olid's horsemen who is given the designation clérigo or chigo is Pedro Castellano, who was perhaps also a secular priest.[5]

But it was during a visit of the Cazonci to Mexico that the real Christian missionary work among the Tarascans had its origin. The Relación de Michoacán tells us that on a certain occasion when the Cazonci and Don Pedro went to Mexico to see Cortés he asked them whether they had any sons. Both denied that they had sons but told him that some of the principales had them. Cortés commanded the sons to be brought to Mexico City to be taught Christian doctrine in the friary of the Franciscans. The Cazonci selected fifteen boys and sent them to Mexico, admonishing them to learn what they were taught and assuring them that they would not be away from home for more than a year. The boys went to Mexico on June 7 and stayed there for a year.[6]

Although the *Relación* does not tell us the year in which this interview between the Cazonci and Cortés took place, the circumstances place it almost certainly in the late summer of 1524. According to the *Relación*, it took place after the Spaniards had taken the census of the towns and had distributed them as encomiendas.[7] The extant initial encomienda grants for Michoacán date from July and August, 1524.[8] The *Relación* also indicates that the Tarascan boys were sent to Mexico a short time before the missionary friars went to Michoacán.[9] As we shall see shortly, the first missionary friars arrived in Michoacán in 1525. But if the Cazonci's visit to Cortés occurred before some date in 1525, it must also have taken place before mid-October, 1524, since Cortés left Mexico City then to go to Honduras and did not return until around mid-June, 1526.[10] The Cazonci's visit may very well have borne a relationship to Cortés' impending departure, since Bernal Díaz recorded that Cortés took some caciques from Michoacán with him on this expedition.[11]

The twelve Spanish Franciscans who are credited with founding the Franciscan Order in Mexico also arrived in Mexico during the summer of 1524, having landed in Veracruz on May 13 or 14. They were not the first Franciscans in Mexico. Two Spanish members of the order served as chaplains to the forces of Cortés, and three Flemish Franciscans arrived in Mexico in 1523. But the two Spaniards returned to Spain before the end of the 1520s, and two of the Flemings died in a shipwreck while returning from Cortés' expedition to Honduras, leaving only the lay brother Peter of Ghent, who did indeed make a great contribution to the good of the Indians in central Mexico. It is justifiably acknowledged, however, that the real founders of the Franciscan Order as an ecclesiastical institution in Mexico were the twelve Spanish Franciscans who arrived in 1524 under the leadership of Fray Martín de Valencia. They had come from the rigorously reformed Franciscan province of San Gabriel in Spain and were committed to a life of poverty and holiness. They are recognized as a remarkable group of religious pioneers.[12]

Having arrived in Mexico City around the middle of June, they held meetings and discussions concerning the problems that faced them and tried to determine the best means of resolving them.[13] Out of these discussions must have grown the idea of establishing a school for Indian boys at the friary that was to be constructed for them in Mexico City. For this they had the example of Fray Peter of Ghent, who had founded a school for boys in Texcoco in 1523. The school in Mexico City became operative in 1525.[14] Thus the fifteen young Tarascan nobles were probably sent off to the school in Mexico City on June 7, 1525.

It was also in 1525, according to Mendieta, that the Cazonci came to Mexico City and, pleased with the good work and teaching of the friars, earnestly requested Fray Martín de Valencia to send friars to Michoacán.[15] As we shall see later, from other sources, it becomes evident that royal Factor Gonzalo de Salazar kept the Cazonci prisoner for a while in Mexico City twice in 1525, once in the spring or early summer and again at the end of the year.[16] It is probable that the friars took advantage of the first opportunity to encourage the Tarascan king to accept Christianity. Mendieta, followed by the other Franciscan chroniclers, states that the Cazonci was baptized while he was in Mexico City in 1525.[17] Although the *Relación de Michoacán* places the Cazonci's baptism at a later date, after the friars had arrived in Michoacán, it appears more probable that he was baptized in Mexico City. Cervantes de Salazar wrote that Motolinía (Fray Toribio de Benavente) had told him that he had seen the baptism of the Cazonci. That must have occurred in Mexico City, since Motolinía was religious superior there during the early years, and there is no indication that he was in Michoacán at that time. Because the Cazonci was the first and most important of their Tarascan converts, the Franciscan priests gave him the Christian name Francisco.[18]

Fray Martín de Valencia, seeing the good will of the Tarascan king and hoping that through his influence the rest of the Tarascan nation would become Christian, sent along with him Fray Martín de Jesús (also known as Fray Martín de la Coruña) and two or three companions.[19] All sources agree that this Fray Martín was the superior of the first group of friars sent to Michoacán. Fray Pedro de Oroz, in the chronicle that he wrote in the 1580s, states specifically that Fray Martín was sent to Michoacán in 1525.[20] There has been a problem with the transcription of the friar's name as given in the *Relación*

because the writer used a paleographic abbreviation that has been
varyingly misinterpreted as Martín de Chaves and as Mindechues.[21]
Actually the final element in the name is a modified Greek form of
Jesus, ihus, to which the scribe added a superfluous *s.* In this case also
it should be transcribed as Martín de Jesús. In his own signature the
friar used the Greek abbreviation for *Jesús.*[22]

The other form of his name, Martín de la Coruña, indicates his
place of origin, Coruña, in Galicia, in the far-northwestern corner of
Spain. Very little is known about his early life. In Spain he had become a member of the reformed Franciscan Province of San Gabriel,
and he had come to Mexico as one of the Twelve. The chroniclers
tell us that he was a man of outstanding holiness, especially noted
for his austerity and prayer. He is said to have been elevated above
the ground in moments of ecstasy. Toward himself he was very strict
in regard to food, drink, sleep, and clothing, but he was full of charity
toward his fellow man, and this won him the hearts of the Indians.[23]

Francisco Gonzaga, a Franciscan minister-general of the late sixteenth century, listed the following friars as companions of Fray Martín
de Jesús: Fray Ángel de Saliceto (or Saucedo, also known as Fray Ángel
de Valencia), Fray Jerónimo, Juan Badiano (or Badillo), Fray Miguel
de Bolonia, and Fray Juan de Padilla.[24] Torquemada rightly judged
that this list represented too large a group to have gone to Michoacán
in 1525, when there were still so few friars in Mexico.[25] Fray Diego
Muñoz, whose description of the Province of Michoacán formed the
basis for Gonzaga's chapter, had actually written that Fray Martín de
Jesús went to Michoacán with the Cazonci and that afterward the five
Franciscans mentioned above went there to help him.[26] Gonzaga, in
summarizing the passage, neglected to mention that not all the friars
went to Michoacán at the same time.

If the traditional list of founding friars in Michoacán is not valid,
who then were the first companions of Fray Martín de Jesús? One of
them was Fray Antonio Ortiz, as we learn from two attestations of
Antonio de Oliver, an early encomendero in the area. In January,
1541, Oliver made the following statement in regard to Franciscan
beginnings in Michoacán: "This witness knows and saw that at the
time stated in the question [1528] Fray Antonio Ortiz was in the city
of Michoacán together with Fray Martín de la Coruña, and they were
the ones who started the monastery of the said city of Michoacán."[27] In
1553, Oliver again noted that, in the first group of friars who went

to Michoacán, Fray Martín de la Coruña went as guardian (local superior), and Fray Antonio Ortiz as preacher.[28]

The name of Fray Antonio Ortiz is not found among those of the pioneer missionaries of Michoacán as given in any of the Franciscan chronicles of the area. But that is no argument against his having been there, since none of the printed sources provides a dependable list of the original group of friars who went to Michoacán. Ortiz had arrived in Mexico with the second group of Spanish friars, about eight or nine months after the arrival of the Twelve.[29] This would place his arrival early in 1525. Perhaps the reason why his name is not mentioned among the missionaries of Michoacán is that he stayed for a comparatively short time. Although he was still in Michoacán in 1528, when Bachiller Juan de Ortega made a visitation of the area, in 1529 he was back in Mexico City, where he preached a famous sermon against the activities of Nuño de Guzmán and the First Audiencia, for which he was hauled down bodily from the pulpit.[30] In 1531 and 1532 he was guardian of the Franciscan friary of Mexico City.[31] He returned to Spain, apparently in 1535, and was immediately elected provincial minister of the Province of San Gabriel. He never returned to the New World but went to Africa to preach to the Mohammedans for a while and was again elected provincial minister in 1544. He lived on in Spain until 1560.[32] His later service to his order so overshadowed his work in Michoacán that his earlier activity there was forgotten.

Fray Andrés de Córdoba, a lay brother who came as one of the Twelve, is mentioned as one of the companions of Fray Martín de Jesús in the chronicle written by Fray Antonio Tello about 1650. Oroz also mentions that this friar labored in Michoacán, without indicating whether or not he went there with the original group.[33]

Regarding the list of five friars given by Muñoz and Gonzaga, it seems probable that these men did not arrive in Michoacán until nearly the end of the 1520s, possibly after the return of Ortiz to Mexico. The references to the friars in documents from Bachiller Ortega's visitation of Michoacán in 1528 seem to imply that only Martín de Jesús and Ortiz were there at the time.[34] A group of friars departed from Mexico City for Michoacán during the tenure of the First Audiencia in 1529–30; perhaps they were the ones mentioned by Muñoz and Gonzaga.[35]

Another friar who was in Michoacán toward the end of the 1520s was Fray Diego de Santa María. In testimony given on March 5, 1532,

Fray Antonio de Ortiz spoke of him as "a friar who had lived in Michoacán, . . . and this friar is an interpreter." The ability to speak the Tarascan language was obviously one that Fray Antonio had not achieved, since he had to ask Fray Diego to interpret for him with some Tarascan Indians who had come to Mexico City to make a complaint against the corregidor of Michoacán in late 1531.[36] Fray Diego's ability to speak Tarascan suggests that he had spent a considerable amount of time in Michoacán. It is difficult to identify this Fray Diego de Santa María among the early friars whose names we know. Perhaps he is the Fray Diego de Almonte whom Mendieta mentioned as having arrived in Mexico in 1525 with Ortiz in the second group of Spanish friars.[37]

We cannot close this consideration of the early personnel of the Michoacán missions without mentioning the arrival of Fray Juan de San Miguel, who became one of the outstanding lights of those missions. Beaumont placed his arrival sometime in the years 1528 to 1530.[38] The earliest documentary evidence that I have found, a letter from Fray Juan written in 1537, indicates that he was laying the foundations of the church and friary in Uruapan in the spring of 1535.[39] His principal activities, especially the founding of mission hospitals, for which his fame would vie with that of Bishop Vasco de Quiroga, do not fall within the time period of the present study. Here we can see only the first beginnings of the efforts to Christianize Michoacán and of the social works for which the Christian community there would become famous.

In regard to the year in which the original group of friars went to Michoacán, Beaumont preferred to place their departure from Mexico City after the beginning of 1526, but his reasons for doing so are not valid. He dated the arrival of the second group of Spanish friars toward the end of 1525,[40] but, depending upon Mendieta's statement that they arrived eight or nine months after the first group, we must place their arrival fairly early in 1525, since the first group had reached Veracruz in May, 1524. Beaumont also maintained that, before leaving for Michoacán, the group assisted at the first ecclesiastical assembly, or synod, which he placed at the beginning of 1526, after the return of Cortés from Honduras.[41] Two historical difficulties are involved here. First, if the friars waited until the return of Cortés before going to Michoacán, their departure would have to be dated not at the beginning of 1526 but in the early summer, because Cortés did not re-

turn to Mexico City until around June 15, 1526.[42] Second, the first
ecclesiastical synod was held not in 1526 but in 1524, fairly soon after
the arrival of the Twelve.[43] There seems to be no reason, therefore,
why we should doubt Mendieta's statement that the first friars went
to Michoacán in 1525.[44]

When the friars arrived in Michoacán, they were reportedly given
an enthusiastic reception by the people, led on by the good will of
their king. He housed the missionaries in his palace in Tzintzuntzan
and showed them royal hospitality. The friars, however, asked him to
give them a place where they could construct a poor house and a
church. They went through all the barrios and chose the place that
suited them best. There, with the help of the Indians, they soon built
a wooden church and a friary formed of thatched cells, which suited
their ideal of poverty more closely than did the royal palace. They
did not require a great amount of space, since they brought with them
only the clothing they wore, their mission crosses and breviaries, and
the necessities for saying Mass.[45]

The church in Tzintzuntzan was dedicated to Saint Ann.[46] Fray
Isidro Félix de Espinosa, a Franciscan historian of the mid-eighteenth
century upon whom Beaumont depended heavily, related that Fray
Martín de Jesús celebrated the first Mass in the little church to the
accompaniment of all the various musical instruments with which the
Indians had been accustomed to honor their gods.[47]

A sketch of the little church appears in a painting preserved in
Beaumont's *Crónica*. The painting, which is related to a lawsuit arising
from the transfer of the diocesan see from Tzintzuntzan to Pátzcuaro
in the late 1530s or early 1540s, shows the Church of Santa Ana in
the upper right corner, a simple gabled structure with a roof that is
clearly sagging in the middle, a bell tower at the front left corner,
and another small tower of some kind at the rear right corner. There
is a small courtyard in front of the church, surrounded by a semi-
circular wall and with a broad flight of steps descending on the right
side. Above it are written the words "Santa Ana, Ynixurin" and on
the side "hy° [*himbó*] de 1526." Partly in Spanish, partly in Tarascan,
it means "Santa Ana, in the year of 1526."[48]

According to contemporary descriptions, this first effort at church
building in Michoacán was not an outstanding success. When Bishop-
elect Vasco de Quiroga came to Tzintzuntzan in 1538 to set up his
diocese, the papal letters assigned him the little Franciscan church as

his cathedral. He immediately asked permission to move his diocesan see to the barrio of Pátzcuaro. To formalize his request, he had an inquiry made regarding the location and condition of the primitive Franciscan church and friary.[49]

The friars had established their church in a valley in the hills above Tzintzuntzan. Quiroga described its location as follows:

. . . a deep valley full of ravines which is between two hills and surrounded almost entirely by a lake of water of bad confluences, where an unpredictable, bad, and sick wind circulates and dominates, coming from over the lake and channeled over the said site and valley where the said church is, so that many people suffer from infirmities of the head.

He added that "the church is in the upper part of a valley" and "at the foot of a hill, and the leveled plot is built up with dry and unstable rock, and it would be very hard to find a foundation there."

He described the church as a structure "of adobes and thatch, old and small, like a little thatch house." The friars who had constructed it when they first came to the province had moved to another place and were no longer caring for the original structure. One witness, Suero Asturiano, stated that since leaving their original church the Franciscans had moved their friary twice.[50] One of these moves, probably the final one, is reflected in two royal cedulas of August 24, 1529. The friars in New Spain had asked for assistance in building their friaries in Michoacán and elsewhere. In one cedula the queen commanded that they be given 500,000 maravedis to help them, and in the other she granted their request that the encomenderos be commanded to lighten the burden of the Indians of the town of Michoacán (i.e., Tzintzuntzan), among others, so that they might build the friary more quickly. The content of the second cedula was reiterated on February 4, 1530.[51]

The change of the location of the church was no doubt motivated at least in part by the complaints of the Spaniards who had attended Mass in the original church. Suero Asturiano was quoted as stating that "many different times he has left off going up there because it is very much uphill and the road is bad." Domingo de Medina said that "the said church is on such a bad site that they cannot go there on horseback because of the ravines and slopes and bridges and pools." According to statements by Diego Calero and Pedro Moreno, the church that the friars were using in 1538 stood on the plain by the lake.[52] This would probably be the church shown below Santa Ana in Beaumont's painting and could very well be on the site of the colonial Franciscan church that is still in use in Tzintzuntzan.[53]

We do not know much about how the friars went about their efforts to Christianize the Indians. The *Relación* tells us merely that they began preaching and trying to rid the Indians of their drunkenness.[54] During the first months or years they had to preach through interpreters, but they worked hard to learn the language to be able to preach in it.[55]

Fray Alonso de la Rea, writing in the seventeenth century, said that the conversion of the Cazonci and the adherence of the Tarascan leaders to the new religion caused dismay among their people, who showed some determination to take up arms in defense of their temples and their gods. But the firmness of their monarch prevented any such movement from gaining momentum.[56] It is probably also true that the severity of the Cazonci in disposing of the *principales* who had urged him to drown himself had lessened the possibility of concerted opposition.

Espinosa and Beaumont give a description of the catechetical method of Fray Martín de Jesús and his companions. It is general in form and may very well present merely the manner of instruction that was common among the friars. They gathered the children together and instructed them carefully, because the young learned the prayers quickly and could teach their elders. All the people were brought together every morning and evening, and they repeated the prayers after the priest word for word. Those who had greater difficulty in learning were given special instruction during the day.[57] The friars soon made use of the Indians' ability to paint. They had pictures and symbols painted on cloth to illustrate their teachings. Placing these visual aids near the pulpit, they used a rod to point out the various elements as they explained them.[58] An illustration of this technique as the friars used it in central Mexico is shown in one of the etchings that Fray Diego Valadés made for his *Rhetorica Christiana* (1579).[59]

We have a description of one such painting that was in use in Michoacán in the mid-1530s. In Uruapan the Franciscans had a painting made that was intended to illustrate the theme of the Last Judgment. It showed Franciscan and Dominican friars in a boat in the middle of Purgatory pulling out souls. The Franciscans were rescuing

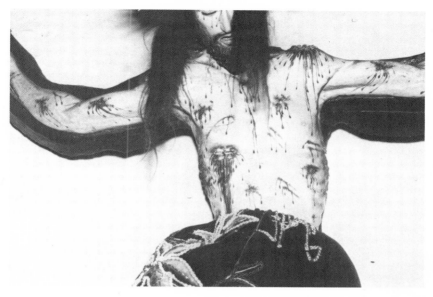

Cristo carved from a single tree trunk and its branches, Santa Fe de la Laguna.

a great number, while the Dominicans were able to get only two, and one of those was slipping back. Obviously it was as much an evidence of the rivalry between the orders as it was an illustration of its intended theological theme. One luckless encomendero, Gonzalo Gómez, remarked that each one depicted it as he wished, meaning that if the Dominicans had painted it the proportions would have been reversed. Unfriendly neighbors used this comment as the basis of a charge of doctrinal relativism against him before the Inquisition.[60]

The general content of the friars' catechesis was such as would be expected in the situation they faced. They first tried to impress their hearers with the horror of human sacrifice and with the falsity of their idols and gods. To this they contrasted the beauty of the Christian belief, explaining to them the existence of only one God of heaven and earth, Creator of all nations, and Lord of all kingdoms, who had sent his ministers to enlighten the nations deceived by the devil. Therefore, the first duties of the natives must be to detest the adoration of idols, to destroy their temples, to execrate human sacrifice, and to cleanse themselves of sin by baptism.[61]

Fiesta of flowers, Ocumicho.

There were serious obstacles in the way of the conversion of the Tarascans. Their customs allowed them to take more than one wife, stressed vengeance on their enemies, and were in general rather loose in their moral restrictions, at least from the friars' point of view.[62] The ritual drunkenness that the Tarascans had accepted as part of their religious rites continued to have an attraction for them.[63]

The priestly caste naturally resented the newcomers, who desecrated their revered gods and made them out as demons. Realizing also that the conversion of the natives to Christianity would mean the loss to their caste of its position of prestige, they made every effort to preserve the old beliefs.[64] They told the people that the friars were really dead people, that their Franciscan habits were winding sheets, and that every night they turned back into bones and went to the under

Procession of Candles, San Andrés Ziróndaro.

world, where they kept their women. They also said that the baptismal water was really blood and that it would break the heads of the children if they were baptized in it.[65]

Yet the natives were amazed at the lives of the friars, seeing that they did not want gold, had no women, and dressed very poorly. They naturally developed certain misconceptions regarding the missionaries. Since they saw that all the priests were full-grown men who never married and who dressed only in their Franciscan habits, they concluded that the friars had come into existence just as they were, already clothed with the habit, and that they had no mothers and had never been children. The author of the *Relación* remarked that even at his time (1540-41) he was not sure whether the Indians believed that the friars had mothers.[66]

The difficulties of the missionary work were very great during the first years. The *Relación* states that, because the natives were so hard to improve, the friars were ready to leave them two or three times.[67] Bishop Juan de Zumárraga, in testimony given in the mid-1530s, asserted that the friars had actually left the Tarascans on two or three occasions because of the slow progress during the years before Vasco de Quiroga made a visitation of the area as *oidor* in 1533.[68] Perhaps this situation is reflected in the fact that Fray Antonio Ortiz was back in Mexico City by the summer of 1529.

We find very little reflection of such a disappointing situation in the chronicles of the Michoacán missions, written mainly in the seventeenth and eighteenth centuries. By that time the discouragements of the early years had been largely forgotten. Fray Antonio Tello relates that in 1527 Fray Martín de Jesús went back to Mexico to report on the abundant spiritual harvest that was ready in Michoacán. Then, with the order and counsel of Governor Alonso de Estrada and Captain-General Cortés, a number of friars were appointed to go back to Michoacán with Fray Martín. It is here that Tello places the arrival of most of the friars mentioned by Gonzaga. He says that at the end of 1527 and the beginning of 1528 Friars Ángel de Salcedo, Jerónimo, Juan de Badía (or Badillo), and Juan de Padilla were appointed to go to Michoacán.[69] It seems more likely, however, that they went somewhat later. Ortiz was still in Michoacán in mid-1528, and there is no evidence of the presence of others.

The visit of Fray Martín de Jesús to Mexico in 1527 was necessitated by the Second Custodial Chapter of the Franciscans in Mexico, and Fray Martín, as superior for Michoacán, was obliged to attend. The chapter was the formal organizational meeting of the order, at which common problems were discussed and new assignments of personnel were made. This must be the chapter of which the *Relación* refers when speaking of the first coming of the friars. It states that the Fathers of Saint Francis held a chapter in Guaxacingo (Huejotzingo) and sent Fray Martín and some other Fathers to Michoacán. This had occurred twelve or thirteen years before the writing of the *Relación*, which would place it as early as 1527.[70] Apparently the *Relación*, with its genius for telescoping events, here confused the first and second missions of the friars, though one would not expect this, since the compiler was himself a Franciscan.

As a few more missionaries entered the field, they began making constantly greater advances. One of the most positive forces for the conversion of the Indians was the exemplary life of the friars. They came among the Indians barefooted and with only the habits they wore. They ate the same food that the Indians ate and lived very plainly. This was something new and astonishing to the Indians— that some of the conquering Spaniards would be willing to give of themselves for the Indians rather than always to be taking from them.[71]

Gradually the work of Christianization gained momentum. During the first year or so the friars were able to work only in the area bordering on Lake Pátzcuaro. They lived in Tzintzuntzan and had *visitas*, or mission churches, in some of the other settlements around the lake. They attended these missions by canoe, visiting the sick, preaching against idolatry, and teaching Christian doctrine. As the number of friars increased, they began to extend their work to towns farther away from the lake, but we do not know anything about the chronological sequence of the later establishments.[72] The *Relación* mentions Ucareo and Zinapécuaro as the first of the later missions.[73] This would be a logical direction of development, since those towns were along the route to Mexico.

The conflict between the Franciscans and the First Audiencia in Mexico City during 1529 and 1530 also had its unfortunate effects on the Michoacán missions, as Diego de Soria testified in 1531:

. . . [this witness] did not see that [the president and *oidores*] fulfilled the ordinances which His Majesty sent concerning the good treatment of the Indians and that they should not be made to bear burdens, except on one occasion when certain friars left this city for the province of Michoacán, and they had some Indians who were carrying a little oil and some books and vestments for saying Mass, and they sent an alguacil after them with an order from Francisco de Ávila, who was alcalde, an they said that it was in accord with the agreement and opinion of the said licenciates, and they took from them the said burdens, or some of them, and they brought back under arrest a Spaniard who was going with the said burdens, and for this reason the friars returned to this city.[74]

In this case the friars were the victims of an unequal and prejudicial application of a royal decree that was observed by no one, least of all by the members of the audiencia.

As the friars established greater ascendancy over the natives in spiritual matters, they undertook a more active offensive against the symbols of native religion. According to Father Muñoz, they gathered the idols from all the places where they were working. They burned all those that could be destroyed by fire, and they threw all the offerings of gold, silver and precious stones into a very deep lake, so as to destroy as far as possible the memory of idolatry.[75] Muñoz gives the impression that this destruction of idols was carried out all at once and definitively, but that was by no means the case. Contemporary documents tell of continuous efforts to eradicate idolatry and even indicate differences of opinion among the friars regarding aspects of the campaign.[76]

The idols were in many forms and were made of many materials. Witnesses who testified for Don Pedro de Arellano in 1532 told of various idols that they had seen in the temples: figures of men, women, and children, as well as of various animals. Some of the anthropomorphic idols were life-sized, while others were small or were only faces or masks. The most commonly mentioned animal figures were those of "tigers" and dogs, although snakes and rabbits were each mentioned once. Apparently, then, the veneration of the ancient feline god of Mesoamerica was still strong in Michoacán. The pottery dogs of Jalisco are a well-known pre-Spanish art form, but apparently the dog statues to which these witnesses referred were of a more resistant material; none of the witnesses mentions pottery as a material. In fact, Alonso Lucas, an apothecary, speaks specifically of dogs made of wood. Some stone statues of dogs are still to be seen in the museums of Michoacán.

The materials most frequently mentioned were gold, silver, copper, stone, and wood. Many witnesses had seen statues of stone and wood, but only a few had succeeded in getting their hands on those made of precious metals. Pedro Veneciano asserted that the Indians kept the idols of precious metals in *cúes*, or temples, at a distance from the roads along which the Spaniards usually passed and that in the other places they made use of those of stone and wood. Such a comment leaves the impression that the knowledge of idols of precious metals was derived more from rumor than from actual contact with them. Bartolomé Aguilar spoke of finding a stone covered with blood and wrapped in blankets on which it appeared that sacrifices had been made. In the *Relación* there is a painting of "those who carried the gods on their backs." The image appears to be wrapped in cloth, much as Aguilar described his find.[77] Martín de Aranda spoke of seeing an idol of "white stone that is like crystal."

The Spanish soldiers and colonists also reported the kinds of offerings that the natives continued to make to their gods during these
early years of Spanish occupation. The sacrifices were varied, including
human, animal, and vegetable sacrifices, as well as precious objects.
Fray Diego de Santa María told Fray Antonio Ortiz of having found
the remains of some men who had recently been sacrificed. Martín
Gómez reported finding hearts, which appeared to be human, hanging in front of idols. The fact of continued human sacrifice and the
reported involvement of the Cazonci in it would be one of the principal accusations against the Tarascan king in his trial by Nuño de
Guzmán.

Blood sacrifice was an important element of native rites. Martín
Gómez, Bartolomé Aguilar, Antonio de Oliver, Pedro de Molina, and
Álvaro Gallego all mentioned finding idols stained with blood. Gallego
found one on which the accumulated blood was a finger's breadth
deep, and Aguilar came upon one with two fingers' breadth of accumulated blood. It is probable that not all of this blood was human.
Oliver reported finding idols covered with blood, in front of which
were offerings of turkeys (*gallinas*) and quail with their heads cut off.

The gods were also given other choice items of the native diet.
Antón Caicedo had seen offerings of beans, chili, and corn; Pedro de
Molina, tamales; and Pedro Veneciano, tamales and drinking water.
Many witnesses mentioned offerings of precious articles of gold and
silver and jewelry. Some also spoke of blankets and clothing.

The Spaniards made every effort to destroy these physical evidences
of the native religion, and they considered idol-offerings of precious
metals justifiable booty. One of the main intents of Pedro de Arellano
in his side of the lawsuit from which the preceding material has been
drawn was to prove that during the previous years it had been considered completely legal for the Spaniards to take such idol-offerings
for themselves.

There appears to have been some disagreement among the friars in
regard to such matters. Hernando Ladrón, who served for a while as
one of Cortés' supervisors (*mayordomo*) testified:

Father Fray Ángel in the province of Michoacán told this witness that in a
cu [temple] he found a quantity of gold and silver offered to the idols and that
he gave it back to the natives. This witness reprimanded him for it, saying

that it was bad to give it back to them so that they could go back to offer it and practice idolatry with it once more, and that it would be better not to give it back but rather to make chalices and ornaments with it so that the divine services could be celebrated, since they would just give it back to the demons to whom they had offered it. And the guardian of the said monastery [Fray Martín de Jesús] told him that it would have been better to do it that way.

Here, then, we have the case of a friar being reprehended for his liberal attitude by a Spanish layman and the Franciscan superior agreeing with the layman. According to Fray Antonio Ortiz, Fray Diego de Santa María had come upon some Indians who were guarding the treasure which the Cazonci had left for his sons. The friar had broken up certain gold-and-silver masks, but he had told the guards to take the treasure to some island, where they could keep it more secure.

Native religious items made of materials other than precious metals were generally broken or burned by the Spaniards who came upon them. Beginning with Antonio de Caravajal, nearly every Spanish official of the period, when speaking of his accomplishments in Michoacán, mentioned the destruction of idols and other religious paraphernalia. Bachiller Juan de Ortega, the most important of them said that he saw "some figures in the *cúes* in the province of Michoacán while he was going around visiting the province, and that he found many figures of dogs and tigers and other figures . . . and that some of them were of metal and of wood and bone, and that this witness had them burned publicly in the presence of Fray Antonio de Ortiz and another Father who was there."

Some of the common Spanish soldiers made a campaign of trying to search out and destroy the vestiges of native religion. Álvaro Gallego, for instance, related that he had frequently entered the temples to take out the images and burn and break them up. On one occasion he had brought many of these native religious artifacts to Mexico before Bishop-elect Zumárraga and the members of the audiencia. When Zumárraga saw them, he had them burned in the plaza of the city.

The work of destroying the evidences of idolatry was far from complete at the time of the Cazonci's death in 1530. Several witnesses reported that Pedro de Arellano, who was corregidor in Tzintzuntzan in 1531, had publicly burned native religious artifacts in the plaza in front of the Franciscan church in Tzintzuntzan. Again in 1533, when Vasco de Quiroga visited Michoacán, he was credited with destroying a considerable number of idols.[78] This negative aspect of the conversion of the Tarascans was, then, a continuing activity, in which Spanish laymen took a leading role.

Individual Spanish laymen also made a positive effort toward giving the Indians for whom they were responsible some training in Christian doctrine. Gonzalo Gómez, in his trial before the Inquisition in 1537, elicited testimony to the effect that at his estancia of Guayangareo he had built a chapel in which Mass was celebrated occasionally and that on Sundays and feast days of obligation he gathered his Indians there to pray the *doctrina cristiana.* Gonzalo López acknowledged that Gómez had always tried to see to it that his slaves and his Indians knew the Our Father, the Hail Mary, the Creed, and the Salve Regina.[79]

Espinosa describes the baptismal practice of the friars, again in rather general terms. They first baptized the little boys whom they had trained near the friary. Infants brought in from outside the town were baptized immediately because of the danger that they might not live to be baptized later and because it seemed that the whole nation would eventually become Christian. Adults were not baptized until they were adequately instructed, although the sick were baptized if they showed that they accepted the Catholic faith, desired baptism, and rejected their old beliefs. During the first years many people were baptized with merely the essential ceremony of baptism with water, there being no bishop in Mexico to consecrate the necessary holy oils, but the additional solemnities were supplied in later years.[80]

In regard to Christian marriage, the friars had a difficult struggle in trying to uproot the traditional practice of polygyny, especially among the nobility. The Cazonci, after his baptism as Don Francisco, reportedly took one woman as his wife, at least officially. Witnesses who were brought forward by his son, Don Antonio Huitziméngari, supported the latter's claim that the Cazonci had married Don Antonio's mother, Guarique Vacujane, by the rites of the Church.[81] Yet there is evidence of a number of "women of the Cazonci" still present as a definable group at the time of his death. The Cazonci's adopted brother Don Pedro also continued to have several wives in his house for several years after his baptism. At the time of Vasco de Quiroga's first visit to Michoacán in 1533, Don Pedro was governor of Michoacán and had three or four women. One of them complained to Quiroga, who discussed the matter with her husband and persuaded him to adopt monogamy.[82]

Once they had established their authority, the friars apparently showed considerable severity toward the natives who were unwilling to carry out the obligations which the new religion imposed upon them. In testimony given in the residencia of Vasco de Quiroga in 1536, two Indians of Michoacán spoke of the coercive methods of the friars, which had the unfortunate effect of forcing some of the Indians to flee into the wilds to preserve their religious customs. Don Francisco, a native of the barrio of Cuyacán, said that

. . . although they [the Indians] were put under much pressure by the friars to go to pray and hear Mass and sermons, and they whipped them and maltreated them in other ways so that they would come to the knowledge of God Our Lord, they did not do it nor did they wish to do it. And for that reason they went into the wilds and stayed there and were not willing to come back, either at that time or for eight, nine, and ten years.[83]

Don Ramiro, a *principal* of the barrio of Pátzcuaro, gave a very similar report:

. . . before the said Licenciate Quiroga went to the province of Michoacán, all of the natives of the said province, at least the greater part of them, were going about without rule, much involved in the practice of idolatry, following the devil and not God Our Lord, in spite of the fact that the friars of Saint Francis who reside in the province preached to them about the matters of God, and whipped them and did other things to them because they were not willing to do it; and the natives went off to the wilds and there they did many of their very despicable customary practices.[84]

In spite of the best efforts of the friars there also developed a certain amount of confusion in the minds of the Tarascans concerning Catholic beliefs and practices. Don Pedro's first reaction to the Mass— that it was a form of divination such as the native priests practiced with water in a vessel—became a general misconception at the beginning. When the friars told them that they had to go to heaven, their ingenuous reply was that they had never seen anyone go there. The friars also followed the practice of placing crosses on the highest hills and in the plazas, barrios, and houses. The natives called the cross Santa María and considered it a god.[85] Such cultural fusion was a natural result of the natives' efforts to understand the new religion within the framework of their own thought and traditions. Certainly it would not be overcome during the infancy of Christianity in Michoacán.

The last five years of the 1520s, then, saw the bare beginnings of the Christianization of Michoacán. The first few friars arrived and established a few churches, the leaders of the Tarascan kingdom accepted Christianity, at least nominally, and beginnings were made in the effort to root out the native religion and replace it with Christian beliefs and practices.[86]

•••

CHAPTER 6

Michoacán, 1524–1526:
The Government of the Treasury Officials

SPANISH civil domination of Michoacán during the 1520s revolved around three interrelated economic activities: the exploitation of the encomiendas, the introduction of elements of European agricultural economy, and the extraction of precious metals either by mining or by exerting pressure on the native nobility to deliver them. The mining was carried out in the fringe areas of the province, to the south along the Río Balsas and its tributaries or to the west among the defiles of the mountains dropping off toward the ocean.

The appointment of Spanish officials in the area was generally motivated by problems arising from these activities although at times such changes merely reflected political turnovers in the superior officialdom in Mexico City. The economic activities, as we shall see in later chapters, were closely bound together, forming a kind of symbiotic relationship. The miners depended upon the encomiendas for provisions, and the sale of provisions to the miners was the easiest way for the encomenderos to convert produce into cash. In the present chapter and in the two following, we shall follow the political history of Michoacán in its new relationship with Mexico from 1524 to 1529, leaving the discussion of its economic exploitation during the same period for later chapters.

The position of the Cazonci in the new order of things was left very unclear and very vulnerable. In many ways he was now an anachronism. He remained as king in the eyes of his people, and possibly in his own eyes, but in the eyes of the Spaniards he became either an obstacle or a tool of control, and eventually, when the new overlords would come to see him as more an obstacle than a tool, he would be removed from the scene by execution.

Cortés' instructions to him, as given in the *Relación de Michoacán*, limited his authority merely to the extent that he could not take tribute from the towns.[1] But he was presumably allowed and expected to retain his jurisdiction as *señor natural* (native lord) of Michoacán. Thus he was lord over a large area that was broken up into many small holdings of Spanish overlords. He was inevitably caught between two fires. When he was later brought to trial before Nuño de Guzmán, as we shall see, he was accused both of exercising his authority, by keeping overseers in the towns, and of not exercising it, by allowing the killing of Spaniards to occur and to go unpunished.[2] The seeds of this conflict were planted at the time of colonization, when the relative jurisdictions of the Spanish and native authorities were not clearly defined.

Troubles were already brewing for the Cazonci soon after the distribution of the encomiendas, troubles brought on by the shifting of political controls in Mexico City.[3] To understand these political changes and the way they affected the Cazonci and Michoacán, we must try to establish the chronology of the period as clearly as possible.

On October 12, 1524, Fernando Cortés, disturbed by the disloyalty of Cristóbal de Olid in Honduras and not knowing that the matter had already been settled by his emissary Francisco de las Casas, led off a large contingent of men bound for Honduras. They eventually reached Honduras after an extremely difficulty overland trek through mountains, swamps, and jungles.[4]

When he departed, Cortés left the royal treasurer, Alonso de Estrada, and the royal accountant, Rodrigo de Albornoz, in charge of affairs in Mexico City. They were to act as his lieutenants, together with the lawyer Licenciado Alonso Zuazo, who as *alcalde mayor* was responsible for administering justice. This arrangement, however, did not work out. By the time Cortés reached the province of Coatzacoalcos, at the south end of the Bay of Campeche, in mid-December, he received word that Estrada and Albornoz could not get along and on one occasion, in a meeting of the town council, had even faced one another with drawn swords. The royal factor, Gonzalo de Salazar, and the royal supervisor (*veedor*), Peralmíndez Chirinos, had accompanied Cortés thus far on the expedition. They now prevailed upon him to send them back to Mexico City to settle matters there. He agreed and gave them two major decrees to take with them. The one appointed them to rule with Estrada and Albornoz if they had settled their differences; the other appointed them to replace Estrada and Albornoz if the latter two had not reached an agreement. The second decree was issued in the town of Espíritu Santo on December 14, 1524.[5] Salazar and Chirinos wasted no time making their way back to Mexico City. Only two weeks later, on December 29, 1524, they appeared before the town council. Concealing the decree that would have made them cogovernors with Estrada and Albornoz, they revealed only the second decree and forced the other two officials to turn over power to them.[6]

Around the middle of February, however, the deceit became known, owing to the arrival of new letters from Cortés. On February 17, 1525, Rodrigo de Paz, Cortés' cousin, whom the Conqueror had left in charge of his properties and business affairs in Mexico City, was accepted by the town council as *alguacil mayor* (chief constable) of the city, by virtue of an appointment from Cortés. When Estrada and Albornoz also appeared before the council and demanded to be reinstated, Paz supported them. Licenciado Zuazo, acting as judge in the case, gave a decision in favor of Estrada and Albornoz, and the town council accepted them, though Salazar and Chirinos rejected the decision.[7]

But the matter would not stay settled. According to a letter that Bishop-elect Juan de Zumárraga later wrote to the king in 1529, those who had opposed Cortés from the beginning and had supported the authority of the governor of Cuba, Diego Velázquez, became the supporters of Salazar and Chirinos and encouraged them in their opposition to the interests of Cortés and his supporters. These same men would later become the principal partisans of Nuño de Guzmán.[8]

In the course of a few weeks Salazar and Chirinos were able to force Paz to come over to their position. On April 19, with his support, they once more ousted Estrada and Albornoz from power. The next day they extracted from the town council a decision that Zuazo's previous decision in favor of Estrada and Albornoz would not be observed and that in the future only decrees issued by Salazar, Chirinos, and Zuazo, or a majority of the three, would be obeyed.[9] This decision obviously gave Salazar and Chirinos the majority vote.

Tensions continued to build in the city, as is evident from the ordinance issued by the town council on May 23 forbidding the bearing of excessive arms in the city.[10] On the same day Salazar and Chirinos placed Zuazo under arrest and sent him back to Cuba to undergo a residencia for an office that he had held there before coming to Mexico.[11] On June 25, Estrada and Albornoz tried to escape from the city under the pretext of taking the king's treasure to Medellín for shipment to Spain, but their two opponents captured them on the road to Chalco and placed them under house arrest in Mexico City.

During the summer relations also deteriorated between the two dominant treasury officials and Rodrigo de Paz, their only remaining major obstacle to dictatorial control. The bitterness came to a head on August 19, when Salazar and Chirinos, deciding that Cortés and his expedition had been wiped out by the Indians, demanded that Paz allow them to inventory Cortés' goods. Paz resisted them, and the situation might easily have resulted in civil warfare within the Spanish community if the Franciscan friars had not intervened and prevailed upon Paz to surrender. With Paz under arrest, on August 22 the treasury officials appointed a new *alguacil mayor* and two new aldermen to the town council from among their own supporters, thus establishing their authority over the city. Then they again demanded recognition of their complete authority, in view of the fact that Cortés had not been heard of for six months and was rumored to be dead. The town council, on which their newly established majority prevailed, swore allegiance to them, as did a large number of citizens.[12]

During the next two months they raided Cortés' possessions and tortured Paz severely in the frustrated hope of making him reveal the location of great treasures that Cortés was rumored to have left behind. Unsuccessful in this effort, they tried Paz for insubordination and on October 16, 1525, executed him.[13] In doing so, they killed a man who was already nearly dead; on September 27 and October 14 Paz had been too sick to sign codicils to his will.[14]

From information given in the trial of Paz, we know that the turmoil of this period had also had its repercussions for the Cazonci. In the list of accusations and the interrogatory that the fiscal Pedro de Escobar presented against Paz on September 13, 1525, one of the charges was that Paz had released the Cazonci from prison in Mexico and allowed him to return to Michoacán in spite of a strict prohibition against it. According to the fiscal, Salazar and Chirinos had collected evidence and had decided that the Cazonci should be imprisoned for the sake of the pacification of Michoacán and neighboring provinces. They also thought that he would reveal to them the location of rich silver mines. Therefore, they imprisoned him in Mexico City, establishing a fine of 4,000 gold pesos for anyone who would release him.

Paz' answer to the charge is not very clear, perhaps indicating the toll taken upon him by the torture. When asked whether he had released the Cazonci, he said that he had told the factor (Salazar) that if he wanted him to keep the Cazonci in a dungeon he would do so but that he was safe. He was then asked when he gave the Cazonci permission to leave. He replied that the Indian had told him that he wanted to leave and that he (Paz) had told him that he should stay until a letter came from the governor (Cortés), and then the Cazonci went away.[15]

From the limited amount of information that these documents give us, it is difficult to fix this episode exactly in the chronology of the period. It seems probable, however, that the arrest of the Cazonci occurred during the first period of dominance of Salazar and Chirinos, between December 29, 1524, and February 17, 1525, and that during the period when Estrada and Albornoz shared power (February 17 to April 9, 1525) Paz allowed the Cazonci to leave. It also appears likely that at this time the friars first went to Michoacán, accompanying the native king.

After the execution of Paz the two officials felt themselves ever more secure in their tyranny. Diego de Ordaz set out to search for Cortés, but he had not gone far inland from the Bay of Campeche when he came upon Indians who assured him that the whole expedition had been wiped out somewhat farther along the way. Accepting their report, Ordaz hurried back to Mexico City, where the officials showed their gratitude by appointing him *alcalde mayor* on November 2, 1525.[16]

At some time during November, probably soon after the arrival of Ordaz, Salazar and Chirinos made an official pronouncement that Cortés and the members of his expedition were dead, and they held a formal funeral ceremony for them in Mexico City. This opened the way for what they surely considered to be a final assault on Cortés' possessions, which they commanded to be sold to pay his debts, the rest to be set aside for his heirs. At the cabildo meetings of November 15, 17, and 28 and December 1, an exceptional number of plots of land *(solares)* were given out in the city, possibly land that had belonged to Cortes' men.[17] On December 15, Albornoz, who, it seems, had settled his differences with Salazar, wrote to the Spanish crown about Cortés' "death" and other matters of government.[18]

Apparently also during December, Chirinos led an expedition southward to Oaxaca to settle an Indian revolt there and reportedly also to block a threatened move by Pedro de Alvarado to bring his army from Guatemala to support the Cortés party. This move probably occurred about the middle of December, since on December 16 Salazar called upon the town council to force Jorge de Alvarado and other messengers and intermediaries of Pedro de Alvarado to leave the Franciscan friary, where they had taken asylum.[19]

In early January, 1526, one of the most infamous acts of Salazar's tyranny took place, showing his anxiety as weaknesses began to appear in his campaign to keep Cortés dead. On January 3, 1526, Juana Ruiz de Mancilla, the wife of Cortés' secretary, Alonso Valiente, received word through Indians from her husband's encomienda town that he and Cortés were still alive. To nip any such subversive rumors in the tenderest bud, on January 4, Salazar accused Juana Ruiz of actions disturbing to good order, took testimony against her without allowing her a defense, and found her guilty. She was condemned to be taken through the streets on an ass with a gag in her mouth, to be given a hundred lashes in public, and to be exiled from New Spain for five years.[20]

Such abuse of power could not stand up indefinitely against the fact that Cortés was very much alive. On January 29, 1526, a messenger from Cortés, Martín de Orantes, slipped into the city with letters in which the governor took from Salazar and Chirinos the right to continue to exercise power in his place, naming in their stead his cousin Francisco de las Casas. Because Las Casas was no longer in Mexico, Cortés' supporters and the cabildo judged that the authority devolved upon Estrada and Albornoz by virtue of their prior appointment.[21] After some jockeying of forces they removed Salazar from office that day and imprisoned him. Chirinos was also captured and imprisoned when he returned from Oaxaca.

To the position of *alcalde mayor* the new authorities appointed Bachiller Juan de Ortega,[22] a relative and loyal supporter of Cortés. By mid-February he was already holding an inquest into the death of Rodrigo de Paz because of criminal charges brought by Paz' mother, Inés Gómez de Paz, against Salazar and Chirinos.[23] From testimony given by witnesses during the inquest, it is apparent that Salazar and Chirinos had summoned the Cazonci to Mexico once more after regaining power and had again imprisoned him. A question in Ortega's interrogatory refers to the fact that Salazar and Chirinos had held the Cazonci imprisoned for a long time, together with his interpreters and favorites. Of itself this might refer to the imprisonment before the death of Paz, but two of the witnesses, the notary Hernán Pérez and the alderman Hernán López de Ávila, asserted that he had been released by Estrada and Albornoz after they took power from Salazar.

In his answer to the charge Salazar claimed that he had imprisoned the Cazonci at the request of all those who had encomiendas in Michoacán, for the pacification of the land and so that the natives of the region would serve the Spaniards to whom they were allotted.

Accountant Albornoz had shown basic agreement with Salazar's assertion in a letter that he had written to the king two months earlier, on December 15, 1525. He complained that the Indians of Michoacán would not reveal to the Spaniards the location of their many silver mines because of their fear of the Cazonci. (This myth that there were many rich silver mines throughout Michoacán continued to plague the Tarascans at least until the time of the Cazonci's execution.) Albornoz asked the king to command that the Cazonci, his two brothers, and the *principales* be sent to the king in Spain, so that Michoacán would serve the Spanish king better, the land would be more secure, and the Indians would be more compliant about revealing their mines. Albornoz wanted to send the Tarascan leaders to the king at the time that he wrote his letter, but others opposed him for reasons that he did not specify but that he characterized as being not very advantageous for the crown.[24]

The witnesses in Ortega's inquest indicate an important reason why Salazar did not want to send the Cazonci to Spain. He was using the Tarascan monarch as a means of extracting treasure from Michoacán. Pedro de Isla testified that Salazar continuously demanded gold and silver from the Cazonci while he held him in prison and that the Cazonci brought him 500 marks of silver and some gold. The factor continued to demand more, and at the time he was removed from office and imprisoned, he was expecting a great amount of gold and silver from the Cazonci. Hernán López de Ávila testified that the factor had told him of the 500 marks of silver and that Pedro de Isla and Vaca had weighed it in the factor's presence. Rodrigo Ximón, a servant of Salazar's, acted as his interpreter with the Cazonci and claimed that he alone went in with Salazar when he talked with the Cazonci. He stated that the treasure was brought in several forms.

There were about 400 silver ingots, some gold ingots, and 20 loads of silver shields and miters. But Salazar was not content with this and demanded more.[25]

Salazar himself admitted that the Cazonci had brought him some silver in Isla's presence and had said that he would bring him 100 cargas of gold and silver for His Majesty. Salazar claimed that he told the Cazonci: "The *veedor* [Chirinos] will come, and we will see whether we can take this in good conscience to help with the expenses that we have undergone."[26] The reference to Chirinos' absence would indicate that the conversation took place after the *veedor's* departure for Oaxaca. There is evidence that the arrival of the Cazonci for this second imprisonment took place around the middle of November, or at least no later than that. On November 18, 1525, Treasurer Estrada received from Salazar, through the latter's servant Juan de la Peña, 48 marks and 4 ounces of silver and 196 ingots of gold weighing 507 pesos, which the Cazonci had brought as service for His Majesty. The gold was apparently quite impure and was sent to the Casa de Contratación in Seville without any determination of its fineness so that it might be refined there.[27] There is no way of knowing whether this was part of the treasure that Isla and Ximón said they had seen Salazar receive, but the wording of the report indicates that the Cazonci came to Mexico at the same time: ". . . the Cazonci, lord of Michoacán, brought them and gave them as a service for His Majesty."[28] The Cazonci, therefore, must have been in prison in Mexico City from at least the middle of November, 1525, until shortly after the removal of Salazar from power on January 29, 1526.

During their period in power Salazar and Chirinos had also been extracting treasures from Michoacán through other means than their heavy pressures on the Cazonci. They sent Antón Caicedo and Cindos de Portillo into the province and its subject areas with a commission to collect gold, silver, and gems from the Indians. Caicedo, besides having been one of the first Spaniards in Michoacán, had also been serving as Cortés' overseer in his encomiendas there. In February, 1526, Caicedo and Portillo testified that the factor and the *veedor* had given them a written command to go to Michoacán to gather treasure, using torture and imprisonment if necessary. They were instructed that if they obtained anything they were to bring it into the city secretly by night and not tell anyone. Portillo reported seeing the Indians of Tzintzuntzan give Caicedo about 80 silver ingots and 20 gold ingots as well as 5 shields that seemed to be of silver. Caicedo testified that at the time of the announcement of Cortés' "death" and the hanging of Paz he had brought 83 marks of silver and 207 pesos of gold from Tuxpan and Amula. He gave the treasure to the accountant Albornoz, but Salazar demanded it, claiming that he had taken those towns for himself. Eventually, Caicedo said, Albornoz and Estrada gave Salazar part of it.[29] The amount that the treasury collected from this last shipment is possibly reflected in entries for November 4, 1525, when it was noted that Estrada received from Caicedo 23 marks of silver and 83 pesos of gold that he had brought from certain towns and *principales* in Michoacán as a service for His Majesty.[30]

Salazar also sent a judicial official into Michoacán, something that was no doubt badly needed, since there was no Spanish municipality in the area, and the Spaniards there were outside the range of effective law enforcement. In this situation Alonso de Ávila was named to go to Michoacán as alcalde. He was, as far as we know, the first alcalde in Michoacán after the departure of the Olid expedition, but we know very little about either his person or his activities. Presumably he was the Alonso de Ávila, *vecino* of Mexico City, who petitioned the town council for land on May 2, 1525.[31] Probably he was also the Alonso de Ávila who in 1528 was encomendero of Cecasta and half of Tepalcatepec, in Michoacán.[32]

Some confusion arises regarding his identity because there was another, more famous, Alonso de Ávila, who had accompanied Cortés in the conquest of Mexico and who would later play a leading part in Francisco Montejo's expedition to conquer Yucatán. But the latter Alonso de Ávila, brother of Gil González de Ávila (or de Benavides), was away from New Spain in 1525. He had been captured by French pirates while accompanying the king's share of booty to Spain soon after the conquest of Mexico. After spending three years in French prisons, he made his way to Spain, where he was appointed *contador* (accountant) of the Montejo expedition. This Alonso de Ávila, therefore, could not have served as justice in Michoacán in 1525.[33] Neither could the *alcalde mayor* of Michoacán be the Alonso de Ávila who was the son of Gil González de Ávila, because his parents-to-be were not yet married in 1525.[34]

From his own narrative of merits and services, compiled in 1526, we learn that our Alonso de Ávila, before his appointment as justice for Michoacán, had fought in the conquests of Mexico and Pánuco and had accompanied Antonio de Caravajal on an inspection trip, on which he had become very ill. It seems that the inspection to which he referred was not Caravajal's survey of Michoacán, since two of Ávila's witnesses spoke of the area of the visitation as being within the jurisdiction of Mexico City ("de los términos de esta ciudad").[35]

Regarding his activities in Michoacán, he said that he went there as alcalde and justice for the miners who were extracting gold and to support and protect the natives, so that no one would do them any harm. His witnesses agreed that he did protect the natives and fulfilled his duty well.[36] Francisco Morcillo, who was notary for Ávila as he had been for Caravajal, said that during the course of their work he saw many sacrifices and idolatries, and he saw that the natives ate human flesh and gave it to the Cazonci and other leading men. He had helped Ávila burn many idols and sacrifices.[37] Juan Tirado testified in the residencia of Cortés that he had heard that Antón Caicedo, Cortés's servant, had nearly killed some *principales* whom he had in the stocks but that Ávila had saved them.[38] We must keep in mind, however, that Caicedo at this time was acting under Salazar's orders to extract treasure from the Tarascan nobility, even by the use of torture. Tirado, who was known as a friend of Salazar and an enemy of Cortés,[39] was pointing his finger at the wrong boss.

We can date the time of Ávila's activities in Michoacán more precisely from testimony that he gave on October 16, 1526. He said that while he was in Michoacán he received a power of attorney from Hernán López de Ávila, incorporating a decree of Salazar and Chirinos, authorizing him to take control of the possessions of Cortés and others who had gone to Honduras and were presumed dead.[40] In the published summaries of the notarial records from Mexico City for this time is listed a power of attorney from Hernán López de Ávila, holder of the goods of the dead, to Diego de Ávila and Juan de Tovar, in Tamazula, Michoacán, dated December 1, 1525. Perhaps Diego de Ávila is a copyist's error for Alonso de Ávila, since the name Diego de Ávila does not appear elsewhere in the documents of Michoacán for this period. Be that as it may, the document indicates the time period when such documents were being sent out. López de Ávila authorized the recipients to collect "all metal tools, slaves, maize, and anything else that belonged to Señor Fernando Cortés, late governor of New Spain." They were permitted to sell these possessions to anyone they wished or at public auction.[41]

Village street, Jarácuaro; threshing grain with animals.

Francisco de Orduña was also active for Salazar and Chirinos in Michoacán. He said that they gave him a "commission, power, and faculty" by virtue of which he went to the provinces of Colima, Zacatula, and Michoacán and distributed the Indians there among the *vecinos* and residents.[42] Undoubtedly they gave him the commission after they had declared Cortés and his followers dead and their encomiendas vacant.

Our information regarding the life of the Spanish residents in Michoacán at this time is so limited that we have great difficulty forming any picture of it. The names that the Indians of Michoacán gave the Spaniards indicate their attitudes toward them. At first, seeing that the Spaniards did not eat the same foods that the Indians ate and did not indulge in drunkenness, the natives called them *tucupacha*, or "gods," and *teparacha*, or "great men," which was also a name for the gods. Another descriptive term given to them was *acatzecha*, or "people who wear hats." Later on the Indians simply called them "Christians," and this title for the Spaniards apparently came into general use.

The Tarascans also arrived at some novel interpretations of Spanish origins and customs. Seeing their form-fitting clothing and armor, so different from the loose-hanging Tarascan robes, they believed that the Spaniards were wearing the flayed skins of men; this was probably the most similar form of apparel in their experience. Since the dance in human skins was associated with the veneration of the goddess Cuerauáperi, the Indians thought that the Spaniards had come from heaven bringing from Cuerauáperi the new blessings of wine and wheat and other European seeds.[43]

••

CHAPTER 7

Michoacán Under the Interim Governors, 1526–1528

CORTÉS finally returned to New Spain on May 24, 1526, when he landed at the port of San Juan Chalchicueca on the Gulf coast. From there he wrote a letter to the town council of Mexico City, making a long comparison in a satirical vein between his rising from the "dead" and that of Jesus.[1] By June 21 he was once more in Mexico City and had accepted the resignations of the officials who had been appointed in his absence.[2]

His return to Mexico City should have led to the reestablishment of political stability in New Spain, but that was not to be. On November 4 of the previous year Charles I of Spain had appointed Luis Ponce de León to go to New Spain as judge of residencia to carry out a judicial review of Cortés' activities as governor. The residencia was to last for no more than three months, during which time Ponce de León was to have the powers of governor.

On July 4, 1526, only a few days after Cortés had returned to Tenochtitlan-Mexico, Ponce de León appeared before Cortés, the *alcalde mayor* Juan de Ortega, the royal officials Estrada and Albornoz, and the members of the town council assembled in the main church of the city. After Ponce de León had presented the royal decree of his appointment, all those present acknowledged his authority, and Cortés gave up his rod of justice, the symbol of his authority as governor.[3] He could not foresee that he would never again hold the office of governor of New Spain.

Unfortunately for the political stability of New Spain, Ponce de León soon became very ill, and on July 20 he died.[4] On July 16, aware that he might not survive his illness, he had appointed Marcos de Aguilar as his successor in case of his death and as *alcalde mayor*

114

to replace Bachiller Ortega. Aguilar had come to New Spain as "inquisitor to attend to matters related to the Holy Office of the Inquisition."[5]

Many of the conquistadors were unwilling to accept the legitimacy of this transfer of power. On July 20, the day Ponce de León died, the representatives of the Spanish towns of New Spain called on Cortés to take power into his own hands once more. But he, apparently afraid that he might be accused of rebellion against royal authority, declined to reassume power, saying that he preferred that his judgment of residencia should proceed.[6] If the residencia had proceeded according to plan, he might have hoped for a fully legitimate return to power in three months. Consequently on July 23, 1526, Cortés' attorney, Francisco Sánchez de Zorita, presented a petition before Aguilar asking him to proceed with the trial, even though there was some doubt about Aguilar's right to succeed Ponce de León as judge of residencia. On August 29, Aguilar declared that, since his authority was in doubt, he would not proceed with the residencia until the king could be consulted.[7]

In the meantime, Aguilar stoutly asserted his right to power as governor of New Spain, even though he himself was sick in bed. In the absence of anyone else trained in the law, the town council finally asked Aguilar to give his own formal judicial opinion regarding the situation, and when he gave his opinion in his own favor, they accepted his authority as *alcalde mayor* of New Spain on August 1, 1526.[8] Aguilar, however, did not survive for a full year. For seven months the meetings of the town council were held in his personal chambers, and finally, on March 1, 1527, came the announcement of his death.[9]

On February 28, 1527, Aguilar had dictated a decree transferring his authority to the royal treasurer, Alonso de Estrada. But there was considerable doubt whether Aguilar had the right to make this transfer of power. Cortés, however, again declined to take over the reins of government on his own authority. On March 1 the cabildo appointed Gonzalo de Sandoval to succeed Aguilar in his powers as *alcalde mayor* of New Spain, but later the same day they accepted Estrada as *alcalde mayor* conjointly with Sandoval. In case of disagreement between the two the town council would make the decision.[10]

Matters continued thus until August 22, 1527. On that day Estrada presented before the town council a royal decree of March 16, 1527, which officially transferred Ponce de León's powers as governor to

Marcos de Aguilar or to the person whom Aguilar might have appointed in his place. Since Estrada had such an appointment from
Aguilar, the decree gave him clear title to the governorship.[11] Sandoval withdrew from the scene, and Estrada alone exercised authority as
governor until the arrival of Nuño de Guzmán in December, 1528.[12]

For Michoacán the short, ineffective periods of rule by Luis Ponce de
León and Marcos de Aguilar do not seem to have had any great importance, though the rule of Alonso de Estrada would prove to have
extraordinary significance for the Tarascan kingdom. The king's instructions to Ponce de León did include a paragraph on Michoacán.
Someone had apparently given the crown a very exaggerated account
of the potential wealth of Michoacán's silver mines. The king wrote
to Ponce:

A report has been made to me that in the province of Michoacán, which is
forty leagues from Tenochtitlan, there is a mountain range where one can take
the earth and smelt it and a large part of it will come out silver, although up
to now this has not been verified by experience, and in order to ascertain
this, it would be good if both the said mountain range and the people who
dwell in it, as well as all the other lands of the province, should be registered and that our accountant should have the book and account of it and
of the *vecinos* and Indians of each province; I command you that you should
do this and decree that an assay should be made in order to know whether
it is true that the said earth has the said silver, or another metal, and let
the secret and truth of it be known, and we command that the said accountant should keep the said register and account, just as is contained in
this paragraph.[13]

There is no evidence that Ponce had an opportunity to attend to this
matter during his very brief tenure of office, and no documentation
has come to light to indicate that Aguilar pursued the matter at all.

In the meantime, during this period of neglect, the relationship
between the Spaniards and Indians in Michoacán deteriorated. Undoubtedly the pressures placed upon the Indians by their encomenderos and by the wandering Spanish miners were the most important
element contributing to the discontent and restlessness. Another no
doubt disruptive element was the movement of goods and men through
Michoacán toward the port of Zacatula, at the mouth of the Río Balsas,
where Cortés was preparing his little fleet to sail to the Moluccas, or
Spice Islands, on the far side of the Pacific Ocean. Cortés had no sooner

conquered Tenochtitlan than he began following the impulse that had led Columbus to open the way to these new lands. As early as 1522, when Cortés was arguing against the appointment of Cristóbal de Tapia as governor of New Spain, he had asserted that he had discovered the "South Sea" (the Pacific Ocean) in three or four places and had commanded that ships be constructed.[14]

We have seen that his first questions to the Tarascan ambassadors concerned the possibility of reaching the South Sea by passing through their lands, that he had the Tarascans carry anchors to Zacatula, and that he had sent Juan Rodríguez de Villafuerte to Zacatula to take charge of the shipbuilding after Olid's withdrawal from Michoacán. Naval supplies had to be carried across from the Gulf coast to the shipyard on the Pacific side. During the summer of 1524, before his departure for Honduras, Cortés sent his servants Juan Ximénez and Juan Morales to Santisteban de Pánuco to get tackle, sail, anchors, and other items from the ships of Pedro de Vallejo and of the deceased Francisco de Garay. They signed a receipt for the items on April 18, 1524, indicating that Cortés had ordered the articles to be taken to the South Sea.[15] On June 4, 1524, Juan Ximénez delivered to Felipe Navarro and Alonso Martín in Ixtlahuaca a large quantity of maritime equipment, including five anchors and six iron cannon. All the items were to be delivered to Juan Rodríguez de Villafuerte.[16] The fact that it was in Ixtlahuaca where they were given over to Navarro and Martín indicates that they were being taken to Zacatula by way of Michoacán, since at that time the route to Michoacán went from Ixtlahuaca to Tajimaroa.

By 1524, however, Cortés realized that the route to Zacatula presented serious problems of communications. In a letter to his cousin Francisco Cortés, who was in charge of the enterprise at the time, he approved Francisco's suggestion that the port should be moved to Acapulco as soon as the ships had sailed for the Spice Islands, because Acapulco was better suited for navigation into the Pacific and for communication with the ports on the east coast.

Francisco Cortés had reported that he had found masts to use in the construction of the ships but that he was having difficulty floating them to the shipyard because of the narrowness of the river. Probably he was trying to bring them down one of the steep-falling tributaries of the Río Balsas. Fernando Cortés did not consider the problem serious. He wrote to his cousin:

If it [the narrow spot] is as wide as you say, there is enough room to bring trees through it for carracks, much more so for ships such as those; therefore, you must make great haste to bring them from one place or another, because until I know that you have them, I will not provide anything for the ships; and when you have done this, write to me immediately, and I will send everything necessary.

He asked his cousin to urge the craftsmen to build the ships quickly, and he recommended special watchfulness over the ships and tackle.[17]

Cortés' expedition to Honduras delayed his plans for the departure of the ships. During that time, however, Albornoz reported in his letter to the king of December 15, 1525, that two ships and a brigantine had been completed in Zacatula and that they could go to the Spice Islands. Assuming that Cortés was dead, he suggested that the crown proceed with the project.[18]

It was not until 1527 that Cortés was able to organize his little fleet for its venture into the unknown distances of the Pacific. Between February and May, 1527, he signed contracts with the sailors who were to man the ships.[19] We can imagine these men traveling west through Michoacán, expecting the natives to supply them with food and porters until, making their way down through the canyons into the tierra caliente, they finally arrived at the mouth of the Río Balsas and there saw the newly outfitted ships awaiting them.

Along the way they must have seen bands of Indian bearers carrying equipment and supplies for the little fleet. Francisco Cortés delivered one such shipment to the care of Pedro Tiscareno in Uchichila (Tzintzuntzan) on Sunday, March 11, 1527. It included four cannon with their cannonballs and equipment; naval stores; materials for making casks; tools such as tongs, hammers, chisels, harpoons, and saws; and other items. All of this was to be delivered to Captain Álvaro de Saavedra, commander of the expedition.[20]

Among the items that the expedition carried for trade were some metal artifacts from Michoacán. Antonio Guiral listed the following among the items that he had received for shipment to the Orient:

122 shields of the metal of Michoacán, which weighed 6 arrobas and 19 pounds.
Plus 100 diadems of the same metal and 100 bracelets and 100 saucers of the same metal, which weighed 2 arrobas and 19 pounds. This was weighed with the cords with which they are tied together.

Further, I received in native rattles of the same metal 4 arrobas and 33 pounds. These rattles are put together like the breast leather of a saddle with heavy cords. They were weighed as they were, all put together.[21]

The "metal of Michoacán" was probably the silver mixed with copper from which many of the metallic objects of Michoacán were made. The nature of the artifacts—shields, diadems, bracelets, saucers, rattles —suggests that they were tribute items that Cortés had obtained from the Cazonci. Possibly, although we have no documentation to prove it, Michoacán was also a major source of provisions and supplies for the expedition, since it was the most accessible agricultural region.

The fleet made its first shakedown cruise from Zacatula along the coast in July, 1527, and finally sailed off into the Pacific on November 1, 1527. Although it succeeded in reaching the Moluccas, it was unable to return to Zacatula. Many years would pass before the Spaniards discovered the combination of winds and currents that would bring sailing vessels back east across the Pacific.[22]

Michoacán, then, played some part in this first effort to establish contact with the Far East from the west coast of Mexico. The demands for supplies and services probably also contributed to the growing discontent among the natives. But a more serious cause of restlessness was the continued growth of mining to the west and south of the Tarascan highlands and the correspondingly greater pressures on the natives for goods and services.

During this time the Spanish judicial and administrative supervision of Michoacán was in the hands of justices and inspectors. We have spoken, for instance, of the activities of Alonso de Ávila during the governorship of Salazar. Another inspector who leaves a very shadowy trace on the history of Michoacán was Martín de Calahorra. In the official record of the smelting house in Mexico City for May 1, 1527, is an entry indicating that Calahorra had brought back 118 pesos and 5 tomines of 21-carat gold, "which are from the fines for the treasury which they owed in the mines of Michoacán."[23] In 1540, Calahorra gave testimony that he knew of the town of Pungarabato and that he had been inspector in the mines of Coyuca thirteen years previously.[24]

That is all that has come to light about his activities. We do not even know whether he was appointed by Estrada and Sandoval or by Marcos de Aguilar, although the fact that he was back in Mexico City by May 1, 1527, only two months after Aguilar's death, suggests that he was appointed during Aguilar's tenure. Two months would not be much time for the journey to and from the mines and the inspection of the mines. The geographical area in which he specifically indicated that he was active, Pungarabato and the mines of Coyuca, was in the far-southeastern corner of Michoacán, near the junction of the Cutzamala and Balsas rivers. We do not know whether his duties also took him into other mining areas of the province, although presumably they did so.

Another region of Michoacán, however, claimed the greatest attention, a region known as Motín. The geographical definition of Motín is somewhat hazy, but we can say that in the first decade after the Conquest the name was applied in a general way to the mountainous region adjacent to the Pacific coast in southwestern Michoacán between Colima and Zacatula. Alonso Álvarez de Espinosa, for instance, defined the region simply as "the provinces of Motín, which lie between the towns of Colima and Zacatula."[25] It is a region of very difficult terrain where even today roads are almost nonexistent.

The chronology of military activity in the province of Motín is difficult to establish with certainty. The name that appears most often in relation to the conquest of Motín is that of Pedro Sánchez Farfán. Carl O. Sauer gave him some attention in his work on Colima, but he was unsure whether to place his activities in 1523, 1526, or 1528. Donald Brand somewhat more accurately placed his campaign in Motín in the period from 1526 to 1528.[26] The best sources of information about Sánchez Farfán's campaign of pacification in Motín are two relations of merits and services by Francisco de Torres (1545 and 1558) and another by Alonso Álvarez de Espinosa (1558), both of whom participated in the campaign.[27] They agree that Sánchez Farfán was sent to Motín by Alonso de Estrada while he was governor. The circumstances indicate that he was sent during the period while Estrada was governing after the death of Aguilar rather than when he governed as lieutenant for Cortés in 1526.

In determining the time of Sánchez Farfán's campaign in Motín, we are aided to some extent by the fact that on February 22, 1527, he became a member of the town council of Mexico City, when Luis de Berrio resigned in his favor. The acts of the town council also show that he was absent for periods during Estrada's tenure as governor. He was not present at cabildo meetings between March 16 and July

31, 1527, and between October 19, 1527, and April 17, 1528.[28]

The problem would seem to be solved by a statement made in 1558 by Diego Hernández Nieto, a member of the expedition, that Estrada appointed Sánchez Farfán as captain to conquer Motín "during the year 1527, at the end of it."[29] This favors the period beginning after October 19, 1527, and cannot be easily discounted. But because of a number of factors that will be mentioned as we go along, I believe that Sánchez Farfán must have made his entrada during the earlier period, between March 16 and July 31, 1527, and that Hernández Nieto was mistaken in his recollection.

There had probably been some military activity in Motín before Sánchez Farfán's arrival. Antonio de Oliver indicated that Antón Caicedo had gone into the province with Spaniards who were in the area and had conquered and pacified some towns before the arrival of Sánchez Farfán.[30] This is the only indication that we have of activity by Caicedo in Motín before the coming of Sánchez Farfán, although there is ample testimony that he entered the region by Estrada's command at a later date. It is possible, however, that, while acting as Cortés' agent in the Tamazula-Zapotlán region, he led a private expedition south into the unsettled Motín.

It is certain that Pedro Sánchez Farfán was the leader of the major expedition of conquest and pacification of Motín at this time. The choice of Sánchez Farfán as leader of the expedition must have been related to his position as encomendero of Tepalcatepec, one of the towns of the Tarascan dominions that was close to Motín.[31] We know very little about the size or composition of the expedition, since none of the records from it have been found. Ángel de Villafaña, according to his own testimony and that of Alonso Álvarez de Espinosa, was *maestre de campo*.[32]

Francisco de Torres gives us a very brief glimpse of the nature of the warfare of the campaign: "I found myself in the pacification of it and in combats among the crags where the Indians had fortified themselves, and I stood watch and went on the incursions with my crossbow."[33] Juan Fernández Ijar, another participant, gives a picture of the physical difficulties of the campaign: ". . . because the land of the said Motín is extremely broken, most of us went on foot; and the rest of those in the conquest, well, the man who went on horseback had to go on foot, and he led his horse by the rein."[34] The rigors of the expedition must have told on Ángel de Villafaña and he must have come back from it dangerously ill, for on June 3, 1527, he registered his last will and testament.[35]

The participants mention two principal benefits of the campaign in Motín: the opening of trade and communications between Zacatula and Colima and the discovery of gold mines and the rush to exploit them. Concerning the first, Francisco de Torres included the following statement in his relation of merits and services of 1558: "After the Spaniards had gone through the said land of Motín, the said Indians remained under obedience to His Majesty, and . . . from that time on the *vecinos* of the said towns of Colima and Zacatula carried on trade because the said land had been pacified for them."[36] Juan Fernández Ijar provided the clearest statement about the effects of the campaign on gold mining:

. . . that time the land remained very well punished and began to serve, and during the conquest some very rich gold mines were discovered, and a great number of slave gangs belonging to *vecinos* of Mexico, Colima, and Zacatula and to other people went there, and, as a result of this, many fifth parts [of the gold mined] came to his Majesty, and they have been valuable to him down to the present day.[37]

Extant notary records in Mexico City for the year 1527 give some indication of a new gold rush to Michoacán. The records show that between January 29 and May 4 there were no new contracts to send slaves and tools to Michoacán; in fact, during that period Pedro de Sotomayor, encomendero of Acámbaro, offered to sell his slaves and tools.[38] But between May 4 and September 7 eleven contracts were registered for sending slaves into the mines of Michoacán and neighboring areas.[39] By that time Ángel de Villafaña must have recovered his health and was once more taking an interest in material gains, because among the contracts is one dated August 4 by which he bought one hundred slaves for mining.[40]

The surge of interest in mining in Michoacán between May and September, 1527, and its absence at a later date is one of the reasons for choosing early 1527 as the period of Sánchez Farfán's campaign in Motín. Another reason is that on January 31, 1528, in the middle of Sánchez Farfán's second period of absence from the cabildo, Ángel de Villafaña, the *maestre de campo* of the expedition to Motín, was in

Mexico City, where he signed a power of attorney authorizing the sale of his slaves in the mines of Michoacán.[41] A third reason is that on September 7, 1527, Hernando Garrovero was serving as alcalde of the mines of Michoacán,[42] and the principal sources on the conquest of Motín indicate that Garrovero was sent to the province by Estrada after Sánchez Farfán had left.

Francisco de Torres and Alonso Álvarez de Espinosa, in their interrogatories of 1558 and their testimony for one another, give us a picture of continuing troubles along the border of Michoacán to the west and south, even after the departure of Sánchez Farfán, probably as a result of the increased interest in mining. They describe the province as being on the point of war, and Torres says:

At that time they killed many Spaniards who were traveling toward the said towns of Colima and Zacatula, and in many parts of it we Spaniards needed to keep watch because many towns were in a state of war and rebellion, as they were when the treasurer Alonso de Estrada, who was governor at the time, sent a captain who was named Garrovero to Motín.[43]

In this threatening situation the Spaniards (presumably this refers only to the Spaniards in southwestern Michoacán) took refuge in Tepalcatepec. Antón Caicedo, who was in Zapotlán, "sent word to them, telling them that the land was rising in revolt and that they should take care."[44]

Both Torres and Álvarez were in Tepalcatepec with Garrovero, and their statements give the impression that they felt themselves to be under siege. Each speaks of the other having sallied forth in search of supplies. Torres' excursion seems to have been the more dramatic. In the words of Álvarez,

the said Francisco de Torres went out with some other Spanish soldiers to the town of Jilotlán to gather provisions by command of the said Garrovero, . . . who had gone with the other soldiers as their leader by command of the treasurer Alonso de Estrada, and along the way the said Francisco de Torres captured and brought back as prisoner a cacique of the province of Jilotlán.[45]

Torres testified that the Spaniards were together for many days, apparently in Tepalcatepec,

until notice of it was given to the said governor, and during that time the said Alonso Álvarez went out to search for provisions by command of the said captain, with other companions whom the captain assigned to him, and this went on until Bachiller Ortega came to the said province to make an investigation and to punish the guilty in the province.[46]

Torres' statement that the situation in Tepalcatepec remained critical until the arrival of Bachiller Ortega would extend it into the spring of 1528. The earliest date that we have for Ortega's activities in Michoacán is the last day of April or the first of May, 1528.

Bachiller Juan de Ortega's visitation of Michoacán was the most important of the judicial-military actions in the province in the years before the Cazonci's death. It continued the custom of trying to control and regulate the problems in Michoacán by means of investigators sent out from Mexico City. In fact, Pedro Sánchez Farfán himself must be included in this series of officials. More than simply a military captain, he was a *visitador*, an inspector general, for the province of Michoacán. In 1532 he testified:

This witness, going as *visitador* of the said province of Michoacán and entering into some *cúes*, which are like granaries, found the said figures of stone and wood, such as the question describes, set up as idols for veneration, and this witness commanded them to be taken out and had them burned, as things pertaining to the devil.[47]

In the first part of the trial of the Cazonci in 1530, Francisco de Villegas introduced a question pertaining to Sánchez Farfán's activities: "Further, [let them say] whether they know, saw or heard it said that Pedro Sánchez Farfán brought accusations against the said Cazonci for sodomy, about which he found sufficient evidence."[48] Only one of the witnesses knew by means other than hearsay of this action by Sánchez Farfán. Cristóbal Romero testified that he knew that Sánchez Farfán had gathered evidence concerning sodomy by the Cazonci but did not know whether he found that the evidence was sufficient, though he did burn some other Indians as sodomites.[49] Sánchez Farfán, therefore, had authority to act as judge in Michoacán, even to the extent of condemning Indians to death.

Another evidence of his judicial powers is that when he returned to Mexico City he gave to Estrada as royal treasurer 115 pesos and 2 tomines of common gold that he as "former *visitador* in the province of Michoacán" had collected "from certain condemnations that he made, applied to the treasury of His Majesty."[50] In most such cases the judge was allowed to keep at least an equal amount for himself. Since Hernando Garrovero had the title "alcalde de minas de Michoacán," he also obviously had judicial powers, although they were probably limited to matters pertaining to mining.

Before the arrival of Ortega, yet another justice had come to Michoacán: Juan Xuárez, apparently the brother of Cortés' first wife, Catalina Xuárez.[51] Again, we know little about his activities in Michoacán. His tenure there immediately preceded that of Bachiller Ortega. This we know from testimony given in 1542 by Juan de Sandoval concerning the notary Juan Martínez de Espinosa. He said that Martínez de Espinosa had been notary for Juan Xuárez "from back before the time when the said Bachiller Ortega went there . . . and that the said Juan Martínez de Espinosa stayed there with him [Ortega] as his notary."[52]

On two occasions Xuárez himself gave testimony concerning his activities, but neither statement gives us much information. In 1536 he said, ". . . this witness went as judge to the said province and made an inquiry concerning the matter that the question mentions, about the killing of Spaniards."[53] In 1541 he made a slightly longer statement:

. . . this witness saw that the other towns [of Michoacán] which were parceled out among the Spaniards served their masters very badly, because this witness saw it while serving as judge at that time, and he saw that in some of the towns the Indians killed some of the Spaniards, because in his capacity as judge this witness made an investigation of it and held the Indian lords and *principales* as prisoners for this reason.[54]

His activities are mentioned by three witnesses in the trial against the Cazonci. Juan de Sámano testified that he had seen that Xuárez freed the lords of Zanzan and Puruándiro from the power of the Cazonci, who was keeping them in Tzintzuntzan.[55] Gonzalo López merely mentioned Xuárez with Ortega in the work of sending native lords back to their towns.[56] But Pedro Muñoz, *maestro* de Roa, provided the most detailed information about Xuárez' work:

. . . when Juan Xuárez was in this city of Michoacán, this witness was also here, and from this city they went together to Pátzcuaro to burn *cúes* and sacrifices; and in some dwellings that they said belonged to the Cazonci, they found many of the paraphernalia of sacrifices. And when the said Juan Xuárez saw those things, he told them that he had not gone there to seek gold or silver or anything else, but to burn up their sacrifices and the idol offerings that they made there, and to seek out the skins of Christians whom they had killed there, and they had told him that they had them there, but he would burn them.[57]

The same witness testified that either Juan Xuárez or Bachiller Ortega had hanged a *principal* who was reportedly from a town that belonged to Santa Cruz.[58] He added that

while the said Juan Xuárez was in this city [of Tzintzuntzan] he took legal action against the lords of it, and when he had gotten fairly far along with the case, there arrived a letter from the treasurer, who was governor at the time, in which he commanded that he should not occupy himself with the justice that should be done to the Cazonci and Pedro Panza and Coyuze (to these three persons as this witness remembers), and this witness saw the letter, and it said that he should not pay attention to the clamor of the Spaniards, letting it be understood that justice should not be done.[59]

It is evident, then, that Xuárez went out in response to reports of the killing of Spaniards, such as we have seen already in the narratives of the troubles in the region of Tepalcatepec. His reports, however, must have convinced Governor Estrada that a stronger show of force was necessary. As a result, sometime in the spring of 1528 Estrada decided to send out Bachiller Juan de Ortega as judge and also as captain of a military force to settle problems in the troubled region.

There is still much that is unclear about the *visita* of Juan de Ortega to Michoacán, even though some documents have come to light that give us a much better idea of his work than could be gained previously. The principal new documents are three letters to Ortega from Governor Estrada and the official record of Ortega's tribute assessment for the towns of Michoacán.[60] Estrada's letters, however, are all answers to letters from Ortega, which we do not have, and they are often hard to interpret.

We do not know Estrada's motives in choosing Ortega to lead the expedition. The choice was certainly contrary to the dying admonition of Marcos de Aguilar, who showed an intense and specific dislike of Ortega in the following paragraph of the document by which he passed on his authority to Estrada on February 28, 1527:

And by the present letter he [Aguilar] said that, insofar as Bachiller Juan de Ortega has been and is a person who has and has had great hatred and enmity with many people in this New Spain, therefore [Aguilar] entreated and charged the said Treasurer Alonso de Estrada and, if necessary, from now on he commanded him in the name of His Majesty, that he should not take counsel with Bachiller Juan de Ortega, nor should he ask his opinion or counsel on anything that should be done or decreed concerning the said government, because His Majesty would be very badly served in that; rather let him command him, and from this moment he commands him, that he should immediately leave this New Spain in fulfillment of a decree of His Majesty, by which he commanded the said Bachiller Juan de Ortega to leave and go out of this said New Spain in a certain manner, as is contained more at length in the said decree, concerning which he said that he burdened the conscience of the said treasurer.[61]

Estrada, however, does not seem to have shared Aguilar's low opinion of Ortega. Ortega had always been a strong partisan of Cortés in Mexico, as we have seen from his action during the spring of 1526. This may have motivated Aguilar's reaction toward him. Perhaps his appointment as inspector general in Michoacán was made out of deference to Cortés, who had major interests in Michoacán and who left Mexico for Spain in the spring of 1528, not long before Ortega led out his expedition to Michoacán.

Ortega must have left Mexico City about April 18, 1528. He could not have left earlier, since on April 16 he recorded a debt in the city,[62] and on April 17 Alonso de Ávalos, who was witness for the first acts of Ortega's tribute assessment, recorded a power of attorney,[63] and Pedro de Bazán, who later asserted that he had accompanied Ortega to Michoacán, recorded a substitution of attorney.[64] A problem is presented, however, by the surviving copy of the first of the letters of Estrada to Ortega, which bears the date March 27, 1528.[65] Both because Ortega and some of his men were still in Mexico City in the middle of April and because of the content of the letter itself, we must judge that the copyist wrote "marzo" for "mayo," an error that would have been easy to make in copying the handwriting of the period. There are references in the letter to Ortega's efforts to regulate the tribute burden, and from the record of the tribute assessment we know that his official acts in this regard began at the end of April or the beginning of May.

Ortega gave his own version of his activities in Michoacán in three

questions of an interrogatory that he presented in Mexico City on
October 19, 1531:

> ii. Further, let them be asked whether they know that, because the province
> of Michoacán was not serving the Spaniards, in view of the many deaths of
> Christians which the Indians of the said province had caused, Treasurer
> Alonso de Estrada, governor at that time in this New Spain, sent the said
> Bachiller Juan de Ortega to the province of Michoacán to pacify it, so that
> the Indians would serve the Spaniards as they were obliged to do.
>
> iii. Further, whether they know, etc., that the said *bachiller*, in fulfillment
> of the said command, went to the said province with many foot soldiers and
> horsemen and sent out a summons to the said lords and *principales* of the said
> province, and in the presence of the Spaniards to whom they were entrusted,
> he established order in their service, both as to how they were to serve and
> what they were to contribute to their masters, and this was done with the
> agreement of everyone.
>
> iv. Further, let them be asked whether they know that before the said
> Bachiller Juan de Ortega went to the said province, they did not serve in
> this way, because the men to whom the Indians were entrusted, mistreated
> the Indians and the Indians had killed many Spaniards; and let them say
> what they know about this question.[66]

It is clear from these three questions that there were two principal
purposes for Ortega's campaign in Michoacán: to punish the Indians
who had been responsible for the deaths of Spaniards and to make
adjustments in the more basic problems of the inequities of the system
of tributes from the encomiendas. Here we will examine the chronology
of Ortega's campaign and his punitive activities, saving for a later chapter a discussion of his decisions regarding the encomiendas.

The first dates that we have for Ortega's inspection come from the
record of his assessment of tributes.[67] Here again, however, we face a
slight chronological problem. Both of the available copies of the record
give the date as April 31, 1528, a nonexistent date, of course. Probably the notary, forgetting that there are only thirty days in April,
wrote April 31 instead of May 1. Assuming this to be true, we begin
with May 1, 1528, as the first known date of Ortega's activities in
Michoacán. On that day, speaking through Juan Martín (or Martínez)
as his interpreter, Ortega summoned Don Pedro before him in Tzintzuntzan and commanded him to assemble all the interpreters of the
province. They were to go to the towns to summon the lords and

principales for the purpose of establishing order in the service of the encomiendas, so that in the future the Spaniards would not mistreat the Indians and the Indians would not continue to kill Spaniards. The towns in which Spaniards had been killed would have to face the requirements of justice. Don Pedro agreed to send the interpreters to summon the lords.

Juan Martín, at Ortega's command, insisted to Don Pedro that he should tell the interpreters to make it clear to the lords of the towns that, unless they appeared before him within the allotted time, he would send or lead his men against them "to kill and burn them and make them slaves, because that is proper for the service of His Majesty and the pacification of these regions, so that the killing of Spaniards should cease."

Don Pedro replied that some of the towns were far away and that they should be given a longer time to respond to the summons. Ortega agreed to allow Don Pedro to set the time limit that seemed best to him. The question may arise in the mind of the reader why Ortega's commands were addressed to Don Pedro and not to the Cazonci. As we shall see below, at this time the Cazonci was once more under constraint in Mexico.

In the record of the tribute assessment there follows a listing of the various towns, including the name of the encomendero of each. In the margin beside each town appears the name of an interpreter and that of a *principal*, presumably the names of the interpreter who was being sent and of the *principal* who was being summoned.

On May 16, 1528, Ortega again commanded Don Pedro to appear before him, together with all the lords of towns who had responded to his summons. Speaking through Juan Pascual as his interpreter, he began to establish order in the system of tributes. He continued this activity on May 17 and 22 and on June 1 and 12. We shall study in detail his reorganization of the tributes later, in the chapters on the encomiendas.

The last of Ortega's commands that was entered in the record of the tribute assessment was apparently given on June 12, 1528. He decreed that whenever Spaniards came to their towns the Indians were to go out to receive them, give them food and lodging, and supply them with two or three bearers and an accompaniment of two *principales* to take them on to the next town.

Probably at about the time that he was completing this part of his work, Ortega received the first of the extant letters from Estrada, which, if my conjecture is correct, the governor sent to him on May 27.[68] Estrada wrote the letter in answer to one from Ortega and a petition from Ortega's men. Both letters had referred to the necessity of keeping a judge in the province, and the men of the expedition, who seem to have been mainly the encomenderos of the province, had petitioned that Ortega be appointed to the office. Ortega, however, had asked that the burden not be placed upon him. Estrada had written to the men that, as long as Ortega was acting as judge, no decision was necessary. To Ortega he wrote that he would be grateful if Ortega would stay on as judge after the completion of his present duties. Otherwise, he thought that Garcí Holguín would be a good choice for the post.

A problem had arisen concerning some versified lampoons (coplas) that were circulating in the region, and Estrada congratulated Ortega on his efforts to eradicate them. He did not indicate the nature of the verses, but he expressed the opinion that they had originated from Gonzalo de Ocampo. Bernal Díaz has preserved for us some small pieces of the works of Gonzalo de Ocampo, who had come to Mexico as one of the leaders of the expedition of Francisco de Garay. The snatches that Díaz has preserved for us give an impression of an irreverent humor that must have angered the authorities.

Referring to the reported leap of Pedro de Alvarado across an opening in the causeway leading out of Tenochtitlan during the retreat of "Noche Triste," Díaz says:

. . . and I never heard anything said about this leap of Alvarado's until after Mexico had been conquered, and then it was in some satirical verses of a certain Gonzalo de Ocampo, which I do not put down here because they are a bit nasty. But among them he says: "Y dacordásete debía del salto que diste de la puente" ["And it must have reminded you of the leap that you made across the bridge"]. But I won't play any further on that key.[69]

Regarding the honor that Cortés accorded to Juana Ruiz de Mancilla after she had been shamed and whipped by Salazar, Díaz records: ". . . and for that honor and gift that they conferred upon her Gonzalo de Ocampo, he of the defamatory verses, said that she took reward from her back as though one would get noses from an arm."[70]

The only complete piece by Ocampo that Díaz preserved lampoons factor Gonzalo de Salazar and his relationship with Cortés.

Díaz wrote:

And I wish to say that for this reason Gonzalo de Ocampo said in his defamatory verses:

¡Oh, Fray Gordo de Salazar	"Oh, Fray Fatso de Salazar
factor de diferencias!	Factor of differences!
Con tus falsas reverencias	With your false reverences
engañaste al provincial.	You deceived the provincial.
Un fraile de santa vida	A friar of holy life
me dijo que me guardase	told me that I should guard myself
de hombre que asi hablase	from a man who would speak
retórica tan polida.	rhetoric so polished."[71]

Verses like these must have brought many an irreverent laugh to the mining camps of Michoacán, to the discomfiture of the authorities. We may well imagine that there was one dedicated to Estrada himself. Estrada thought that the reason for the continuing problem with the verses in Michoacán was that Ocampo had left his writings to Gonzalo López, whose miner, Alvaro Gallego, was going about singing them. Both men were encomenderos, López of Cuitzeo and Gallego of Chucándiro. López also had charge of Comanja for Juan de Solís.[72]

The governor commanded Ortega to investigate the matter and, if he did not wish to punish López, to send the report to Estrada so that he might take the necessary action. But Ortega was commanded to punish Gallego thoroughly, as well as anyone else who was composing or singing them or who had them written down. If Ortega could get his hands on copies of the offensive verses, he was to burn them.

Ortega was seemingly unhappy that no significant opportunities for reward had appeared for himself. Estrada assured him that he would receive a reward when the opportunity arose, but no member of the expedition was to return to Mexico until Estrada decided what was best, and Ortega was not to give permission for anyone to leave without first notifying Estrada.

Very soon after completing his assessment of tributes, Ortega went to Cortés' encomienda towns in the northwest corner of the Tarascan kingdom. In his letter of July 12, Estrada mentioned that he had received two letters from Ortega, both written on June 29 in Zapotal (Zapotlán, present-day Ciudad Guzmán). Alonso de Mata also placed Ortega in the far-western part of the province at this time. He indicated that when he took Ortega a commission from Estrada, dated in Mexico on June 13, he found the *visitador* as he was coming from Tamazula.[73]

Estrada's letter of July 12 opens with an expression of his pleasure at hearing from Ortega once again, because some time had passed since he had last received a letter from him. The governor congratulated Ortega on the good work that he was doing both in punishing the guilty and in setting the encomiendas in order. Estrada agreed that Ortega might keep the money from the fines that he imposed as something toward a salary for himself and his men.

Ortega had asked to be allowed to give permission for some of the men to return to Mexico. Estrada did not object but thought that the men should not scatter. When the expedition had returned to Tzintzuntzan, Ortega himself might return to Mexico if he thought it best.

In this letter Estrada included the important information that he was allowing the Cazonci to return to Michoacán: "I am giving permission to the Cazonci that he may go in the company of the friars. He is leaving so tamed that I think that he will not dare do anything for which he should return here. There you will be able to confer about everything more at length." This explains why the Cazonci's name did not appear in the acts of the assessment of tributes. The friars with whom he was returning were probably also coming back from their chapter at this time.

By the time Estrada's letter of July 12 reached Ortega, he had surely returned to Tzintzuntzan. From there on July 19 he wrote a letter to Estrada, which Estrada received on July 27. During the week from July 24 to July 31, Ortega gathered testimony about Alonso de Mata's cruelty to the Indians of Tuzantla, in the presence of the friars and the Cazonci.[74] This incident will be discussed in detail later.

Estrada's reply to Ortega's letter of July 19, which Estrada wrote on July 28, is almost entirely devoted to matters related to encomiendas, and the greater part of its contents will be considered in later chapters. He did, however, discuss one other matter of importance, that of Ortega's successor in office. He had decided to take the burden from Ortega's shoulders, but he had changed his mind about appointing Garcí Holguín, whom he now considered to have too many friends and acquaintances in Michoacán. Instead he had determined to replace Ortega with Gonzalo Xuárez, whom he described as "this man of good will who is in your household and, because he is a good person and not partial to anyone, and so that he may have something to look after and to profit from, it has seemed good to me that he should go to take charge of that province." Xuárez could not have delayed long in going to Michoacán so that Ortega could return to Mexico. Ortega was in the capital by August 29, 1528, when he registered some silver at the royal smelting house.[75]

The punitive aspect of Ortega's campaign, although it constituted an important motivation for the expedition, is the least well documented of his activities. In an interrogatory presented in 1541, Ortega asserted that the Indians in Michoacán had killed sixty to seventy Spaniards. This is the only estimate that we have of the number of Spaniards who had lost their lives in the province. Ortega suggested that the cause of the unrest was the Spaniards' maltreatment of the Indians.[76]

It is difficult to find specific information about the killings. The greatest detail concerning an individual killing is the narrative of the death of Antón Caicedo's interpreter as told in the *Relación de Michoacán*. The *Relación* does not mention the man's name, but the evidence points to the conclusion that he was the Spaniard and interpreter named Juan who had told Caicedo about homosexual prostitution in Michoacán.[77] Two witnesses in Guzmán's trial of the Cazonci also mentioned the murder of the interpreter Juan, but no one seemed to know his surname.[78] In the words of the *Relación:*

And [Caicedo] had with him an interpreter, a good linguist, a Spaniard they say; and because of mistreatment of the Indians, while the Cazonci was absent in Pátzcuaro, those *principales* got drunk and they took their bows and arrows and went after him. He fled from them, and he was a great runner. But four of them caught up with him and shot him with their arrows. But before they shot him, he stabbed one of them and killed him. Afterward the justice found out about it, and Bachiller Ortega came from Mexico to do justice, and he set dogs on those *principales* who had been involved in the death of that young interpreter.[79]

The Cazonci claimed that he was in Mexico when the murder of the interpreter Juan occurred.[80]

The *Relación* also mentions that another Spaniard was later killed at Xicalan, a subject town of Uruapan. For this killing Ortega enslaved most of the residents of the town, almost depopulating it.[81] It is worth noting that it was the encomendero of Uruapan, Francisco de Villegas, who brought the first accusations against the Cazonci in the lawsuit that resulted in his death.[82]

Juan Infante later alleged that Ortega had destroyed or enslaved the population of Sevinca (Sevina) and its subject area because they had reportedly killed a Spaniard. Infante's assertion was supported by testimony given at various times by Antonio de Oliver, Hernando de Jerez, and Diego de Motrico, all of whom asserted that they had been present and had seen what happened.[83]

Alonso de Mata remembered San Remo as the name of one of the Spaniards who had been killed while passing through Michoacán.[84] A man named San Remo had accompanied Olid to Michoacán in 1522 as a crossbowman.[85] The records of Ortega's tribute assessment indicate that the natives of Comanja had killed a black man.[86] In separate testimony given in 1540, Ortega noted that the natives of Cipiajo had killed a Spaniard and that he had scolded the Cazonci and Don Pedro about it because the town was subject to the city of Michoacán and they had consented to the killing.[87]

During the trial of the Cazonci by Nuño de Guzmán, Gonzalo López testified that

they had some Indians of Urucuaro imprisoned because they had killed two Spaniards, and he [López] heard them say that the Cazonci had commanded them to be killed. And when Bachiller Ortega made an investigation concerning it, he found that the clothing and arms of the said Spaniards were in Pátzcuaro, and he commanded that they be brought before him. And when they had been brought, those who brought them confessed that they were bringing them from Pátzcuaro, which is a league from this city [Tzintzuntzan] and that they had been kept there by command of the said Cazonci.[88]

Juan Hernández asserted during the same trial that Ortega "made the said Cazonci bring certain prizes, among which there was a sword and a machete and a helmet and some fetters and other things, and they brought them from the town of Cuaraquaro."[89]

It is evident, then, that there was an ample number of cases in which the natives of Michoacán expressed dissatisfaction with their treatment after the Conquest by taking vengeance on the Spaniards who ventured through the region without adequate protection. We can also see that the principal means of punishment that Ortega used were to set dogs on them and to enslave them. Domingo Medina, testifying in 1541, stated that Ortega had also burned Indians whom he found guilty.[90]

Estrada referred to enslavements and confiscations of goods in his letter of July 12. After agreeing that Ortega could take the fines that he imposed upon Spaniards as something by way of salary, he continued:

What I wrote to you, sir, that you should take the slaves that were made as something toward the reckoning of your salary, was done under the impression that it would be of some profit to you, since there was not anything else at the time. And I say it again now, that you should take them, and His Majesty's fifth, also. Concerning the silver, gold, and clothing, which you say, sir, were found in the towns where they killed the Christians, I believe that it must be a jest; but if it were the truth, I would be happy about it, so that those gentlemen and hidalgos might have some part.[91]

He seems to make a reference to this also in his letter of July 28:

And in regard to the first paragraph, where you complain, sir, because I wrote you something, I do not know what, I do not remember what it was, concerning the silver, gold, and clothing that was found, you are mistaken, sir, because my intention was not such as you say, sir, because in truth in this case I believe that you owe me thanks instead, because every time that I see letters from your grace and know what is happening there, I rejoice greatly over it, and I consider it as something very well done and ordained.[92]

It is impossible to surmise with certainty what had upset Bachiller Ortega; perhaps he did not appreciate the governor's conclusion that what he had written about the silver, gold, and clothing was a matter of jest.

It is possible that some of the items were confiscated in raids on temples where the practice of native rites had continued. Gonzalo López, encomendero of Cuitzeo, asserted in testimony given on February 1, 1532:

. . . While this witness was in Michoacán during the time of the treasurer, Bachiller Ortega, who was there as judge, said publicly—and this witness does not know whether it was proclaimed by the crier—that whoever would find jewels, gold, or clothing in the *cúes* might take them for himself, provided he paid the fifth to His Majesty; and, while there, this witness saw that certain Spaniards went out one night to search for the *cúes*, and they brought back clothing and many Indians, whom the said Bachiller Ortega commanded to be branded, and he gave them out as slaves, after His Majesty's fifth had been paid, and this witness bought a good number of them.[93]

In this way Ortega, like his predecessors in civil authority in Michoacán, continued the attack upon native religion.

Although Ortega returned to Mexico in the summer of 1528, according to some witnesses he did not consider that he had been allowed to settle the problems of Michoacán completely. Both Gonzalo Gómez and Juan Hernández testified two years later at the Cazonci's trial that Ortega had said that the Cazonci was deserving of death, but they both asserted that they had seen a letter from Estrada commanding Ortega not to touch the lords of the province.[94]

In accordance with Estrada's decision about Ortega's successor, Gonzalo Xuárez went to Michoacán as judge and lieutenant governor after Ortega's departure, and he stayed there until he was replaced by Nuño de Guzmán's representative in the spring of 1529.[95] We do not know anything about his activities in office except that he was the first who resisted the expansionism of the new encomendero of Comanja, Juan Infante.[96] We shall see more about that later.

At about this same time the Indians of Motín rebelled again, and Estrada appointed Antón Caicedo as captain of another expedition of pacification there. Some individuals were unhappy about the appointment. Both Antonio de Serrano and Ruy González complained later that Caicedo was nothing more than a groom for Cortés' horses and that other gentlemen in New Spain deserved the appointment more than he did.[97] Yet Caicedo's years of experience in Michoacán surely stood him in good stead as a preparation for this duty. He was also encomendero of Tarecuato and surrounding towns in western Michoacán, which put him in an advantageous geographical position for conducting a campaign into Motín. Two of the men who went with him were Juan Gallego and Alonso Álvarez de Espinosa.[98] Álvarez had returned only five months before from the dangerous experience with Garrovero in Tepalcatepec. Again, he said, "they took many days to pacify it and put it under the dominion of His Majesty."

Thus, on the eve of the arrival of Nuño de Guzmán as president of the First Audiencia of Mexico and governor of New Spain, Michoacán had passed through a time of trial and readjustment in the relationship between the conquerors and the conquered. If a more humane and less greedy person had come to govern the colony, the results might have been beneficial. But the arrival of the new royal representative foreshadowed nothing but further destruction for the Tarascan king and his kingdom.

•••

CHAPTER 8

The Rule of Nuño de Guzmán

NUÑO Beltrán de Guzmán arrived in Tenochtitlan-Mexico as president of the First Audiencia of New Spain in December, 1528.[1] By that time his name and character were already well known in the Spanish colony because of his activities as governor of Pánuco. A member of the Spanish nobility, he was born in Guadalajara, Spain, in the late 1480s or early 1490s. Little is known of his youth; it seems that he had some training in law, though he did not gain a degree. Probably in 1518 he was given the post of a *contino*, a member of the royal bodyguard. In that capacity he performed some important services to the king, for which he was rewarded with the appointment as governor of Pánuco, a jurisdiction of unclear but extensive dimensions along the east coast of Mexico north of Veracruz. He received this appointment on November 4, 1525, while he was in Toledo, but he took a long time getting to his post. He left Spain from Sanlucar de la Barrameda on May 14, 1526.[2]

In a memorial that he wrote to the king in later years, he stated that after arriving in Santo Domingo he was sick for several months with fevers, at first with "continuous tertians and afterwards with double quartans" (probably a form of malaria). From there he went on to Santiago de Cuba, where he again fell sick. It has been assumed that during his stay in the Caribbean he absorbed from Cortés' enemies there some of the hatred that he would later show for the Conqueror of Mexico.

Finally he moved on to his governorship, arriving in Santisteban de Pánuco on May 24, 1527 (in his memorial he gave the year as 1526, but that is clearly impossible, since, as he also asserts in the

138

same document, he ruled there for a year and seven months, and there are ample sources to show that he went from Pánuco to take over the presidency of the audiencia in Mexico City in December, 1528). His period of rule in Pánuco was characterized by extensive enslavement of Indians, who were sent to the islands of the Caribbean in exchange for livestock. It was also a time of conflict with the citizens of Mexico City. The boundaries between the jurisdictions of New Spain and Pánuco had never been clearly defined because Cortés had sought to bring the area under the direct control of New Spain. Now, with an aggressive new autonomous authority in Pánuco, the latent conflicts quickly came to the surface.[3]

As early as June 14, 1527, the cabildo of Mexico City noted that the new governor of Río de Pánuco was exceeding his authority, apprehending caciques and lords who were subject to the jurisdiction of Mexico City. They decided to send a complaint to Guzmán and to demand that he show the documents of his appointment.[4] On December 2, 1527, there was another bitter complaint against Guzman's activities, because of which the citizens of Mexico City were nearly ready to send an expedition against him.[5] By February 19, 1528, Gil González de Benavides, alcalde of the city, had led out a group of men to defend the boundaries of Mexico City's jurisdiction against Guzmán's incursions. Because of the danger of civil war, possibly leading to a rebellion among the Indians, the cabildo suggested a compromise be reached, dividing the border towns between the two jurisdictions.[6]

By April 27, 1528, there seems to have been a rising fear among the members of the cabildo that they might be losing the more important battle of retaining the favor of the king. On that date they noted that Guzmán and his lieutenant Sancho de Caniego were impugning their loyalty to the crown and were destroying Pánuco by their slave raiding. Therefore, they commanded their attorney to gather testimony to send to the king concerning the matter.[7]

After this they were silent about the conflict with Guzmán, perhaps because they had heard rumors about his appointment as president of the audiencia that was being sent out to govern New Spain, or perhaps because the departure of Cortés and many of his close friends for Spain in March, 1528, had reduced the cabildo's will to resist.

Cortés at first had been willing to accept Guzmán as a man of honor. On June 12, 1527, he had written to García de Llerena, his representative in Santisteban:

. . . and you should not be disturbed by what they have told you along the road; it frequently happens that most of the news that people talk about publicly does not turn out to be true, because, according to the knowledge that I have, Señor Nuño de Guzmán is a very noble person, and in everything he will look out for what is best for the service of His Majesty, without giving hearing or credit to troublemakers.

But in the letters that followed on June 22 and August 11, Cortés indicated that he recognized the danger of the developing conflict between his interests and those of the new governor of Pánuco.[8]

It is partly in this context that we must understand Cortés' decision to depart for Spain. We must also note, however, that for well over a year he had been under royal command to return to the court. In a decree of November 24, 1525, the king had commanded him to return to Spain without delay on the first available ship to discuss matters related to the government of New Spain.[9] The purpose of the order seems to have been to get Cortés off the scene to make way for the activities of Luis Ponce de León, whose appointment had been issued only three weeks earlier. But it was not until early 1528 that Cortés actually embarked on the voyage.

Probably in order to have more impressive gifts to offer to the king, Cortés turned once more to the Cazonci. According to the *Relación*, before the arrival of Guzmán as president, Cortés sent Andrés de Tapia to the Cazonci with the following message:

The Marqués has sent me, and he says that another lord is coming to the land; and he will be in Mexico and will be governor, and that I should let you know about his coming and that if he should ask you for gold you should not give it to him, but you should send all of your treasures of gold and silver to where I am, and not hide or keep anything. If Nuño de Guzmán asks for it, you should tell him that you already sent it to me to take it to the Emperor.

(It seems probable that the first person in the last part of this message indicates Cortés rather than Tapia.)

The Cazonci replied: "This must be the truth. There is still a little bit of gold and silver that they left us. Take it. Why do we want it? It belongs to the Emperor."

Twice they took a quantity of gold and silver to Cortés, and afterward Tapia went away.[10]

This episode apparently occurred during 1527; Tapia was reported to be in Michoacán on November 15, 1527.[11] Since he himself later said that he was "*mayordomo* for the lord Don Fernando Cortés,"[12] he may have gone into western Mexico on some errand related to the departure of the fleet to the Moluccas, which left Zacatula on November 1, 1527.

Two entries in the treasury records, however, suggest dates earlier in the year for the two shipments of treasure from Michoacán. On August 3, 1527, Pedro de Isla paid the royal fifth for Cortés on "common silver from Michoacán in shields, plates, and mitres" weighing 1,188 marks, 2 ounces, 1 real. Again on October 8, Isla paid the fifth on 383 marks, 4 reales of common silver for Cortés, and a shield of poor-quality silver for Andrés de Tapia weighing 5 marks, 4 reales.[13]

These dates would seem to be too early for Cortés to have known about the appointment of Nuño de Guzmán. But by that time he surely knew that his political position in New Spain was in danger. On August 22, 1527, Estrada had presented the decree that confirmed him in the position of governor in place of Cortés, and it is not improbable that Cortés had received some prior notification of the decree through his representatives at court. Also in August 1527, the king began to issue the first decrees directed to the newly established audiencia of New Spain.[14]

We have no information to indicate that at this early date the crown had actually selected the president for the audiencia. This seems unlikely, since the *oidores* had to send a messenger to Guzmán to notify him of his appointment after their arrival in Veracruz in November 1528.[15] Very probably, however, Cortés knew of the discussions that preceded the decision to establish an audiencia in New Spain. It is possible that when he realized that the king was not going to return the governorship to him he sent his messenger to the Cazonci telling him that someone was coming to replace Cortés. Guzmán's name may have been inserted later through hindsight by the author of the *Relación,* just as he referred to Cortés in the passage by the title Marqués, even though Cortés would not receive the title until after he had arrived in Spain and Guzmán had already been governor for several months.[16]

Perhaps some of the items that the Cazonci sent to Cortés at this time were the Tarascan artifacts that made their way into the shipments to the Moluccas. In any event, the communication between

Cortés and the Cazonci must have taken place before the visitation of Bachiller Ortega, since Cortés left for Spain in March 1528,[17] and Ortega did not go to Michoacán until April of that year.

The instructions from the crown to Guzmán were issued on April 5, 1528, while Cortés was in midocean on his way to Spain. They dealt very little with Michoacán, except to repeat the substance of the command that the king had given to Ponce de León to investigate the report of the existence of a mountain range in Michoacán that was rich in silver ore.[18]

But bad news for Cortés and his interests in Michoacán was contained in the secret instructions to the audiencia, also issued on April 5, 1528. The audiencia was commanded to place Cortés' encomiendas Tamazula and Tzintzuntzan directly under the authority of the crown.[19]

It was another eight months, however, before the audiencia actually assumed office. On November 13, 1528, the cabildo of Mexico City indicated that they had received word that the *oidores* of the audiencia had arrived in Veracruz and that Nuño de Guzmán, governor of Pánuco, was to be the president of the new body. The cabildo dispatched various prominent individuals to go out to meet the new officials.[20] At their meeting on December 4, 1528, the cabildo took note that the president and the *oidores* were approaching the city. This was the last meeting in which Alonso de Estrada participated as governor.[21]

The *oidores* of the audiencia took office soon afterward. Perhaps their first day of work was December 9, for on that day they took away the rods of office from the *alcaldes ordinarios* (municipal judges) of Mexico City because of irregularities in their elections.[22] Also on that day Cortés' attorney, Pedro Gallego, presented before them a royal decree that was intended to protect Cortés' rights to his encomiendas.[23] Guzmán himself did not arrive until a few days after the *oidores*.[24] He assisted at a meeting of the cabildo for the first time on January 1, 1529.[25]

The audiencia of which Guzmán was the president consisted of Alonso de Parada, Francisco Maldonado, Juan Ortiz de Matienzo, and Diego Delgadillo. Within two weeks after their arrival Parada and Maldonado died, leaving only Matienzo and Delgadillo to cooperate with Guzmán in a policy of self-enrichment at the expense of the Indians and of Cortés and his friends. This policy would affect both Spanish and native interests in Michoacán.[26]

When Guzmán and the audiencia arrived in Mexico, they attracted to their side a man named García del Pilar, a self-seeking leech who was to guide them in sucking up the wealth of the Indians, always diverting some of it to his own use. Bishop-elect Juan de Zumárraga, a Franciscan priest who had been sent out by the king with the audiencia to take control of the ecclesiastical jurisdiction in Mexico City, described Pilar as

an interpreter of the tongue of the Indians of this land and, of a truth, I assure Your Majesty that, in the opinion of all who desire the service of God and of Your Majesty, this tongue should be taken out and cut off, so that he would no longer speak with it the great evils that he does speak and the robberies that he invents daily, because of which he had been on the point of being hanged by the past governors two or three times; and thus he was commanded by Don Fernando not to speak with an Indian under penalty of death.[27]

The friar here plays on three meanings of the word *lengua,* as the physical tongue, a language, and an interpreter, making the passage hard to translate.

This image of Pilar is reinforced by other contemporary testimony. In the investigation that Bachiller Ortega had made against Salazar and Chirinos in 1525, Martín de Calahorra had testified that "they sent García del Pilar to collect gold and make a visitation of the purses of the Indians, and because he told people why he was going, they had him arrested and said that they were going to hang him."[28] In Cortés' residencia Bachiller Ortega himself testified that he had arrested Pilar "for crimes and robberies that he had committed, stealing from the Indians" and that later Cortés had been on the point of hanging Pilar for his robberies from the Indians.[29] In his own relation of merits and services, written in 1529, Pilar gave the reason for his influence with both the Spanish officials and the Indians. He stated that, having come to Mexico with Cortés, he was the first one who learned the language of the Indians, and as a result the Indians put their trust in him.[30]

Zumárraga had remonstrated with Guzmán about having such a person in his hire, but the only results were insults from Pilar and an assertion by Guzmán to the effect that Pilar was a servant of His Majesty through whom Guzmán would do a great deal.[31] Later, however, Pilar turned against Guzmán, and the latter, through his lawyer, described Pilar as

a bad Christian, a perjurer, a man of ill-repute, drunken, cursing, slandering, living in public concubinage with an Indian woman, bearing false witness, a fickle man who went with the times, speaking ill about the past governors to those who came to govern, in order to stand in well with them. Thus, he spoke very ill of both the Marqués and Treasurer Alonso de Estrada to my aforementioned party [Guzmán] and to Licentiates Matienzo and Delgadillo, former president and *oidores*, . . . and the said Pilar used to dress like an Indian with a loincloth and blanket over his naked body and with his feathers and gold ornaments, and he performed dances with the said Cazonci and ate and drank with them and performed sacrifices so that they would give him gold.[32]

Although these are the sentiments of one who obviously considered himself betrayed by Pilar's disloyalty, they certainly do not speak well of the man whom Guzmán chose as his principal interpreter and adviser with the Indians.

One of Guzmán's initial acts after taking office was to send out Indian messengers in all directions to summon the leading native lords to appear before him. To quote Zumárraga again:

. . . as they [the lords] would arrive, the said Pilar would make long discourses to them secretly in the house of the President; and therefore I believe, and do so affirm to Your Majesty, that the purpose was not so that they should come to holy Baptism. And it is believed and has been seen that the lords did not come empty-handed, . . . and there was not wanting one of them who did not come with his offering, and with these presents the will to covetousness was opened even further.[33]

In this plan the Cazonci, the richest native ruler still alive, was caught with special force. A *principal* and *naguatlato* [interpreter] from Michoacán who had taken the Christian name Gonzalo Xuárez was residing in Mexico City to notify the Cazonci about whatever the new Spanish rulers might command. On the very afternoon of the day on which Guzmán arrived, Pilar summoned Xuárez and took him before Guzmán. The latter commanded him to go to Michoacán and summon the Cazonci and other lords and *principales* to Mexico City. There is some confusion about what happened next, but it seems that the

Cazonci did not come at this first summons. Instead he sent another interpreter to Guzmán with gifts.[34] The amount of treasure that he sent is uncertain. Don Pedro later testified that it was sixty little silver plates and that Pilar took all of them for himself.[35] Pilar, on the other hand, stated that it was about 100 marks of silver in plates and shields and 600 pesos of gold in cups and adornments and that the Tarascans had given the treasure to Guzmán in his presence.[36] Such contradictions are typical of the documentation of this period; even one and the same witness, questioned on different occasions, gives different answers.

At the time of the arrival of Guzmán and his companions, the representative of royal authority in Michoacán was still Gonzalo Xuárez, the justice whom Estrada had appointed to assume the judicial office there after the return of Bachiller Ortega to Mexico City.[37] But fairly soon Xuárez was replaced by someone more to Guzmán's liking, Antonio de Godoy. Bishop-elect Zumárraga described Godoy, without naming him, as follows:

. . . to Michoacán they sent with the office of justice a muleteer who up to this time has lived by that work, with his beasts, because he took to Guzmán in Pánuco the news of his presidency. And with this muleteer it is said that they have sent to Michoacán much merchandise from the President and Oidores in order that he might sell it to the miners who go about there gathering gold. They sent such things as trousers, jackets, wine, vinegar, and oil and other things. And to carry them he took along a great number of Indian porters, a very detestable and forbidden thing.[38]

another significant service for Guzmán besides informing him of his appointment as president. He had gone to Michoacán at Guzmán's command to bring in the Cazonci and the *principales*. Godoy described his assignment in the following words:

. . . it could be about two years ago, more or less, right after Nuño de Guzmán came to this city to exercise the office of president, that the said Nuño de Guzmán sent this witness with an order for the former lieutenant governor of Michoacán, commanding him to give this witness Don Francisco Cazonci and Don Pedro, lords of Michoacán, and all the other lords of the said province and that this witness should bring them to this city; and the said *alcalde mayor* summoned the said lords and told them that they should come with this witness.[39]

The *Relación* takes up the story more fully from there.[40] When Godoy arrived, he apprehended the Cazonci; Don Pedro; a *principal* named Tareca, supposedly very important, from an encomienda town belonging to Antonio de Oliver; and many other *principales*. He gathered them together in Cuitzeo. This town was the encomienda of Gonzalo López, who would continue to be involved with Godoy and Guzmán in their activities in Michoacán.[41]

Godoy told the Tarascan lords not to be sad, that they were being summoned by the president, Nuño de Guzmán.

The Cazonci answered, "Let us go. Why should we be sad? Perhaps he wants to say something to us."

Godoy encouraged them, saying: "You will not stay there for a long time. He will be happy about your visit."

When they arrived in Mexico City, Guzmán was very pleased and said to them: "Welcome. I had you summoned. We will talk tomorrow. Go and enjoy yourselves, and come back here in the morning."

Godoy asserted that when he brought the Tarascan lords to Guzmán's house they gave the president some silver plates. Godoy did not know how many of them there were, because he left while the Indians were presenting them to Guzmán. But he said that later García del Pilar told him that there were "twenty silver plates and some gold ingots, and that the said president had not wanted to accept it because it was a small thing."[42]

Guzmán's expression of displeasure is recorded descriptively in the *Relación*. On the morning after the arrival of the Tarascan lords Guzmán summoned them into his presence and said: "How is it that you have come here empty-handed? What do you bring me? Did you not know that I had come?"

They replied, "Lord, we did not bring you anything because we left in a hurry."

There follow some passages in the *Relación* that seem to belong to a later period, when Guzmán was preparing to go to war in the west.[43] But the narrative soon returns to the question of precious gifts.

Guzmán said, "Send for the gold that you have there in Michoacán."

The Cazonci gave the reply that Cortés had suggested through Tapia: "Lord, I do not have any gold. Tapia took it all."

Guzmán was upset at this: "Why did you give it to him?"

The Cazonci gave a very direct answer: "Because they asked us for it, just as you are doing now."

Guzmán again expressed his frustration at finding that the treasure was already gone. "Why did you believe Tapia?"

In the face of this fury the Cazonci gave a conciliatory answer: "Don Pedro will also go, and he will see to it that a search is made to find whether there is any left."

Then Guzmán told the Cazonci the terms of his imprisonment: "You must remain here for the time being, and a Christian will be with you to guard you. Don't be upset. What, aren't you in your own house here when you are in mine?"

The Cazonci did not like Guzmán's proposal. "It would be better if I went to stay in some other place."

But Guzmán insisted, making the imprisonment more evident: "I do not want you to go. You will be well off here in my house. If you wish to go somewhere, take a walk along that terrace."

The Cazonci submitted, saying, "Good. What you say is enough."[44]

Antonio de Godoy confirmed that he had seen the Tarascans locked up in the room in which Guzmán put them and which he did not let them leave, and they were still there when he returned to Michoacán about a month later, except that he took Don Pedro back to Michoacán with him.[45]

The Cazonci's case was so singular as to warrant Zumárraga's giving him special attention in his letter to the king. The bishop-elect wrote that Guzmán kept the Cazonci in his house, next to the room where he was accustomed to retire, for more than two months, as in a simulated prison, without allowing him to leave. There, speaking through Pilar as his interpreter, he would hold long discourses with the Cazonci every day, trying to convince him that his vassals should ransom him. He asked for eight hundred ingots of gold at half a mark each and a thousand ingots of silver at a mark each, and he showed them a wax model of the size of the ingot he wanted. Zumárraga added that the Cazonci was well ransomed.[46]

In 1554, Don Francisco Quiróngari, governor of Tiripetío, remarked that he had seen the large quantity of gold bars and the ingots that were made in Michoacán to be taken to Guzmán.[47] He is the only Indian witness, however, who mentions that precious metals were prepared in this form for delivery in Mexico. The *naguatlato* Gonzalo Xuárez, who was most active in conducting treasure to Mexico at this time, made three statements about what was brought. Each statement lists the same kinds of articles but gives different quantities. Two things are worthy of note regarding Gonzalo Xuárez's lists of treasure. First, all the articles of silver are given in numbers divisible by twenty, as would be expected of one making an estimate in the Mesoamerican vigesimal system of counting. Second, in spite of the fact that the lists appear to be estimates and are given in a different way each time, the total number of articles in each statement is the same — 244. The various statements by Xuárez are compared in table 1.

TABLE 1

Statements of the *Naguatlato* Gonzalo Xuárez Regarding
Precious Articles Given to Nuño de Guzmán

	Date of Statement		
Item	February 14, 1531*	June 11, 1531†	June 23, 1531‡
Silver plates	40 + 40§	120	40
Silver shields	20	40	60
Silver diadems (also called *penachos*)	40 + 40	40	60
Silver bracelets	40 + 20	40	80
Gold shields	2	2	2
Gold plates	2	2	2

*"Ceinas toma información, 1531," AGI, Justicia, leg. 226.

†"Información de don Pedro Arellano sobre qué oro y plata recibió Nuño de Guzmán de los indios de Michoacán, 1531," AGI, Justicia, leg. 226.

‡"Juicio seguido por Hernán Cortés contra los Lics. Matienzo y Delgadillo, año 1531," *BAGN* 9 (1938):361.

§The numbers in the second column are items brought by another *principal*.

Xuárez supports Zumárraga's statement that the treasure was given as a ransom, saying that it was brought so that the Cazonci might be freed from prison.[48] But his description of the nature of the Cazonci's imprisonment disagrees with that of Zumárraga and Godoy. According to Xuárez, the imprisonment was fairly lenient, since the Cazonci was allowed to move about in the city during the day but had to return to Guzmán's house at night to sleep.[49] After the ransom was paid, the Cazonci was allowed to return to Michoacán.

It seems probable that this imprisonment occurred in the early spring of 1529 and that the Cazonci returned to Michoacán before the middle of May. When Godoy returned to Michoacán with Don Pedro a month

after the Cazonci had been imprisoned, he went as *alcalde mayor* of
the region, replacing Estrada's appointee, Gonzalo Xuárez. On May
14, 1529, the audiencia sent him a command ordering him to take
the encomienda of Tzintzuntzan from Cortés for the crown and instructing him to inform the Cazonci of this change.[50] If the Cazonci
had still been in Mexico, there would have been no object in telling
Godoy to notify him.

At the time Zumárraga wrote his report to the king, which he dated
August 27, 1529, he referred to the Cazonci's imprisonment as something in the past that had lasted for more than two months. Yet at
that very time a new storm was gathering over the Cazonci, a storm
that within six months would destroy him entirely.

Zumárraga wrote that for three or four days previously well-informed
sources had reported that the president and the *oidores* had been noti-
fied of the approach of ships. Suspecting that they were bringing
back Cortés with authority over the land, they had determined not to
receive him but to seize him. To carry this out more easily, they had
warned all of Cortés' relatives, friends, and well-wishers to prepare
to go on an expedition with Nuño de Guzmán to a region to the
northwest called the Teules Chichimecas. Zumárraga asserted that he
had also heard that Guzmán was planning to make war in provinces
that were already conquered and to rob their caciques of whatever
gold and silver they had; this plan especially included the Cazonci
in Michoacán.[51]

Probably the matter that had come to Zumárraga's attention only
a few days previously was not the decision to organize the expedition
but the determination to force Cortés' allies to accompany them. Already on May 15, 1529, Guzmán and the audiencia had made a formal
decision to organize the expedition to the province of Teules Chichimecas.[52] The records of the cabildo for July 26, 1529, also noted that
some members of that body were planning to go to the war with
Guzmán.[53] Thus Guzmán's preparations for an expedition were well
known in the city for a considerable time before the date of Zumárraga's letter.

It was apparently in connection with these plans that Guzmán commanded that the Cazonci be brought to Mexico City again. Although
the *Relación* mentions only one summons of the Cazonci to Mexico
City, that of Godoy, here as in other instances the *Relación* seems to
have telescoped events. We know from several sources that the Ca-

zonci was imprisoned in Mexico City twice during Guzmán's presidency. First, there is the testimony of the two Tarascan interpreters, Gonzalo Xuárez and Alonso de Ávalos. Xuárez went to Mexico with the Cazonci when Godoy took him, but later, when Gonzalo López took the Cazonci to Mexico, Xuárez stayed behind to look after the provisioning of Guzmán's slaves in the mines.[54] The interpreter Alonso de Ávalos, on the other hand, arrived in Tzintzuntzan from Cortés' mines in Motín a few days after Godoy had taken the Tarascan leaders to Mexico, but he went to Mexico with them later, when they were taken there by Gonzalo López and seven other Spaniards.[55] This second imprisonment must have occurred in late August or early September, 1529, very soon after Zumárraga wrote his letter to the king. Martín Gómez, who accompanied the Cazonci to Mexico the second time, said that the Cazonci was put into irons about ten days after his arrival and was kept under guard in Guzmán's house for about four months before Guzmán went to Michoacán.[56] As we shall see, Guzmán left Mexico City to begin his famous expedition to Jalisco shortly before Christmas of 1529.

Even stronger evidence regarding the time when the second imprisonment occurred is contained in a letter from Guzmán to Godoy dated August 20, 1529. It is obvious from the context of the letter that Guzmán had previously sent a command, either to Godoy or to Gonzalo López, ordering the arrest of the Cazonci and Don Pedro. Godoy had then written to Guzmán on August 15, telling of difficulties between the Cazonci and his brother (Don Pedro) and of the problems that might arise from sending them to Mexico under evident arrest. In Guzmán's letter of August 20 he told Godoy to confer with Gonzalo López and, if López agreed with Godoy, then Don Pedro was to remain in Michoacán, and the Cazonci was to come to Mexico. Apparently someone had told the Cazonci about the king's decree that commanded the audiencia not to take Cortés' encomiendas away from him, a decree that the audiencia had chosen to disregard. Guzmán determined to use this as a pretext for commanding the Cazonci to come to Mexico City. He advised Godoy to tell the Cazonci that Guzmán had not ordered his arrest but had only asked him to come there to inform him about who had told him that he did not have to serve the king but should rather serve Cortés. Guzmán also instructed Godoy to lead the Cazonci to believe that Guzmán would be setting out on his expedition soon. If, with these various forms of persuasion, the Cazonci would come freely, he was to be allowed to do so; otherwise, he was to be brought in under arrest.[57]

On the back of Guzman's letter is an undated note from Godoy to Gonzalo López in which Godoy asks López to order Don Pedro to come back, even against his will, "because here, sir, everything is lost, and they will not even give us a drink of water. . . . What good is it if both lords go there? Command that Don Pedro come back and that the Cazonci go."[58]

Thus, in late August 1529, the Cazonci once more followed the familiar path to imprisonment in Mexico City. For him it was at least the fifth such journey in as many years, but, unfortunately, it would be his last.

What were Guzmán's motives in bringing the Cazonci to Mexico once more? Did he simply want to extract more precious metals from this continuously rich mine? Did he want to punish him for siding with Cortés in the political and economic struggle? Was there a power struggle between the Cazonci and Don Pedro in which Don Pedro was winning out because he was more pliant to the wishes of the Spaniards? Did Guzmán suspect that this strongest surviving native king might organize resistance against his proposed expedition? Or was he giving ear to the constant carping of the Michoacán encomenderos about the Cazonci's incursions into the area of their assumed rights? Probably something of all of this was involved in his decision, but it seems that his intentions centered on the hope that he could extract more wealth from the Cazonci to help finance his proposed expedition, for which in the end he would have to borrow funds from the royal treasury.[59] Much of the information given by Don Pedro in the *Relación* concerning the Cazonci's imprisonment must surely be placed in this period, even though Gonzalo López is nowhere mentioned in it.

When they arrived in Mexico City, Guzmán told the Tarascan nobles: "I have some important business. Have you not heard of the place called Tehuculuacan [perhaps he was speaking of the Teules Chichimecas], and of another town called Cihuatlan, where there are only women?"

They told him that they had not heard of those places, but he insisted: "Didn't the old men, your ancestors, speak to you about it?"

"They didn't say anything to us about it," they answered.

Guzmán then told them about his plans: "Well, we are going to go to those lands. Make many arrows and shields and twenty bows with their copper tips and many fiber sandals and other footwear. Entrust it to one of you so that he may go and look after it."

The Cazonci indicated Don Pedro: "This one will go, my brother, Don Pedro."

Then Guzmán informed the Cazonci of his immediate fate: "You will remain here and wait for me, and we will go together, for I must go to the war."[60]

All sources indicate that the conditions of the Cazonci's imprisonment on this occasion were rather severe, at least at first. He was kept in a room in Guzmán's dwelling and was committed to the care of two Spaniards named Placencia and Lobón. Ávalos, the *naguatlato*, was the only Indian allowed to stay with him. If the Cazonci wanted to talk to the Tarascan *principales*, he had to bribe a guard, who would then let him speak to them at the door. Ávalos testified that when Guzmán imprisoned the Cazonci he put his feet in irons.[61]

Guzmán subjected him to threats and ridicule to get more treasure from him. The *Relación* records the following exchange between them on the second occasion on which the *principales* brought treasure:

Guzmán asked, "Why do you bring so little? Don't you have any shame? What is it? Am I not the lord?"

The Cazonci expressed a certain degree of desperation: "Where are we going to get it? Is there anything else out there? Haven't they already brought it all?"

Guzmán became angry and began making threats: "There is a lot. Are you an unimportant lord? If you do not bring it to me, I will treat you as you deserve, for you are a villain and you skin Christians. Well, knowing this, how have I treated you? Why do you want the gold? Bring it all, because the Christians are all angry with you, and they say that you steal the tributes from their towns and that you rob their towns, and they say that I should kill you for the trouble that you give them. But I do not believe them. Why don't you believe me when I tell you this? Do you want to die?" In this threat were contained nearly all the accusations that would later be brought against the Cazonci in his trial.

The Cazonci, speaking perhaps with the anguish of his loss of authority and prestige, or perhaps with the pride of a warrior who does not show fear in the face of death, replied, "It pleases me to die."

This infuriated Guzmán even further, and he said, "That is good." Then he commanded his servants, "Throw him inside there, this one who wants to die, and don't let him go out." Then, addressing the Cazonci, he warned him to take the threat seriously: "Perhaps you laugh about it when I tell you why I have not mistreated you."

Then they put the Cazonci back in his prison room, and he began to weep and to try to find more treasure to offer to Guzmán. The *Relación* leaves one with the impression of a frantic search through all corners of Michoacán, seeking out caches of precious objects that still remained.[62]

The estimates of the amounts of treasure that were brought to Guzmán at this time vary greatly. Certainly large amounts of precious metals were brought to him. Alonso de Ávalos, the *naguatlato*, subsequently gave three estimates of the amounts that were given and, since he was the Cazonci's interpreter at the time, a comparison of them may be worthwhile (see table 2). The *Relación* mentions far greater amounts, but since the statements of Ávalos are more detailed and were made under oath within two years of the occurrence, they may be considered more trustworthy.[63]

TABLE 2
Statements of the *Naguatlato* Alonso de Ávalos Regarding
Precious Articles Given to Nuño de Guzmán

	Date of Statement		
Item	February 14, 1531*	June 11, 1531†	June 23, 1531‡
Silver plates	300	300	300
Silver shields	180	120	170
Silver crests	—	100	100
Silver bracelets	120	100	100
Gold shields	3	2	2
Gold bracelets	5	5	5
Total	608	627	677

*"Ceinos toma información, 1531," AGI, Justicia, leg. 226. In this source the *naguatlato* is called Alonso de Ávila, but since he tells of having been tortured by Guzmán, having his feet burned during the trial of the Cazonci, he must be the *naguatlato* Alonso de Ávalos, who was subjected to that torture during the trial. Scholes and Adams, eds., *Proceso contra Tzintzicha Tangaxoan*, p. 63.

†"Información de Arellano, 1531," AGI, Justician, leg. 226.

‡"Cortés contra Matienzo y Delgadillo," p. 364.

A salient fact that presents itself in the documentation of this period

is that García del Pilar was feathering his own nest out of every shipment of treasure that was brought in for Guzmán. The custom of
the go-between taking a generous *mordida* (money obtained by graft)
for himself goes back to the very beginnings of the colony in Mexico.
Zumárraga had suspected this at the time of the Cazonci's first imprisonment. He reported that after the arrival of the audiencia Pilar
paid off a large debt and became rich and well outfitted. His credit
with the Indians was so great that they brought tribute to him as well
as to the president and the *oidores*.[64] In the case of the Cazonci, Guzmán used Pilar as a Spanish-Nahuatl translator to remonstrate with
the Cazonci to send more treasure. The *naguatlatos* who accompanied
the Cazonci served as Tarascan-Nahuatl interpreters. Pilar did not
understand Tarascan.[65]

The Indians' testimony indicates that Pilar was taking part of nearly
every shipment of gold and silver that they brought in from Michoacán.[66] He did so under the pretext that he would use his influence
with Guzmán on the Tarascans' behalf. On one occasion when he
took a great amount for himself, the *principales* complained: "Sir, what
will we do, since you are taking all this? Would you not speak for us,
so that we could go with our lord the Cazonci to a house away from
here in the city where we must go? Tell this to Nuño de Guzmán."

But Pilar assured them: "Let's go. Don't be afraid. I will speak to
him about it."[67]

Licentiate Matienzo, one of the two surviving judges of the audiencia, was also receiving a share of the loot from Michoacán. Juan Ochoa
de Lejalde remembered seeing Pilar enter the dwelling of the licentiate
with a *principal* from Michoacán "and under his blanket he was carrying about five or six marks of silver." Another witness, Sancho de
Frías, said that in Matienzo's house he had seen some little silver
plates that seemed to be the workmanship of Michoacán and that the
household pages had told him that the Indians from Michoacán had
brought them. He also estimated that they weighed five or six marks
but added that it was "very bad silver which is worth only about
two or three pesos a mark."[68]

The *naguatlato* Ávalos testified that after the Cazonci gave the third
shipment of treasure to Guzmán the president released him from
imprisonment and allowed him to move freely about the city but did
not permit him to return to his own land. He commanded him to remain in Mexico until the time came to accompany Guzmán to the war,

since it would be necessary for the army to go through Michoacán. The Cazonci, therefore, stayed in Mexico during the intervening time and went back to Michoacán only when Guzmán was ready to leave.[69]

In the meantime, in Michoacán, Antonio de Godoy was exercising power as the principal local Spanish authority. This man who was supposed to represent Spanish law in the province testified on one occasion that he did not know how to write,[70] although at other times he made an effort to sign his name.[71] His principal activities in Michoacán involved provisioning the president's slaves from towns that had previously been Cortés' encomiendas and gathering supplies for Guzmán's expedition. I will discuss these activities in the course of the following chapters.

For his own profit Godoy engaged in the enterprise of sacking Indian tombs. In 1531, when Cortés sued the judges of the audiencia for depriving him of the income of his towns, he included a question on this grave robbing and elicited some interesting replies. Three Indian witnesses, Alonso de Ávalos, Gonzalo Gómez, and Sebastián, mentioned the names and places where Godoy broke open tombs: Tzintzuntzan, Pátzcuaro, Apasanaro, and Ibaceo, or Ibazaro (probably Ihuatzio).[72] Gregorio Gómez testified that Godoy had told him that from one tomb he had taken more than 600 pesos of gold, which he had sent to Nuño de Guzmán.[73] Another witness, Antonio de Oliver, in his usual chatty style, gives us an enlightening view of Godoy's grave robbing.

In regard to the matter of the tombs, he [Oliver] says that one day during the month of October of the year 1529 this witness came to this city of Uchichila and found here Antonio de Godoy and Hernán Pérez de Bocanegra, citizens of the city of Mexico, and Juan de Sámano, citizen of the city of Mexico who has gone to the war with Nuño de Guzmán. And the said Hernán Pérez de Bocanegra and Juan de Sámano said to this witness, very secretly by themselves, "Oliver, do you have any *cúes* in your town?" And this witness said, "Yes." Then the said Hernán Pérez de Bocanegra and Juan de Sámano said, "Then examine them and see if there are tombs, because we are letting you know that this Godoy who is here has taken from tombs much gold and silver, amounting to more than ten thousand *castellanos*." And that is what happened. And later this witness knew that the said Antonio de Godoy had sacked many tombs, from which he had taken great amounts of gold and silver, he and Bernaldino de Albornoz, to whom, because he had helped him sack certain tombs, he gave a thousand pesos of gold.[74]

It is impossible to verify from other sources that the amount of precious metals that Godoy took from the tombs was anywhere near as great as Oliver indicated. Francisco de Villegas testified that Diego Hernández, a cooper, brought to Mexico City the articles that Godoy had found. There they were smelted down by order of Guzmán and came to only about 140 pesos.[75] The official records indicate an even smaller amount. The registers of the smelting house show that on November 16, 1529, Diego Hernández brought in 122 pesos of 20-carat gold for Antonio de Godoy.[76]

With this desecration of the ancestral tombs the stage was set for the destruction of the last Tarascan king. But because conflicts over the encomiendas played such an important part in the downfall of the Cazonci, we will consider these conflicts before proceeding to the final days of the Tarascan monarch.

•••

CHAPTER 9

Politics and the Encomienda

THE development of the encomienda system is one of the most complex aspects of the first decade of Spanish domination of Michoacán because of the large number of individuals involved, the basic and unresolved conflicts between Spanish and Tarascan political and economic systems, and the varied and contradictory political interests that influenced the distribution and functioning of the encomiendas. Among such political interests we must count those of the Tarascan imperial leaders, the native leaders at the town level, the first conqueror-encomenderos, later Spanish colonists, the Spanish political leadership in Mexico City, and the Spanish monarchy.

In this chapter we will look at the political influences exerted on the encomienda, especially the impact of the political turmoil in Mexico City and political decisions in Spain about the tenure of the encomiendas in Michoacán. Chapter 10 discusses the economics of the encomiendas under the aspects of their administration, the amount and use of tribute, the relationship to mining, some instances of abuse of the system, and the increasing resentment of the encomenderos against the Cazonci. Alphabetical listings of the individual encomenderos and of the encomiendas are found in appendix B, together with short histories of the tenancy of individual towns when that information is available. With the list of towns the reader will also find the tribute assessments in those instances where they are given in the record of Bachiller Ortega's visitation.

It is not my intention here to explore deeply the legal history of the encomienda. That has been undertaken in works by Silvio Zavala and Lesley Byrd Simpson.[1] Here I try to follow the factual development of the encomienda in Michoacán during the period preceding the death of the Cazonci, insofar as factual information is available.

157

Political considerations played a part in the first grants of encomiendas in Michoacán, and political changes in Mexico City constantly produced changes in the tenure of the encomiendas. We have seen that during the summer of 1524 Cortés distributed the encomiendas of Michoacán, keeping the best towns for himself but also giving out some of the good ones to the treasury officials and their relatives as a form of political appeasement. Such political influence on decisions regarding encomiendas continued to be the norm during the rest of the decade. Each new political authority would try to consolidate his position by assigning encomiendas to his supporters, at the expense of opposing political interests in the colony. This activity was made all the easier because none of the governors seems to have kept an official register of grants of encomienda as a general administrative practice. Thus it continued to be true that the only proofs that a person had of his right to an encomienda were his cedula of the grant and the testimony of his friends.

When Salazar and Chirinos declared Cortés and his followers dead in late 1525, one of the first things they did was redistribute the encomiendas. They sent Francisco de Orduña to Michoacán, giving him "commission, power, and faculty" to distribute the Indians among the citizens and residents and to administer justice in the provinces of Colima, Zacatula, and Michoacán. By virtue of this authorization he distributed many towns in those provinces to the citizens and conquerors who were living there. For example, he gave one-third of the province of Ávalos to Jorge Carrillo and another third to Pedro de Bazán.[2] The treasury officials took Cortés' towns from him for their own benefit.[3]

As soon as Cortés returned from Honduras, he issued a decree declaring null and void all grants that his lieutenants had made during his absence.[4] It is obvious from this decree that Cortés planned to make a complete review of the encomiendas, and he did begin to redistribute the towns. The cedulas of Alonso de Mata for Tuzantla-Ocumo and of Antón Sánchez for half of Turicato date from July 2, 1526.[5] But because Ponce de León arrived almost immediately, on July 4, and took away Cortés' authority, the Conqueror was not able to complete the reassignment and actually left greater confusion than had existed previously, as is evident in the cases of Turicato and Tuzantla-Ocumo (see below and appendix B).

Ponce de León arrived with instructions to make a full investigation of the question of the encomiendas, including the possibility of terminating them entirely and making them all tributaries directly to the crown. Having made his investigation, he was to send a report to the crown. The king, however, added a significant prohibition: "And until I, having seen your report, shall send a command regarding what is to be done in this matter, you shall not make any innovation in it from the way that it is at the present."[6]

This order apparently prohibited Ponce de León from making new assignments of encomiendas. He lived such a short time after assuming office that he had little chance to do anything about the encomiendas. But since both Marcos de Aguilar and Alonso de Estrada held power only insofar as it had been given to Ponce de León, there was a question whether they had authority to tamper with the encomiendas. But this did not deter them from acting as if there were no limitation on their authority. Aguilar, for instance, added to the confusion in Turicato by making Antón Sánchez sole encomendero of the town and in Pungarabato by giving confusing cedulas to Pedro de Bazán and Alonso Gutiérrez de Badajoz.[7]

Estrada seemed to have no doubts about his complete authority regarding encomiendas. The evidence of his intervention in the tenure of encomiendas appears frequently in the histories of the individual towns. Especially is this evident in the case of Juan Infante, reviewed below. In the course of Infante's dispute regarding the towns that he claimed, Alonso Lucas made a statement that is enlightening not only regarding Infante's grant but also regarding the general degree to which Estrada intervened in the tenure of the encomiendas:

[Alonso Lucas] said that, at the time when the Treasurer Alonso de Estrada was governor of this New Spain and the said Alonso Lucas was notary of the said government, the said Treasurer Alonso de Estrada gave and entrusted Indians to many persons and took away and removed Indians from some persons who had them in the said trust, as often as he wished and considered it good, and for this reason, because he gave out and took away Indians every day, no register was kept of the grants and trusts that he made, nor did this witness keep it, nor did he nor does he have a register of any cedula that the said treasurer issued, neither does he have it of the one that he gave to the said Juan Infante. This he said and swore, and he swore, by God and Holy Mary and the sign of the cross that he made with his hands, that it is the truth, and he signed it with his name. Alonso Lucas.[8]

For his personal benefit Estrada tried to take Pátzcuaro as a separate encomienda, but when he was informed that it served Cortés as part of the subject area of Tzintzuntzan, he did not pursue the effort.[9]

Not only did Estrada show little concern about the royal prohibition to Ponce de León in regard to treating of individual encomiendas, but he sent out Bachiller Ortega to make a full-scale revision of encomienda tributes, the first such general revision of tributes in Michoacán since the original distribution of the encomiendas.

With the appointment of the First Audiencia, royal political decisions began to enter more directly into decisions regarding the status of encomiendas in Michoacán, particularly by way of a direct attack on Cortés' holdings there.

From the beginning Cortés had made himself the most important encomendero in Michoacán by taking for himself Tzintzuntzan, which included the whole tributary area of the Lake Pátzcuaro Basin, as well as Huaniqueo in the north and the silver-producing towns to the west—Tuxpan, Amula, Zapotlán, and Tamazula—and probably also Mazamitla. Afterward he continued to accumulate towns in Michoacán. Immediately upon returning from Honduras, he agreed to take Comanja from Juan de Solís in exchange for supporting that sick and crippled conqueror. At that time he also annulled the grant of Tajimaroa to Diego López Pacheco and took it for himself. He reacquired Huaniqueo from Fernando Alonso, apparently only a short time before the Ortega *visita*. He got Naranja from García del Pilar in exchange for half of Mestitlan shortly before his departure for Spain. It is unclear how he gained control of Tiripetío from Juan de Alvarado, but the Ortega *visita* also lists him as encomendero of that town. There is some evidence that he also took control of Matalcingo (Charo), even though it was in dispute between Juan Fernández Infante and Rodrigo de Albornoz. It is obvious, then, that before he went to Spain in 1528 Cortés had established his control over a very large and very rich area in Michoacán.[10]

In other regions of New Spain he had also taken the richest towns for himself, and the Spanish crown was not happy with the reports that it received of his expansive greed. In the secret instructions that the king issued for the audiencia on April 5, 1528, he commanded the *oidores* to place a number of Cortés' encomiendas directly under the authority of the crown. Among them were "Tamazula, where there are silver mines, with its land; [and] Uihtzilan [Tzintzuntzan] in Michoacán, which is the chief town of the province, with its land."[11]

Cortés must have learned about these instructions soon after his arrival in Spain in May 1528, because on June 29, 1528, a royal cedula was drawn up for him, addressed to the president and *oidores* of the audiencia, which commanded that Cortés' towns should be left to him just as they had been at the time when he departed for Spain.[12] Cortés' attorney, Pedro Gallego, presented this cedula before the audiencia on December 9, 1528, almost as soon as the members had taken office. On December 13, 1528, the *oidores* gave formal obedience to the decree and said that, as far as its fulfillment was concerned, "they were ready and prepared to do everything that might be fitting for the service of His Majesty."[13] In other words, they reserved judgment regarding its fulfillment until they could decide what to do about it.

By May 1529, they had decided to obey their original instructions and disregard the cedula that was intended to protect Cortés' rights. On May 14, 1529, they sent an order to Antonio de Godoy, commanding him to take the city of Uchichila for the crown and to send away those who were there in Cortés' name. Godoy was also to call in the Cazonci and let him know that he was now to give his tribute to the crown and to no one else. On May 26, Godoy informed Hernando Ladrón of the content of the order and took possession of the Tarascan capital in the king's name. Three days later he called in Ladrón and Sebastián Rojo, "stewards and helpers of Don Fernando Cortés," and commanded them, under penalty of five hundred pesos of gold from the mines, not to take tribute from Uchichila or Huaniqueo.[14] On May 26, Godoy sent another command to Alonso de Zamudio in the towns Zapotlán, Tuxpan, Amula, and Tamazula, ordering him not to receive any more tribute from those towns, under penalty of one hundred pesos of gold.[15]

The Indian interpreter Gonzalo Xuárez later testified that as the message came down to the Indians it was expressed in different terms, indicating that they belonged to Nuño de Guzmán:

[The representatives of Guzmán] told them that they did not belong to the Emperor nor to the said Marqués but to Nuño de Guzmán; and they said no, that they belonged to Captain Malinche [Cortés]; and Godoy and Bernaldino de Albornoz told them no, that [Cortés] was under arrest in Castile and that they did not belong to anyone but Nuño de Guzmán.[16]

Godoy sent Guzmán a report that he had taken Cortés' towns from his overseers, but on June 12 Guzmán wrote him a short letter scolding him for having exceeded his authority in taking more than Uchichila and Tamazula.[17] Nevertheless, although Guzmán reined in Godoy to some extent in regard to the number of Cortés' towns that he could place under the direct authority of the king, he and the audiencia allowed a continued erosion of the Conqueror's claims by private individuals. They permitted Infante to take Comanja, Naranja, some of the subject area of Huaniqueo, and a large part of the subject area of Tzintzuntzan. They gave Tajimaroa to Gonzalo de Salazar, and Albornoz tried to establish his rights to Tiripetío, although Juan de Alvarado was able to gain the advantage there.[18]

On September 12, 1528, Cortés had obtained a second decree from the emperor, incorporating the previous one of June 29, 1528, which was supposed to protect his rights to his encomiendas. García de Llerena presented it before the audiencia on September 13, 1529, in one more effort to force the *oidores* to return Cortés' towns to him. Their reply in regard to Tzintzuntzan was that Cortés had first placed it under the direct authority of the king and later had taken it for himself. By way of a general statement regarding the return of Cortés' encomiendas, they said that they would do "what they see is most fitting for the service of His Majesty and the colonization of the land."[19]

The empress reissued the cedula in Cortés' favor in a covering cedula of October 8, 1529, addressed to Guzmán, Bishop-elect Zumárraga, and Licentiate Matienzo of the audiencia. Cortés' lawyers presented this new decree before Matienzo and Zumárraga in May 1530. Finally, on July 23, 1530, Matienzo decided that Comanja and Naranja should be returned to Cortés but he withheld a decision on Tiripetío because Albornoz had presented a cedula for it, signed by Cortés himself, and a lawsuit in regard to it was in process.[20] Cortés also brought suits against Guzmán, Matienzo, and Delgadillo for income of which they had deprived him during the time when they had taken his encomiendas from him in obvious contradiction to royal decrees.[21] Yet none of the towns in Michoacán except Matalcingo (Charo) was included in the grant of the Marquesado del Valle de Oaxaca when it was given to Cortés in 1529.[22] The result was that Cortés's influence, which had been of primary importance in Michoacán in the 1520s, nearly disappeared during the 1530s.

Besides fulfilling with excessive zeal their instructions regarding Cortés' encomienda towns, Guzmán and his companions also shuffled the tenure of the other encomiendas to their own advantage and that of their friends, relatives, and supporters. The most famous instance was that of Capula. Dr. Cristóbal de Ojeda, who claimed one-half of the encomienda, obtained permission to trade it for Talcozatitlán. Guzmán and the audiencia then gave Ojeda's half of Capula to Luis de Berrio, a cousin of Licenciado Delgadillo, in exchange for one-half of Teupatlan. Berrio received the tribute for a while, but then Delgadillo began taking the tribute for himself. Guzmán appointed Berrio *alcalde mayor* of the Zapotecs. While Berrio was with the Zapotecs, Delgadillo sent him a cedula for half of Chinantla in exchange for his half of Capula and also asked him to sign a letter releasing Delgadillo from all obligations for tribute that he had already taken from Capula.[23]

In another instance the audiencia gave Sinagua to Antonio de Godoy, Guzmán's representative in Michoacán, upon the death of the previous encomendero of the town, Juan de la Plaza. This was an obvious reward for Godoy's services, but when the Second Audiencia replaced the First, the new judges revoked the grant.[24]

Two cases that show the particular complexity of the lengthy legal struggles that could result from the political manipulations of the encomiendas in the 1520s are those of Pungarabato and Turicato. In the case of Pungarabato, in the tropical hot country of the Río Balsas basin Pedro de Bazán conducted a series of four lawsuits regarding it which were taken on appeal to the Council of the Indies. From a comparative reading of them the following sequence of encomienda grants presents itself, though not without some remaining confusion. In 1524, Cortés originally gave the town to Juan Velázquez de Salazar, brother of Factor Gonzalo de Salazar. Only a short time afterward Velázquez de Salazar returned to Spain, accompanying Cortés' famous silver cannon. Cortés then gave the town to Fernando Alonso de Villanueva. But before Cortés returned from Honduras, Estrada gave it to Ángel de Villafaña, and Alonso was given a better town. Marcos de Aguilar, however, gave the encomienda to Pedro de Bazán on September 17, 1526. Although the terms of Bazán's grant appear to have given him sole control of the town, Aguilar also gave half of the encomienda to Alonso Gutiérrez de Badajoz. A further element of confusion enters the picture from the fact that in the Ortega assessment Fernando Alonso was still listed as holder of one-half of the encomienda of Pungarabato.

The confusion is not relieved by the fact that on April 12, 1529, Guzmán and the audiencia gave Antonio de Anguiano half of Pungarabato on the basis of a trade with Fernando Alonso de Villanueva for Tianguesteco. But in a judicial inquiry made at Anguiano's request, he indicated that he had made the trade for Pungarabato with Alonso Gutiérrez de Badajoz.

Pedro de Bazán was deprived of his half of the encomienda by Guzmán and the audiencia because he at first refused to accompany Guzmán on his expedition to New Galicia. On October 15, 1529, they gave his half of the encomienda to Luis Sánchez. Bazán spent the rest of his life in an effort, eventually successful, to reestablish his complete rights to the town and to exclude all other claimants. In 1532 he sued the *oidores* Matienzo and Delgadillo for the return of his half of the encomienda, along with the income that it had produced while he had been deprived of it.[25] In 1537 he and Anguiano fought off an attempt by Juan Veláquez de Salazar to reclaim the town.[26] In 1541, Bazán brought suit against Anguiano to exclude him from the encomienda.[27] Even after Bazán's death his son Hernando had to defend his right to the town against a claim by Luis Sánchez.[28] The success of these various efforts of the Bazans is indicated in both the *Relación de los obispados* and in the *Suma de visitas,* where Hernando de Bazán, Pedro's heir, is named as the sole encomendero.[29]

The history of Turicato as an encomienda is about as complicated as that of Pungarabato and is summarized here from an even longer series of lawsuits. Cortés gave the town to Diego Hernández Nieto and Hernán Rodríguez in 1524 after the Caravajal *visita.* Hernández Nieto, a personal servant of Cortés, accompanied him to Honduras. Upon returning from that expedition, Hernández Nieto and Rodríguez renounced their rights to the town to Cortés, who promised to give them better encomiendas. Cortés did not have an opportunity to fulfill his promise before he had to give up his authority to Luis Ponce de León, but he did dispose of Turicato. On July 2, 1526, he gave half of the encomienda to Antón Sánchez and, apparently, the other half to Francisco Martínez, the pastor of Zacatula. On September 17, 1526, Marcos de Aguilar gave Sánchez the entire encomienda.

Hernández Nieto and Rodríguez contested the grant to Sánchez, and on March 22, 1527, Estrada and Sandoval restored Hernández Nieto's half to him. Presumably they also restored Rodríguez's half, since Antón Sánchez promptly brought suit against the two of them. A decision by Estrada and Sandoval on July 30, 1527, awarded the encomienda entirely to Sánchez. Less than two months later, on September 25, 1527, Estrada allowed Sánchez to transfer the encomienda to Antonio de Oliver, one of Estrada's servants.

In 1528, Hernández Nieto went to Spain with Cortés, where he obtained a royal cedula on August 29, 1528, commanding that his encomienda should not be taken away from him. In 1531, Hernández Nieto and Rodríguez made a demand against Oliver before the audiencia, but apparently they did not follow it up. In 1540, Hernández Nieto finally brought serious action against Oliver for his half of the town, and he won a favorable decision from the audiencia of Mexico, confirmed definitively by the Council of the Indies on March 15, 1548. Apparently Rodríguez was dead by this time, because Hernández demanded that the fiscal (the crown's attorney) take action to gain control of the other half of the encomienda for the crown. His insistence on excluding Oliver from the encomienda may have been due to slurs regarding Hernández Nieto's origins that Oliver made against him during the course of the legal struggle. Oliver had accused him of being the son of a black slave woman, trying in this way to exclude him from active participation before the court. Hernández Nieto asserted that he was the son of Gonzalo Hernández Nieto and his *free* black servant woman. Although the fiscal won a decision against Oliver, the latter managed to retain his half of the encomienda for the rest of his life through various appeals. At his death about 1572 his half was allowed to pass to his aged wife, who had no heirs.[30]

Juan Infante and the Grand Encomienda

A discussion of the establishment of the encomiendas at this period would not be complete without some attention to the arrival of Juan Infante and the beginnings of his grandiose encomienda. His claims led to what was undoubtedly the most serious and far-reaching dispute over an encomienda in Michoacán. It would involve him in conflicts with the Marqués del Valle, Francisco de Villegas, the native lords of Tzintzuntzan, and, most important, Vasco de Quiroga.

Juan Infante was not a conquistador. Rather, he was an early example of those who gained more by wielding the pen than most conquistadores did by wielding their swords. He arrived in New Spain in the service of a notary, Rodrigo de Baeza, in whose house he had lived as a boy in Cuba. They and Antonio de Godoy came to Mexico on the same ship.[31] When Infante arrived in Mexico, he was still a very young

man, "un mozo sin barba" ("a beardless boy"), as Cristóbal de Benavente later described him.[32] He had ambition and ability, however,
and he soon entered the employ of Alonso de Estrada, serving as official of the treasurer in the smelting house.[33] His name appears in the
records of the smelting house as early as August and September, 1526.[34]

His work in the smelting house naturally led him to engage in mining. On February 11, 1527, he and Diego Ramírez registered a debt
of 225 gold pesos to Martín Soldado for the purchase of 50 male and
female slaves. On May 4 of the same year he acknowledged a debt
of 50 gold pesos to Juan de Herrera for the remainder of the payment
for slaves whom he had bought. Undoubtedly these were Indian slaves,
since African slaves brought much higher prices. Also on May 4, 1527,
he entered into a partnership with Comendador (knight commander
of a military order) Frey Ramón Bernal to gather gold in the mines
of Michoacán. Infante agreed to put in "100 Indian slaves, male and
female, with their tools and trays"; Bernal obligated himself to "maintain the slaves with corn, beans, chili, salt, and, twice a week, pork."
The contract was to last until the Feast of Saint John (June 24) of 1528.
Either the agreement with Bernal was inadequate or Infante had other
slaves working in the mines, because on January 4, 1528, he acknowledged a debt of 90 gold pesos to Hernando Ladrón for provisions for
the mines.[35]

Because of the cost of supplies he must have begun looking for a
vacant encomienda in Michoacán that he could persuade Estrada to
assign to him. His opportunity came in mid-1528 with the death of
Juan de Solís, a captain of artillery. Solís had been given the encomienda
of Comanja in the original distribution of the towns of Michoacán.
Comanja, a small town on the road from Tzintzuntzan to Zacapu, did
not give Solís much income. In fact, there is considerable doubt that
it still legally belonged to Solís in 1528. Solís, "sick and paralyzed" and
on crutches, had lived in the house of Juan Bernal, who took care of
him. He gave Bernal the income of Comanja, which Francisco Morcillo, encomendero of Indaparapeo, collected for him. Solís was in
Medellín when Cortés returned from Honduras, and, according to
Juan de Jerez, he approached Cortés and said: "Lord, your lordship
gave me a town in Michoacán called Comanja, but I have not used it
or gotten any income from it. Therefore, I entreat your lordship to take
it and do what you wish with it and provide me with my food here."
Cortés answered, "You wish it thus, thus it shall be, and very gladly."

Cortés then took the town for himself and received its tributes until he left for Spain. Then Gonzalo López took charge of the town, claiming that he had a power of attorney from Solís.[36]

On May 16 and June 12, 1528, when Ortega assessed the tribute of Comanja, Conzalo López, acting for Solís, reached an agreement with Don Pedro Cuinierángari, allowing Don Pedro to have control of the town in exchange for delivering 60 cargas of corn and 20 cargas of beans to the mines every twenty days.[37]

Ortega later testified that he had allowed this arrangement because Don Pedro asserted that the city of Michoacán [Tzintzuntzan] did not have adequate lands for farming and that the people could not give the tribute that they owed to Cortés unless they could use the lands of Comanja. A short time later, while Ortega was still serving as lieutenant for the governor in Michoacán, Solís died, and Estrada assigned his Indians to Juan Infante and Rodrigo Ruiz.[38] Infante sent his cedula of the encomienda with his power of attorney to Diego Rodríguez de Valladolid, in Michoacán.[39] Once more Ortega called in Don Pedro and made an agreement that he should give to the new encomenderos the tribute that he had previously given to Solís.[40]

This first cedula gave to Infante and Ruiz only Comanja, as Solís had held it before his death. Cristóbal de Cáceres, who "at the time had a certain partnership with the said Juan Infante" and saw the cedula, said that it gave Comanja and its subject area to Infante and Ruiz. When Cáceres went to the town and asked what subject towns Comanja had, they named Purecho and Axaxo and some other small settlements.[41]

Antonio de Oliver said that he and Rodríguez de Valladolid had frequently asked one another "why the said Juan Infante had taken such a little thing when he took the half of the said Indians, because they were few and were not willing to serve."[42] Alonso Lucas, notary of the government of Estrada, also asserted that Estrada had intended to give Infante and Ruiz only the Indians that had been left open by reason of the death of Juan de Solís.[43]

It was a surprise to everyone, then, when Infante later appeared with a cedula assigning him twenty-six towns, many of which had always been considered major towns, or subjects of major towns, belonging to other encomenderos.[44] The towns were listed as follows: Comanja, Naranja, Chocatan, Tacaro, Coaneo, Sebinan, Cepiajo, Matuxeo, Araçapo, Charanpuato, Guayameo, Erongarícuaro, Axaxo, Citandaro, Cuymato, Chupicuaro, Capaquareo, Porunjacuaro, Guanamoco, Orunbaquaro, Aquiscuaro, Chincharo, Corunda, Parachone, Aguaqueo, and Noritapani.

Some of these names are not recognizable in terms of modern counterparts. Perhaps the names changed drastically, or the towns themselves may have disappeared. But those that are clearly recognizable give us an idea of the potential conflicts inherent in Infante's claim. Naranja had been a separate encomienda and had belonged to Cortés. Coeneo was a subject town of Huaniqueo. Erongarícuaro, Purenchécuaro, Chupícuaro, and Guayameo (where Santa Fe was later built) were on the shores of Lake Pátzcuaro and had traditionally been considered subject towns of Tzintzuntzan. Francisco de Villegas had collected tributes from Sevina and Capaquareo (Capacuaro) as subject towns of his encomienda of Uruapan. Altogether they incorporated a large area west, northwest, and north of Lake Pátzcuaro.

The date of the cedula, October 20, 1528, places it well after the conclusion of the Ortega visitation. It was issued in the name of Juan Infante alone; Rodrigo Ruiz had died in the meantime.[45]

Few people ever saw the original of this cedula. Cristóbal de Cáceres said that Infante told him, apparently in late 1528, about a new cedula that gave the whole encomienda to him, but Infante did not show it to him.[46] Infante later claimed that he had taken the cedula to Michoacán and asked Gonzalo Xuárez to put him in possession of the towns contained in it, but Xuárez had answered that "he could not dispossess anyone unless he brought an express command for it."[47] Antonio de Oliver, however, indicates that what Infante brought was not a cedula but a list of towns. He said that one day he (Oliver)

went to the said city of Michoacán, and the said Gonzalo Xuárez said to this witness, "Señor Oliver, didn't you see what Juan Infante came with?" And this witness said, "With what, Señor Gonzalo Xuárez?" And he answered, "He came with a list (*memoria*) of towns so that I would entrust and deposit them to him until he should go to Mexico to ask Governor Alonso de Estrada for them." And this witness asked him, "Well, what did you answer him?" And the said Gonzalo Xuárez told this witness that he had answered him that he was not willing to do it because he did not have authority to be able to do it and that he should go and ask the lord governor for them, and so he bade him farewell.[48]

Several months later ("the Royal Audiencia was already in this city

[Mexico] for possibly seven or eight months, because the Audiencia came about November or December, and what this witness has said happened about August or later") Cáceres again met Infante in the public plaza of Mexico City, and Infante said to him, "Look here at a cedula that my lord the treasurer made for me of the towns that I told you about, and my lady Doña Marina [Estrada's wife] has kept it safe for me." Cáceres read it and noted that it contained the names of many towns "and that it had a signature that said Alonso de Estrada," but it was not countersigned by a notary.[49]

Infante must have been disturbed by this close scrutiny of his cedula. On August 25, 1529, he had a copy made by Miguel López de Legaspi and on August 27, 1529, had another copy made by his former employer Rodrigo de Baeza. Both copies indicated that the original had been countersigned by Alonso Lucas.[50] But, as we have seen above, Alonso Lucas later denied that Estrada had given Infante anything more than the Indians whom Solís had held.

No evidence has appeared that anyone ever saw the original cedula after this. In all the lawsuits in which Infante was involved over the encomienda, he always offered the copies as proof of his right to the grandiose claim. He gave various contradictory excuses for the disappearance of the cedula. On November 24, 1535, he stated that Francisco de Villegas and others had stolen it. In 1540, Antonio de Oliver testified that Infante had told him that Cortés and his men had stolen it when they passed through on their way to [Baja] California but that on another occasion Infante had called upon him to testify that Diego Rodríguez de Valladolid had taken it back to Spain with him.[51]

Although Infante had been unable to get recognition of his claim from Gonzalo Xuárez, he had greater success with Antonio de Godoy. On that occasion Infante returned to Michoacán armed with a mandate from Guzmán and the audiencia that he was to be protected in the possession of the towns listed in his cedula and that other Spaniards were not to interfere in them. Godoy issued the corresponding document of protection on October 25, 1529, in the city of Michoacán, on the basis of the copy of the cedula of encomienda made by Baeza.[52] Nevertheless, Alongo de Veas, who resided in Comanja for Infante for six months, stated definitely in 1534 that Infante did not make use of more than Comanja before Guzmán passed through on his way to New Galicia.[53]

The important fact, however, was that before the death of the Cazonci the audiencia and Godoy had given Infante the first fully legal recognition of his exaggerated claim.

Two questions present themselves regarding Infante's cedula. First, how did he obtain it? Second, how did he succeed in having it accepted? One answer to the first question was given by Don Pedro de Arellano, corregidor of the city of Michoacán, in 1531:

I say that the cedula which the said Juan Infante has from Alonso de Estrada, on the basis of which he asks for the said towns, was issued because of false and untrue information at the time when the First Royal Audiencia arrived in this New Spain, leading the said Treasurer to think that the said towns, with others which he had previously taken from this city, were subject to Comanja; and in order to do this, he came to the said towns which he is requesting and took the lords and *principales* who were in them, and he kicked and beat them many times until he got them to say that they were part of the subject area of Comanja; and then he put down the names of the said *principales* on a paper, and with this memorial that he made he went to the Treasurer Alonso de Estrada before the said *oidores* arrived in Mexico City, and he entreated him to give him a cedula for all of those towns, giving him to understand that all of the said towns were subject to Comanja and that they had thus belonged to Solís, through whose death the town of Comanja and its subject area had been given to Juan Infante as his encomienda.[54]

Arellano, however, was not in Michoacán at the time these events took place, and it is possible that his knowledge of the facts was not exact. It is also possible that Infante forged the cedula and then had it copied so that no faults would become evident. Although both Rodrigo de Baeza and Miguel López de Legaspi later asserted under oath that the cedula that Infante had presented to them to copy had appeared to be genuine and that there was nothing written between the lines,[55] nevertheless, the disappearance of the original cedula and Infante's contradictory statements about what happened to it leave a suspicion that there had been something visibly wrong with it.

Infante's success in gaining legal acceptance of his cedula was dependent upon several coincidental factors. First, the subject towns of an encomienda were often not adequately specified in the cedulas of the encomienda. Thus when Infante claimed towns that Francisco de Villegas considered subjects of Uruapan, Villegas could not show written proof of prior possession.[56] Infante also had a politically opportune time for establishing his claim in Michoacán. He moved into a convenient political vacuum there. Cortés had departed for Spain, and his interests in Mexico were suffering from the disfavor of the political authorities in the colony. Thus there was no dominant political figure to oppose Infante when he claimed several towns that had given tribute to Cortés. Further, he did not try to make his possession effective in the towns around Lake Pátzcuaro until after Nuño de Guzmán had passed through, executing the Cazonci and taking with him the other leading lords of the region. It is not surprising, then, that Infante later commented that after the Cazonci's death the towns of Michoacán served their encomenderos better than they had previously.[57]

Infante's aggressiveness naturally made enemies for him and resulted in the first recorded instance of a hired assassin in colonial Michoacán, though the assassination attempt was unsuccessful. Gonzalo Gómez, defending himself against witnesses who had testified against him before the Inquisition in 1537, said that Infante was his mortal enemy

because for the past eight years [i.e., since 1529] neither of them speaks to the other, because since that time, because of some very rude and insulting words which the said Juan Infante spoke against the said Gonzalo Gómez, the said Gonzalo Gómez brought it about that a certain Montemolín stabbed the said Juan Infante, and he did stab him, and the stabs were so serious that the said Juan Infante came to the point of death because of them and was in bed for a long time.

Antonio de Oliver added further verification of the matter:

. . . the said Gonzalo Gómez told this witness that he had sent a colt and a mare to a certain Montemolín so that he would stab the said Juan Infante, and that the said Montemolín gave three or four stabs to the said Juan Infante, and the said Juan Infante, being a friend of this witness, showed them to him, and this witness saw them, and he saw that the said Juan Infante had the said Montemolín apprehended because of the said stabbing.[58]

It is not possible here to go into the lifelong struggle that Infante waged to retain control of the small barony that he had staked out for himself. I have surveyed elsewhere the aspects of the struggle that brought him into conflict with Vasco de Quiroga, and the interested reader is referred to that work. Suffice it to say here that Infante was able to maintain control over all the towns that he claimed until 1554, when the crown took from him the towns on the islands and shores of Lake Pátzcuaro. He passed the other towns on to his son and heir.[59]

•••

CHAPTER 10

The Economics of the Encomienda

THIS chapter draws together a number of themes related to the eco-nomic exploitation of the encomiendas of Michoacán in the 1520s. It includes discussions of administration and "marketing," showing the close relationship between the encomiendas and mining, and looks at some resultant instances of maltreatment of Indians. It also considers the functioning of the system under Guzmán and the First Audiencia, the estancia as a forerunner of the hacienda, and the importance of the encomienda in the increasing conflict between the Cazonci and the Spaniards.

The Administration of the Encomiendas

The encomenderos were not usually the Spaniards who had the most direct day-to-day contact with the natives of Michoacán. The fact that no municipality was founded there during the 1520s and that nearly all the encomenderos were *vecinos* of Mexico City meant that few of these men of prime importance in the colony spent much time in Michoacán. Most of them had homes in Tenochtitlan–Mexico, where they received the income from their towns and usually had some na-tives of the towns to perform personal services in their houses. In fact, on May 26, 1524, the town council of Mexico City issued an ordinance that, so as not to leave the city undefended, no encomendero should absent himself personally to gather gold or to live in his encomienda or hacienda but should send out miners and *estancieros* to perform such tasks.[1]

It was such people as these who made up the initial resident Span-ish population of Michoacán: miners who wandered through the area prospecting for precious metals or who oversaw gangs of Indian slaves panning for gold, overseers (*mayordomos*) whom the encomenderos sent into the province to supervise the exploitation of their encomiendas, and other individuals who served as herdsmen for encomenderos' livestock or established their own estancias on unoccupied land. They are generally faceless men whose names appear occasionally on contracts and lawsuits but who left little imprint on history. Yet they were the managers, the local administrators, often called *calpisques*, who saw to it that the encomiendas functioned as they were expected to. Generally they seem to have signed contracts obligating them for a year or so, and after the contract expired, they might go to work for someone else. For example, in 1532, Luis de Cabrera had been Francisco de Villegas' overseer in Uruapan for about five years.[2] By contrast, Martín Gómez, who by 1532 had worked in Michoacán for seven years, had been employed by Cortés for a while, then he had taken charge of Indians for Juan Infante, and finally in 1532 he was a servant of Guillén de la Loa.[3]

Sometimes such men changed their line of work. For example, Mateo de Vera was a miner for Juan de Ortega as of November 6, 1528, but after the arrival of the First Audiencia he was put in charge of Pátzcuaro for Licenciado Matienzo.[4] Hernando Ladrón was a miner in Michoacán on April 2, 1527, when Francisco de Santa Cruz empowered him and Diego de León to recover his encomienda Indians and other goods from Alonso de Mata and other persons.[5] On October 24, 1527, Santa Cruz and Nicolás de Palacios Rubios put Ladrón and Juan Martín de Calvete in charge of their towns, Tuzantla and Cutzio.[6] Ladrón must have served well, because shortly after Cortés left for Spain in 1528, Ladrón began to serve as his overseer for the city of Michoacán.[7]

On August 25, 1525, Gonzalo Sánchez contracted to serve as swineherd for Fernando Alonso and Francisco de Villegas in Villegas' town, Uruapan.[8] On February 11, 1528, Pedro López Galbito indicated that he had pigs in his towns in Michoacán, but his name does not appear among those of the encomenderos. Perhaps the explanation is found in the record that on the following day, February 12, 1528, Andrés de Monjaraz gave formal permission to Pedro López Galbito and Miguel de Mesa to reside in his towns, Jaso and Teremendo.[9] For the nearby town of Huaniqueo, on November 15, 1527, Juan Mateos made a contract with Hernando Alonso and Marcos Ruiz to serve them there.[10] Both Juan Ochoa and Miguel de Espinal asserted that they had served

Juan Infante in his towns in Michoacán for a few months in 1529 before Nuño de Guzmán passed through on his way to New Galicia.[11]

Conflicts arose at the local level among these representatives of the Spanish overlords. In 1537, Gonzalo Gómez recorded that about eight years previously (around 1529) Martín de Aranda had been *calpisque* for Villafuerte in his towns.[12] Aranda had stolen some of Gomez' pigs, whereupon Gómez had gotten Villafuerte to dismiss Aranda. Gómez also brought criminal action against Aranda and obtained a judgment against him. But Aranda then went into the service of Cristóbal de Valderrama, who was hostile to Gómez because he claimed that Gómez' estancia Guayangareo fell within the area of his encomienda, Tarímbaro.[13]

These were also the men who suffered most from the wrath of the Indians, because they were the ones who saw to the collection of tribute and made other daily impositions on them. Most of the deaths of Spaniards mentioned in the trial of the Cazonci were those of miners who were working in or passing through Michoacán or of *calpisques* of towns.[14]

They were also, however, the first Spaniards who learned the Tarascan language. We have noted the instance of the interpreter Juan who was killed by the Tarascan *principales*.[15] Both Juan Martín and Juan Pascual served as interpreters for Bachiller Ortega in 1528,[16] and Martín Gómez claimed to have done the same,[17] although his name does not appear in the record of the visitation. None were encomenderos; they must have learned the language while serving as overseers or miners in the Tarascan area.

A few encomenderos appear to have spent considerable time in their towns, and they sometimes also served as *calpisques* for others. We have seen that Gonzalo López, encomendero of Cuitzeo, was also collecting tribute from Comanja for Juan de Solís just before Infante took control of the town.[18]

The most important encomendero-*calpisque*, however, was Antón Caicedo. Besides holding Tarecuato and other neighboring towns in western Michoacán as his encomiendas, he also served as overseer of Cortés' towns in Michoacán. Apparently he was a good man with the natives. The *Relación de Michoacán* honors him, saying, "The lord Marqués sent to the city [of Michoacán] a man of good repute named Caicedo, that he should take charge of the Indians of the city."[19] Alonso de Estrada, in his letter to Bachiller Ortega, of July 12, 1528, included an exhortation that Caicedo should not by any means desert what he had under his charge for Cortés. Santa Cruz had written something to Caicedo that disturbed him, but Estrada expressed confidence in him: "I know that he does it well, and the lord Don Hernando charged and entrusted it to me more than anything else. I am writing to him that he should not make any change, because it would displease me." Evidently a certain Juan Serrano also had some authority from Cortés and was causing problems. In his letter of July 28, Estrada expressed his hope that Caicedo would not be angered because a certain Zamudio had been sent to replace Serrano, and he asserted that he did not intend to remove Caicedo from his position. But he thought that Caicedo should come to Mexico City to give him a report. Perhaps these conflicts led Caicedo to withdraw from Cortés' service, for in May, 1529, when Godoy took over Cortés' towns for Guzmán, Hernando Ladrón was in charge of Tzintzuntzan and its area, and Alonso de Zamudio was overseeing Tuxpan, Amula, Tamazula, and Zapotlán.[20]

The presence of African slaves in Michoacán during the first colonial decade is a shadowy reality that is hard to document adequately. In Ortega's record regarding Comanja it was noted simply, "They have killed a Negro."[21] The notarial records show that Hernando Ladrón sold to Francisco Oliveros a black slave named Cristóbal on April 17, 1528, and another named Francisco on May 4.[22] Presumably Ladrón had had the slaves with him in Michoacán.

Gonzalo López, encomendero of Cuitzeo, bought a black slave named Pedro from Hernán Pérez on December 30, 1527, and another named Juanillo from Pedro López Galbito on February 11, 1528. On January 31, 1528, Ángel de Villafaña noted that he had a black slave named Antón working under Francisco Parrado with a gang of (Indian) slaves in the mines of Michoacán.[23] It appears that in Michoacán as elsewhere the Spaniards used African slaves to oversee Indian workers.

The Encomiendas and the Mines

Most of the towns of highland Michoacán were not in mineral-producing areas and could not give tribute in precious metals, even though their encomenderos constantly suspected them of hiding mines from the Spaniards. Their tributes were of a more bulky sort, such as corn, beans, chili, fish, salt, and products of local industry, such as blankets, footgear, and pottery containers.[24] The encomendero and his household could consume only a limited amount of such products. The problem for the encomendero, then, was to find ways to convert them into precious metals. Two principal ways of doing so presented themselves. One was to carry the products to the nearest mining area and sell them to the miners to support the Indian slaves whom they had working for them. The other was to feed the produce to pigs or other livestock that could be driven to the mines or to the Spanish urban areas and sold there.

To understand the market presented by the mines, we must give some consideration to that industry, an important element in the economy of early colonial Michoacán. The treasures that had been brought back from Michoacán by the Caicedo and Olid expeditions merely whetted the appetites of the Spaniards for more of the same. The members of the Olid expedition must have gotten an inkling that the treasures of central Michoacán were mostly imported accumulations. Although Michoacán was probably the source of much of the silver of aboriginal New Spain, the mines were not in the Tarascan area proper but in the western dependencies that had been brought under the control of Michoacán by force of arms, notably Tamazula, Zapotlán, Tuxpan, and Motín to the west and southwest and some areas along the Río Balsas drainage to the south. It is possible that these areas had been subjugated by the Tarascan empire precisely because they were sources of metals.[25]

Cortés took control of the silver-producing towns of Tamazula, Zapotlán, and Tuxpan for himself soon after the Conquest, probably after the return of the Caravajal expedition, though one source indicates that Cortés was deriving silver from the Michoacán mines as early as 1523. Luis de Cárdenas, writing to the king in 1527, stated that in 1523 Cortés had taken five hundred cargas of silver from the mines of Michoacán and also that the Spaniards had been informed by the Indians that Cortés had forbidden Christians to go there under pain of a hundred lashes.[26] Probably this was an instance of exaggeration through envy; there is no solid evidence to support Cárdenas's statement. He also wrote that, after Cortés had gone to Honduras, "Governor" Albornoz (the royal accountant) had put his Indians into the mines and in five days had taken out five hundred marks of silver.[27] Domingo Niño, one of the witnesses in Cortés' residencia, claimed that Olid's colony failed because Cortés discovered the richness of the region and took it for himself.[28] Regarding these statements we must keep in mind that both Cárdenas and Niño were bitterly opposed to Cortés. Niño in particular was noted as an enemy of Cortés and a friend of Gonzalo de Salazar,[29] and in 1527 he had engaged in a lawsuit with Cortés over two towns that Salazar and Chirinos had given him on October 25, 1525.[30] Their testimony also contradicts the obvious fact that Cortés did distribute many encomiendas in Michoacán and that there were many Spanish miners there.

More exact information about the amount of precious metals that Cortés was obtaining from Michoacán during the first years after the Spanish occupation of the region is found in accounts taken by Cortés soon after his return to Mexico from Honduras. On May 25, 1526, he received an accounting of receipts and expenditures made in his name by his *mayordomo* Andrés de Barrios.[31] This is the most detailed listing of Cortés' income that we have for this early period, but unfortunately the account does not give dates for the receipts, and we are uncertain whether they represent the whole period of Cortés' absence or merely the months in 1526 after Salazar and Chirinos were deposed. But since four deliveries of silver by Caicedo are listed, they surely must pertain to a longer period of time than February to May 1526. Otherwise Caicedo would have been doing almost nothing but traveling back and forth between Mexico City and Michoacán. Probably, then, the receipts span the period of Cortés' absence, except for the last months of 1525 and January 1526, when Salazar and Chirinos were taking his income.

The account includes the following entries from Michoacán: 25 pesos of gold of an uncertain fineness given by the Cazonci; 20 gold ingots brought from Tuxpan and Tamazula by Caicedo; 10 gold ingots given by the Cazonci; 67 ingots of the purer gold called *oro de minas* (about 22 carats) brought by Caicedo; 83 pesos of *oro de minas* brought by Alonso de Ávila and Juan Méndez, a miner; and 48 ingots of gold weighing 132 pesos, brought by Tobar from Tuxpan, Amula, Tamazula, and Zapotlán. The total comes to 150 pesos of *oro de minas*, 157 pesos of gold of uncertain fineness, and 50 gold ingots for which no weight is given. Of this total the Cazonci gave 25 pesos and 30 ingots of gold of uncertain fineness, and from the region of Tuxpan, Tamazula, and Zapotlán came 20 ingots of unspecified weight and 48 ingots weighing a total of 132 pesos.

In regard to silver, Caicedo was credited with four deliveries in which he brought 149 ingots and 5 shields, 100 ingots, 90 ingots, and

60 ingots, respectively. Altogether they weighed 47 marks, 2 ounces, 4 reales. The Cazonci brought 60 ingots which weighed a total of 4 marks, 6 ounces. Juan de Tovar brought 440 ingots weighing 37 marks, 7 ounces, from Tuxpan, Amula, Tamazula, and Zapotlán. The total weight of the silver was 89 marks, 7 ounces, 4 reales, contained in 899 ingots and 5 shields.

Barrios indicated that all but 37 marks of silver had been used to make bowls, candlesticks, pitchers, plates, and ornaments for spurs. Among many other expenditures he had also spent 84 pesos, 3 tomines, for tools for Tamazula and 395 pesos for tools that were divided between Michoacán and Oaxaca.

Cortés was by no means the only Spaniard who was operating mines in Michoacán at that time. Among the alleged reasons why he could not find a very large force to lead to Honduras in 1524 was that some of the soldiers had heard of the discovery of mines in Michoacán and had gone there to work them.[32] In 1525 a very rich silver mine was discovered by a certain Morcillo, presumably the Francisco Morcillo who had acted as notary for both Caravajal and Ávila and who was encomendero of Indaparapeo, in Michoacán. The mine was considered to be the richest yet discovered in New Spain, so rich that, when the discoverer went to register it, the royal officials, not content with the royal fifth, took the whole mine for the crown. The chroniclers tell us that the mine either disappeared or played out as a punishment for such greed. But when Father Alonso Ponce, the Franciscan commissary general, visited Tamazula in 1587, the mine was still, or again, in operation.[33] It sounds as though this may have been the mine from which Albornoz was said to have taken five hundred marks of silver in five days. Herrera mentioned that after its discovery there followed a small mining rush to Michoacán and that the Indians came near to rebelling.[34]

The notarial records for Mexico City for the 1520s are quite incomplete,[35] but they do give some indication of what was happening in Michoacán. On November 18 and December 1, 1525, Juan Ximénez and Blasco Fernández, respectively, recorded that they had Indian slaves in the mines of Michoacán with their washing trays (bateas) and metal tools. This indicates that the precious metal was being obtained by placer mining. But perhaps the more significant fact is that both of these individuals were offering to sell their slaves and tools.[36] The miners who had rushed into Michoacán upon hearing of Morcillo's discovery had perhaps not found enough precious metal to pay for the maintenance of the operation. The man whom Juan Ximénez authorized to sell his slaves was Alonso de Ávila, the alcalde and justice. It seems probable that Ávila's work in Michoacán was connected with the near rebellion of the Indians which Herrera mentioned as one result of the mining rush following Morcillo's discovery in 1525.[37]

Another indication of the traffic between Mexico City and Michoacán at this time is that on July 26, 1525, the cabildo of Mexico City gave Juan de la Torre, cousin of Alonso de Estrada, permission to establish an inn in the unsettled region on the way to Michoacán between Ixtlahuaca and Tajimaroa.[38] He must not have taken advantage of the permission immediately, since again on October 12, 1526, the cabildo gave him permission to found inns in Cuertlavaca (Ixtlahuaca?) and the uninhabited area of Tajimaroa.[39]

In the letter that Rodrigo de Albornoz wrote to the king on December 15, 1525, he showed considerable concern over certain irregularities that he feared were developing in silver production in Michoacán. He advised the king that it would be necessary to establish a smelter in Michoacán where the silver ore could be processed, after which the silver would be taken to Mexico City for refining. His reason for this suggestion was that local Indians, slaves, and even Spaniards were taking the ore and smelting it and even refining it in their own houses, and, surprisingly enough, they were not paying the king's fifth or tenth to the royal officials. In fact, some were even taking the silver to the port and bribing the officials there to let it pass. When the accountant's deputy at the port had tried to do something about this state of affairs, he had not been allowed to interfere. Albornoz, therefore, wanted the crown to insist that all smelting in Michoacán be done at a royal smelting house which would be established there, after which the silver, accompanied by an affidavit regarding the amount, was to be sent to Mexico City, where the royal officials could take the crown's due share during the refining. This procedure would necessitate the appointment of an assistant accountant to reside at the smelter.[40] The crown, however, does not appear to have taken any serious action on the accountant's suggestion.

The notarial records, which are extant for the period January 29 to November 15, 1527, and from December 27, 1527, to December 1, 1528, give us some idea of the activities in the mines, though we must suspect that they show us only the tip of the iceberg. They show nothing, for instance, of the activities of Cortés, which were probably more extensive than those of any other individual. They do, however, show some of the surges of interest corresponding to the periods of the expeditions of Sánchez Farfán and Ortega.

In early 1527 there was very little notarial activity in relation to mining in Michoacán. The only item recorded before May 4 was a negative one: on March 30, Pedro de Sotomayor authorized Esteban Miguel, a miner, to sell his slaves, tools, and washing trays in the mines of Michoacán.[41] From May to early September, however, interest increased greatly. On May 4, Juan Infante formed a partnership with Frey Ramón Bernal for working mines in Michoacán, Infante furnishing 100 slaves, male and female, with their tools and trays, and Bernal supplying the food to support them.[42] On May 23, Alonso Cardenel empowered the priest Cristóbal Bello to recover his slaves from Antón Muñoz.[43]

On June 21, Gaspar Ramírez sold 20 Indian slaves and other items in the mines of Michoacán to Antón Bravo and Fernando Alonso.[44] On June 26, Hernando de Cáceres, Luis Hernández, and Gonzalo del Castillo formed a partnership to work the mines in Michoacán, with a black slave named Antón and 77 Indian slaves.[45] The next day Juan de Nájera authorized Juan Pérez de Herrera to reclaim 67 Indian slaves who were being used to gather gold in the mines of San Cristóbal in Michoacán.[46]

On July 15, Alonso Lucas agreed to go to the mines of Michoacán to gather gold with 100 slaves who belonged to Hernán Rodríguez, an apothecary.[47] On August 3, Gonzalo López, encomendero of Cuitzeo, paid 500 pesos to Peralmíndez Chirinos for male and female slaves, with their tools and trays, whom Chirinos had held in a partnership with Juan de Jaso, encomendero of Arimao.[48] The following day Ángel de Villafaña, who had been Sánchez Farfán's *maestre de campo*, bought 100 Indian slaves, "expert in the work of the mines, with all of their tools and trays," from Sebastián de Grijalva, who had been employing them in partnership with Riobó, the encomendero of Araró.[49] On August 8, Andrés Alonso and Jacome Ginovés agreed to put 30 slaves each, with their tools and trays, into the mines of Zacatula.[50]

A declining or disappointing profit may be indicated in the subsequent series of notarial acts. On August 14, Pedro de Villanueva gave his power of attorney for the recovery of 56 slaves and their tools in the mines of Michoacán.[51] On September 7, Juan Rodríguez Cerezo empowered Hernando Garrovero to recover his 22 slaves and sell them for the price that seemed best.[52] And on the same day Juan Jiménez, encomendero of half of Arimao, sold 36 slaves and their tools to Francisco de Orduña, *vecino* of Zacatula, and Juan de la Plaza, encomendero of Sinagua.[53]

After that no more contracts related to the region appear until December 30, when Gonzalo Riobó de Sotomayor, encomendero of Araró, bought some slaves, presumably for use in Michoacán.[54]

The first half of 1528 showed some activity. Ángel de Villafaña offered his slaves for sale on January 31.[55] Juan de Cabra and Serván Bejerano formed a partnership on February 6 to exploit mines in "Zacatula and Michoacán or wherever may be best for them."[56] Gonzalo López purchased 8 slaves in the mines of Zacatula on February 11. Pedro de Bazán, encomendero of half of Pungarabato, bought 50 slaves on March 21 and 65 more on April 1.[57]

On April 20, 1528, probably soon after Bachiller Ortega had departed for Michoacán, Fernando Alonso, blacksmith, and Nicolás López de Palacios Rubios, encomendero of Cutzio, formed a partnership for mining. Alonso was to supply Indian slaves (200, if necessary) with their tools and trays. Palacios Rubios would support them with pork, corn, and beans, with turkey if they got sick, and with Indian women to make bread and Indian men to build huts for them. The profits were to be divided equally. This Fernando Alonso appears to have been the one who was executed as a heretic on October 17 of that year, rather than Fernando Alonso de Villanueva, who was encomendero of half of Pungarabato.[58]

Until the end of August no more contracts were registered that appear to have been related to mining in Michoacán. This period corresponds very closely to that of the stay of Ortega and his expedition in Michoacán. Then, between August 28 and September 20, there are five notarial acts by persons with interests in the region. On August 28, Andrés de Monjaraz and Blasco Hernández formed a partnership for mining; on September 4, Hernando de Torres listed about 100 slaves in the mines of Coyuca as part of a pledge to pay a debt; on August 28 and September 10, Juan Fernández de Ijar made purchases of slaves; and on September 20, Francisco Morcillo sold slaves and tools to Diego de los Olivos.[59]

During the rest of 1528 only one more act was registered that appears to have been related to the region. On November 6, 1528, through a third person, Juan de Ortega acknowledged a debt for slaves and tools for gathering gold, and the miner Mateos de Vera acknowledged that he owed 50 pesos for pigs that he had bought for feeding the same slaves.[60] These slaves were probably being used in conjunction with the encomienda of Tuzantla, which Ortega had confiscated from Alonso de Mata during the summer of the same year and which Estrada had assigned to Ortega.[61]

The Indians who were put to work in the mines in Michoacán were those who had been enslaved in various wars by the Spaniards against rebellious Indian towns or those who had been slaves in their native society and had been acquired by the Spaniards as tribute or by other means.[62] Michoacán does not seem to have suffered extensively from enslavement through warfare because of the relatively peaceful nature of the Conquest there, although we have seen that Bachiller Ortega made slaves in a few towns because they had killed Spaniards or were otherwise rebellious. We do not have any records of slaves being given as tribute in Michoacán at this time.

But there must have been many slaves who were brought into Michoacán from other parts of Mexico. We have no way of knowing how many there were, but it appears that there were many hundreds. Cortés claimed that at the time when his towns were taken from him by Guzmán and the audiencia he had six gangs of slaves working in the mines,[63] and many others had slave gangs working there, as we have seen.

The low price of Indian slaves also indicates their relative abundance. For instance, on July 15, 1527, Hernán Rodríguez paid 450 pesos for 100 slaves. On March 21, 1528, Pedro de Bazán paid 150 pesos of gold for 50 slaves, or three pesos each. On April 1, 1528, he paid 3 pesos, 3 granos, of gold apiece for 65 slaves.[64] By contrast, imported and scarce African slaves were expensive. Gonzalo López on December 30, 1527, bought an African slave who was eighteen to twenty years old for 250 pesos.[65] On April 17, 1528, Hernando Ladrón sold a black slave for 110 pesos of *oro de minas*, and on May 4 he sold another for 125 pesos.[66] Horses were about equally expensive. Pedro de Maya bought a horse for 140 pesos of gold on March 23, 1528, "which he received lame in one hoof." On March 24, Juan López, a muleteer, went into debt for 190 pesos of gold for "a chestnut pack horse, with all of its packsaddles for the road and two wineskins." On the same day for 200 pesos of gold, Juan de Gallegos bought a horse "shod on the rear hooves and on the left front hoof."[67]

Little information has survived regarding the treatment of the slaves in the Michoacán mines. The human misery involved in the hard work in the tropical lowlands, where most of the mining was done, is incalculable. Men and women appear to have been used indiscriminately in the slave gangs. They worked under Spanish overseers, or *mineros*, who signed contracts of limited duration to serve in that capacity. Amador Martín, for instance, made a contract with Lucas Montánchez to serve him for a year as a miner in Michoacán or elsewhere. Alonso Lucas signed such a contract with Hernán Rodríguez and Gonzalo Fernández on July 15, 1527.[68] Cortés had eight Spaniards in charge of his slaves in Motín at the time when Guzmán and the audiencia took his towns from him.[69]

Juan Rodríguez Cerezo mentioned that with his slaves he had an "iron chain of six branches, with twenty collars," indicating that the slaves were sometimes chained, but this is the only mention of such a chain that I have encountered, and it is hard to judge how widespread the practice was.[70]

The slaves' food was the produce of the Michoacán encomiendas — corn, beans, chili, sometimes fish, and salt. Some of the pork from the pig farms that the Spaniards established in Michoacán also went to feed the slaves. We have noted that Frey Ramón Bernal contracted to give pork twice a week to Juan Infante's slaves, and Palacios Rubios mentioned it among the foods that he promised to supply to Fernando Alonso's slaves. A touch of humanity appears in the latter contract, in which Palacios Rubios agreed to give the slaves turkey if they became sick.[71]

We have also seen that Palacios Rubios promised to supply Indian women to make bread and Indian men to build huts. These workers were undoubtedly from Palacios Rubios' encomienda. Since it was not allowed to use the Indians of the encomiendas for the actual work of the mines, they were used in this way so that the working time of the slaves could be entirely dedicated to mining.

Most of the extracts of the notarial contracts mention mining tools and trays in only a general way, but occasionally a contract lists them in greater detail. Pedro de Villanueva had, with his 56 slaves, 50 washing trays, 47 hoes, 14 small bars, and 10 grub hoes; Juan Jiménez, with 36 slaves, had 10 small bars, 20 hoes, and 9 grub hoes; Francisco

Morcillo, with 23 slaves, had 20 hoes, 8 small bars, and 7 grub hoes.[72] These tools were for breaking and loosening the soil, which the slaves then washed in the trays to separate the gold from it.

I have found only one statement giving a more or less precise estimate of the actual production of gold from a mine. Pedro de Bazán said that at the time when the First Audiencia took his half of Pungarabato from him it was supporting 200 slaves in the mines of Coyuca, five leagues away, and that the slaves were collecting twelve to fifteen pesos of gold every day.[73] Since Bazán's statement is part of a claim for damages, it is quite possibly exaggerated.

Subsidiary industries and services economies grew out of the mining activities. Diego Alcalde and Gonzalo Díaz are named as *bateeros*, or makers of washing trays, in Michoacán.[74] The demand for trays in the mines must have given them plenty of work.

We have already mentioned the permissions given to Juan de la Torre to found an inn in the uninhabited area between Ixtlahuaca and Tajimaroa, to give lodging to the people traveling to and from Michoacán. The miners were also willing to pay to have some of the comforts of home brought to them. Cristóbal de Ojeda asserted that Estrada had formed a partnership with his servants Juan Infante and Rodríguez, allowing them to use Indians to carry jugs of wine and oil from Veracruz to the mines in Michoacán and Zacatula, even though it was far more than the legally allowed distance for using bearers.[75] Probably the eleven pack mules and "seven pairs of skins for transporting wine" that Gaspar Ramírez sold to Antón Bravo and Fernando Alonso on June 21, 1527, were also used in this service, since Ramírez also sold twenty slaves who were collecting gold in Michoacán.[76]

Income from the Encomiendas

For the first four years of the existence of the encomiendas in Michoacán we have only bits and pieces of information regarding the income that the encomenderos received from their towns there. For instance, Antón Yringua, *principal* of Turicato, testified that after Cortés gave the town to Diego Hernández Nieto and Hernán Rodríguez the Indians on one occasion brought to their encomenderos in Mexico City 100 ingots of silver as tribute.[77] Probably this occurred between the time of the distribution of the encomiendas and Hernández Nieto's departure for Honduras with Cortés.

Cortés' income from Michoacán was, by his own statement, considerable. In his lawsuit against Peralmíndez Chirinos for damages, he claimed that in 1525 he was getting an income of at least 2,000 pesos of gold a year from Uchichila (Tzintzuntzan) and Tamazula and at least another 2,500 pesos of gold from Tuxpan, Amula, Zapotlán, and Huaniqueo. This evaluation, however, included the production of his mines as well as tribute in cloth, services, and provisions and income from his herds.[78] The statement is so general as to be of little use for precise information, and it is very possibly exaggerated, as damage claims tend to be, but at least it indicates that Cortés' income from his Michoacán encomienda towns was large enough to be of some importance to him.

The Spaniards began to introduce domestic livestock, especially pigs, into Michoacán very early. We have already seen the fate of the ten "pioneer" pigs that were first admitted to the presence of the Cazonci. But the exploding pig population could not long be excluded from Michoacán, and they soon began moving across the border in droves. On August 25, 1525, Gonzalo Sánchez, a farmer and a native of Coria de Galisteo, agreed to take one hundred sows to Michoacán for Fernando Alonso the blacksmith and Francisco Villegas. Alonso was to supply the sows, the corn to feed them, the Indians to care for them, and the necessities for Sánchez and the Indians. They were to be taken to Villegas' encomienda, Uruapan, where Sánchez was to build pigsties and to see to their increase. When the contract expired at the end of a year and a half, the tithe having been paid, Sánchez was to receive one-fifth of the increase, while the other four-fifths were to go to Alonso and Villegas.[79]

The first systematized account that we have of the legitimate income from the encomiendas of Michoacán is the Ortega assessment of 1528. With the list of towns in appendix B is also given the amount of tribute that each town agreed to pay its encomendero. Some fairly obvious observations can be made regarding the shortcomings of the list. First, the assessment is incomplete. Although the major towns of the tierra caliente of southeastern Michoacán are listed, with the names of their encomenderos, no tribute assessment is listed for any of them. Thus we do not have assessments for Ajuchitlan, Tuzantla, Coyuca, Cutzamala, Cutzio, Guayameo, or Pungarabato. Apparently Ortega did not personally into the tierra caliente. He offered to do so to investigate the complaints of the Indians of Tuzantla against Alonso de Mata (see below), but Mata declined the offer, and there is no evidence that Ortega made the journey on his own initiative. It is unfortunate that we do not have more information regarding these towns during the 1520s, since they were the towns closest to the mines of the Río Balsas valley.[80]

The following towns are named as the encomiendas of Alonso de Ávalos: Cindangualo, Chavinda, Guaraqueo, Sacandalo, Tacandaro, and Tucate (text B gives the names as Sindinguara, Chaudan, Quaraquio, Zirándaro, Tacandaro, and Tucatl; see appendix B). No tribute listing is given for any of them, but it is possible that they are a duplicate list of towns that are otherwise given as encomiendas of Alonso de Ávalos and Fernando de Saavedra.

For a significant group of towns in eastern Michoacán, Araró, Indaparapeo, Maravatío, and Tajimaroa, no tribute is listed, and Matalcingo and Zinapécuaro are not even mentioned. Since these towns lay along the route from Mexico, it is possible that Ortega had made decisions regarding them as he came into the province and that those decisions were not put into the official record of the assessment.

In the northwestern sector a few towns (Guaracha, Sahuayo, Jiquilpan, and Mazamitla) are listed for which no tribute assessment is given. That there was a considerable amount of unrest in the region is evident from statements in the assessment record to the effect that Guaracha and Sahuayo were unwilling to serve and the Indians of Jiquilpan had fled to the towns of Ávalos.

Four other towns, Amula, Arimao, Cecasta, and Zanzan, also appear without assessments. Amula was perhaps included as a subject town with one of the other of Cortés' towns in the northwestern area. Cecasta and Zanzan are not identifiable as modern towns in Michoacán.

Another observation, not so evident, concerning the assessment record is that it is incomplete even for those towns for which it gives a listing of tribute. It lists only the cargas of provisions that the encomenderos could demand that the Indians carry to the mines. But the encomenderos also expected to receive other forms of tribute. On March 12, 1532, Pedro Cornejo, Juan Infante's *calpisque* in Guayameo (where Santa Fe de la Laguna was later built), testified concerning the tribute of the town. He was in charge of Guayameo, Sarandachoa, Cucharo, and two other estancias. During the two months that he had served Infante, the towns had given two tributes, and in each tribute they had given eighty cargas of corn and thirty pieces of cloth. They had

Fishermen on Lake Pátzcuaro.

also built "some houses for the livestock that might be there by command of the said Juan Infante." They also gave "as much as half a
fanega of corn every day" for the pigs. For food for Cornejo and the
Indians who took care of the livestock, "on days when meat can be
eaten, they give him three chickens [turkeys] and salt and chili and
tamales for the Indians who watch the livestock, and now that it is Lent
they give this witness the fish and eggs that this witness asks of them."[81]
    On March 10, 1532, Diego de Escobedo testified that, besides the
usual foodstuffs, "every thirty or forty days" Infante's towns of Comanja
and Naranja and their subject towns "give him possibly 120 pieces of
cloth and an equal number of cups and an equal number of sandals,

Taking home reeds for weaving, Lake Pátzcuaro.

. . . and every day they give to this witness and three other Spaniards
whom the said Juan Infante has in the said towns, they give him every
day six hens and chili and fish and eggs and everything that they ask
of them for their support." He estimated that Infante had 600 to 700
pigs in the towns.[82] Infante himself, in letters to Cristóbal de Cáceres,
his *mayordomo* in Michoacán, mentioned items of tribute as varied as
blankets, sandals, cups, pots, pottery griddles, jugs, seats, and pelts of
cats (probably large felines).[83]

   In regard to Coyuca, one of the towns of the tierra calienta for which
no assessment was given in 1528, we find the following report of the
Indians' tribute to Guillén de la Loa in 1534: they planted for their

Pottery market, Tzintzuntzan.

encomendero three fields of corn (planting 50 fanegas) and four pieces of land in chilies and beans (planting 5 fanegas). They had also been obliged to give 1,500 fanegas of corn from their houses each year, but they had been relieved of this obligation, which was apparently commuted to work in the mines. Moreover, "every two months, when the chili is gone, they buy what is necessary for the slaves." Every two months they also gave the necessary salt. Three times a year they gave 400 items of clothing for the slaves: 100 *jicales*, 100 *mastiles* (probably loincloths), and 100 shirts and skirts.[84]

In making any computation based on Ortega's tribute assessment, therefore, we must be conscious of its limitations; it is incomplete in regard both to the number of towns and to the amount of tribute that it gives for the towns for which it lists tribute. Cognizant of this, let us see what data it does provide in regard to the total amount of tribute. The tributes are listed by cargas, the amount that would be carried by an individual Indian. Most of the tributes were to be given every twenty days, a Mesoamerican month, except for those of Cortés' towns, which contributed every thirty days, and a few others, which contributed more frequently. In the following calculations all the tribute is converted into the amount that it would total in 30 days, approximately a European month.

Table 3 shows the amounts given to Cortés, the amounts given to other encomenderos, and the totals.

TABLE 3
Cargas of Tribute Due to the Encomenderos Every Thirty Days

Item	Cortés	Others	Total
Corn	1,400	3,630.0	5,040.0
Beans	110	525.0	635.0
Chilies	55	156.0	211.0
Salt	—	138.0	138.0
Fish	23	70.5	93.5
Various other provisions	—	2,835.0	2,835.0
Total	1,588	7,354.5	8,942.5

The total number of cargas of foodstuffs specified by Ortega's assessment was, therefore, 8,942.5, and of this amount Cortés' towns gave 1,588 cargas, or about 17.8 percent of the total. It would be incorrect, however, to conclude that Cortés was receiving 17.8 percent of the tribute from Michoacán, since only two of the many towns whose tribute is not given belonged to Cortés. Those two towns were Mazamitla and Amula.

But the production of the foodstuffs was only part of the tribute burden. The towns were also obligated to supply an equal number of bearers to deliver the produce to the mines. Moreover, some towns provided bearers who were used for carrying provisions grown on special fields for the encomendero or provisions purchased by the encomendero. The two groups must be added together to arrive at the total number of bearers involved in service to the mines every 30 days, insofar as this is indicated by Ortega's assessment. These totals are shown in Table 4.

TABLE 4
Number of Bearers Supplied Every Thirty Days

Kinds of Bearers	Cortés	Others	Total
Bearers of tribute	1,588	7,354.5	8,942.5
Other bearers	300	1,278.0	1,578.0
Total	1,888	8,632.5	10,520.5

We arrive at a total of 10,520.5 as the number of bearers allowed to be used in the course of 30 days. (The fractional number is the result of multiplying the 20-day tributes by 1.5 to find the equivalent for a 30-day period.)[85]

Another question that may be asked is how much labor this burden-bearing involved. We have some information for the 1530s regarding the towns of Juan Infante that gives us something of an answer. On March 12, 1532, Buenaventura, lord of Comanja, said that it took 10 days for the bearers to go to the mines of Colima and 5 days to return, a total of 15 days.[86] On April 18, 1534, Juan Infante wrote to Cristóbal de Cáceres that from Pomacoran it took the bearers 6 or 7 days to arrive at the mines and 4 days to return, a total of 10 or 11 days.[87] Perhaps, for the sake of a rough estimate, we can take 13 days as an average time that the bearers spent on the road. Certainly it required much less time to go from towns near the mines, such as Tepalcatepec, but more days would be necessary to reach them from the northeastern towns, such as Yuriria, Cuitzeo, or Acámbaro. If we multiply the 10,520.5 bearers by 13 days spent on the road, we arrive at 136,766.5 as a rough estimate of the number of days of work involved licitly each 30 days in delivering the assessed provisions to the mines. This does not take into account the work involved in growing the provisions, which we have no way of estimating.

Ortega's assessment was obviously an effort to systematize a very disorderly situation. At the beginning of the record, on April 31 (May 1), 1528, he stated his purpose: ". . . that [the natives] might have order in serving the Spaniards, and that they might not be subject to the ill-treatment that had been done to them, and that the killings of the Christians might cease." He sent out interpreters to summon the lords and *principales* of the towns, threatening them that if they did not come he would go out against their towns with his men "to kill and burn and enslave them."

A settlement in the tierra caliente of the Río Balsas basin.

On May 16, speaking to several lords of towns, he made an important ruling. After that day they were to make two deliveries of provisions *(caminos de bastimentos)* to the mines, and thereafter, beginning
after the Feast of Saint John the Baptist (June 24), they were to be
free of the obligation for the three following months, and later they
could lay off for one more month when they chose. After this rest
they were to carry the tribute to the mines every twenty days. He
threatened death to any lord who did not fulfill his obligation. He
also threatened the encomenderos that if they did not respect the
period of rest he would suspend their encomiendas until the governor
made a decision on the matter. He reiterated this ruling on June 12.[88]
Ortega reported his decision to Estrada, who approved it in a letter
of May 27, telling Ortega to punish the lords who did not fulfill their

obligation "so that the witnesses will take warning." The governor also discussed the distance over which the Indians could be forced to carry tribute. Some encomenderos claimed that Estrada had allowed them a distance of 45 leagues, but he denied this. He did allow distances of up to 40 leagues but suggested that agreements should be made with lords of other towns to change bearers so that they would not have to travel more than 25 or 30 leagues from their towns.

The Spaniards also complained about the period of rest. In his letter of July 12, Estrada suggested that the four months might be divided more evenly into two parts but left the decision to Ortega until such time as they were able to discuss the matter. In his letter of July 28, however, he told Ortega twice that the period of rest should be observed as Ortega had ordained it and that it should not be broken.[89]

Abuse of the Encomiendas

In his letters Estrada made some general references to the need to punish those encomenderos who had exceeded the ordinances, but the only two names that he mentioned were those of Juan de Sámano and Alonso de Mata. Not much has come to light about the matter of Juan de Sámano and his encomienda of Chilchota. On May 17, 1528, Ortega indicated a problem with Chilchota when he specifically commanded the cacique of the town to observe the three months' rest during the rainy season and another month's rest at a later time, under threat of depriving Sámano of the encomienda. He also reduced the tribute burden of provisions from 300 cargas to 250 cargas.[90]

Estrada also made reference to the matter in his letter of July 28:

The other day I had written to your grace that, because of the *veedor's* need, you should give a pass or license for Juan de Sámano to take a shipment [of tribute] for the slaves that the *veedor* has there. I think that before this gets there the other thing that you mention, sir, will have been done. If it is so, let him be punished like the others, and in this there must not be any father or *compadre*.

From other data presented in the lawsuit between Ortega and Alonso de Mata, it is evident that Ortega found the accusations against Sámano serious enough that he decided to take the encomienda away from him. Estrada approved the decision and gave the town to Ortega himself.[91] Yet the kind of political influence that Estrada told Ortega not to take into consideration did in the end prevail for Sámano. As indicated in the section from Estrada's letter quoted above, Sámano was supporting slaves for the *veedor*, Perálmindez Chirinos. He also had the support of Chirinos's close friend Gonzalo de Salazar, who prevailed upon Estrada to give Chilchota back to Sámano.[92] Undoubtedly influential in this decision was the fact that Sámano was the son of the very important royal secretary of the same name. On October 8, 1528, he had a document drawn up in which he gave general power of attorney to his father, an act that may have had some relationship to his problems over his encomienda.[93]

An instance of mistreatment of Indians about which we have ample information is that involving Alonso de Mata. He was the kind of sociopath upon whose actions the "Black Legend" was built. There is no evidence that he was typical of the encomenderos in Michoacán; in fact, the evidence indicates just the opposite—that he was so exceptionally abusive that he was one of only two encomenderos whose towns Bachiller Ortega confiscated and he, alone of all the encomenderos, lost his Indians permanently. We follow his career here because it shows the extremes of abuse that were possible in the encomienda system when it delivered a town into the hands of a petty tyrant.

Mata became encomendero of Ocumo (now known by the Nahuatl form of its name, Tuzantla) by virtue of a grant from Fernando Cortés, issued on July 2, 1526, two days before the arrival of Luis Ponce de León.[94] Mata's grant also included Tamaloacan, in the jurisdiction of Zacatula. Ocumo had previously belonged to Francisco de Santa Cruz. In 1527, Santa Cruz gave his power of attorney to Hernando Ladrón and Diego de León to reclaim his Indians and other goods that Mata and other persons had taken against his will.[95] Also in 1527 he brought suit against Mata over possession of Ocumo, and in 1540 he made a claim before the audiencia that the town had been unjustly taken from him.

Mata used his encomienda to support gangs of slaves in the mines. Andrés Núñez testified that Mata's Indians from Ocumo had maintained about 200 slaves in the mines for Núñez for about eight months. Álvaro Gutiérrez, a miner, testified that he had worked a gang of Mata's slaves in the mines of Coyuca, presumably supported by Ocumo. But

Mata was not satisfied with slaves obtained elsewhere. Indian witnesses testified in 1541 that he had branded as slaves 20 of 200 Indians who carried supplies from the town to the mines.

Mata's tyranny took on more pathological aspects. In late 1531 several of the native *principales* testified regarding his cruelties. They said that on one occasion, when a *principal* and a commoner refused to bring Mata some Indian girls whom he wanted, he beat them on the testicles so badly that they died about twenty days later. For the same reason he killed two other commoners, one from Cutzamala and the other from Tuzantla, by setting dogs on them. He demanded slaves as well as pretty girls, and the *principales* gave him slaves from the town. Some of the slaves escaped, and when a *principal* of Tuzantla named Ococetequitato refused to tell him where they were, Mata subjected him to the water torture and kept him tied upside down for half a day. The *principal* died about twenty days later. When Mata recaptured the slaves, he cut off their noses. He beat another slave to death because he had lost a hoe. The lord of Tuzantla, Canaoci, one of the witnesses against Mata, had been imprisoned, chained to a post, for four moons (eighty days), because he had not taken corn, beans, and other things to the mines as quickly as he was commanded. Andrés Núñez also also testified that Mata had imprisoned an Indian *principal* in a house because he was taking tribute to the Cazonci.

On May 29, 1528, Canaoci appeared before Ortega to make a complaint of maltreatment against Mata. He brought with him the two slaves whose noses Mata had cut off. Ortega apparently considered the matter too important for him to decide and sent the Indians to Estrada, in Mexico City.

Mata later testified that he also went to Mexico City to complain that, while the Indians of his town of Tuzantla were serving in his mining gang (which was illegal), suddenly one night they all left and absconded with twenty-five or twenty-six of his slaves. He went to Estrada to ask whether Estrada had commanded them not to serve him. Estrada said that he had not issued such an order but that he had received reports that Mata had mistreated his Indians. Estrada sent Mata back to Michoacán with a commission to Bachiller Ortega to investigate the matter. The commission, which was dated June 13, 1528,[96] also instructed Ortega to review an investigation that Alonso de Vargas, inspector of the province of Zacatula, had made concerning Mata's mistreatment of Indians in his other town, Tamaloacan. Mata met Ortega as he was returning from Tamazula, but Ortega does not appear to have taken action immediately.

Ortega reported that Mata joined him when he was in Tamazula or one of its subject places and that, besides communications from Estrada, he carried letters from many people in Mexico City who entreated Ortega to act humanely with Mata in the matter of the maltreatment of the Indians. Ortega received Mata with honor and allowed him to eat at his table. (In this testimony Ortega was trying to show that he had not acted with ill will toward Mata in taking Tuzantla away from him, even though he himself was later given the town as his encomienda.)

Estrada was very insistent that Ortega should do justice in regard to Mata, in spite of all protests. In his letter of July 12, 1528, he wrote to Ortega:

I also sent a certain commission to your grace that out there you should look into the matter of Mata's maltreatments. Take note, sir, that in the matter of maltreatment of Indians I do not want there to be any father or *compadre*; and even if he were my son, I would want him to be punished. And because I committed it to your grace and Mata is there, do not neglect to ascertain the truth in its entirety, and let the evil deed be punished, because, if you do not do so, sir, you will load upon yourself a very great burden of conscience. And because, as I have said, when your grace comes to Michoacán [Tzintzuntzan], we will be in communication with one another about everything, I will not delay over this matter.

When Ortega returned to Tzintzuntzan, he began an active investigation of Mata's cruelties. On July 24, Canaoci once more presented his complaint, and Mata presented the record of the investigation that Alonso de Vargas had made on February 8 regarding Mata's cruelties in Tamaloacan. Later that day Ortega also took testimony from Xanaco, a *principal* of Tuzantla. The friars Antonio Ortiz and Martín de la Coruña, who had recently returned to Michoacán in company with the Cazonci, were present for the questioning of the witnesses. Mata later stated that the Cazonci, Malinal, and Don Pedro were also present, and he claimed that for this reason the witnesses did not speak the truth.

Antonio de Oliver, in his usual dramatic fashion, described how

Mata used him as a go-between to try to persuade Ortega not to confiscate his encomienda:

. . . while the said *bachiller* was in the city of Uchila [Tzintzuntzan] this witness saw that the said Alonso de Mata came up to this witness and said to
him, "Sir, I beg your grace to talk to Bachiller Juan de Ortega so that he
will not take away my Indians from me and that, in regard to the penalty,
he should do what he pleases." And this witness at the request of the said
Alonso de Mata went to the said *bachiller* to ask him not to suspend Mata's
[grant of the] Indians of the town of Ocumo, which he had as his encomienda.
And Bachiller Juan de Ortega answered this witness, "Sir, I don't know why
you come to ask what you don't know about; if you saw the record of the
investigation, you would not say this to me. But for love of you, I will do
everything possible in accordance with justice." And this witness immediately
again entreated the said *bachiller* to take into consideration that he [Mata]
was one of the first conquerors. And the said *bachiller* again told this witness
that he would do everything that he could for him, without neglecting to administer justice. And this witness left the city of Uchila to come to this city
[Mexico], and it came to his knowledge that the said *bachiller* had suspended
[the grant of] Indians to the said Alonso de Mata and of other Indians to
Juan de Sámano.

On July 29, Ortega presented the testimony to Mata and twice offered to go to Tuzantla to gather more information. On July 31, Ortega questioned another *principal* of Tuzantla named Cozoci. Again
Ortega twice offered to go to Tuzantla for further investigation, but
Mata declined the offers.

Ortega later recorded the following conversation with Mata concerning his willingness to make the difficult journey down to Tuzantla
to collect further evidence:

. . . the said Bachiller Juan de Ortega asked the said Mata whether he had
any defense against what the Indians were saying against him and said that
he would go to his town, even though it would be a great deal of work, to
receive the said defense so that he might defend himself. And the said Alonso
de Mata said that they were dogs and his enemies. . . . The said Bachiller
Juan de Ortega said to him two or three times, "See how it looks to you,
Mata, concerning what the said Indians say against you. If you have any defense in your town, I will go and record it, even though it means work." And
the said Alonso de Mata answered, "Sir, since the Indians say this here in
my presence, they will also all say it there. There is no need for the trip."
And so the said Bachiller Ortega did not go.

Since Mata was not interested in continuing the investigation, Ortega pronounced sentence on July 31. He forbade Mata to use the town in the future under pain of death, and he fined him 32 pesos of *oro de minas* (eight days' salary for Ortega). He reserved further judgment for the maltreatment of the Indians to the royal justice.

Estrada had already taken Mata's encomienda from him. In his letter of July 28 he wrote to Ortega:

In regard to Mata, the Indians came here whose noses had been cut off and who had been mistreated, and their testimony was taken; and I sent them to your grace so that you might make a more ample inquiry with the others there. Do it, sir, and send it to me so that it can be judged together with this other one. I have already suspended [the service of] his Indians.

We have no documentation to indicate whether any further criminal action was taken against Mata. He was still living in Mexico in 1552 when, as an old man, he appealed to the king for a larger pension as a conqueror because all his encomiendas had been taken away from him.[97]

The later history of Tuzantla as an encomienda is an example among many of how the encomienda system was used as a tool of political favoritism. Alonso de Estrada gave Tuzantla to Factor Gonzalo de Salazar, who had returned to favor, and to Ortega he gave Chilchota, which Ortega had taken from Juan de Sámano. At the same time Estrada took from Ortega an encomienda that he had held in Oaxaca. Salazar, however, used his influence to have Sámano reinstated in Chilchota. Since this left Ortega without an encomienda, Salazar agreed to give up Tuzantla so that it could be given to Ortega. On September 30, 1528, Estrada issued a cedula making Ortega encomendero of the town. According to testimony of Suero Asturiano, Ortega used the tribute of Tuzantla to maintain a gang of slaves for Cristóbal Martín Camacho and a few of his own slaves.

Mata later brought suit against Ortega, claiming that he had been unjustly deprived of the town. Although Mata was unsuccessful in proving his claim, the lawsuit preserved invaluable information about Ortega's inspection of Michoacán.

The Encomiendas After the Ortega Visitation

Many of the practices that Bachiller Ortega allowed during his visitation were limited or made illegal by a royal ordinance issued later that same year, on December 4, 1528, addressed to the Audiencia of Mexico, Bishop Garcés of Tlaxcala, Bishop-elect Zumárraga, and the Dominican and Franciscan friars. The king allowed the encomenderos to demand that the Indians carry tribute to the place where the encomendero lived, provided the distance did not exceed twenty leagues. They could carry the tribute to the mines only if the service was voluntary, if they were paid beforehand, and if the distance was no more than twenty leagues. The audiencia, however, was allowed to moderate the rule of twenty leagues if it found that the limitation was not in accord with right and reason.

Further, the Spaniards were forbidden to use Indians to carry to the mines the nontributary provisions that they raised on lands within the area of their encomiendas. They were forbidden to use Indian women from their encomiendas to make bread for the slaves in the mines or to serve in their houses. Nor were they to use Indian men of their encomiendas to dig ditches from rivers to the mines, to build any other structure related to the extraction of gold, to build houses for the slaves, or to carry the tools and trays when the owners moved their slaves from one mine to another. The slaves themselves were to do these tasks. The encomenderos had been using the Indians from their towns for such works so that all the working time of the slaves could be utilized in the gathering of precious metals.

In one respect the royal ordinance reinforced Ortega's command regarding the period of rest for the tributary Indians. The king ordained that during planting time the Indians' burdens should be lightened. He also commanded that Spanish vagabonds, who went about demanding food and other forms of support from the Indians, should be thrown out of the land. It seems probable that many of the Spaniards who were killed by the Tarascans before Ortega's visitation were men of this kind. The king further commanded that even those Spaniards who had legitimate reasons for traveling from town to town should pay for anything they received from the Indians. Among other things the king also ordered those who had slaves or Indians in encomiendas to provide them with priests to teach them the Catholic faith and to celebrate Mass for them on Sundays and the principal feasts.[98]

There seems to be little indication, however, that these ordinances had any positive effect on the way labor was actually utilized in the encomiendas and mines of Michoacán during this period. When the audiencia arrived in Mexico in late 1528, the officials simply moved into the existing system of utilizing the encomiendas and began using it for their own benefit. Cortés claimed that when they took his towns in Michoacán from him the towns were supporting six gangs of slaves in the mines, and he estimated the value of this support at 6,000 gold castellanos. Because his slaves did not receive the needed support after the towns were taken away from him, they were scattered and lost. He placed the value of the slave gangs at 1,000 castellanos each, probably a greatly inflated valuation in view of some of the prices given in the notarial records of the period.[99]

Guzmán and the *oidores* wasted no time putting their own slaves to work in the mines. We do not have much information on how they acquired their slaves. Gonzalo Gómez, however, said that when he was in prison and under sentence of torture for some undisclosed crime he was pressured into selling 100 slaves to Matienzo at a reduced price. The slaves were working in the mines at Zacatula. He also testified that within two months of assuming office Guzmán had two gangs of slaves gathering gold in the mines of Zacatula.[100] The president may have brought from Pánuco some of the Indians whom he had enslaved there, and it seems probable that he added more slaves later.

Although Cortés' large encomienda of Tzintzuntzan with its subject area surrounding Lake Pátzcuaro was nominally placed under direct tribute obligation to the crown when Godoy took it over in May, 1528, in actuality its tribute was used to support Guzmán's slaves in the mines of Zacatula. Godoy gave the following statement regarding his instructions from Guzmán:

. . . the said Nuño de Guzmán sent this witness, and with him Don Pedro, the brother of the Cazonci, so that the said Don Pedro would support for him certain gangs of slaves which the said president was sending to the mines of Zacatula to take out gold; and the said president told this witness that if the said Don Pedro did not give him all the provisions and support for the said slave gangs he should write him about it immediately, because he would not set free the said Cazonci, who remained under detention in his house.

Don Pedro did go back to Michoacán with Godoy and saw to it that supplies were sent to Guzmán's slaves.[101] Gonzalo Xuárez, the interpreter, declared that every twenty days they gave as tribute 400 cargas of corn, 40 cargas of beans, 40 cargas of chilies, 40 cargas of fish, 20 cargas of salt, 200 pairs of sandals, and 400 blankets.[102] Moreover, they were required to supply Indian women to grind corn and make bread for Guzmán's 300 slaves.[103] This was considerably more tribute than had been allowed to Cortés in Ortega's assessment. Every *thirty* days he had been allowed 600 cargas of corn, 45 cargas of beans, 25 cargas of chilies, and 20 cargas of fish.[104]

It seems that when the Cazonci returned to Michoacán in the summer of 1529 he had heard of the cedula that should have prevented the audiencia from taking Cortés' encomiendas away from him. We have seen that one of Guzmán's motives for commanding the Cazonci to return to Mexico in August was that "he should come here to inform me about who had told him that he did not have to serve the king but Fernando Cortés." Apparently the Cazonci had cut off the supplies to Guzmán's slaves, because later in the same letter Guzmán added: "And the Cazonci will pay for the slaves who because of him went away and died." Although Guzmán had commanded Godoy to start collecting supplies for his projected expedition to the northwest, he did not want him to neglect the mines: "And regarding the matter of the mines, I did not wish that you should turn your attention away from it but that you should send whatever gold there is, and that you should see to it that my slave gangs are put to work in that river that has been found."[105]

The officials of the royal treasury were not happy about the way in which Guzmán was taking the tribute of Tzintzuntzan for himself. Francisco López, who had been a servant and official of Contador Rodrigo de Albornoz, testified that Guzmán did this "against the will of the *contador* and even of the treasurer Alonso de Estrada."[106] Guzmán, however, was able to withstand the pressure until he left on his expedition to the northwest. Godoy attested that when Guzmán was on his way to the war Pedro de Ortiz came with a deputation from the *contador,* and because of this Guzmán commanded Godoy that in the future he should buy supplies for his slaves. Godoy said that he had sent Guzmán 1,000 pesos of gold dust that the slaves had gathered while they were being supported with the provisions from Tzintzuntzan.[107]

Gonzalo Gómez asserted that Guzmán was also obtaining supplies for his slaves from Tacanvora (Tacámbaro?) and Sinagua, towns he had assigned to Godoy, and that he was also getting corn and chilies from Xalxocotitlan, an estancia of Francisco Rodríguez.[108]

Diego Delgadillo paid 500 pesos for a gang of 100 slaves whom Gonzalo Mejía had working in the mines of Coyuca, with the understanding that Mejía, who was going to Spain, would let him support them from Mejía's town of Copulilcolulco, which was near the mines.[109] Delgadillo also had other slaves in the mines of Zacatula. Juan de Salcedo testified that Delgadillo maintained his slaves in Zacatula from Capula, a town that, as we have seen, he took from his cousin Luis de Berrio. He was also getting support from several towns in the province of Matalcingo (the Valley of Toluca) and from a town near the mines that Salcedo said he had taken from Alonso de Ávila.[110] In regard to the last town, however, Ávila said that what had happened was that he had 600 or 700 fanegas of corn in his estancia Áquila with no way of transporting it, and therefore he traded it to Delgadillo for an equal amount in Mexico.[111] Both Cortés and Francisco de Santa Cruz asserted that Delgadillo shared in the fruits of Tzintzuntzan and Tamazula for the support of his slaves.[112] From conversations with several of Delgadillo's intimates Francisco de Herrera estimated that Delgadillo had about 500 slaves in Michoacán.[113] Delgadillo had one of his servants, Juan Ruiz Martínez, appointed as justice and placed in charge of Tamazula so that he might better oversee the slaves.[114]

Oidor Juan Ortiz de Matienzo does not seem to have engaged in the exploitation of the Michoacán encomiendas to the same degree as his fellow judges did. Although Cortés accused him of sharing in the tributes of Tzintzuntzan and Tamazula to support two slave gangs in the mines, other witnesses indicated that Matienzo bought most of the supplies that his slaves needed. Juan de Salcedo said that Matienzo got a little bit of support also from Copúndaro.[115] Gonzalo Riobó de Sotomayor, encomendero of Araró, said that at times Matienzo's slaves were so badly provided for that he, because of affection and obligations that he had toward Matienzo from Española, provided supplies for them without any command or consent from the *oidor*. A certain Frías, Matienzo's overseer, was upset about this and wrote to Riobó that "he should not concern himself with that because if the *licenciado* knew about it he would be angry about it and that he should look after his own hacienda and take care of it and not concern himself with that of the said *licenciado*." Riobó, however, said that he continued to look after Matienzo's slaves.[116]

A rather dismal picture of the results of the first year of the audiencia's activities in Michoacán comes from a statement that Father Francisco Martínez, pastor of Zacatula, made in Mexico City on January 2, 1531. About fourteen months previously (about November 1529) he had left Concepción, a town in the province of Zacatula, to come to Mexico City, and he was very sick. He arrived at La Huacana, and from there he expected to spend three days' journey on the road to the city of Michoacán, passing through a region that had previously been populated with Indians both along the road and away from it. But on this occasion he did not find any sign of human habitation, neither house nor field nor anything else except trees and temple pyramids. He could not even find anyone to give him a drink of water, and he had to sleep in uninhabited areas all three nights.

When he arrived in Tzintzuntzan, he went to the house of a *principal* to rest and asked the reason for the depopulation of the region, which once had so many people. The *principal* told him that a large part of them had died of hunger and others had fled. (The latter reason would seem to be supported by the fact that they had apparently moved their houses also.) Because they had lived along the road to the Zacatula mines, they had been the objects of all manner of abuse. The *principal* told Father Martínez that the travelers had inflicted many mistreatments upon them, taking them to the mines and keeping them there for many days, forcing them to build houses and to work in the mines. Because the Spaniards had kept the men working in the mines and building houses and the women making bread for the slaves, they had not been able to plant their fields, and since they had nothing to eat but the plants, they could not survive.

Father Martínez said that along the road he had met with many Indians, men and women, one of the latter pregnant, carrying corn, beans, chilies, fish, pots, and other things. They told him that they were from Tzintzuntzan and were taking the provisions to the mines of Zacatula for the president (Guzmán) to feed his slaves. The priest estimated that the distance was forty-five leagues. It appears that almost every prohibition of the ordinances of 1528 was being openly violated.

Father Martínez went to lodge in the house of the Cazonci in Tzintzuntzan. There the interpreters came in to him, weeping, to tell him that Godoy had put Don Pedro Panza in prison because he had not supplied enough corn or enough bearers to carry the corn to the

mines. On another day the priest went to the house of Godoy to talk
to Don Pedro. He had to do this surreptitiously, posting spies to tell
him when Godoy was not there, because Godoy kept Don Pedro in
a secret prison where no one could see him. He found Don Pedro
with his feet locked in stocks. Don Pedro explained the reasons for
his imprisonment in the same terms as those the interpreters had
given.

Later Father Martínez spoke to Godoy and begged him for the love
of God to release Don Pedro because he was such an important nobleman. Godoy, however, said that he would not do so until Don Pedro
had fulfilled the total number of bearers and cargas of corn that Godoy
had commanded. Then the priest got angry at Godoy and told him that

he should keep in mind that now at the present he had many Christians
with him and that with their favor he had thrown him into prison, but that
when the president had gone he would be left alone and he could pay for
the imprisonment of the Indian, and that if the people of Michoacán have
killed some Christians, the cause is that they have been subjected to such
maltreatments.

From this statement it appears that a major reason why Godoy was
putting such pressures on Don Pedro to bring together bearers and
corn was that he was assembling them to send with Guzmán's expedition. The double imposition — to supply the mines and to provision a
major expedition — must have constituted a very severe burden on the
economy of Michoacán.

Father Martínez had no success in getting Godoy to release Don
Pedro, and when he left Tzintzuntzan to continue his journey to Mexico
City, the Tarascan nobleman was still in prison.[117]

The Estancia

In the economic picture of the first decade of colonial Michoacán the
estancia is an element about which we have only limited information.
But it does seem to have been a predecessor of the hacienda as an
independent economic unit operating within the jurisdictional area of
an encomienda.

We must be aware, however, that the term *estancia* was used with
several different meanings in the 1520s. We find frequent mention of

estancias of livestock that the encomenderos had in their towns. For example, Pedro, *principal* of Huaniqueo, said tha. "the said Marqués had . . . an estancia of pigs near the town of Naranja, and the Indians of Naranja served in the said estancia, and from there they moved it to Huaniqueo in a location that is called Xiripitio, and this witness helped to move the said estancia."[118] Nicolás de Palacios Rubios stated that "he had heard the said Antón Caicedo, manager for the Marqués, say . . . , regarding some estancias of pigs of the said Marqués which he had near the lake, that a stream next to the said estancias had risen and that many of the pigs had drowned."[119] In these cases the word *estancia* seems to indicate the herd of livestock, the place where they were kept, and the associated structures.

But sometimes the term *estancia* was used to indicate a small settlement that was subject to a major town, as when Cristóbal de Cáceres said that "the said Comanja had as its subjects Purecho and Axaxo and other estancias of these towns which he does not remember."[120] Pedro Cornejo also spoke of "Sarandagachoa and Cucharo and Guayameo and two other estancias whose names this witness does not remember."[121] More to the point here, however, is the way in which Gonzalo Gómez used the term when he spoke of Itacaro and Guayangareo as his estancias. Both intruded into areas claimed by other encomenderos. The Indians of the city of Michoacán accused him of having taken over part of their tribute area in his estancia of Itacaro, which Estrada had granted him in a cedula of 1528.[122]

The place where Gomez resided "as its lord"[123] was Guayangareo, an estancia that Cristóbal de Valderrama claimed as part of his encomienda of Tarímbaro. It was Valderrama who first presented accusations against Gómez before the Inquisition as one who engaged in Jewish practices.[124] And Gómez indicated a territorial basis for Valderrama's ill will in his defense before the tribunal of the Inquisition:

The said Martín de Aranda knew that the said Gonzalo Gómez has had and does have differences with Cristóbal de Valderrama over the estancia and lands which the said Gonzalo Gómez has in the province of Michoacán, and the said Martín de Aranda agreed on a wage with the said Valderrama to make trouble for Gómez, as he has done to the said Gonzalo Gómez concerning the said lands and estancia before the lord viceroy.[125]

Gómez spoke of the Indians of Guayangareo as though they were an encomienda: ". . . the said Gonzalo Gómez also asked and obtained from the said friars that they would baptize the Indians whom he had *en encomienda,* and he has been the cause that in his said town and in others in the province of Michoacán more than two thousand souls have been baptized."[126] He also treated them as though they were an encomienda. Speaking of Itacaro, he said:

> . . . it must have about forty-five Indians, and with these said Indians this witness guards his livestock and cows and mares and sheep, and they take care of certain plants and other enterprises that this witness has in his said estancia of Guayangareo where this witness has his residence, and it is three leagues from the said estancia of Itacaro; and also they give him a hen [turkey] every two days, and this is what he knows, under the oath that he made, and he signed it.[127]

It is obvious, therefore, that what Gómez meant by an estancia was a small-scale equivalent of an encomienda, from which he received a limited amount of tribute and services. Because it fell within the area of another encomienda and included the use of some lands in that area, it can be considered a forerunner of the hacienda. We do not know how many estancias of this kind there were; those of Gómez are the only ones about which we have any information.

The Conflict Between the Cazonci and the Encomenderos

We must not imagine that the Cazonci was despoiled of all of his income by the distribution of the towns as encomiendas. To do so would be to underestimate the astuteness of the native monarch. There is testimony in this regard by Juan Catao, *principal* of Paracho, a subject town of Turicato. Catao said that he had been present when Caravajal visited Turicato, and he saw that, regarding "Cartoque and its estancias, which are Enanenpacaro and Caquitaro and Guatanangueo and Yurepetaro, the Cazonci commanded that they should not say anything about them, and they served him until the Cazonci died, and since then they have served with the town of Turicato."[128] As the encomenderos or their overseers became better acquainted with their encomiendas, such tactics as this could not escape their notice.

There was also an administrative custom of the Tarascan kingdom that seriously conflicted with the encomenderos' ideas of their rights. In each town it was customary to plant fields for the needs of the state and religion, "for the wars and offerings for their gods." These were known as the "fields of the Cazonci," and there was a local overseer over each one as well as a general overseer in charge of all of them.[129] When Cortés told the Cazonci that he should cease taking tribute from the towns because Cortés was going to distribute them to the Spaniards, it was like telling him that he could no longer be king. The Cazonci, however, was not very scrupulous about observing the prohibition of Cortés, and he continued to receive tribute from towns other than those directly subject to Tzintzuntzan. The lords of the towns continued to regard the Cazonci as their lord and master.[130] At first all of this probably did not make much difference to the encomenderos, since they did not know their areas well enough to realize that tribute from their areas was still going to the Cazonci. But as the Spaniards came to have a better understanding of their holdings, they also came to resent the drain of tribute going to the native king. We have a statement by Andrés Núñez, for example, that "once this witness saw that the said Alonso de Mata took an Indian *principal* by the hair and threw him into a house because he was taking tributes to the Cazonci of Michoacán."[131]

Mata's encomienda, Tuzantla, was in the distant tropical country of the Río Balsas basin. Another encomendero of that region, Juan de Burgos, who had half of Cutzamala, said that in 1531 it had been verified that his Indians had continued to carry tribute to the Cazonci, even though they were forty-five leagues from Tzintzuntzan.[132] We can assume that the tribute service to the Cazonci was even greater from the closer, more populous upland towns.

The Indians were forced, however, to become more secretive about such activities. Martín Gómez reported that

many nights as he was going along the road he met many Indians loaded with corn which they were bringing from other towns, and this witness would ask them for whom they were carrying that, and they would say that it was for the said Cazonci and Pedro Panza, and they said that they were bringing it from the Spaniards' towns.[133]

During his visitation, Bachiller Ortega recognized this as a serious problem. On May 17, 1528, he warned Don Pedro under pain of death not to take tribute from the towns that were entrusted to Spaniards, and under the same penalty he warned the lords of the towns not to give tribute to the Cazonci. On June 12 he repeated the warning to Don Pedro and another group of lords.[134]

Another focus of conflict between the encomenderos and the Cazonci and the native nobility was the custom of the native lords to spend most of their time in the court of the Cazonci rather than in their towns. As the *Relación de Michoacán* puts it: "Likewise, most of the time the caciques of the province were with the Cazonci."[135] The Spaniards' view of this can be seen in a statement by Diego Rodríguez de Soria in May, 1531: ". . . and the said Cazonci and Pedro Panza hid the lords and caciques of the said towns that were entrusted to Spaniards, and they even put in overseers and said that they were lords of the said encomienda towns."[136]

The Spaniards found this custom a serious obstacle to the control of their encomiendas, and they resented it because the local caciques were not readily accessible to implement their wishes and commands. One of the major charges that Francisco de Villegas brought against the Cazonci at the beginning of his trial in 1530 was that he interfered with the proper operation of the encomiendas. The third and eighth questions of his interrogatory refer to the Cazonci's alleged interference:

3. Further, [let them be asked] whether they know that all of the *vecinos* who have these allotments cannot nor have they been able to make use of the said towns because the said Cazonci keeps from them the lords of the towns, and if there are any, they are his overseers who rob the towns for him and depopulate them so that they may not serve the Spaniards to whom they are allotted, and this is public and well known. . . .

8. Further, [let them be asked] whether they know, saw, or heard it said that, if some lords have been taken from some towns, the said Cazonci had them, and it has been in order to keep them in stocks and imprisoned and intimidated, especially from Bachiller Ortega, who took from him the lord of Puruándiro and the lord of Zanzan and the lord of Capula.[137]

The difficulty of such a situation, from the point of view of an encomendero or his overseer, can be judged from the answer of Cristóbal Romero to the eighth question: ". . . while this witness was in a town of Tiripetío, if anything had to be done or if he had to command the lords to have anything done, he would come to this city to tell the Cazonci that he should command it, because they were with him in this city."[138]

Both Juan Xuárez and Ortega had to deal with cases of native lords who were in Tzintzuntzan with the Cazonci rather than in their towns. Much of the friction seems to have arisen because the Spaniards did not understand that many of the Indians who appeared as lords of towns held their offices merely by appointment of the Cazonci. Gonzalo López testified that he once went to the Cazonci and Don Pedro to ask for the lord of Cuitzeo, his encomienda. The Cazonci told him that in Cuitzeo, as in other towns where no lord appeared, there were no lords except the overseers whom he placed there.[139]

In his own defense in his trial the Cazonci explained the absence of some specific native lords. He asserted that the lord of Puruándiro had fled upon the arrival of the encomendero Juan de Villaseñor and had come to Tzintzuntzan, where he had remained for a year until Ortega commanded him to return to his own town. The lord of Zanzan was a native of Tzintzuntzan, married to a woman of Zanzan, and he was in his native city when Ortega ordered that the lords be returned to their towns.[140]

In the early summer of 1529, Bernardino de Albornoz made a criminal complaint and took testimony against Don Pedro, whom he designated as "Indian lord of this province of Michoacán," and against the interpreters Gonzalo Xuárez and Francisco, who he said "now have command in this said city." The brief investigation was made between June 25 and 28, 1529, presumably before Antonio de Godoy. In the interrogatory the native lords were accused of depopulating towns belonging to Spanish encomenderos, of having fields planted within the boundaries of Spanish encomiendas and having them cultivated by Indians from the encomiendas, and, in general, of continuing to behave like lords and preventing the Indians from giving complete and undivided service to their Spanish masters.

Juan de Ripa, who was living in Tacámbaro, testified that he had met an Indian going to Tiripetío at Don Pedro's command to get blankets and corn and that in Cuitzeo the Indians had planted fields for the accused lords. Juan López Patiño, who was in Uruapan for Francisco Villegas, stated that the accused had planted fields in Uruapan and that he believed that they had used Indians from Uruapan for it. Also, one day when one *principal* of Uruapan had beaten another, the victim had complained to Don Pedro and Francisco as his lords.

The encomendero of Puruándiro, Juan de Villaseñor, said that the accused lords had depopulated two towns and two estancias subject to his town and that he had complained about it to Gonzalo Xuárez. He said that he had also seen that, by command of the Cazonci and Don Pedro, fields were planted in his encomienda and tended by his Indians and that the lords of Tzintzuntzan had collected part of the crop. The interpreters had also arrested one of his principales and imprisoned him in Tzintzuntzan for a while because he would not give them tribute.

Jaime Trías, encomendero of Zanzan, complained that Don Pedro had taken one of his *principales* with his people and sent him to a town belonging to Arriaga (the encomendero of Tlazazalca), among the Chichimecas, to plant fields. The people had been unwilling to come back and settle again in their own town. When the lords of Tzintzuntzan planted fields in the jurisdiction of Trías's town, he had harvested them for himself.

It is fairly evident, then, that even under the threat of death Don Pedro had not obeyed Ortega's prohibition against taking tribute from other encomiendas. In fact, Villaseñor testified that even when he had gone to complain to the *justicia mayor* Gonzalo Xuárez about the depopulating of his towns Don Pedro had refused to send the people back and had said that the penalty should be carried out against him.[141]

Thus the conflict between the new lords of the province and the former king was growing critical. The king's domain had been cut away from beneath him, but he was still considered responsible for the acts of his people.

•••

CHAPTER 11

The Death of the Cazonci

DURING the winter of 1529–30 all the forces, political, religious, and economic, that threatened the Cazonci reached a climax. The occasion was the expedition that Nuño de Guzmán organized to expand Spanish domination into the region north and northwest of Michoacán, a region that would be known in the colonial period as Nueva Galicia.

An eyewitness report of the manner in which Guzmán and the *oidores* reached the decision to undertake the expedition comes from testimony of Francisco López:

One day of the year 1529 (he does not remember what month), in the afternoon while the said president and *oidores* were going over accounts with the treasury officials of His Majesty, and Licentiate Delgadillo was going over their accounts with President Nuño de Guzmán, they began to talk about the province of Michoacán and about how the Teules Chichimecas who were doing harm to the Spaniards were there nearby, and that it would be good if President Nuño de Guzmán went to the said province to pacify it and bring it under the dominion of His Majesty; and then immediately the said Licentiate Delgadillo had Juan Sánchez bring paper and ink, and he composed a paragraph to be written down in the *libro de acuerdo* [register of decisions] concerning the aforesaid, and it was written into the *libro de acuerdo* in the presence of the accountant and treasurer. In that said paragraph it was agreed that the said Nuño de Guzmán would go to the said province. And this witness saw that it bothered the said treasurer and accountant that the said president should go on the said expedition because the said officials of His Majesty would have to loan some gold from the gold of His Majesty to the said president. And this witness saw that the accountant did not sign the said paragraph and agreement until many days later when the said licentiates sent for the *libro de acuerdo*, and this witness brought it to the said licentiates, and they asked him why the

211

accountant had not signed, and this witness said that he did not know; and so they made the said accountant sign against his will.[1]

The written resolution that incorporated the decision to make the expedition against the Teules Chichimecas bears the date May 15, 1529.[2]

The officials of the royal treasury had ample reason to be wary about giving approval for Guzmán's planned expedition. The president eventually borrowed a total of 10,000 pesos of common gold from the royal treasury (6,000 pesos on one occasion, 3,000 on a second, and 1,000 on a third) "so that the persons who would go with him to the war of the Teules Chichimecas would be assisted, because this would be good for the service of His Majesty, because otherwise the said war could not be waged and the Spaniards would not be assisted."[3]

Many Spaniards had no desire to go with Guzmán. He, however, used all of his authority as captain-general to draft men, horses, and equipment for his army, in spite of the opposition of Bishop-elect Zumárraga and the friars. Some Spaniards, such as Francisco Morcillo, claimed that the campaign was unnecessary. Morcillo said that he had visited the Chichimecas twice and that they had received him peacefully and fed him. Other Spaniards believed that the purpose of the expedition was to remove Cortés' supporters from the city before his return from Spain, as Zumárraga had asserted.[4] Many took refuge in the friaries of the city, while others fled from the city and stayed away until early in 1531, when the Second Audiencia arrived to relieve Guzmán and his companions of their duties. Guzmán was able to capture some of them and took them along as prisoners during the first part of his campaign. He also gave his constables permission to enter houses and confiscate horses, hardware, and arms. All of this caused great discontent in the city, but there was no legal recourse against it, since the judges of the audiencia sided with Guzmán.[5]

Guzmán also asserted authority over the encomiendas as a means of forcing men to accompany him. For instance, in Tenochtitlan on September 9, 1529, he issued an order for Pedro de Bazán, in the mines of Michoacán, threatening him with the suspension of his right to collect tribute from his Indians and a fine of 300 pesos of *oro de minas* if he did not come with his horses and arms to accompany Guzmán to the war. The notary Lope de Brizuela, who served as the executor of the order, caught up with Bazán on September 23, but the encomendero, who already had his horse saddled and bridled, rode away without waiting to listen. Brizuela caught up with Bazán and informed him of the order before witnesses as they were riding along. On September 25 the notary again read the order in the mines where Bazán had his usual residence, but the encomendero was not to be had. Bazán went to Tenochtitlan soon afterward and offered his services to Guzmán,[6] but the audiencia took away his half of Pungarabato, and he was not able to get it back until after the arrival of the Second Audiencia.[7]

Guzmán also demanded that the Indians of the various pacified provinces of the Valley of Mexico and surrounding regions should support him with men and supplies. As usual, we do not have much precise information concerning the number of Indian allies. Indian witnesses from Huejotzingo, east of Mexico City, disagreed in 1531 about the number of warriors from their city who accompanied Guzmán, one saying 600 and the other 1,000, while the painting which accompanied their testimony indicates 320. Huejotzingo also contributed a gold banner with an image of the Virgin and Child, as well as footwear, clothing, arms, and other supplies for their men.[8]

The same pattern was probably followed in the other major towns, and when the army was assembled and ready to depart, it was a major expedition. Guzmán described the Spanish contingent to the crown in considerable detail, without acknowledging the far larger force of native warriors:

I got together about four hundred Spanish foot soldiers and cavalry to go to discover and conquer that land of the South Sea, . . . and they were well outfitted with arms and a change of horses, besides the thirty that I took at my own expense to assist those who might need them or whose horses might die; and I did this, going to the war with seventy crossbows and fifty muskets and twelve small bronze cannons with their stands and many lances and a large supply of bolts [for the crossbows] and arrowheads and bowstrings and powder, fiber sandals and leather armor for the foot soldiers and Indians, and cloth for bartering and other things for gifts and two bellows and much iron and hardware and tools and nails in order to build a brigantine if necessary, and wine, vinegar, oil and flour, and a store of medicines, and three thousand head of my pigs and sheep besides another six or seven thousand head that went with the army and besides other extensive provisions of bacon, cheese, conserves, and things necessary for the sick.[9]

There are a number of other estimates of the size of the expedition. For instance, Cristóbal de Barrios, said that there were 150 cavalrymen, 200 foot soldiers, and 10,000 to 12,000 Indian allies.[10]

At the same time preparations were also being made in Michoacán, which was to serve as an advance base for provisions and supplies for the army. We have seen that, when Don Pedro accompanied the Cazonci to Mexico, Guzmán sent him back to Michoacán with orders to have the artisans make "many [quilted] cotton vests and many arrows and shields and twenty bows with the copper arrowheads for them, and many fiber sandals and other footgear."[11] He also imposed on the towns a heavy levy of food—corn, beans, and chilies—and he sent officials to collect it.[12]

This was undoubtedly what Guzmán was referring to when he wrote to Antonio de Godoy in his letter of August 20, 1529:

And regarding the levy of corn, I think that it will not be possible to get it, since this is the end of the year; neither do I think that it can be had in such great quantities. Levy as much as possible of it on the new crop and a thousand or two thousand fanegas of beans and the corresponding chili and salt; and let this be levied by the lords of the towns so that at the proper time they may come to where you command them.[13]

Because the towns along the Río Balsas were some distance from the route of his march, Guzmán worked out a trade. He either took or was given provisions belonging to the accountant Albornoz in the city of Michoacán, and he allowed Ortiz, a servant of Albornoz, to replace them with levies on the towns of Coyuca, Ajuchitlan, Pungarabato, Cutzamala, Cutzio, and Guyameo.[14]

In December, 1529, Guzmán finally had his grand force assembled and ready to leave Mexico.[15] They departed shortly before Christmas. The author of the "Fourth Anonymous Relation" wrote that they left on December 20. (He erroneously gave the year as 1530.)[16] García del Pilar was probably more accurate when he said that they left three days before Christmas, since on December 21 Guzmán's chamberlain Pedro de Guzmán, acting in Don Nuño's name, registered a great number of gold jewels of Indian workmanship weighing 467 pesos and silver worked by a Castilian silversmith weighing 116 marks, 4 ounces, 4 reales.[17] This probably indicates that the final preparations for the departure were being made at that time. (For a chronological table of these last weeks of the Cazonci's life, see appendix C.)

Leaving Mexico probably on December 22, the army took three days to reach a town belonging to Pedro de Muñoz, *maestro* de Roa, probably Jiquipilco. Another journey of two days brought them to Ixtlahuaca.[18] We know that they were in that town on December 27, 1529, because Guzmán issued a set of instructions for his *alcalde mayor* there on that date.[19] Juan de la Torre, encomendero of Ixtlahuaca, was unhappy about their visit. He later complained that they took a great amount of corn from him and that they burned the wheat in his granaries and the flax that he had collected.[20] From Ixtlahuaca their route into Michoacán probably went by way of Tajimaroa. We do not know how long it took them to reach Tzintzuntzan, though we can make an estimate from information given by García del Pilar. He stated that the Cazonci was free for about three days after the arrival of the army in Tzintzuntzan, he was imprisoned for about fifteen days before being threatened with torture, and he was held for another seven days before the army moved on, about twenty-five days in all.[21] The army probably left Tzintzuntzan on January 29, which would place their arrival around January 4.

With the arrival of Guzmán's host in Tzintzuntzan, we face a number of historical questions about which there is abundant but frequently contradictory testimony. The first such question is whether or not the Cazonci accompanied Guzmán from Mexico. As we noted in the discussion of the Cazonci's last imprisonment in Mexico City, Guzmán allowed him his liberty after a certain amount of treasure had been brought but told him to wait in the city and return to Michoacán with the expedition.[22] Pilar's "Relation" gives the impression that the Cazonci was in Michoacán when Guzmán arrived there,[23] but Pilar's "Dicho," Guzmán's *Memoria*, and the *Relación de Michoacán* record that the Cazonci returned to Michoacán with the army.[24] The "Fourth Anonymous Relation" tells us that when the expedition departed from Mexico City the Cazonci accompanied it in conditional liberty, but under watch and with a guard.[25] The contradiction is more apparent than real. The solution is found in a statement by Juan de Burgos: ". . . this witness saw that at the time when the said Nuño de Guzmán was ready to depart, the Cazonci was in this city [Mexico], and when he was ready to go, he sent him ahead with certain Spaniards in the status of a prisoner, and they found him in the said city [Michoacán] at the time when they arrived in it."[26] The Cazonci, therefore, went on ahead of the main expedition under guard, but his departure from

Mexico City preceded that of the main force by such a few days that many witnesses simply did not make any distinction. Having arrived in Tzintzuntzan, he may have been allowed to go to his own dwellings, although the *Relación de Michoacán* states that Guzmán did not permit him to do so.[27] Pilar and the "Fourth Anonymous Relation" both say that Guzmán had the Cazonci summoned shortly after the army had established itself in Tzintzuntzan, suggesting that he was not required to stay with Guzmán.

The *Relación de Michoacán* records a conversation between Guzmán and the Cazonci shortly after the Spaniard's arrival in Tzintzuntzan. It is difficult to interpret the conversation because the manuscript lacks punctuation to indicate which sentences are interrogatory and which are declarative. The following interpretation seems the most likely one.

According to the *Relación*, Guzmán said to the Cazonci, "Now you have come to your house. Where do you wish to be? Do you wish that we should be together in my dwelling or do you wish to go to your house?"

Naturally the Cazonci answered, "I would like very much to go to my house for a while and see my children."

Guzmán's next statement indicates that he may have been simply toying with the Cazonci in his first question: "Why do you need to go? Have you not come to your land, and are not these your houses where you are now? Have someone summon your wife and children here. No Spaniard will enter your dwelling. And here they will make up a bed for you and you will be there."

By now the Cazonci realized that it would not be possible for him to oppose Guzmán's will: "So let it be. How can I go against your words? Let it be as you wish. What you say is good."

After this the Cazonci seems to have resigned himself to the fact that he would not come out of the ordeal alive. Guzmán had already threatened him with death in Mexico, and he had accepted the threat. Now he spoke to his servants, giving them something of a last testament:

Go and tell the elders and my wives that they will not see me any more. Tell the elders to console my wives. Tell them that I do not feel well about what I have done, that I think that I must die, and that they should look after my children and not leave them unprotected. How can they see me here? Tell them that they should ready themselves, and give food to the Spaniards, so that the Spaniards will not blame me if anything is lacking. The *principales* are here who have charge of the people for whatever may be necessary.[28]

The next day the Tarascans brought Guzmán the armor and armaments that they had made at his command for the campaign. They delivered four hundred cotton vests (thick, quilted cotton armor for the upper body) and the other articles that he had asked for. Guzmán, however, became very angry, saying that the amount was far too small, and he accused them of sending the armaments to a place called Cuinao, where he suspected them of setting up an ambush. He was so angry that he took out his sword and hit Don Pedro with the broad side of it several times. Then he commanded that both the Cazonci and Don Pedro be imprisoned.[29]

Antonio de Godoy gives another account of a confrontation between Don Pedro and Guzmán that occurred soon after the arrival of the expedition. He said that about three days after the president's arrival in Michoacán he summoned Godoy and told him that he wanted to send the king as much gold and silver as possible. Godoy was to go with Pilar to try to convince the Cazonci and Don Pedro that they should give him the precious metal to send to Spain in the ships that were ready to leave. Don Pedro was able to gather four hundred silver articles and some gold articles but said that he could not get any more. Godoy, Pilar, and Juan Pascual accompanied him to Guzmán, and Don Pedro told the president that "he could not get any more together unless they gave him more time to collect it and have it brought, because that was not earth and water that they should get it together so quickly." Angered at this, Guzmán "attacked the said Don Pedro and hit him several times, saying to him that, of the twenty thousand pieces that he had promised him for sending to His Majesty, he was giving no more than four hundred."[30] Probably Guzmán had counted on this precious metal as a means of repaying the gold that he had borrowed from the royal treasury, although he may truly have planned to send it directly to the king in the hope of regaining the favor that seemed to be slipping from his grasp.

This brings us to another question regarding Guzmán's passage through Michoacán: How much treasure was he able to extract from the Tarascans at this time? Pilar spoke of having seen considerable amounts of gold and silver taken to Guzmán, but he hesitated to estimate its value.[31] Guzmán, on the other hand, flatly denied having received any treasure from the Indians, and he accused Pilar of having taken it if any was brought. In 1532 Guzmán took testimony from witnesses, trying to prove that he had not received anything. His witnesses were at that time still accompanying his army in New Galicia and were obviously under pressure to give answers that would support his interests.[32] We see evidence of this in two different depositions given by Juan Pascual, who served Guzmán as Tarascan interpreter. In 1532 he testified that the Cazonci had not given Guzmán any gold or silver and that "this witness as interpreter spoke to him everything that he [Guzman] asked him. Therefore, this witness believes that if the said Cazonci had given any gold or silver to the said lord governor, this witness would have known it, because the lord governor did not speak to him with any other interpreter except this witness."[33] Later, however, when Juan Pascual was free of Guzmán's control and testified in the judicial review of Guzmán's tenure as governor of New Galicia, he told quite a different story:

. . . through the tongue of this witness, who was interpreter of the said Indians, the said Nuño de Guzmán asked them for a great amount of gold and silver, and he saw that the said Indians gave him once in the said city a quantity of gold and silver, and another time at the ford of the River of Our Lady [Río Lerma] they gave him more gold and silver, and another time more gold and silver in a town called Cuyna, and all of it might be worth as much as five thousand pesos of gold of the Indians, because this witness saw it given to him and all of it passed through his hand because he was translator of the said Indians.[34]

The evidence is entirely against Guzmán. The statements of all the Indians who were not in his power indicate that he was given treasure in considerable amounts. Of special interest is the testimony of Sebastián, Don Carlos, and Tiripiti, *principales* of Tzintzuntzan. Testifying on June 11, 1531, they agreed on the following list of items that were given to Guzmán while he held the Cazonci prisoner in Tzintzuntzan: 100 silver plates, 100 silver shields, 100 silver crests (*penachos*), 60 silver bracelets, 40 silver saltcellars, 5 gold saltcellars, and 5 gold bracelets.[35] On February 14, 1531, Sebastián had given a different description of the treasure, but it totaled about the same amount: 100 shields, 100 crests, 160 plates, and 40 bracelets, all of silver, and 3 plates and 3 bracelets of gold. Sebastián said that Pilar, Godoy, and Juan Pascual took the treasure from Don Pedro's house to Guzmán late one night when the Spaniards were already gathered to go on toward Jalisco.[36] Both of his statements agree with Godoy's estimate that Don Pedro gave Guzmán 400 pieces of silver and a few pieces of gold. Godoy also said that the next day Guzmán ordered him to find two small chests and that Álvaro de Ribera told him that they were for carrying some gold and silver to Mexico City. The following day Ribera left, taking the gold and silver and some letters for Licenciado Delgadillo.[37]

While Guzmán was in Tzintzuntzan, he also paid a large part of a debt that he owed to Alonso de Ávila. The latter said that Guzmán, who owed him a little less than 1,200 pesos, paid him about 1,050 pesos in silver of Michoacán and some gold bracelets.[38]

There is an indication that Pilar was still taking his *mordida* at this time. On January 28, 1530, in the smelting house of Mexico City there was registered for him a shipment of 8-carat gold that amounted to 169 pesos.[39] Gold of such low quality generally came from native ornamental articles. Spaniards often complained of the amount of copper in the gold articles from Michoacán.

Later, when Guzmán was taking action against the Cazonci at the Río Lerma, there was a common suspicion in the camp that he was again trying to extract treasure from the Indian king. Yet although a number of sources speak of this rumor, no Spaniard except Pascual claimed to have actually seen the gold and silver.[40] The *Relación de Michoacán* records that Indian bearers brought the Cazonci 400 gold half moons and shields and 80 gold pincers, but he gave Guzmán only 200 of the precious items at this time and sent the rest of them back. But none of the other Indian witnesses, even those who had been subjected to torture by Guzmán, spoke of any shipments of precious metals to Guzmán between the time of his departure from Tzintzuntzan and the execution of the Cazonci.[41] As we have seen, Juan Pascual spoke of gold and silver being given to Guzmán at the ford of the river.

There is definite evidence that Guzmán received a large shipment of treasure after he had the Cazonci put to death. In 1531 the Indian Alonso de Ávalos, in his testimony for Cortés, asserted that, after the execution of the Cazonci, Guzmán had threatened to burn both Ávalos and Don Pedro within five days unless they told him about the Cazonci's treasure.[42] The "Fourth Anonymous Relation" states that when the army arrived at Cuinao certain messengers of Don Pedro and Don Alonso arrived in camp, and it was rumored that they brought more gold and silver this time than they had delivered at any other time.[43] Juan Pascual supported this in the statement quoted above. Penata Coriste, an Indian servant of the Cazonci, witnessed the shipments of treasure that were taken to Guzmán at this time. In 1531 he testified that after the burning of the Cazonci he chanced to be in the dead king's house one day when messengers came from Don Pedro. They told Coryme, the guard of the Cazonci's treasure, that he should take a large amount of the treasure to the river, where Don Pedro was held prisoner by Guzmán. The shipment consisted of 1 carga of gold, 4 cargas of silver, 100 gold ingots, 800 silver ingots of the size that was to be sent to Mexico, 200 gold ingots of the same size, 100 silver crests, 125 silver shields, 100 silver bracelets, 100 silver plates, 5 gold pincers, 5 silver pincers, 40 gold lip plugs, 2 chests of precious stones, and some ear plugs of emeralds enchased in gold. Also twenty-five women of the Cazonci and of the greater *principales* were sent to Guzmán. Penata Coriste stated that there were no other witnesses except those who were directly involved and that none of them had yet returned to Tzintzuntzan at the time of his deposition.[44] Fray Martín de Jesús, however, speaking in the same year (1531), corroborated this testimony. He reported that the women of the Cazonci had told him that all the Cazonci's precious articles and twenty-five of his women had been taken to Guzmán because he demanded them.[45]

It must have been part or all of this treasure that Guzmán's messenger Álvaro de Ribera later brought to Mexico to Licenciado Delgadillo. On February 17, 1532, he testified that he had transported from Guzmán to Delgadillo an amount of gold and silver that he estimated at about 300 marks of silver and 4,000 or 5,000 pesos of gold. It would appear that he made this trip in July 1530. Ribera stated that Guzmán gave him the gold and silver in Omitlán and that along with the treasure he took some idols and the skins of some Christians to Mexico City.[46] As we shall see, these last items were physical evidence in Guzmán's case against the Cazonci, and they were undoubtedly sent to Mexico City with the transcript of his action against the Cazonci. The copy of the trial record was made in Omitlán on July 6, 1530.[47] Guzmán also wrote to the king from that town on July 8, 1530,[48] and Ribera probably took the treasure, the documents, and the items of evidence to Mexico City soon after the latter date. On August 16, 1530, in the smelting house of Mexico City, Pedro Regidor registered for Nuño de Guzmán 1,949 pesos, 4 tomines of 11-carat gold; 1,832 pesos of 10-carat gold; 1,204 pesos of 9-carat gold; and 256 pesos of 8-carat gold. On August 31, Delgadillo, acting in Guzmán's name, paid the royal fifth on 349 marks of silver in ingots, shields, miters, and small plates.[49] According to various witnesses, Delgadillo had kept the silver articles in a strongbox in his house and had taken the royal fifth from them there rather than in the smelting house, because he said that if he let anyone take them across the open plaza those to whom the president owed debts would demand the silver.[50]

Having gone ahead of our story to discuss the question of the treasure that was given to Guzmán, we must now consider the involved circumstances surrounding the trial and death of the Cazonci.

All the sources agree that Guzmán imprisoned the Cazonci soon after the army reached Michoacán but disagree about his reason for the action. Guzmán himself stated that he imprisoned the Cazonci because of charges that he interfered with the encomiendas, charges that were brought against him by some of the encomenderos themselves.[51] This statement agrees with the first section of the trial record of 1530. On the other hand, the "Fourth Anonymous Relation," Pilar's "Relation," and the *Relación de Michoacán* assert that he was imprisoned because he did not deliver enough supplies for the army.[52]

The imprisonment occurred three or four days after the army arrived in Tzintzuntzan.[53] The place of the Cazonci's imprisonment was a small room (*recámara* or *retrete*) behind Guzmán's chamber, with a door opening into Godoy's apartment.[54] There, we are told, Guzmán instructed Godoy, Pilar, and Juan Pascual to try to get more treasure from the Tarascan king. Pascual, the Spaniard who knew how to speak Tarascan best, was stationed in Godoy's apartment at the door of the room where the Cazonci was imprisoned.[55] Pilar stated that he himself went in frequently to talk to the Cazonci and to encourage him to give more treasure to Guzmán. The president himself also sometimes went in to talk to the Cazonci, using Pascual as his interpreter.[56]

After continuing in this way for several days (Pilar says that it was about fifteen days), Guzmán decided to resort to more drastic action. He commanded the three Spaniards to take the Cazonci into Godoy's living quarters and torture him,[57] allowing them the option of burning his feet. Pilar said that Godoy put him on guard at the door with a cocked crossbow because there were so many Indians around who might kill them.[58] The interrogation, according to the *Relación de Michoacán*, centered on two points: whether the Tarascans had made an alliance with the Indians of Cuinao and whether they had more gold and silver to give Guzmán. The *Relación* indicates that the torture was first directed against a *naguatlato* named Juan de Ortega, "and they tortured him in his private parts with a green stick."[59]

Godoy had begun to "tie up the said Cazonci, he being naked to the skin, and to have fire brought," when suddenly two Franciscans appeared on the scene, carrying a crucifix covered with a cloth of mourning. One was Fray Martín de Jesús, to whom some boys had run with the report as soon as the torture started.[60] Pilar fled as soon as the friars appeared and left Godoy to argue with them.[61] When Fray Martín demanded to know why they were treating the Indian leaders in this way, they told him that the Indians were unwilling to show them the road. The father then asked the Indians, "Well, do you know the road?" They answered: "We do not know it. We must say that we do not know it." Fray Martín then scolded the Spaniards for what they had done, and the friars returned to their friary.

The Spaniards then had the Indians carried to Guzmán, and he became very angry: "Scoundrels! Who told the Father? Should I give up the idea of taking you along to the war just because the Father goes along after you?"[62]

Pilar said that he went to see the Cazonci the next morning and that "the said Cazonci wept with this witness, saying that he had not done ill to any Christian, and why were they treating him so badly."[63] This incident occurred on about January 22; Pilar said that it happened about seven days before the army departed from Michoacán.[64]

Soon afterward Guzmán initiated the trial of the Cazonci. Until recent years it has generally been believed that Guzmán did not hold a formal trial of which an official transcript was preserved. The basis for this belief was a letter from the queen of Spain to Guzmán, written on April 20, 1533, and preserved in the collection of decrees compiled by Vasco de Puga. In this letter the queen noted that in a previous letter, dated January 25, 1531, she had commanded Guzmán to send to the Council of the Indies a notarized copy of the trial of the Cazonci and a complete list of the Cazonci's goods that Guzmán had taken. In the second letter she reiterated the command in case it had not been carried out.[65] Because of the repetition of the command and the fact that the trial record was not found, it was assumed that no such record was made or that it was not considered adequate to send to Spain. This line of reasoning goes back as far as Father Antonio Tello, who wrote his chronicle in the mid-seventeenth century.[66] But the story was changed when France V. Scholes found the copy in the Archivo General de Indias, Seville, and he and Eleanor B. Adams published it in 1952. It is evident from that edition that a copy of the trial record was made on July 6, 1530. Guzmán probably sent it to Mexico City immediately, long before the queen wrote her first letter to him. In Mexico City another copy was made on January 25, 1532, but apparently there was some delay in sending the copy to Spain, because it was not presented to the Council of the Indies in Toledo until February 23, 1534.[67]

The text of the trial record consists of three separate sections, all of which have been mentioned previously. First there is the record of a suit prosecuted against the Cazonci by Francisco de Villegas between January 26 and January 28, 1530. Within this there is included, as a document of evidence, the record of an investigation by Bernaldino de Albornoz against Don Pedro and the Indian interpreters Gonzalo Xuárez and Francisco, made between June 25 and June 28, 1529. The third section is the record of the trial, condemnation, and execution of the Cazonci by Guzmán at El Paso del Río de Nuestra Señora de la Purificación. The trial was carried out between February 5 and February 14, 1530. The action by Villegas and that by Guzmán actually form parts of a single case against the Cazonci.

The record appears to be authentic. If Guzmán and his henchmen had wanted to prepare a fake trial document, they would surely have made the evidence against the Cazonci in the first part more telling, and the defense for the Cazonci would surely have been somewhat more complete. The record also agrees closely with what we know from other sources, except for certain statements by Pilar and the "Fourth Anonymous Relation."[68] For example, in opposition to Pilar, the trial record contains nothing about demands by Guzmán for the Cazonci's treasure or women, but we would not expect him to let such things enter the permanent record. The only possible evidence of such questioning is found in an unelicited statement by the Cazonci under torture: ". . . and that his [or their] women are in Michoacán," but this statement would seem rather to refer to the wives of the war captains who were supposedly in Cuinao and who are mentioned immediately before and afterward.[69] It seems, therefore, that we can put our confidence in the trial record as an authentic document.

Francisco de Villegas, encomendero of Uruapan, opened the case in Tzintzuntzan on January 26, 1530, by presenting a judicial complaint against "the Cazonci, called Don Francisco," His principal complaint was that the Cazonci had interfered with the proper functioning of the encomiendas by keeping the lords of the towns with him and that he had previously prevented justice from being done to himself by using his "copious amount of gold and silver." Villegas mentioned sodomy and the killing of Spaniards as crimes for which the Cazonci had not been punished.

Guzmán accepted the accusation, had Juan Pascual sworn in as interpreter, and offered the Cazonci a choice of Juan de la Peña or Francisco de Godoy as his defense attorney. The Cazonci chose Juan de la Peña.[70]

La Peña had been close to the anti-Cortés faction in Mexico for many years. In late 1525 he had been close to Salazar and Chirinos. As a servant of Salazar he had delivered to Estrada the treasure that the Cazonci had brought as service to the king in November, 1525. He had also countersigned a grant of encomienda by Chirinos and Salazar to Gonzalo de Ocampo on October 17, 1525.[71]After Cortés' departure for Spain in March, 1528, La Peña's star rose once more. On August 14, 1528, the city council of Mexico City awarded him two orchards, and in October of the same year he was attorney for the city council.[72] On June 16, 1529, he was accepted as one of the notaries of the city by virtue of a royal decree.[73] In September and October 1529, he presented before the audiencia briefs for Salazar and Chirinos against Cortés' interests.[74] He also served as prosecutor for the First Audiencia.[75] From such a defense attorney the Cazonci could hope for very little, and he got very little.

After La Peña had accepted the office of defense attorney and had sworn to carry it out faithfully, Villegas presented an interrogatory of nine questions for his witnesses against the Cazonci. The accusations contained in the interrogatory can be reduced to five: that the encomenderos could not make use of their Indians because the Cazonci kept the lords of the towns with him under restraint and put in their place his own overseers who robbed and depopulated the towns; that in all of the towns of the province there were silver mines and the Indians carried on trade in silver from them but that the Cazonci prevented the Indians from making the mines known to their Spanish masters, collecting the silver for himself to use in his defense; that a great number of Spaniards had been killed in the province, mainly at the command of the Cazonci, and that many of the valuables of the dead

Spaniards had been found in the possession of the Cazonci; that Pedro Sánchez Farfán had taken legal action against the Cazonci for sodomy and had found ample evidence; that Bachiller Juan de Ortega had made an inquiry concerning the Spaniards whom the Cazonci had commanded to be killed and had found enough information to conclude that the Cazonci deserved death, but that he had been commanded not to execute the penalty.

As witnesses for the preliminary inquiry Villegas presented Gonzalo López, encomendero of Cuitzeo; Juan López Patiño; and Juan de Sámano, encomendero of Chilchota. After they had given their testimony, Guzmán issued an order for Juan de Burgos, constable major of the army, or his deputies, to arrest the Cazonci. About an hour later Burgos returned and said that he had the Cazonci imprisoned.[76] Burgos later gave the following description of his manner of fulfilling Guzmán's order: ". . . at the time when he went to arrest him he was already imprisoned in a room of the president with stocks and a chain, and this witness called certain persons to witness how he was imprisoned and how he left him there in the lodging of the said Nuño de Guzmán in a room of that lodging."[77]

The next day, January 27, Guzmán went to the room where the Cazonci was imprisoned and interrogated him through the interpreter Juan Pascual. The Cazonci identified himself as "Don Francisco, and in the Tarascan language Cazonci," and acknowledged that he was a Christian. When asked whether he was lord of the province, he answered that "he used to be lord of it, but that now he is like a common laborer." He had served the Spaniards for nine years, and he knew that the province had been divided up for service to the Spaniards since Caravajal had come to visit it.

Then Guzmán began to get to the heart of the accusations, asking first about the lords of the towns whom the Cazonci was accused of keeping from their towns. The Cazonci explained one by one the cases in which specific accusations had been made, as mentioned above.

Asked if there were gold and silver mines in the province, he said no, that what had been given to Olid and Cortés had been in the possession of his parents and ancestors for a long time. Regarding the silver that had come from mines over toward the towns of Ávalos, he said that the Christians had taken it and that it had disappeared, and he denied that he had taken gold and silver from towns belonging to Spaniards.

Guzmán then questioned him about the killings of Spaniards in the province, and the Cazonci denied complicity in any of them. When Guzmán asked whether the death of a miner in Uruapan had not been done at his command, the Cazonci asked "why should he kill any Christian; if he had wanted to kill them he would have done so before, as soon as the land was conquered, at the time when they came to this province." The Cazonci also asserted that the killings had occurred while he was in Mexico.[78]

After concluding the examination of the Cazonci, Guzmán told Villegas that he should continue the presentation of witnesses against him the next day. Juan de la Peña presented a weak defense statement that did not address itself to any of the real issues of the case. Then Guzmán issued a decree to the effect that both sides should present their witnesses before noon the next day. La Peña asked for a longer term, but Guzmán refused, saying, ". . . thus it is fitting for the service of His Majesty that justice be done summarily."[79]

On Friday, January 28, Villegas presented eight more witnesses to answer the questions of his interrogatory. They were Pedro Hernández, servant of Gonzalo López; Juan de Ojeda; Juan Fernández Ijar; Francisco de los Ríos; Miguel de Mesa: Pedro Muñoz, maestro de Roa; Cristóbal Romero; and, finally, Don Pedro, the adopted brother of the Cazonci. None of the Spaniards held an encomienda in Michoacán.[80]

The testimony of the witnesses shows clearly that the most important of the charges were those of interfering with the encomiendas and of killing Spaniards. Regarding the others, only one Spaniard knew of the Sánchez Farfán inquiry regarding sodomy, and there was no evidence of mines of precious metals in most of the towns, since central Michoacán was not a silver-producing area. As we have seen, the conflict over the interference with the encomiendas had been building over a long period, and it went back to basic questions of jurisdiction that were left unclear at the time of their distribution. On this matter there was probably sufficient evidence presented against the Cazonci, though it came from interested witnesses, the Spaniards of the area.

The more serious charge was that the Cazonci had commanded his people to kill Spaniards. The testimony given in this regard was primarily circumstantial. The usual line of reasoning ran something like this: The Cazonci was the absolute lord of Michoacán; therefore, he had complete control over what happened in the area; therefore, the deaths of the Spaniards could not have occurred without his having commanded them.

It is difficult to calculate exactly the number of Spaniards whose deaths are mentioned in the course of the trial because of the irregularity of the spelling of place-names and the difficulty of detecting duplications. The total, however, seems to fall somewhere between thirty-six and forty-seven. But one gets the strong impression that at least the great majority of these killings had occurred before the visitation of Bachiller Ortega and had been judged at that time.

The truly surprising element in this part of the trial is the testimony of Don Pedro. It was also the most damaging for the Cazonci. He supported fully the two basic accusations, that the Cazonci had continued to take service from the towns that had been granted to the Spaniards and that he had commanded the killing of Spaniards. Don Pedro mentioned specifically the killing of two Spaniards in Uruapan two and a half years previously and two others in Tacámbaro four years previously, and he said that he had heard the lords of those towns say that the Cazonci had commanded the killings.

To support his case, Villegas submitted the investigation regarding interference with the encomiendas that Bernaldino de Albornoz had made a few months previously, in June 1529.[81]

For the defense of the Cazonci, Juan de la Peña composed a superficial list of four questions about the Cazonci's character, which were presented to three witnesses, none of whom had been in Michoacán very long. They disclaimed knowing even the most fundamental facts about the Cazonci. One of them, Alonso de Arenas, even harmed the cause by saying that he had heard that the Cazonci was a bad man who had killed many Spaniards. No Tarascan witnesses were called.[82]

With this testimony the first part of the trial was brought to a close. Villegas said that he could not accompany Guzmán on the road and withdrew from the case, leaving it up to Guzmán to proceed with it in his official capacity.[83]

The next day, January 29, Guzmán once more mustered his expedition and started the march northward toward the unconquered regions. To his previous force there was now added a large number of Tarascan warriors and bearers. The *Relación de Michoacán* says that Guzmán commanded the Cazonci to assemble 8,000 men, with a threat: "Send through all of the towns. If you do not bring as many as I say, you will pay for it."

The Cazonci answered, "Sir, you send through the towns, since they belong to you."

This response forced Guzmán to admit, no doubt with considerable displeasure, that he still needed the Cazonci: "You alone must do it. What is this? Are you not the lord?"

The Cazonci then sent for the men.[84]

The *Relación* indicates the the 8,000 men did assemble but that when the Spaniards began distributing them among themselves, without any account or order, many of them fled.[85] The Spaniards then used chains to make sure that no more of them ran away. Pilar, in his relation, indicates that some of them were put in chains, but in his "Dicho" he says that there were 4,000 or 5,000 men and that "they went along with chains and collars around their necks" and that he did not see any who were not chained.[86] It seems doubtful, however, that so many chains would have been available on such short notice. It appears more likely, as the "Fourth Anonymous Relation" and the *Relación de Michoacán* indicate, that the lords of the towns were put in chains as hostages for the service of their subjects.[87] The Tarascans also supplied "four thousand loads of corn and an infinity of chickens [turkeys]."[88]

The Cazonci was carried along in a hammock-type litter, still in restraints. He seems to have lost hope, and his health was failing. The *Relación* says, "The Cazonci's color was now bad and he did not want to eat anything, and his face was almost black."[89]

No one gives explicit dates for the movements of the army, but because we know that the expedition reached the Lerma River on February 2, we can calculate back to January 29 as the date of their departure from Tzintzuntzan by using information given by Pedro de Carranza. Carranza, a member of the expedition, wrote that, after leaving Tzintzuntzan, Guzmán went on the first day (January 29) to a town of Juan Infante. On the second day (January 30) they reached a town of Villaseñor (probably Puruándiro), and the next day (January 31) they went on to another town belonging to Villaseñor. Two days later (February 1 and 2) they proceeded to a river (the Lerma).[90] This river, which the natives called Chiconave or Chiconavatengo,[91] Guzmán named Río de Nuestra Señora de la Purificación, because his expedition arrived there on February 2, the Feast of the Purification of the Virgin Mary.[92]

After the army had established itself beside the Lerma, Guzmán reopened the trial of the Cazonci with a partly new set of accusations. On February 5 a Tarascan named Cuaraque testified that seven months previously the Cazonci had sent a large group of warriors under the war captain Cipaque to the town of Cuinao, where they were preparing to ambush the Christians. The plan was that the Indians at Cuinao would attack Guzmán and the expedition from the front, and at the same time the Cazonci and the several thousand Tarascans who accompanied Guzmán would attack from the rear. He also accused the Cazonci of having sent to the men much native armor (probably the "vests" mentioned in the *Relación* that Guzmán had accused the Cazonci of sending to Cuinao). This was a very serious accusation, since Guzmán's army of fewer than 500 would have been hopelessly outnumbered by the Tarascans, especially if the Mexican Indians had also decided to rebel.

Cuaraque further accused the Cazonci of having retained certain idols in secret, of having sacrificed Spaniards to them, and of having danced in the skins of those Spaniards, which he still kept near his idols. Thus to the accusation of murder there was added that of practicing idolatry and human sacrifice after baptism. Cuaraque also named two Indians with whom he said the Cazonci had engaged in homosexual acts. Guzmán then interrogated a Chichimeca named Guanax, who admitted that the Cazonci had warriors under the command of a captain named Cipaque.[93]

Guzmán now determined to resort to torture. For this purpose he had a thatched hut built outside the camp, probably fearing that if the other Indians became aware of the torture they might rebel.[94] The *Relación de Michoacán* says that it was "separate, where the Spaniards did not go, in some weedy patches along the bank of the river."[95]

Guzmán had a ladder brought to the hut, ordered the Cazonci placed on it and began tying his arms with cords. The Cazonci then admitted that he had hidden the lords of Jacona and Uruapan. He was then stretched out on the ladder and tied, and he admitted that he had kept the lord of Cuitzeo hidden but that he was dead. The Cazonci's legs were then tied, and they began to tighten the cords on his right arm, giving them two twists. The Cazonci gave up his resistance at this point. He asked that the constables should leave, and when they had done so, he confessed that he had many warriors under three captains in Cuinao and Cinapácuaro, enemy towns, that he had sent the men there to fight the Spaniards after he had returned from Mexico City and that he had sent them much armor and many weapons after Guzmán's arrival in Michoacán. He had done this at the request of the people of Cuinao. He had commanded that some Spaniards be killed in Chilchota as they were coming from Zacatula. He had three idols to which he offered adoration, and the skins of the Christians, and he would bring them before Guzmán. After making this confession, he was released from torture. A little later his confession was read and translated to him, and he ratified it.[96]

The next day, February 6, Guzmán interrogated Don Pedro. Immediately the *principal* accused the Cazonci of having commanded many Spaniards to be killed, two in Turicuaro, two in Tacumbaro, one in Uruapan, four in Pazondano, two in Tlazazalca, one in Guacinba, and two in Ponzadona. He said that Cuinao was subject to the Cazonci and that the Cazonci had placed many warriors there from all parts of Michoacán. Then he corrected himself and said that the warriors in Cuinao were from Jacona and other towns and did not belong to the Cazonci.

For the present Guzmán seemed content with these answers, but later the same day he called Don Pedro before him once more and, when the Indian leader denied that he knew anything more, Guzmán commanded that he be tortured. Throughout the tightening of the ropes on his arms and legs and the stretching of his whole body by the tightening of the *maestra* (main rope?), Don Pedro denied that he knew anything more.

Then they began the water torture, placing a cloth over his mouth and pouring water over it and into his nose. He asked them to stop after the first little pitcher of water and amplified his accusations. The Cazonci, he said, had 8,000 men in Cuinao to attack the Spaniards, and he had sent them cotton armor. But he denied the charge that they had dug pits for the Spaniards to fall into. He had seen the Cazonci and Don Alonso dance in the skins of Spaniards, in honor of a golden idol called Yornacusi. The Cazonci had also performed homosexual acts with Indians, especially one named Juanico. Guzmán then released him from torture, and after a short time Don Pedro ratified his testimony as it was read and translated to him.[97]

On February 7, Guzmán did not proceed with the trial; on that day he held a formal ceremony to take possession, in the name of the crown, of the country that lay ahead.[98] In the words of the "Fourth Anonymous Relation," "There he took the banners into the countryside with all of the foot soldiers and horsemen, sounding the trumpets, and commanding it to be proclaimed that as president of the New

Spain and governor of the Province of Pánuco he was carrying out the formal act of possession in these lands." Pedro de Carranza adds, ". . . he laid his hand to his sword and slashed at the trees as a sign of possession."[99]

Guzmán also commanded that a little chapel should be build on a promontory, "with its crenellated wall roundabout and gates like a fortress." With this he kept his men and the Indian allies busy while he continued with his investigation of the Cazonci and the possible ambush ahead.[100]

The next day, February 8, he summoned Don Alonso, named Vise in Tarascan, who was married to a daughter of the Cazonci. Don Alonso would not admit anything or accuse the Cazonci of anything, and Guzmán condemned him to torture. After he was tied to the ladder, they brought in Don Pedro, who said that Don Alonso knew of the warriors whom the Cazonci had sent to Cuinao. Don Alonso agreed that some Indians had gone from Michoacán to that place, but he maintained that they were not warriors. Don Pedro asserted that Don Alonso had danced in the skin of a Spaniard before idols, but Don Alonso denied it. Guzmán ordered the torture to proceed. They gave two twists to the cords on each arm, but Don Alonso admitted nothing. Then they gave a twist to the cords on each of his legs, and he admitted that there were warriors in Cuinao, but he maintained that he did not know by whose command they were there. He was given another twist on each leg, and his body was stretched with the tightening of the *maestra*, but he said that he did not know anything more.

Then they started the water torture. After the first little pitcher of water, he admitted that the Cazonci had commanded the killing of the Spaniards and that he kept idols. After a second pitcher of water he said that Cuinao was subject to the Cazonci and that he had sent warriors there to kill the Spaniards. After a third pitcher was poured over the mask, he admitted that the warriors in Cuinao were from Michoacán. After two more pitchers he revealed that there were idols in the mountain of Iricuaro. He was subjected to two more pitchers of water but confessed nothing more. Finally Guzmán stopped the torture, and after a little while Don Alonso ratified his testimony.[101]

For two days Guzmán did nothing more in the case, at least nothing that appears in the record. On February 11, however, he brought in the interpreter Gonzalo Xuárez, known in Tarascan as Cuycique. The Indian denied knowledge of any of the accusations. He was given the torture of the ladder and cords but continued to deny any knowledge. He was given seven pitchers of water with the cloth in his mouth, and he continued his denial. Then Guzmán ordered him to be stretched on the ground with his hands tied behind his back and his feet tied to a pole. The constables washed the soles of his feet with water and stuck cotton to them. Then, bringing a brazier with fire to the soles of his feet, they ignited the cotton on his feet and let it burn. The interpreter then admitted that the Cazonci had commanded the execution of the Spaniards killed in Tacámbaro. The soles of his feet were then placed in the fire itself, but he would not confess anything more. After that Guzmán released him from torture.[102]

Next Guzmán had them bring in the other interpreter, Alonso de Ávalos, known in Tarascan as Acanysante. After denying knowledge of any of the charges, he was given the torture of the ladder and cords, he was tortured with seven pitchers of water, and cotton was burned on the soles of his feet, but he still denied knowledge of the accusations. Finally Guzmán released him.[103]

That is the course of the torture of the Tarascan leaders as given in the trial record. The order in which they were tortured is essentially the same as that given in the *Relación de Michoacán*, in Carranza's "Relation," and in testimony given by Martín Gómez in Cortés' case against the judges of the audiencia.[104] It is the opposite of the order given in the two relations of Pilar and in the "Fourth Anonymous Relation."[105]

The questions are the same as those given in the *Relación de Michoacán*, except that the *Relación* puts considerable emphasis on questions about holes that the Indians were said to have dug in the road so that the Spaniards' horses would fall into them. The *Relación* also mentions questions about treasure.[106] Ávalos and Xuárez both testified in 1531 that they had been asked about the holes,[107] though there is no mention of this question in the record of their interrogation and torture. When Ávalos testified for Cortés against the judges in 1531, he said that they had been tortured to disclose the Cazonci's treasures.[108] Xuárez stated in 1531 that his feet had been burned so badly that he still had to be carried on someone's back.[109] When the *Relación de Michoacán* was written in 1540-41, Don Pedro still bore the marks of the ropes on his arms.[110]

After having taken this testimony under torture, on February 11 Guzmán also heard two more witnesses, Xacuipangua, lord of Zanzan, and Juanico, an Indian of Zanzan, both of whom said that all the accusations against the Cazonci were true. On the same day Guzmán commanded Don Pedro to bring the idols of the Cazonci and the skins of the Spaniards. Don Pedro said that he would send for them and would bring them in the next day.[111] Apparently this was the hurried trip of Pedro de Guzmán and other Spaniards, mentioned by Pilar, that set the camp talking about more treasure being brought to Guzmán.[112] There can be no doubt that idols and human skins were brought back. On February 13 the Cazonci was confronted with two idols and confessed that they were his.[113] We have seen that they were taken to Mexico City by Ribera, probably in July 1530.[114] When the copy of the trial record was presented in the Council of the Indies in 1534, it was accompanied by two idols and the skin of one Christian.[115]

Guzmán now considered that he had enough evidence to convict the Cazonci. On February 14 he pronounced sentence:

I find that I must condemn, and I do condemn, the said Cazonci, named Don Francisco, to the penalty for the crime that he has thus committed, and I condemn him that he shall be taken from the prison where he is, his hands and feet being tied, with a rope around his neck, and with the voice of a crier to make known his crime, and he shall be put into a pannier, if one can be had, and, tied at the tail of a nag, he shall be dragged around the place where the camp is situated, and he shall be taken to the side of the ford of this river and there he shall be tied to a timber and burned in living flames until he dies naturally and becomes dust. And if the said Cazonci should wish to die as a Christian, since he has received the water of baptism, even though after he received it he went back to commit idolatry as is evident and apparent from his confession and this trial, I command that before he is burned, he shall be given a garrote at the neck so that the said Cazonci shall die and be separated from the living spirit, and afterward let him be thrown into the fire and burned, as has been said. And because it is presumed that the natives of the said province will take the ashes of his body and will carry them off to commit idolatry with them, from which God Our Lord will be ill-served, I command that the ashes that remain from his body and flesh shall be thrown into this said river in such a way that they cannot be had. And, moreover, I condemn the said Cazonci to the loss of all of his goods, and I adjudicate them to the chamber and treasury of His Majesty and to the costs justly made in this lawsuit, the assessment of which I reserve to myself. And judging it to be thus, by this my definitive sentence I pronounce and command it in and through these writs. Nuño de Guzmán.[116]

Pedro de Carranza said that he went to the dwelling of Guzmán that morning and found the Cazonci there as preparations were being made for his execution. The Cazonci lamented that "he had done good to the Christians and that he had not waged war on them but that he had fed them and given them of what he had and that he had given gold and silver for that great *tetuán* (lord) of Castile; and if he had given all this, why were they killing him?"[117]

But the sentence was executed immediately, in spite of a perfunctory appeal by La Peña, which Guzmán simply brushed aside. The Cazonci was dragged around the camp, and the crier who accompanied him proclaimed:

This is the justice which the Emperor and Queen our lords and the very excellent lord Nuño de Guzmán, president of the New Spain and captain-general of the army in their name, command to be done to this man as an idolatrous traitor, and because he has killed many Spaniards, he commands him to be dragged around and burned for it. Let him who does such pay such.[118]

When they had tied the Cazonci to the stake and surrounded his body with wood, they called Don Alonso, and the Cazonci spoke to him. García del Pilar, who was standing next to the interpreter Juan Pascual, asked the latter to translate for him. Pascual answered:

. . . you know that he is saying that he [Don Alonso] should observe the reward that the Christians and Nuño de Guzmán are giving him in payment for the services that he has done them and the gold and silver that he has given them and for having surrendered the land in peace and without war; and he commanded him that after his burning, he should collect the dust and ashes that remained of him and take them to Michoacán and that there he should gather all of the lords of the said province together and that he should tell them what had happened, and that he should tell it all and should show them his ashes and should guard and keep them in his memory. And this is what the said interpreter Juan Pascual told him.[119]

The Cazonci must have shown sufficient repentence to satisfy Guzmán, because he was given the garrote before he was burned.[120] The odium that attached to Guzmán's name, however, would not even give him credit for this small humanity. Padre Tello asserted that the

Cazonci had not been able to withstand the torture and had died because of it before reaching the stake.[121] Pilar and the "Fourth Anonymous Relation" stated that he was burned alive.[122] But the *Relación de Michoacán*, which gives Don Pedro's version, and the depositions of the two Tarascan interpreters, who had most reason to speak out against Guzmán, all indicate that the Cazonci was strangled before being burned.[123]

As far back as Gómara is found the accusation that Guzmán "burned him [the Cazonci] with many other knights and principal men of that realm, so that they would not bring complaints, because a dead dog does not bite."[124] Many later writers have accepted Gómara's opinion as fact, but there is no support for it in the contemporary records. As we have seen, the two interpreters testified at least three times in 1531. Don Pedro, who was most deeply implicated with the Cazonci, was the source for much of the last part of the *Relación de Michoacán* in 1540-41. Don Alonso, whose later testimony we have not had occasion to use, appeared as a witness for Guzmán in 1539.[125] These were the outstanding *principales* of Michoacán, the ones who knew most about what Guzmán took and who might have done the most harm to him. If he had wanted to kill the *principales* to protect himself, these would certainly have felt the flames first.

Guzmán commanded that the Cazonci's ashes were to be thrown into the river, but the Cazonci's request that his ashes be taken back to Tzintzuntzan seems to have been fulfilled. According to the *Relación de Michoacán*, some of the Cazonci's servants recovered the ashes from the river and took them back to Michoacán, where part were buried at Pátzcuaro and part elsewhere. At the second place a woman was killed, apparently to continue the Tarascan custom of burying wives and servants with the Cazonci.[126] Unwittingly Guzmán had also fulfilled the ancient Tarascan custom of burning the body of the Cazonci after his death.

Were the accusations of treason verified? Don Pedro, in the *Relación de Michoacán*, reported that when the army reached Cuinao all the people fled and the Spaniards found no great Tarascan force hidden there.[127] That is undoubtedly what motivated the last entry in the trial record. On March 8, in the town of Acucio (probably Cuitzeo, in Jalisco) Guzmán called Don Pedro before him and asked him under oath about the location of Cuinao, where the Cazonci had his warriors. Don Pedro answered that they were in another town called Cuinao, near Ystlan.[128] That may have been true, or, on the other hand, it may have been that Don Pedro, to save his own skin, had the warriors dispersed, just as he claimed to have done when the Spaniards first came to Michoacán under Olid.

The execution of the Cazonci was the most symbolic act marking the end of the pre-Spanish kingdom of Michoacán and the completion of the Spanish conquest of the region.

•••

CHAPTER 12

Concluding Thoughts

THE drama of the conquest of Michoacán had a cast of many characters, involved in deep and often bitter conflict with one another. The
central figure was that of the Cazonci Tzintzicha Tangaxoan, or Don
Francisco; among the secondary characters two who played very prominent parts, though sinister ones, were Don Pedro Cuinierángari and
Nuño de Guzmán. In the next few pages we will draw together some
concluding thoughts regarding each of these personages.

The Cazonci's docile submission to Spanish rule has often been interpreted as cowardice. Such a conclusion surely oversimplifies the
problem. It may be true that the young king was afraid to face the
Spaniards, but there were less inglorious reasons for his reluctance
than cowardice. First, it must be remembered that he was not yet very
firmly in control of the Tarascan throne when the invaders first appeared on his frontier. He had felt obliged to execute his three brothers
because of their alleged disloyalty. Even if we do not entirely accept
Don Pedro's version of the conquest, it does at least indicate that a
serious struggle was still taking place between the Cazonci and his
principal lords, especially Timas. Moreover, the Cazonci knew of the
great tactical advantage that the Spaniards possessed in their firearms
and horses. He had heard of the terrible vengeance that they had
wrought on the Aztec capital for its resistance. In such circumstances
was it not more prudent to come to terms with the invaders? Further,
why should he be expected to fight against those who had crushed
his worst enemies? There was no sense of pan-Indian solidarity between the two kingdoms, which had warred so bitterly against one
another.

But there was probably a deeper reason for the Cazonci's submission to Cortés: the nature of his religious beliefs and attitudes. The *Relación de Michoacán* indicates that the Cazonci considered the Spaniards gods and gave them divine honors, even attributing their thirst for gold to a divine appetite. With such an attitude of mind he must have felt that it was futile for him to try to resist these mysterious, seemingly superhuman personages. Thus he submitted his kingdom to the great sovereign across the sea, whom he probably envisaged as one of the supernaturals. In one of his statements to Guzmán he indicates that he felt later that he could have put up a stiff resistance if he had desired to do so. When asked whether he had commanded a Christian to be killed, he said no, that if he had wished to kill Christians he could have done so when they first came to the province.[1]

It is also probable that the Cazonci believed that he was entering into something like a treaty of friendship with Cortés, which would leave him on a certain level of equality with the Spaniards. If that was his concept of the situation, he made some serious errors of judgment. He did not understand how insecure Cortés' authority was, authority that Cortés' followers accepted only as long as it seemed to have royal support. If Cortés had remained in power, the Cazonci's position would also have been more secure. But Cortés' hold on power was very short-lived, and those who substituted for him or came after him in authority did not respect the Cazonci's rights. Moreover, in his complete submission to Cortés the Cazonci did not retain any expressed rights for himself, as he would have done in a treaty in the European style. Thus the later Spanish governors treated him as though he had no particular rights.

Charles Gibson has commented on the absence of formal treaties between the Spanish conquerors and the native rulers of the New World.[2] Certainly that was true of the conquest of Michoacán. Perhaps because the Spaniards overran the native American kingdoms with such comparative ease, they did not see any need for making the kinds of concessions that a treaty implies. Whatever may have been the cause, the result was that a native king such as the Cazonci was left without even the minimal degree of protection that a treaty with Cortés might have given him.

The Tarascan king must have wished many times that he had eliminated the invaders when they were few and weak and he was still in control of his forces. He first began to feel the cost of his submission when repeated demands were made on his store of treasure, but that was only taking the stored fruit of his kingdom. A far more difficult state of affairs was created when Michoacán was divided among the encomenderos, and the Cazonci was left a king without a kingdom. Nothing but strife could be expected to develop from the undefined relationship between the two powers. The Cazonci, still considering himself a king and respected as such by his former subjects, had to resort to secret means of supporting himself and his household. As king he was expected to meet special exactions of the Spanish authorities, necessitating clandestine tribute from the towns. The people still revered him as their sovereign, and, when troubles arose, they turned to him rather than to the Spanish authorities. The Spaniards, on the other hand, resented his interference in what they now considered their domain. They wanted to use the people of their towns for their own purposes and to be the sole beneficiaries of the tribute. They realized that they could not have complete control of their encomiendas as long as the native lords of the towns could be withdrawn at the will of the Cazonci. In sum, it was an impossible situation — two civil governments ruling the same people, in the same area, at the same time. Violence was inevitable.

The violence took the form of a gradual attrition rather than a full revolt. The mistreatment of the Indians by the Spaniards led to retaliation by the Indians. The Spaniards laid the responsibility for every Spanish death at the door of the Cazonci, and he became the scapegoat for all the crimes committed against the Spaniards. And there is indeed evidence that he was personally implicated in some of these deaths. The accusations that were made against him in his trial by Guzmán cannot be merely shrugged aside. All the Indian witnesses except Alonso de Ávalos confessed that the Cazonci had been responsible for the death of one or more groups of Spaniards.

Moreover, after having outwardly professed the Christian faith, the Cazonci continued to practice idolatry, even to the extent of sacrificing Spaniards and retaining their skins for his native rituals. Perhaps during the hard times that came upon him during the late 1520s he decided to turn back to the old familiar gods under whom he had enjoyed a more prosperous existence. As in any culture faced with drastic change, there must have been strong conservative forces pushing him back into the old ways. Don Pedro, who was involved in this regression to the native religion, may have been one of the impelling forces behind it, being the son of a native priest.

The part played by Don Pedro during this whole last period of the Cazonci's life is mysterious and sinister. In the *Relación de Michoacán* he pictured himself as a devoted adopted brother of the Cazonci, always looking out for the sovereign's good. But the documents of the Guzmán period give us quite a different impression, leading us to think that perhaps here we have the Indian version of García del Pilar, always trying to stay on the winning side. This may have been Don Pedro's meaning when, in his testimony for Guzmán against Pilar, he assured his hearers that he had no ill will against Pilar, since Pilar had taught him how to get along with the Christians.[3]

In 1529, while the Cazonci was in Mexico City with Guzmán, Don Pedro was the headman in Michoacán, and Bernaldino de Albornoz referred to him as "Indian lord of this province of Michoacán."[4] Possibly at that time he became attached to the high position and determined to keep it for himself. A desire for power seems to be indicated by his appearance of his own accord to give testimony for Villegas against the Cazonci. An interesting expression of Don Pedro's ambition for independent power is found in a statement in the testimony that he gave at that time. Speaking of the Cazonci's continuing efforts to control the native nobility, he said: ". . . and he [the Cazonci] gave that command to this witness even though this witness is governor of this city."[5] If the Cazonci was put out of the way, Don Pedro would obviously be the next one in line of authority, since the Cazonci's sons were still very young.

In 1540, Don Pedro was Indian governor of Michoacán, and since nothing was now to be lost by proclaiming the Cazonci innocent, Don Pedro gave a story in the *Relación de Michoacán* that declared the Cazonci free of responsibility for those things of which the same Don Pedro had accused him in 1530.

But was the Cazonci innocent? Guzmán has been criticized very severely for his action against the Cazonci, and this action has been made the prime exhibit for accusations against him of excessive cruelty. For those who sided with Cortés, the Cazonci became an impeccable martyr, sacrificed to Guzmán's greed. This attitude is exemplified by the following quotation from Hubert Howe Bancroft: "I believe that there is no circumstance to be urged in behalf of Nuño de Guzmán which can justly relieve him of the black crime of having foully and without provocation murdered the kind-hearted Caltzontzin."[6] The evidence now available, however, indicates that neither was the Cazonci as kind-hearted nor was Guzmán's crime as black as was supposed.

Those who can see nothing but black when the name of Guzmán is mentioned will perhaps reject the validity of the trial record and continue to hold that the execution of the Cazonci was a black and inexcusable crime. But those who accept the document as a valid legal record must admit that Guzmán had ample evidence against the Cazonci for what were, from the Spanish point of view, very serious crimes. There was damaging evidence both on the charge of having murdered Spaniards for his sacrificial rites and on that of having set up an ambush against Guzmán's army. The question of whether or not the latter accusation was later verified does not change the fact that Guzmán had strong evidence, even from Don Pedro, of treachery by the Cazonci. The trial was admittedly summary because of the imminent danger to the comparatively small army of Spaniards. Guzmán's army did delay for several days over the trial of the Cazonci, a delay that was expensive, for the army's supplies were limited.

Other judges had investigated the Cazonci for these same crimes, except the accusation of imminent treachery, and had not executed him for them. Why did Guzmán consider the execution necessary? One fact that we cannot overlook is that the sentence against the Cazonci gave Guzmán the right to confiscate the Cazonci's goods, and this may have been a major motive for finding him guilty. We have mentioned the raid on the Cazonci's house for treasure after his execution. I do not think that anyone can deny that Guzmán was a very greedy man, willing to do almost anything to the natives to enrich himself.

Apparently the Cazonci's wives were also considered part of the booty. We have, for instance, the following testimony reported for one of them:

On the tenth day of the said month of January of the said year [1532] the said lord judge summoned before him Leonor, who says she is a servant of Don Pedro de Arellano, who has been corregidor in this said city of Michoacán. She was asked if she is a slave. She says that, despite the fact that she has a brand on her head, she is not a slave and that her father and mother were not slaves but free, and that she who is testifying was the wife of the Cazonci, and that Godoy put on her the brand that she has on her face, and that he also branded three other women on the face when the said Antonio de Godoy was justice here in this city, and that she and one of the other three women were wives of Don Pedro, Indian lord of this said city.[7]

It appears from this that Don Pedro must have taken some of the Cazonci's wives as his own after the king's death.

Perhaps an even more important element in Guzmán's decision to execute the Cazonci was a conflict of politics and personalities between the two. The Cazonci seems to have remained loyal to Cortés even after Guzmán's arrival. We have seen this in the fact that he cut off the provisions for Guzmán's slaves after he returned to Michoacán in the spring of 1529, maintaining that he was subject to Cortés. Further, Guzmán was arrogant and racist. This is evident in his statement about the place of his imprisonment in Mexico City in 1537–38: ". . . the public prison, where there were Negroes, thieves, and other people."[8] How could he accept that the Cazonci was a monarch among his own people and that they gave him regal veneration? We have seen his arrogant treatment of the Cazonci during his imprisonment, and there are evidences that the Cazonci could reply with equal arrogance. It must have shocked Guzmán to see the royal honors given to the Cazonci by his people when he arrived in Tzintzuntzan. He probably not only resented the prestige of the Cazonci but was afraid to leave alive the monarch who had command of the populous kingdom that he was leaving at his rear as he marched on to the northwest.

Regarding Guzmán's later career, he led his army on north and west to conquer the region that would later bear the name New Galicia. There he held the position of governor until 1536. In that year he returned to Mexico City, and he was living there in the house of Viceroy Antonio de Mendoza when he was arrested in early January 1537 by Diego Pérez de la Torre, judge of residencia of New Galicia. He was kept in the public prison of Mexico City from January 1537 until June 30, 1538. By command of the Council of the Indies he returned to Spain, probably in late 1538. There he spent the rest of his life, still listed as a *contino* (member of the royal bodyguard), but with the royal court as a prison.[9] He died, almost penniless, in Valladolid on October 26, 1558.[10]

What were the effects of the Cazonci's death? The army of Tarascans with Guzman's expedition were kept under control, partly by the army of Spaniards and Mexicans and partly because the Tarascan nobles were held as hostages. In Michoacán there was apparently

Plaza, San Andrés Ziróndaro.

some disturbance during the days immediately after the burning of the Cazonci, but it was soon quieted.

The Cazonci was able to hide away some gold and silver for his sons. In the words of Cuini, one of the guards of the treasure:

At the time when Nuño de Guzmán went to the province of Michoacán, Don Francisco Cazonci, lord of the said province, had the said gold and silver put there out of fear, so that they would not take it from him; and this witness and the others who were there were slaves of the said Don Francisco Cazonci; and he commanded them that they should not have any other care but to guard the said gold and silver that he left under guard; and he said that he left it for such a time as he should need to get together the tributes for His Majesty, and that what they might lack for what they were obliged to give, they should make up from there; and since the said Cazonci went

Canoe race, Janitzio.

with Nuño de Guzmán, this witness and the others maintained the said guard, fulfilling the command of the said Cazonci.[11]

Don Pedro de Arellano, the new corregidor of Michoacán, found out about the deposit of treasure, possibly while he was making his investigation of Guzman's activities. In late 1531 he raided the rocky outcropping where it was hidden, tortured the guards until they revealed its location, and took it for himself. Although the audiencia later retrieved part of it from him, there is no evidence that any of it was ever returned to the sons of the Cazonci.

The family of the Cazonci remained prominent in Michoacán for many generations. His two legitimate sons were given a Spanish education. The older son, Don Francisco Tariácuri, became governor of Michoacán after the death of Don Pedro in 1543 but died in 1545,

House of the Huitziméngari, Pátzcuaro.

apparently without offspring. The second son, Don Antonio Huitzi-méngari, then became governor and continued in that office until his death in 1562. He left a young son, Don Pablo, who apparently did not reach majority, dying in 1577. There, according to the "Relación de Pátzcuaro," ended the legitimate male line of the Cazonci. But Don Antonio had other children by other women, and through them the name of Huitziméngari was kept alive at least into the seventeenth and eighteenth centuries.[12]

Some brief general conclusions should be mentioned regarding the encomiendas and land usage. The development of the hacienda as an institution independent of and distinct from the encomienda seems to have been foreshadowed in the presence of an *estanciero* such as Gonzalo Gómez in an area that fell within the boundaries of an encomienda.

There are hints in the documentation that there were other estancias of this kind, but the evidence for them is not entirely clear.

In regard to the relationship between the encomiendas and land tenure, it is clear that at this period the encomenderos felt free to utilize land within the area of their encomiendas. They did so for planting fields in which they grew foodstuffs over and above what the Indians were obliged to give as tribute. Even the royal ordinances of 1528 acknowledged the existence of such fields. The encomenderos also used the land for the establishment of their estancias of livestock, especially pigs and cows at this time. Both of these types of land utilization, however, depended upon the right of the encomenderos to demand labor as tribute, whether for planting and cultivating the fields or for feeding and caring for the animals. The right to labor as tribute was not taken away from the encomenderos until the 1540s, when the crown prohibited it in general terms in the New Laws of 1542 and more specifically in a royal decree of 1549.[13] Afterward such land utilization by the encomenderos became illegal unless it was carried out with salaried labor or slave labor. As these laws were gradually enforced more stringently, the distinction between the tenure of an encomienda and the utilization of land became more and more clearly differentiated, and the encomienda and the hacienda went their separate ways.

Appendices

Data from the Five Known Fragments of the Caravajal Visita

Town	Subject to	Lord	Mountain	Water[a]	No. of Houses		Distance (In Leagues)[b]
					Indian Count	Spanish Count	
			Espopuyuta (or Comanja), October 9–11, 1523[c]				
Espopuyuta (Espopoyutla)	Cazonci	Ayuxeanare (Axuxecuari)	Cupanvan	Chirano (Chirameo)	40	65	5.00
Tetenamatal	Espopuyuta	—	Oringuara	Chuchijo	6	14	1.00
Ayunequichi	Espopuyuta	—	Panbanmuchato	Tirimacuro	5	13	0.50
Tox	Espopuyuta	—	Matox	Amboxo	5	9	1.00
Huytla	Espopuyuta	—	Terecuaro	Chirapen	5	15	0.50
Xachongoytula	Espopuyuta	—	Tapusco	Atenda	20	95	1.00
Atenda			Xaltepec	lake			
Nida			—				
Tetenabo	Espopuyuta	Ybache	Trebintacoato Chichro	Buya	2	7	2.50
Chanchiro	Espopuyuta	—	Piraban	Uchiquiro	3	15	2.00
Orinda	Espopuyuta	—	Guara	Cupazechique	3	10	1.00
Cuxinbano	Espopuyuta	—	Cuxiban	Cuiniquichio	2	8	1.00
Tipuculta	Espopuyuta	—	Huytepetla Taltepec	Urumo	3	10	0.25
Chiltecan	Espopuyuta	—	—	Capundi lake	7	13	1.00
Marixo (Cipiajo)	Espopuyuta	—	Marixo (barranca)	Atenba	5	15	1.50
Tixicato (Tipicato)	Espopuyuta	Oacuinjo (Guacuinuio)	Chichayoquarohato (Chichayquarohato)	Urepetio	3	10	2.00

Quaraqui (Caracua)	Taxicaton (Tipicato)	—	Uricapan (Bracapa)	Urepetan (Urepetio)	5	10	0.25
Tachibeo	Tipacato (Tipicato)	—	Chichaxiguaro (Chichaxicaro)	Xideon (Xabeo)	5	8	0.50
Tacaro	Espopuyuta	Caras (Haraz)	Chichatoquarofato	Tarinbaro	4	11	2.50
Maranja (Naranja)	Espopuyuta	Chichanpano (Chichanpan)	Ichantepec (Ichartepeque)	Guaxucar (Guayna) arroyo	25	40	2.00
			Quanitepecan (Coadtepeque)				
Copanban	Maranja	—	Coantepecan (Coattepecat)	Chichidaron	6	15	1.00
Otlatli	Maranja	Inacopil	Coxmabofato	Chichandaro	10	25	0.50
Terexeron	Otlatlan	Taquipuy	Acatlan	Materexeron	15	25	0.50
Tutepec	Espopuyuta	Tetenepia	Tutepec	Amimuchato marsh	20	40	2.00
Guanamocontero	Tutepec	—	Tescalco	Animuchato marsh	10	20	0.50
Caringo	Tutepec	—	Quixucato	Acabcito	4	15	1.00
			Norixaro				
Tescalco	Espopuyuta	Techinitica	Tescalco	Cuymofato arroyo and marsh	20	45	2.00
Tacatlan	Tescalco	—	Tescalco	Zacatlan	15	25	1.50
Usapala	Tescalco	Uchichila	Palan	Orireguara	10	20	1.00
			Origuara				
Istlauaca	Tescalco	—	Istlauaca	Istlauaca	4	10	0.50
Apundaro	—	Characi	Apundarofato	Casatrico lake	15	30	2.50 (From Tescalco)

Town	Subject to	Lord	Mountain	Water[a]	No. of Houses		Distance (In Leagues)[b]
					Indian Count	Spanish Count	
Ocinibo (Ocambo)	Apundaro	—	Apundaro	Casatiro lake	10	15	0.50
Taricaco	Apundaro	—	Tamapufato	Chitaapen	10	40	3.00
Agungarico	Apundaro	Pibaran	Apuxa	Hararo	10	30	4.50
Inchazo	Tescalco	—	Cherepuato	Cometyron	8	15	2.00
Caqueon	Tescalco	—	Chirapequaro	Epariquaro river	10	10	2.00
Uraquiteon	Tescalco	—	Chirapequaro	Pundaro	3	7	2.00
Orinebequaro	Tescalco	—	—	Uranvequaro marsh	3	7	1.50
Chincharo	Tescalco	—	Eruchiron	marsh	10	20	1.50
Total					341	782	

Uruapan, December 22–24, 1523[d]

Town	Subject to	Lord	Mountain	Water[a]	No. of Houses		Distance (In Leagues)[b]
					Indian Count	Spanish Count	
Uruapan	Cazonci	Hornaco (Horimco)	Tarecinta	Arlecici (Atacece), Zenzun (Zenzum) rivers	30	150 (115)	15.00
Cupacuaro	Uruapan	—	Xaguarochito (Xiguarohato)	Xaraquaro river	6	25	—
Chichanguataro (Chichanguatiro)	Uruapan	—	Chantadavan (Chantatavan)	Charachanda (Charahanda)	6	15	1.00
Anguagua (Anguangan)	Uruapan	—	Ichanquaro Chapata	Vyehara	10	55	3.00
Chicaya (Chacaya)	Uruapan	Quarasco	Chaca	Chata	60	90	4.00

Charangua (Chirangua)	Uruapan	—	Taxuatan Charagua Antan a pine grove	Areche	5	8	0.50
Chire	Uruapan	Tangua		Chire (Chiren) arroyo	3	7	1.00
Quequecato (Quetacato)	Uruapan	Carachato	Capayo (Pirinda)	Pacayo, arroyo	5	12	0.50
Arenjo (Harenjo)	Uruapan	Macamijo (Macuymijo)		Pantau (Patau) river	(7)	15	0.25
Cachaquaro (Cachiquaro)	Uruapan	—	Ichavatiro	Chirapan (Chiripan) river	5	12	1.00
Arechuel (Harecho)	Uruapan	—	Churata	Atayaque (Ataya) river	3	8	1.50
Chirusto	Uruapan	Antayo	Chapacavan (Chacapavan) Huamuda	Chirasto	40	70	3.00
Chirapan (Charapa)	Chirusto	—		Chananpa (Charanpan) arroyo	5	30	—
Total					185	495 (462)	
Turicato, January 21–23, 1524[e]							
Turicato	—	Yoste	—	Cuzpangarico, Chucureo rivers	30	85	10.00 (from Uchichila)
Cuzengo	Turicato	—	—	Yorequaro river	1	2	0.50

Town	Subject to	Lord	Mountain	Water[a]	No. of Houses		Distance (In Leagues)[b]
					Indian Count	Spanish Count	
Hinchameo	Turicato	—	Avamuhato	Huchamoato	1	5	1.50
Papaseo	Turicato	—	Chizintoato	Acuichapeo river	9	24	1.50
Icharo	Turicato	Corache	Charapeteo	Atoyaque river	5	8	0.25
Macada	Turicato	Guaratud	Charapetio	Coruxaneo river	5	10	1.00
Hurutaquaro	Turicato	Tanga	—	Curuxanio river	5	7	0.50
Catao	Turicato	—	Huramuhato Coringorima	Tuyaque arroyo	4	10	1.50
Vapanio	Catao	—	—	Tuyaque river	3	7	0.50
Acuychapeo	Turicato	—	—	Toyaque river	2	3	2.00
Uranapeo	Turicato	—	Ichapeto	Chizandaro river	3	7	3.00
Chupinguaparapeo	—	Guaratucupen	—	Chichiscapeo, Cutzparangueo arroyos	5	12	2.00
Casindagapeo	Chupinguaparapeo	—	—	Irequaro river	4	13	1.50
Corinquaro	Chupinguaparapeo	—	Atuquaro	Coringuaro river	4	12	3.00
Unguacaro	Coringuaro	Chenque	Catan	Ungueenaro river	5	10	0.50
Tocumeo	Chupingaparapeo	Otmipe	Batupachao	Maris	5	15	5.00

Tetenxeo	Turicato	Caringa Camecuato		river Xupacarureca arroyo	5	9	5.00
Aroaquaro	Tucomeo	Tumescatuato		Urequaro arroyo	3	7	0.50
Total					99	246	

Huaniqueo, March 25, 26, 30, and 31, 1524[f]

Guaniqueo	Calsunsi	Aymotupe (Aynotape)	Tucapachirato (Tucapachuato)	Uripitio (Viepetio) river (arroyo)	10	45	6.00
Atapuato (Ataxuato)	Guaniqueo	—	Cutuxuato (Cutaxuato)	Urepitio (Viepetio) river (arroyo)	2	5	1.50
Tavanquaro	Guaniqueo	—	Cucutejo (Aranquetero)	Tabanquaro river (arroyo)	2	15	1.00
Cuynio	Guaniqueo	—	Corichichan (Corochachin)	Uripitio (Viepetio) river (arroyo)	5	12	0.50
Yoriquataquaro (Yoricotaquaro)	Guaniqueo	—	Yurecutaquaro	Cochao river (arroyo)	5	8	0.50
Charico (Chapucho)	Guaniqueo	Poronga (Parogan)	Tamapuato	Cochao arroyo	4	10	0.25
(Choropeceo)	Guaniqueo	Zucindie (Zusanda)	Chuquejuato	Yurequi (Yurequa)	5	20	0.50

Town	Subject to	Lord	Mountain	Water[a]	Indian Count	Spanish Count	Distance (In Leagues)[b]
Tuyquaro (Tuycaro)	Guaniqueo	—	Tuyquaro	river (arroyo) Hatesteo (Haresteo)	5	16	1.00
Hachocato	Guaniqueo	—	Checato (Achochato)	Quinceo	20	30	1.00
Quinceo	Guaniqueo	—	Vipicho (Quinceo)	(Vipecho) (arroyo)	3	8	1.00
Haruteo (Aruteo)	Guaniqueo	—	China (Chapanchuato)	China (arroyo)	3	10	1.00
Chimo (Chinao)	Guaniqueo	—	—	Chinoo (Chinao) river (arroyo)	1	5	0.50
Chinandaro	Guaniqueo	—	Haunpo (Harapo)	Tarinbaro	6	13	1.00
Puruaco	Guaniqueo	—	Puruaco	Terexajaro (Tereparaco)	10	10	1.50
[Name missing]	Guaniqueo	Cusca (Cuaca)	Tucuxuato (Tucupachuato)	Tendaxaraco (Tendeparaco)	10	35	1.50
Cochequeta (Cochiquita)	Guaniqueo	Parangua	Hanyquato	Parapeo	5	14	1.00
Curunxao	Guaniqueo	—	Cuarijato (Carijuato)	Comao	5	5	0.25
Cucharro	Guaniqueo	—	Jaraquarofito (Xaracuarohato)	Carixaheo marsh	15	25	0.25
Cinhaxeciro	Guaniqueo	Acoraquan	Tamaxuato	Cinhaxecio	5	15	0.25

(Cuchapeceo)		(Conracoa)	(Tamapuato)	(Cochapaceo) river (arroyo)			
Carachao	Guaniqueo	—	Caraquaro (Xaraquaro)	Curuchao (Carachao)	6	17	0.50
Poromo	Guaniqueo	—	Tamapuato	Uruena	10	40	1.00
Curindecutero	Guaniqueo	—	Cuchandecutero (Cuchindecutero)	Chandecutero (Chindecutero)	4	9	1.00
Cherequaro (Cheraquaro)	Guaniqueo	—	Harequaro (Cherequaro)	Aherequaro (Cherequaro) arroyo	5	12	1.50
Pareo	Guaniqueo	Iquinao (Iquincio)	Pareo	Turimoro	10	15	1.50
Tabinao	Pareo	—	Pecheo (Pacheo)	Anix, river (Cuixo, arroyo)	8	12	0.25
Pamo (Pano)	Guaniqueo	—	Herequaro (Cherenquaro)	Chincharro (Chancharro)	10	18	2.50
Cipiajo and Axinda (Axuda)	Guaniqueo	Quetuquipa (Taquipa)	Chanachetio (Charachetio)	Xanitiro (Junitio)	10	45	2.50
Chichachequaro (Chichachoquaro)	Cipiajo	—	Chichachequarohato	Vipicho (Vipecho) arroyo	2	10	0.50
Haxistio (Chiristio)	Cipiajo	—	Chequechuhato	Yurequa river	6	8	1.00
Chichavemo (Chichanvemo)	Guaniqueo	(Chara)	Chechanvemo	(Chichanvemo) (marshes)	5	35	1.00
Machendao (Chendao)	Chichandaro	—	Chendaro (Chendao)	Chipiatio (Chipuatio)	10	15	0.25
Unjequaro	Chichandaro	—	Unjuquaro	—	3	20	0.25

Town	Subject to	Lord	Mountain	Water[a]	No. of Houses		Distance (In Leagues)[b]
					Indian Count	Spanish Count	
Aneplayo (Cuexerio)	(Chichandemo) Chichandaro (Chichandemo)	—	(Unjequaro) Puruato	Apario, river (Aperio, arroyo)	7 (10)	30	0.25
Guandararo (Guadacoro)	Chichavemo (Chichademo)	—	Chaxaranduhato Xara (Xaraque)	Xararemio (Xareremio) arroyo	7	12	0.25
Chubero (Chavero)	Chichanvemo	—	Carapuato Caputo (Cacapuato)	Chaueto arroyo	10	25	0.50
Areno	Guaniqueo	Xureque (Xareque)	Chinchamato (Caparacatero)	(Chanchamatato)	20	25	2.50
Tarinbaro	Areno	—	Taranbaro (Tarinbaro)	Turimicho river (arroyo)	3	30	0.25
Tamapuato (Tamapusto)	Areno	—	Cuanamo (Cuypuato)	Chinchimacito (Chinchimatato)	5	12	0.25
Chacurco (Chacuaco)	Areno	—	Anipuato (Cuipuato)	Chaquato	20	45	0.50
Guaguo	Areno	—	Punamuaro (Pimanuhato)	Guaguo (Guanguao)	10	35	1.00
Carachao	Areno	—	Hamanco (Hanicuaco)	Matayraco (Matachiraco)	3	3	0.50
Carajo (Carijo)	Areno	—	Anipufato (Aniputo)	Arijo (Carijo)	3	3	1.00
Acanbaro	Areno	—	Caparicutero	Chanchimaro (Chinchimacaro)	15	25	0.25
Cumuxoz	Guaniqueo	Curinde	Guarararo	Cario, arroyo	5	15	0.25

(Cumuxao) Xarepitio (Xarepetio)	Guaniqueo		(Xaracuaro) Tuxacutero (Tapancutero)	(Carijo) Yurequa			
Total					5	10	0.50
					323 (326)	827	
Erongaricuaro, April 19–21, 1524[g]							
Eranguariquaro	Cazonci	Quaca	Uchataro	Apunda de Uchichila	20	65	2.00 (by water) 3.50 (by land)
Cabaro	Punguaricuaro	—	Curopechao	Herao	3	7	1.00
Cuyropeo	Punguaricuaro	—	Umeo	Atucori	5	12	1.00
Uramagaro	Erunpuritareo	—	Quexoque	Uruguamaro	6	25	1.00
Tanbbo	Eranguaricaro	—	Iraguetio	Iramaro	15	25	1.00
Tacuyxao	Eranguaricaro	—	Acunboringui	Atorcari	2	10	1.50
Chacharachapo	Eranguaricaro	—	Charachapo	Iraquaro	2	8	1.50
Aramontaro	Coringuaro	Tarequequere	Aramontaro	Andahoa	3	20	1.00
Andaparato	Coringuaro		Aguaparato	Paraxori	4	9	0.50
Maharazo	Eronguaricuaro	—	Haracheo	Cupamo	4	10	1.50
Toricaro	Eronguaricuaro	—	Canacoran	Aran	6	15	2.00
Aran	Eronguaricuaro	—	Guacuxua	Aran	6	16	2.00
Pechequaro	Eronguaricuaro	—	Quapacuaro	Haran	2	6	2.00
estancia baja	Eronguaricuaro	—	Uaxa	Xuyba	4	9	1.50
Navache	Eronguaricuaro	—	Chapita	Chapitamcho	6	20	2.00
Charan	Eronguaricuaro	Amita	Chapitan	Bequaro	10	35	2.00
Mirio	Eronguaricuaro	Nocorandi	Tarare	Cundiro	6	20	3.50
Se—— [Sevina?]	Eronguaricuaro	—	Pundo	Punjaquaro	10	35	4.50
[Lacuna in text]			Pinguacara				
Paracho	Eronguaricuaro	Curichi	Parachuato	Punjuacuro	6	25	3.50

Town	Subject to	Lord	Mountain	Water[a]	No. of Houses		Distance (In Leagues)[b]
					Indian Count	Spanish Count	
Uquacato	Eronguaricuaro	—	Chiquian	Aranja	4	23	3.00
Aranja	Eronguaricuaro	—	Chicuyan	Xanaban	10	45	3.00
Guaraguao	Coringuaro	—	Parita	Purato	6	13	0.50
Cheranazcon	Araxa	—	Chiran	Condiro arroyo	6	15	0.25
Tanpangatiro	Aranxa	—	Cuyguaticuaro	Arangueo	3	20	0.50
Uricho	Eranguariquaro	Jepeno	—	Apunda de Uchichila lake	20	60	0.25
Puchumeo	Eranguaricuaro	—	Ingachue	Catlabe	5	15	0.25
Pecurajo	Eranguaricuaro	Nuiteniba	Bacapan	Uchichila	7	20	0.25
Pechataro	Eranguaricuaro	Pereche	Tinguara Guanjareme	Apunda, lake Cuyxeo	10	45	1.50
Yaorochio	Pechataro	—	Zazapuato	Xurequaro	6	12	0.25
Opomaratio	Pechataro	—	Custe	Bapariquaro	3	10	1.00
Xuyna	Pechitaco	Apache	Brixero	Xanaxua	15	25	1.00
Canagua	Pechitaro	—	Tupeticostahato	Zanagua	5	14	0.25
Cuyxo	Pechitaro	—	Tupeti	Arixono	10	25	0.25
Vaparicuto	Pechataco	—	Purexrero	Anagua	2	7	0.25
Urequero	Pechataco	—	Bibaman	Ire	5	12	0.50
Icheparataco	Eronguariquaro	—	Ichachiachaco	Ichepaquaro	5	30	0.50
Opunqueo	Eronguaricuaro	—	—	Lake of Uchichila	4	15	1.00
Uristibpachco	Uricho	—	—	Apunda, Lake	15	30	0.25

Ceremotaro	Necotan de Uchichila	—	Tupe	—	of Uchichila Lake of Uchichila	25	35	0.25
Capacadane	Necotan	—	—	Apunda, Lake of Uchichila	3	20	0.50
Total						289	863	

[a] A spring, unless otherwise indicated.

[b] This distance seems to refer always to the immediate *cabecera* (superior town) or *subcabecera* indicated in column 2.

[c] Data from AGI, Justicia, leg. 130, fols. 952v–59. There is a partial second copy in ibid., fols. 1984–85v. Variant spellings in the second copy are shown in parentheses.

[d] From AGI, Justicia, leg. 138. Another copy in AGI, Justicia, leg. 130, fols. 1636–38. Variant names, spellings, and numbers in the second copy are shown in parentheses.

[e] From AGN, Hospital de Jesús, leg. 292, exp. 119, fols. 432–34.

[f] From AGI, Justicia, leg. 130, fols. 1177–84; another copy in ibid., fols. 1856v–63v. Variant spellings and entries in the second copy are shown in parentheses.

[g] From AGI, Justicia, leg. 130, fols. 1145–52.

The Encomenderos and Encomiendas
of Michoacán

NO complete listing of the original grants of encomienda for Michoacán is available to us. In chapter 4, I spoke of the grants that clearly date from the summer of 1524. The first relatively complete listing of the encomiendas is in the record of the Ortega tribute assessment, made in 1528, four years after the original distribution of the encomiendas.

The Ortega assessment, therefore, represents the status of the encomiendas in Michoacán at the time that it was made, 1528. We do not know how many changes had occurred since Cortés made the first grants in the summer of 1524, but to judge from the cases about which we have information, there had been a considerable number of trades, confiscations, vacancies through death, and so on, during the intervening years. There are also some encomiendas missing from Ortega's tribute assessment. Those that have come to light are given separately at the end of the lists extracted from the Ortega assessment.

Regarding the text of the record of Ortega's assessment, the original has not been found, but at least two copies are extant. One (which I call text A) is preserved in a copy of a lawsuit between Vasco de Quiroga and Juan Infante over control of towns along the west and north shores of Lake Pátzcuaro (AGI, Justicia, leg. 130). The other (text B) is found in a nineteenth-century copy of a late sixteenth-century lawsuit by Don Constantino Huitziméngari, grandson of the last Cazonci, over an annual pension granted to him by the royal crown (Archivo Histórico del Institutio Nacional de Antropología e Historia, Col. Gómez de Orozco, MS 171).

A serious problem arises from the wide variation in the spellings of the names of the towns. The Spaniards wrote down the names as they heard them, generally without a knowledge of the linguistic nuances of the sounds. The copies of the document that we have come to us through the hands of copyists who had no knowledge of Tarascan and who increased the confusion. The copy of the *tasación* from AGI, Justicia, leg. 130, is a third-hand copy, having been copied from Ortega's original for the record of the lawsuit in Mexico and then recopied when a clean copy was made to be sent to Spain. The copy in the Colección Gómez de Orozco (MS 171, fols. 17–28v) was made in the nineteenth century from a copy made on January 18, 1595, from the copy in the record of the lawsuit between Quiroga and Infante, which had remained in Mexico. It is, therefore, a fourth-hand copy. Although in general it is the less trustworthy of the two copies, in a number of instances it gives a better interpretation of the names than does the other copy.

In the following pages I give first an alphabetical listing of the encomenderos with their encomiendas, followed by an alphabetical listing of the towns with their encomenderos and with the tribute burden assigned them by Ortega. In both lists are included commentaries to clarify problematic points and to give additional information of interest. Annotations regarding sources are included in the commentaries rather than at the foot of the page. Complete citations are found in the Bibliography.

The Encomenderos, with Their Towns

1. Alonso, Fernando: half of Pengarabato. (A Fernando Alonso had previously held Huaniqueo.)

There were two Fernando Alonsos in Mexico in the 1520s. One of them, Fernando Alonso de Villanueva, was encomendero of half of Pungarabato and was still alive in 1529. (See below, under Pungarabato.) The other Fernando Alonso, a blacksmith, was executed as a heretic on October 17, 1528. (*IP*, 1:353.) I suspect, without proof, that the latter was the Fernando Alonso from whom Cortés had reacquired Huaniqueo (*q.v.*) at some time before the Ortega visitation.

2. Argueta [Hernando de Ergueta]: Half of Tepalcatepec.

Text A gives the name as Argueta on both fol. 967 and fol. 971, without giving a first name. Text B has Urgueta. The only similar name that I have encountered is Hernando de Ergueta, whose name appears many times in the notarial records of the period. (Cf. *IP*, vol. 1, index, p. 424.) This is confirmed by a statement in Alonso de Estrada's letter of July 12, 1528, to Bachiller Ortega: "Now, sir, you know that an estancia was discovered between Tepalcatapeque and Motín, and concerning this matter Alonso Dávalos [sic] and Hernando de Ergueta, his partner, are at law with Requena." (AGI, Justicia, leg. 135, no. 3.) Alonso de Ávila shared Tepalcatepec with Ergueta (see below). Perhaps the estancia to which Estrada referred was Coalcomán, which does not appear in Ortega's tasación.

3. Arriaga, [Antón de]: Tlazazalca.
Text B has Artlaga. Neither copy gives a first name for him. Antón or Antonio de Arriaga had accompanied Olid among the horsemen ("Relación e la plata . . . ," AGI, Justicia, leg. 223), appears a number of times in the notarial records for the period (cf. IP, vol. 1, index, p. 408), and gave testimony for Juan Infante in 1533 (AGI, Justicia, leg. 130, fol. 1970). A Sebastián de Arriaga also appears in the notarial records, but there does not seem to be any relationship between him and Michoacán.

4. Ávalos, Alonso de: Contuma. "Pueblos de Ávalos," Cindangualo, Chavynda, Guarequeo, Sarandala, Tacandaro, Tucata.
This list of towns, beginning with Cindangualo, is given as "the towns of Ávalos" on fol. 962 of text A of the tasación (April 31, 1528). Text B gives the names as Sindinguara, Chaudan, Quaraquio, Zirandaro, Tacandaro, and Tucatl. Later in the acts of the tasación (June 12, 1528), when the lords of the towns appear for the assessment of tribute, the following, entirely different, list of towns is given as subject to "the lords who are entrusted to Alonso Dávalos and to Fernando de Sayavedra, his brother" (f. 972):
(With his brother Fernando de Saavedra), Sayula, Atoyac, Teocuitatlan, Techaluta, Zacoalco, Cocula.
All the names on this list are recognizable as the names of still-surviving towns west and southwest of Lake Chapala, and they are the ones that were usually identified as the towns or province of Ávalos. Perhaps the discrepancy between the two lists indicates that there was more than one language group in the region and that each town had more than one name. This was true of Tarecuato (q.v.), in western Michoacán. Cortés had originally granted these towns to three brothers, Alonso

de Ávalos, Juan de Ávalos, and Fernando or Hernando de Saavedra. Both Juan de Ávalos and Fernando de Saavedra went to Honduras, Fernando de Saavedra with Cortés, Juan de Ávalos perhaps earlier. Neither of them returned. Juan apparently died before Cortés returned to Mexico; Fernando stayed on as lieutenant of the captain-general in Higueras. It seems that he also later died there, though he is still listed as encomendero here in 1528. ("El fiscal con Jorge Carillo sobre ciertos pueblos," AGI, Justicia, leg. 198, no. 3; "Probanza de los méritos y servicios de Gonzalo de Sandoval [sic — de Francisco de Saavedra Sandoval], México, 5 noviembre 1562," AGI, Patronato, leg. 65, no. 1, ramo 19; "Probanza de los méritos y servicios de Alonso de Ávalos y Hernando de Saavedra, hecha por Hernando de Ávalos Saavedra, 6 mayo 1582," AGI, Patronato, leg. 77, ramo 12.) After Salazar and Chirinos officially declared Cortés and his followers dead, they sent Francisco de Orduña to visit the provinces of Colima, Zacatula, and Michoacán and redistribute the encomiendas. Orduña gave Jorge Carrillo, *vecino* of Colima, the share of the province of Ávalos that had belonged to Juan de Ávalos. Cortés upon his return annulled all grants of encomienda made by Salazar and Chirinos. Apparently Cortés did not have an opportunity to redistribute this share of the province of Ávalos before the arrival of Ponce de León, and it was later taken by the crown. ("El fiscal con Jorge Carrillo," AGI, Justicia, leg. 198, no. 3.)

Pedro de Bazán was given Fernando de Saavedra's part of the encomienda, also by Orduña. Under Marcos de Aguilar he was given in its stead half of Pungarabato. ("Juan Velázquez de Salazar con Pedro de Bazán y Antonio Anguiano sobre Pungarabato y Charcharando, 1537," AGI, Justicia, leg. 126, no. 5; "El fiscal con Jorge Carrillo," AGI, Justicia, leg. 198, no. 3.) Although Fernando de Saavedra was again listed as one of the encomenderos in 1528, Bishop-elect Zumárraga wrote to the king in 1529 that Guzmán and the audiencia gave "to Manuel de Guzmán, servant of the president, the Indians which they took away from Fernando Saavedra, which are very good, in the mines of Michoacán" (Zumárraga, "Carta a su Magesdad, 1529," p. 193).

The denomination of the towns shows great variation. There are notable differences in the spelling between the two copies of the Ortega *tasación*. In the lawsuit between the fiscal and Jorge Carrillo each side gave a list of the towns, and these lists differ from one another and from the Ortega lists. The following is a comparison between them:

Ortega's *Tasación*		AGI, Justicia, leg. 198, no. 3		Modern Name
Text A	Text B	Carrillo's List	*Fiscal's* List	
Çayula	Zasuta	Çayula	Çayula	Sayula
Atoyaque	Atoyac	—	—	Atoyac
Tusitatan	Tansitata	Teoquitatlan	Tentiquitatlan	Teocuitatlán
Chilutia	Chiluntia	—	Atachelutlan	Techaluta
Çacualco	Tzaqualpa	—	—	Zacoalco
Cocula	Cocula	—	—	Cocula
—	—	Tepeque	Tepeque	Tepec
—	—	Amaqueca	Maneque?	Amacueca
—	—	Metramexalpa	—	?
—	—	Chalapa	—	Chapala?
—	—	—	Tutequi	?
—	—	—	Tomultlanque	?
—	—	—	Semecemepala	?

5. Ávila, Alonso de: Cecasta, half of Tepalcatepec.

6. Bazán, [Pedro de]: half of Pungarabato.
Bazán's first name is not given in the record of the Ortega assessment, but the fact that he was Pedro de Bazán is clear from the number of lawsuits in which he engaged over Pungarabato. (For citations, see chapter 9, nn. 25–27.)

7. Burgos, Juan de: half of Cutzamala.

8. Caicedo, [Antonio]: Tarecuato (Tepehuacán).
Caicedo's first name is not given in any of the four instances in which he is mentioned in the texts of Ortega's record, probably because he was well known in Michoacán. We have seen that Antón or Antonio Caicedo was one of the first Spaniards in Michoacán and that he was active there throughout the 1520s. After his death the royal fiscal of the audiencia brought suit against his daughter Isabel, claiming that Antón Caicedo's towns should have reverted to the crown. The towns that are mentioned are Perivan (Peribán), Tepevacan (Tarecuato), Tenguandin (Tingüindín), and Tecasquaro (Tacatzcuaro). ("El fiscal con Isabel Caicedo sobre que se restituyan los pueblos de indios que tuvo encomendados su padre Antonio Caicedo, 1535," AGI, Justicia, leg. 188, no. 4.) The fact that Tepehuacán and Tarecuato are names for

the same town is clear from a statement by Motolinía in which he writes of "a town of the province of Michoacán, which in that language is named Tarecuato, and in the language of Mexico is called Tepehuacan." (Motolinía, *Memoriales*, p. 162.) Tarecuato is listed as the encomienda of Antón Caicedo's wife and heir, Doña María de Montesdoca, in *Relación de los obispados de Tlaxcala, Michoacán, Oaxaca y otros lugares en el siglo XVI*, ed. García Pimentel, pp. 48–49; and it and Peribán appear as encomiendas of her second husband, Francisco de Chávez, in *Suma de visitas de pueblos* (vol. 1 of *Papeles de Nueva España*, ed. Francisco del Paso y Troncoso), pp. 179–80, 254.

9. Cortés, Fernando: Amula, Tamazula, Tuxpan, Zapotlan, Mazamitla, Tiripetío, Naranja, [Tzintzuntzan], Huaniqueo, Tajimaroa. For discussion of the encomiendas of Fernando Cortés in Michoacán, see below under the names of the individual towns and in chapter 10.

10. Écija, Andrés de; Cuycoran.
Text A calls him Andrés de Cea on the first appearance of his name (fol. 961v). Text B has Andrés de Asija.

11. Gallego, Álvaro: Chucándiro.

12. [Gómez, García]: half of Capula.
Neither text gives the name of the encomendero of Capula, but the extracts of the notarial records indicate that on May 13, 1528, García Gómez made a contract with Cristóbal de Ojeda that Ojeda would reside in Gómez' town "Catula," in Michoacán (*IP*, 1:289, no. 1341). See also below, under Ojeda.

13. González de Benavides, Gil: Guayameo.

14. Holguín, García: Ucareo.
On the first occasion when Ucareo is mentioned in the assessment record, the encomendero's name is given as Gonzalo Holguín (fol. 968), the second time as García Holguín (fol. 968). García Holguín was a witness to the acts of the *tasación* on May 16 and June 12, 1528 (fols. 964, 968). Within two or three years Holguín went to Guatemala, and from there he went on to Peru, where he remained. ("El fiscal con Juan de Bezos, vecino de Mexico, sobre derecho al pueblo de Ucareo, 1542," AGI, Justicia, leg. 197, no. 2.)

15. Hurtado, Diego: Taimeo.

16. Isla, Pedro de: half of Tancítaro.
Text A gives the encomendero's name as Ayala on the first occasion; Text B gives Isla. In all other instances his name is given as Isla or Pero Isla. In the notarial records Pedro de Isla is referred to as a servant of Fernando Cortés. (*IP*, 1:42, no. 74; ibid., pp. 267–68, no. 1222.)

17. Jaso, [Juan de]: half of Arimao.
Jaso's first name is not given, but it seems probable that he was the Juan de Jaso who was active in Zacatula and Michoacán at this time ("El fiscal contra Arellano, AGI, Justicia, leg. 187, no. 1, ramo 2; *IP*, 1:235, no. 1035).

18. Jerez, [Hernando de]: Zacapu.
Spelled Xeres in the manuscript. Text B gives Aeves on the first occasion. No first name is given. The *Relación de obispados*, p. 177, indicates that Hernando de Jerez was the first encomendero of Zacapu, and he was succeeded by Gonzalo de Ávalos, husband of Jerez's daughter. Both Gonzalo Gómez and Alonso de Veas commented during the course of the Inquisition trial of Gonzalo Gómez that Hernando de Jerez was the encomendero of Zacapu ("Proceso contra Gonzalo Gómez," AGN, Inquisición, vol. 2, exp. 2).

19. Jiménez, Juan: half of Arimao.

20. Leonardo: Jiquilpan.

21. Loa, Guillén de la: Coyuca.

22. López, Gonzalo: Cuitzeo.
Also called Sancho López (text A, fol. 970).

23. Martín de Gamboa, Cristóbal: Ajuchitlan.

24. Mata, [Alonso de]: Colutia [sic—Tuzantla].
That Mata's first name was Alonso is clear from "Alonso de Mata con Ortega y Santa Cruz, 1541," AGI, Justicia, leg. 135, no. 3. For the identification of the town, see below, under Tuzantla.

25. Medina, [Domingo de]: half of Tancítaro.
According to a statement by his heir, Domingo de Medina received a
cedula of encomienda for half of Tancítaro on August 24, 1524. ("El
fiscal de S. M. con Diego Enríquez de Medina y Doña Luisa de Velázquez sobre el pueblo de indios de Tancítaro, México, 1573," AGI,
Escribanía de Cámara, leg. 100.) He is also given as the encomendero
of half of Tancítaro in *Suma de visitas*, pp. 254–55.

26. Monjaraz, [Andrés de]: Teremendo and Jaso.
Although his first name is not given in the Ortega assessment, it appears that this encomendero is Andrés de Monjaraz, because on February 12, 1528, he gave permission to Miguel de Mesa and Pedro López
Galbito to reside in his towns in Michoacán. (*IP*, 1:244, no. 1086.)

27. Morcillo, [Francisco]: Indaparapeo.
Text A (fol. 968) gives the surname as Morillo. Francisco Morcillo is
named as the first encomendero of Indaparapeo in *Suma de visitas*, p.
133; and in *Relación de las encomiendas de indios hechas en Nueva España a los conquistadores y pobladores de ella. Año de 1564*, eds. France
V. Scholes and Eleanor B. Adams, p. 33.

28. Ocaño: Maravatío.
Text B gives the name as Cotanio. No further identification of this
encomendero has come to light. *Suma de visitas* (p. 150) names Pedro
Juárez as the encomendero of Maravatío.

29. [Ojeda, Cristóbal de]: half of Capula.
No encomendero is given for Capula in the record of Ortega's assess-
ment. Dr. Cristóbal de Ojeda later claimed that at the time when the
First Audiencia arrived he was encomendero of half of Capula (AGI,
Justicia, leg. 226).

30. Oliver, [Antonio de]: Turicato.
Antonio de Oliver tried to prove his legitimate possession of Turicato
through a long series of lawsuits with Diego Hernández Nieto. See
chapter 9, n. 30. Text B gives the name as Olviedo.

31. Oñate, Cristóbal de: Tacámbaro.

32. [Palacios Rubios, Nicolás de]: Cutzio.

The *tasación* identifies the encomendero of Cutzio simply as *"el camerero"* ("chamberlain"). In documents dating from 1527, it appears that the *camerero* of Fernando Cortés was Nicolás de Palacios Rubios (AGN, Hospital de Jesús, leg. 203, fols. 33, 77, 107). Palacios Rubios is also indicated as one of the first encomenderos of Cutzio in "El fiscal con Rui González, vecino y regidor de México, sobre derecho a los pueblos de Teutalco, Centeupan, y Cuiceo que le fueron encomendados, 1541," AGI, Justicia, leg. 193, no. 2. See below, under Cutzio, for the more complicated picture of the tenure of the town that is given in this lawsuit.

33. Pantoja, [Juan de]: La Huacana.

No first name is given in the *tasación*, but Juan de Pantoja is listed as the encomendero of La Huacana in the *Relación de los obispados,* pp. 47–48, 168; and in *Suma de visitas,* pp. 294–95. He is one of the few encomenderos of Michoacán who had accompanied Cristóbal de Olid ("Relación de la plata . . . ," AGI, Justicia, leg. 223, fol. 340v; AGI, Justicia, leg. 130, fol. 1365).

34. Plaza, [Juan de la]: Sinagua.

Text B gives the name as Raza on the first occasion. That the first encomendero of Sinagua was Juan de la Plaza, *vecino* of Zacatula, is clear from information given in "El fiscal con Antonio de Godoy sobre el derecho del pueblo de Cinagua que le había sido encomendado, 1542," AGI, Justicia, leg. 197, no. 4. Juan de la Plaza was also one of the horsemen of Cristóbal de Olid's expedition. ("Relación de la plata . . . ," AGI, Justicia, leg. 223, fol. 338.)

35. [Riobó de Sotomayor, Gonzalo de]: Araró.

Text A gives only the surname Riobón. Text B interprets it as Rodrigo Bon. It seems that this encomendero must have been Gonzalo de Riobó de Sotomayor, servant of Fernando Cortés (*IP,* 1:214, no. 904; in this instance his name is printed as Rioboz). According to testimony in the residencia of Nuño de Guzmán (AGI, Justicia, leg. 226, fols. 377v–79), he had slaves in the mines of Michoacán, and in testimony that he gave in the Inquisition trial of Gonzalo Gómez, he showed great familiarity with Michoacán ("Proceso contra Gonzalo Gómez," AGN, Inquisición, vol. 2, exp. 2).

36. Rodríguez, Diego: half of Cutzamala, Urapa ⟵

37. Saavedra, Fernando (see above, with Ávalos, Alonso de). ⟵

38. Sámano, Juan de: Chilchota.

39. Sánchez [Farfán?], Pedro: Tepalcatepec.
Sánchez' name appears only with the first mention of the town in
Ortega's *tasación*. Later, when Ortega made the tribute assessment for
the town, two other men were listed as the encomenderos (fols. 962,
967r–v, 971). See below, under Tepalcatepec. It seems probable that
this Pedro Sánchez was the Pedro Sánchez Farfán who led the expedition into Motín, though it must be acknowledged that the documents
of the period uniformly refer to the leader of that expedition with the
double surname. In the notarial records Pedro Sánchez is also named
as the encomendero of Jilotlan, neighboring town to Tepalcatepec (*IP*,
1:343, no. 1646).

40. Sandoval, [Gonzalo de]: Guaracha and Sahuayo, Jacona.
Only the surname is given, and one might easily assume that the reference was to Juan de Sandoval, who witnessed the acts of Ortega's visitation on April 31 (May 1), 1528 (fol. 960) and was Diego Hurtado's
representative in Taímeo (fol. 969). But, in fact, the encomendero at
that time was Juan's more famous cousin Gonzalo de Sandoval, as is
clear from "Juan de Albornoz, vecino de la ciudad de México, con el
veedor Pedro Almíndez Cherino, sobre derecho a la mitad del pueblo
de Xacona, 1536," AGI, Justicia, leg. 123, no. 1. (Cf. *IP*, 1:236, no. 1040.)

41. Solís, [Juan de]: Comanja.
The record of Ortega's assessment refers to the encomendero of Comanja
simply as "Solís el artillero" (Solís the artilleryman). From testimony
given in AGI, Justicia, leg. 130 (fols. 1284–86, 1929r–v, 1956r–v), it is
clear that this Solís was Juan de Solís. His death at the very time of
the Ortega visitation opened the way for Juan Infante's extravagant
claim to encomienda holdings west and north of Lake Pátzcuaro, dis- ⟵
cussed in chapter 9.

42. Sotomayor, [Bachiller Pedro de]: Acámbaro. ⟵
Although his first name is not given in the Ortega record, probably

this encomendero was Bachiller Pedro de Sotomayor, who first entered Michoacán with Cristóbal de Olid as regidor ("Relación de la plata . . . ," AGI, Justicia, leg. 130, fol. 1305). He had slaves working in the mines of Michoacán in 1527 (IP, 1:129, no. 469) and served as *alcalde mayor* and captain in the province of Zacatula (AGI, Justicia, leg. 130, fol. 1308).

43. Tovar el comendador: Yuriria.

44. Trías, Jaime: Zanzan.
Text B gives the name as Ecoyme. The name Jaime Trías is clear in text A, and he is also referred to as encomendero of Zanzan in Scholes and Adams, eds., *Proceso contra Tzintzicha Tangaxoan* (p. 63).

45. Valderrama, [Cristóbal de]: [Tarímbaro] Estapa.
The Ortega assessment does not give Valderrama's first name, but in both the *Relación de obispados* (pp. 41–42, 160) and the *Suma de visitas* (p. 251) Cristóbal de Valderrama is given as the first encomendero of Tarímbaro. Regarding the identification of the town, see below, under Tarímbaro.

46. Villaseñor, [Juan de]: Puruándiro.
In 1540, Juan de Villaseñor testified that Cortés had given him his encomienda in Michoacán (AGI, Justicia, leg. 130, fol. 1239). Juan de Villaseñor witnessed the acts of the Ortega *tasación* on April 31 (May 1), 1528 (fol. 960), and in 1531 he served as inspector of the province of Michoacán (AGI, Justicia, leg. 130, fols. 1232, 1483–85).

47. Villegas, Francisco de: Uruapan.

The Encomienda Towns, with Their Encomenderos and Tributes

The tribute amounts given here are those that appear in Bachiller Ortega's *tasación*. The assessment of the tribute was sometimes changed during the course of the visitation so that different numbers sometimes appear for the same town in different parts of the record. The numbers below are those that appear to have been the final assessment. The tribute figures are given in terms of cargas, the amount that an adult bearer could reasonably carry. In one entry for Cuitzeo, the measures fanega (1.58 bushels) and carga are used interchangeably. The tributes were to be delivered to the mines every twenty days (a Mesoamerican month) unless otherwise noted (fol. 963). In the list below the town is listed first, followed by the encomendero and the tribute amount.

1. Acámbaro: Bachiller Pedro de Sotomayor; tribute: 300 cargas of corn, to be delivered in the mines

2. Ajuchitlan [otherwise known as Thitichuc umo]: Cristóbal Martín de Gamboa; tribute: not listed.
Variants: text A, Suchitlan; text B, Axuchitlan. Text B gives Deque as another name, confusing the phrase of the text, "El pueblo de ——— que por otro nombre se dice Suchitlan" ("the town of ——— which by another name is called Suchitlan"). The *relación geográfica* for the area indicates that the other name of the town was Thitichuc umo, in Cuitlateca, the language of the natives of the region (RGM, 1:69). Cortés gave the town to Cristóbal Martín de Gamboa on July 3, 1526, shortly after Cortés' return from Honduras (AGI, Patronato, leg. 67, ramo 2). This probably indicates that there had been a previous encomendero who had either died or lost favor. The *Relación de las encomiendas, 1564* (p. 16) names Andrés de Roças as "settler and first holder."

3. Amula: Fernando Cortés; tribute: not listed.

4. Araró: Gonzalo de Riobó de Sotomayor; tribute: not listed.

5. Arimao: Juan de Jaso and Juan Jiménez; tribute: not listed.
Variants: text A, Harimao; text B, Animaro.

6. Atoyac: Alonso de Ávalos and Fernando de Saavedra; tribute: 60 cargas of corn, 20 cargas of beans, [text B, 12 cargas of beans], 5 cargas of chili, 5 cargas of salt; to be delivered in the mines of Motín or others equidistant.

7. Capula: García Gómez and Dr. Cristóbal de Ojeda; tribute: 200 cargas of corn to be delivered in the mines.
The record of Ortega's assessment does not indicate the name of the encomendero of Capula. Cristóbal de Ojeda later claimed that he held

half of the encomienda at the time when the First Audiencia arrived (AGI, Justicia, leg. 226). The other half must have belonged to García Gómez, who on May 13, 1528, made an agreement with Ojeda that the latter would reside in Capula and collect tributes from the town for him (*IP*, 1:289, no. 1341). At Ojeda's request Guzmán and the audiencia gave him Talcozatitlan in place of Capula, and they gave his half of Capula to Luis de Berrio, Licenciado Delgadillo's cousin. Later Delgadillo took Capula for himself to support his slaves in the mines and gave Berrio half of Chinantla. (Testimony of Cristóbal de Ojeda and Luis de Berrio, AGI, Justicia, leg. 226.)

8. Cecasta: Alonso de Ávila; tribute: not listed.
Variant: text B, Sicascan.

9. Chavinda: Alonso de Ávalos; tribute: not listed.
Variant: text B, Chaudan.

10. Chilchota: Juan de Sámano; tribute: 250 cargas of provisions to
    be delivered in the mines.
Variants: text A, Echilchotla; text B, Chilchotla. The lord of the town had offered to supply 300 cargas, but Ortega reduced the amount to 250.

11. Chucándiro: Alvaro Gallego; tribute: 100 cargas of provisions,
    6 cargas of chili, 6 cargas of salt, 2 cargas of fish; to be delivered
    in the mines.
Variants: texts A, B, Chocandiro, Chocandaro.

12. Cindangualo: Alonso de Ávalos and Fernando de Saavedra;
    tribute: not listed.
Variant: text B, Sindinguara.

13. Cocula: Alonso de Ávalos and Fernando de Saavedra; tribute:
    60 cargas of corn, 20 cargas of beans [text B, 12 cargas of beans],
    5 cargas of chili, 5 cargas of salt; to be delivered in the mines of
    Motín or others equidistant.

Colutia: see Tuzantla.

14. Comanja: Juan de Solís (Gonzalo López in charge); tribute: Under control of Don Pedro, who agreed to give 60 cargas of corn and 20 cargas of beans to Gonzalo López in exchange and to deliver them to the mines.

For With?

Because the history of this encomienda is so intimately related to the rise of Juan Infante as a political force in Michoacán, it is discussed in chapter 9.

15. Contuma; Alonso de Ávalos; tribute: 60 cargas of corn, 20 cargas of beans, 5 cargas of chili, 5 cargas of salt; to be delivered in the mines.

Text B gives Colima as the name of this town, but it is certainly not to be confused with the city of Colima, which was always considered a jurisdiction of its own, not subject to Michoacán.

16. Coyuca: Guillén de la Loa; tribute: not listed.

On the first occasion when this town was mentioned in the assessment, it was misspelled Colutla. There was a lawsuit over Coyuca between Pedro de Meneses and the children of Guillén de la Loa, which started in 1543 and was finally judged in favor of Meneses in 1560 ("Pedro de Meneses con los hijos de Guillén de la Loa, sobre que se deshaga el cambio que éste hizo del pueblo de Coyuca por el de Guayacocotla, 1543," AGI, Justicia, leg. 141).

17. Cuitzeo: Gonzalo López; tribute: 300 cargas of corn, 30 cargas of fish, 40 cargas of beans, 4 cargas of chili, 4 cargas of salt; to be delivered in the mines.

Variants: text A, Cuyzeo; text B, Cuiceo, Quitzeo, Cuiseo. The lord of the town offered 400 cargas of corn, but Ortega limited it to 300 cargas. The second time the tribute for this town is listed, the number of cargas of chili is given as 40 in text A. Text B gives the number as 4, and this agrees better with the total number of cargas as given in the margin, 388.

18. Cutzamala (otherwise known as Tusantran): Diego Rodríguez and Juan de Burgos; tribute: not listed.

Text B gives the second name as Tusantla, but Tuzantla (*q.v.*) was a separate encomienda.

19. Cutzio: Nicolás de Palacios Rubios; tribute: not listed.
Variants: text A, Cuçio; text B, Cuihseo. According to information given in "El fiscal con Rui González, vecino y regidor de México, sobre derecho a los pueblos de Teutalco, Ceteupan y Cuiceo, que le fueron encomendados, 1541" (AGI, Justicia, leg. 193, no. 2), Cutzio was originally granted in halves to Nicolás de Palacios Rubios and Alonso Martín the Asturian. On October 29, 1530, after Martín died, the First Audiencia gave his half to Ruy González; they also declared that Palacios Rubios had left his half vacant, and they gave it to Gonzalo Ruiz. A few days later, on November 6, the audiencia approved a trade by which Ruy González gave Gonzalo Ruiz his half of Cutzio in exchange for Ruiz' half of two towns in the Valley of Toluca that the two encomenderos also shared equally. Thus Gonzalo Ruiz became the sole encomendero of Cutzio. At one time the crown took it away from him, but on December 31, 1541, it was restored to him. (AGI, Justicia, leg. 267, fol. 387v.) He is named encomendero in the *Suma de visitas* (pp. 80-81). By 1564 his daughter, Juana de Torres, had inherited it from him (*Relación de las encomiendas, 1564*, p. 29). The spelling of the town's name is frequently closer to Cuitzeo than Cutzio, but the *Suma de visitas* (pp. 80-81) gives the location of Ruiz' encomienda precisely, as situated in the tierra caliente, bounded by Turicato, Zirándaro, Genuato, Coyuca, Pungarabato, and Cutzamala. This could be only Cutzio.

20. Cuycoran: Andrés de Écija; tribute: 13 Indians [text B, 12 Indians] every 5 days to carry provisions to the mines.
Variants: text B, Guaviquaran, Caviquaran.

Estapa: see Tarímbaro.

21. [Guaracha and Sahuayo]: Gonzalo de Sandoval; the Indians were not willing to serve.
For these two towns text B gives the names Guarahchan and Cabayo [Çabayo?]; text A has the unintelligible Coraynzanguayan.

22. Guarequeo: Alonso de Ávalos; tribute: not listed.
Variant: text B, Quaraquio.

23. Guayameo: Gil González de Benavides; tribute: not listed.
Variants: text A, Guaymeo; text B, Guaimeo.

24. La Huacana: Juan de Pantoja; tribute: 100 cargas of provisions and beans to be delivered in the mines.
Variant: texts A, B, Guacana.

25. Huaniqueo: Fernando Cortés; tribute: 360 cargas of corn, 10 car- *Lacusme* gas of chili, 3 cargas of fish; to be delivered in the mines every 30 days.
Variant: texts A, B, Guaniqueo. This spelling is fairly standard in the sixteenth century. Cortés had apparently claimed Huaniqueo for himself during the first distribution of towns in Michoacán (see chapter 6, n. 6), but perhaps he had not been able to reestablish his claim to the town adequately after his return from Honduras. As late as November 15, 1527, it was controlled by Fernando Alonso and Marcos Ruiz, as we learn from a contract that they made with Juan Mateos for his service in that town (*IP*, 1:209, no. 894). It is unclear how Cortés regained control of the town. A Fernando Alonso was burned as a heretic on October 17, 1528 (*IP*, 1:353; see above, under Fernando Alonso). If the man who was burned was this encomendero, perhaps he was already in trouble before Cortés left for Spain in March, 1528, and Cortés took advantage of the opportunity to reassert his control over the town.

26. Indaparapeo: Francisco Morcillo; tribute: not listed.
Variant: text A, Andraparapeo.

27. Jacona: Gonzalo de Sandoval; tribute: 300 cargas of corn and beans, 10 cargas of chili, 10 cargas of salt; to be delivered in the mines.
Variants: text A, Xacona; text B, Aacona. Jacona had originally been granted to Juan de Albornoz by Cortés on August 24, 1524. According to Albornoz, when Cortés returned from Honduras in 1526, angered by the behavior of his lieutenants in his absence, he took away the encomiendas of many of their friends and relatives, among whom was Juan de Albornoz, relative of the royal accountant Rodrigo de Albornoz. Juan de Albornoz was at this time engaged in the pacification of Pánuco. Cortés gave Jacona to his faithful captain Gonzalo de Sandoval. Sandoval accompanied Cortés to Spain in 1528 but died almost immediately upon his arrival there. He must have been seriously ill already before his departure, because on February 1, 1528, he authorized that his will be drawn up in favor of his cousin Juan de Sando-

val (*IP*, 1:236, no. 1040). When Estrada heard of Sandoval's death, he entrusted Jacona to the royal *veedor* Peralmíndez Chirinos on August 4, 1528. Juan de Albornoz brought suit for the town before the audiencia in Mexico on June 23, 1536, but on November 21 the audiencia judged in favor of Chirinos. Albornoz appealed to the Council of the Indies, but no definitive decision is found with the copy of the case. ("Juan de Albornoz, vecino de la ciudad de México, con el veedor Pedro Almíndez Cherino, sobre derecho a la mitad del pueblo de Xacona, 1536." AGI, Justicia, leg. 123, no. 1.) Later listings, such as the *Relación de los obispados* (p. 43) and the *Suma de visitas* (p. 302), give it as a *corregimiento*, or town that gave its tribute to the royal authorities rather than to an encomendero. This was probably a result of the provision of the New Laws of 1542, which prohibited royal officials from holding encomiendas ("Códice de leyes nuevamente hechas . . . ," *DII*, 16:388).

Jaso: see below, with Teremendo.

28. Jiquilpan: Leonardo; tribute: the Indians had fled and taken refuge in the towns of Ávalos.
Variants: text A, Xiquilpa; text B, Xiquilpan.

29. Maravatío: Ocaña; tribute: not listed.
Variant: text A, Mariatio.

30. Mazamitla: Fernando Cortés; tribute: not listed.
Variant: text A, Masamytra.

31. Naranja: Fernando Cortés; tribute: 40 cargas of corn, 5 cargas of beans, 5 cargas of chili; to be delivered in the mines every 30 days.
Variant: text A, Naranjo. According to the testimony of Antonio de Oliver, Naranja had belonged to a certain Medina, wine master of Cortés, who later became a Franciscan. Then it was given to García del Pilar, who, according to Francisco de Villegas, traded it to Cortés for half of Mestitlan a few days before Cortés left for Castile (AGI, Justicia, leg. 130, fols. 1293, 1301, 1845.)

32. Pungarabato: Pedro de Bazán and Fernando Alonso de Villanueva; tribute: not listed.

Variant: text A, Punjaravato. For the complicated history of the tenure of this encomienda, see chapter 9.

33. Puruándiro: Juan de Villaseñor; tribute: 400 Indians to carry provisions to the mines.
Variant: texts A, B, Purandiro.

34. Sarandala: Alonso de Ávalos; tribute: not listed.
Variant: text B, Zirandaro.

   Sahuayo: see above, with Guaracha.

35. Sayula: Alonso de Ávalos and Fernando de Saavedra; tribute: 60 cargas of corn, 20 cargas of beans [text B: 12 cargas of beans], 5 cargas of chili, 5 cargas of salt; to be delivered in the mines of Motín or others equidistant.
Variants: text A, Cayula; text B, Zasuta.

36. Sinagua: Juan de la Plaza; tribute: 40 cargas of provisions to be delivered in the mines every 10 days.
Variant: texts A, B, Cinagua. Because of the death of Juan de la Plaza, the First Audiencia gave Sinagua to Antonio de Godoy in 1529. The Second Audiencia took it away from Godoy and placed it directly under royal authority. ("El fiscal con Antonio de Godoy, sobre el derecho del pueblo de Cinagua que le había sido encomendado, 1542." AGI, Justicia, leg. 197, no. 4.)

37. Tacámbaro: Cristóbal de Oñate; tribute: 200 cargas of corn to be delivered in the mines.

38. Tacandaro: Alonso de Ávalos; tribute: not listed.

39. Taimeo: Diego Hurtado; tribute: 300 cargas of corn to be delivered to the mines.
Variant: texts A, B, Taymeo. The tenure of Taimeo was actually much more complex than it appears from the Ortega record. It had been given by halves to Gaspar de Ávila and Diego Hurtado. Hurtado had gone to Spain, returned to Mexico, and gone back to Spain again. (This is undoubtedly why the Ortega record speaks of Juan de Sando-

val as acting in his name; fol. 969.) Soon after Ortega's *visita*, Estrada decided that it was best to take Hurtado's half of the encomienda away from him, and on November 17, 1528, he gave it to Francisco Quintero. Later, under Viceroy Mendoza, Quintero traded his half of the encomienda to Francisco Rodríguez de Zacatula. Upon Rodríguez' death, according to the opinion of the royal fiscal, Rodríguez' half went to his son Pedro Sánchez and, upon his death, to the crown (March 14, 1549). Rodríguez' wife, Inés Álvarez de Gabraleón, was married a second time, to Guido de Labezares, and he conducted a lengthy lawsuit with the fiscal in his wife's name, claiming that the half of Taimeo should have gone to her. But in 1562 the Council of the Indies decided in favor of the fiscal. (AGI, Justicia, leg. 202, no. 1.) Gaspar de Ávila apparently possessed his half of the encomienda peacefully and passed it on to his son Pedro de Ávila at the end of his days. (*Suma de visitas*, p. 252; *Relación de los obispados*, p. 45; *Relación de las encomiendas, 1564*, p. 36.)

40. Tajimaroa: Fernando Cortés; tribute: not listed.
Variants: text A, Ximaroa; text B, Taximaroa. Tajimaroa, modern Ciudad Hidalgo, was not originally an encomienda of Cortés. Under the name of Taxinda or Tajinda, Cortés granted it to the royal factor Gonzalo de Salazar on July 24, 1524. But after Estrada and his supporters imprisoned Salazar in 1526, Estrada took the encomienda from Salazar and gave it to Diego López Pacheco. When Cortés returned, he voided the grant to López Pacheco and took the town for himself. Salazar, however, returned from Spain in 1529 and sued the representatives of Cortés for the return of the town. On September 18, 1529, Guzmán and the audiencia judged in favor of Salazar. Cortés was not able to regain control of the encomienda, and Salazar passed it on to his son Juan Velázquez de Salazar. ("El fiscal con Gonzalo de Salazar y Pedro Almíndez Cherino, factor y veedor en México, sobre el derecho a un pueblo de indios llamado Taximaroa, 1529," AGI, Justicia, leg. 185, no. 1, ramo 1; "Proceso del factor Gonzalo de Salazar contra Hernando Cortés, 1529," AGN, Hospital de Jesús, leg. 265, exp. 12; *Suma de visitas*, p. 253; *Relación de los obispados*, p. 45; *Relación de las encomiendas, 1564*, p. 40; see also "El fiscal con Gonzalo de Salazar, factor que fue en Nueva España, sobre derecho a los indios del pueblo de Taximaroa y sus sujetos, 1552," AGI, Justicia, leg. 202, no. 2, ramo 2.)

41. Tamazula: Fernando Cortés; tribute: 100 Indians to carry provisions to the mines of Motín.
Variants: text B, Tacamazula, Tamazulapam.

42. Tancítaro: Pedro de Isla and Domingo de Medina; tribute: 5 cargas of corn, 5 cargas of beans, 1 carga of chili daily; to be delivered in the mines.
Variants: texts A, B, Taxitaro; text B, Tanchitaro.

43. Tarecuato (otherwise known as Tepehuacan): Antón Caicedo; tribute: 200 cargas of provisions to be delivered in the mines.
Variants: text A, Tarecuaco; text B, Tarequato; texts A, B, Tepeguacan. For the identification of Tepehuacan as Tarecuato, see above, under Caicedo. Tartacha, the lord of the town, had not come at Ortega's first summons, and Ortega ordered him whipped, but the lord had one of his *principales* take the lashes for him. Ortega commanded him to feed the Spaniards in his town and to bring back the Indians who had fled to the wilds, under the threat of death or enslavement for them. He ordered the lord to hang anyone who would not serve and threatened the lord with hanging unless he obeyed. (Fol. 967.)

44. [Tarímbaro], otherwise known as Estapa: Cristóbal de Valderrama; tribute: 180 cargas of corn, 20 cargas of beans, 10 cargas of chili, 5 cargas of salt, 5 cargas of fish. At least the corn and beans were to be delivered in the mines.
The Ortega *tasación* does not use the name Tarímbaro but gives the name of Valderrama's town in the following variations: text A, Stapa, Estapa; text B, Iztapa, Yztapa. But in the *Relación de los obispados* (pp. 41-42, 160) and in *Suma de visitas* (p. 251), Cristóbal de Valderrama is given as the encomendero of Tarímbaro, and Iztapan is given as an alternate name for Tarímbaro.

45. [Techaluta]: Alonso de Ávalos and Fernando de Saavedra; tribute: 60 cargas of corn, 20 cargas of beans [text B, 12 cargas of beans], 5 cargas of chili, 5 cargas of salt; to be delivered in the mines of Motín or others equidistant.
Variants: text A gives the name of the town as Chilutia; text B, as Chiluntia. See above, under Alonso de Ávalos.

46. [Teocuitatlán]: Alonzo de Ávalos and Fernando de Saavedra; tribute: 60 cargas of corn, 20 cargas of beans, [text B, 12 cargas of beans], 5 cargas of chili, 5 cargas of salt; to be delivered in the mines of Motín or others equidistant.

Variants: text A gives the name of the town as Tusitatan; text B, as Tansitata. See above, under Alonso de Ávalos.

47. Tepalcatepec: (Pedro Sánchez), Alonso de Ávila and Hernando de Ergueta; tribute: 100 cargas of corn, 20 cargas of beans, 2 cargas of chili, 5 cargas of salt; to be delivered in the mines. They were also warned to feed and guard Christians who would pass through and to provide them with bearers.

Variants: text A, Tapaltatepeque, Talpatepeque. The Ortega *tasación* gives Pedro Sánchez as the encomendero on the first occasion when the town is mentioned, but on the two other occasions, when the tribute assessment is made, it names Alonso de Ávila and Argueta (Hernando de Ergueta) as the encomenderos. Text B gives the tribute of salt as 100 cargas, surely in error.

48. Teremendo and Jaso: Andrés de Monjaraz; tribute: 140 cargas of corn, 7 cargas of chili, 2 cargas of salt, [text B, 7 cargas of salt, 2 cargas of chili] to be delivered in the mines.

49. Tiripetío: Fernando Cortés; tribute: 400 cargas of corn, 60 cargas of beans, 15 cargas of chili to be delivered in the mines every 30 days.

Variant: text A, Tripityo. Juan de Alvarado claimed that Cortés had given him this town in 1524 (AGI, Justicia, leg. 130, fol. 1333). We do not know how Cortés came to control it in 1528. According to a letter of Nuño de Guzmán to Antonio de Godoy (June 20, 1529) the *contador* Albornoz claimed to have a cedula for the town (AGI, Justicia, leg. 130, fol. 1505r-v). Alvarado is given as the encomendero again in the *Suma de visitas* (pp. 251-52), although the *Relación de los obispados* (p. 41) lists it as a *corregimiento*.

50. Tlazazalca (otherwise known as Uralca): Antón de Arriaga; tribute: 160 cargas of provisions to be delivered in the mines.

Variants: texts A, B, Taçaçalca. For the alternate name text B gives Urazato.

51. Tucate: Alonso de Ávalos; tribute: not listed.
Variant: text B, Tucatl.

52. Turicato: Antonio de Oliver; tribute: 130 cargas of corn, 10 cargas of beans, 25 small bags of salt, 10 cargas of chili [text B, 20 cargas of chili]; to be delivered in the mines.
For the history of Turicato as an encomienda, see chapter 9.

53. [Tuzantla]: Alonso de Mata; tribute: not listed.
Although the Ortega *tasación* gives the name of Mata's encomienda as Colutia (text A) or Colantia (text B), the lawsuit over Mata's town, which resulted from Ortega's confiscation of it, names it Ocumo or Tuzantla ("Mata con Ortega y Santa Cruz, 1541," AGI, Justicia, leg. 135, no. 3). For greater detail concerning this case, see chapter 10.

54. Tuxpan: Fernando Cortés; tribute: 100 Indians to transport provisions to the mines of Motín.
Variants: text A, Tuspa, Taspa; text B, Tuchpa. This is Tuxpan in present-day Jalisco, named in the assessment and elsewhere with its neighboring towns, Tamazula and Zapotlán. It is not to be confused with the Tuxpan, in present-day Michoacán near Zitácuaro.

55. [Tzintzuntzan]: Fernando Cortés, tribute: 600 cargas of corn, 45 cargas of beans, 25 cargas of chili, 20 cargas of fish; to be delivered in the mines every 30 days.
Ortega's record does not give an assessment that is specifically assigned to Tzintzuntzan (or Uchichila). The tribute assessment given here is listed as the obligation of the Cazonci and Don Pedro, who would have gotten the tribute from Tzintzuntzan and its subject towns around Lake Pátzcuaro.

56. Ucareo: García Holguín; tribute: 200 Indians to transport provisions to the mines.
García Holguín went to Guatemala and from there to Peru (1531), where he remained. The First Audiencia then gave Ucareo to Juan Bezos. The Second Audiencia, following their instructions to take away all suspicious grants made by the First Audiencia, took the town away from Bezos and placed it directly under authority of the crown. ("El fiscal con Juan Bezos, vecino de México, sobre derecho al pueblo de Ucareo, 1542," AGI, Justicia, leg. 197, no. 2.)

57. Urapa: Diego Rodríguez; tribute: 80 cargas of provisions to be delivered in the mines.

Although both texts give the spelling of this town as Uruapa, it is not to be confused with Uruapan, which was the uncontested encomienda of Francisco de Villegas. In an investigation that Vasco de Quiroga made concerning copper mining in Michoacán in 1533, both Antonio de Godoy and Alonso Lucas mentioned Diego Rodríguez as encomendero of Urapa. ("Cierta información sobre lo del cobre, 1533," AGI, Indiferente General, leg. 1204.) In his letter of July 12 to Bachiller Ortega, Alonso de Estrada mentioned that he had been told that nearly all of Rodríguez' Indians had fled into the wilds, and he asked Ortega to try to bring them back to service. (AGI, Justicia, leg. 135, no. 3.)

58. Uruapan: Francisco de Villegas; tribute: 200 cargas of corn, chili, and beans to be delivered in the mines.

59. Yuririapúndaro; Tovar, *el comendador*; tribute: 220 cargas of provisions, 10 cargas of fish; to be delivered in the mines.

Variants: text A, Ururapundaro, Urirapundalo, Urirapundaro; text B, Yorirapundaro, Yuriraquadaro. In the first statement of tribute the lord of the town also offered six loads of salt (fol. 965).

60. Zacapu: Hernando de Jerez; tribute: 200 cargas of corn and beans to be delivered in the mines.

Variants: text A, B, Çacapo; text B, Tzacapu.

61. Zacoalco: Alonso de Ávalos and Fernando de Saavedra; tribute: 60 cargas of corn, 20 cargas of beans [text B, 12 cargas of beans], 5 cargas of chili, 5 cargas of salt; to be delivered in the mines of Motín or others equidistant.

Variants: text A, Çacualco; text B, Tzaqualpa.

62. Zanzan: Jaime Trías; tribute: not listed.

63. Zapotlán: Fernando Cortés; tribute: 100 Indians to carry provisions to the mines of Motín.

Variant: texts A, B, Çapotlan.

A number of towns appear in later lists as encomiendas or *corregimientos* in Michoacán that are not named in the Ortega *tasación*. Some were probably considered as subjects of other towns. For instance, the heirs of Antón Caicedo claimed that he was encomendero of Peribán and Tingüindín besides Tarecuato, which is the only one attributed to him in the assessment. Peribán passed on to his heirs as a separate encomienda according to *Suma de visitas* (pp. 179-80), but Tingüindín became a *corregimiento* (ibid., p. 254).

Undameo (Necotlán) was considered part of the encomienda of Charo (Matalcingo) until Viceroy Mendoza separated it from Charo and made it a *corregimiento* (*RGM*, 1:42).

Ario-Guanajo, which was treated as a *corregimiento* in *Suma de visitas* (pp. 117-18), had previously been considered part of Diego Rodríguez' encomienda, Urapa. In 1533, Alonso de Escobar mentioned "Guanajo, which is entrusted to Diego Rodríguez, who has gone to Spain, and the treasurer has this town." ("Cierta información sobre lo del cobre . . . , 1533," AGI, Indiferente General, leg. 1204.)

Chiquimitio also appears as a *corregimiento* in *Suma de visitas* (p. 77), but it does not appear among the encomiendas of Ortega's period.

Two other towns of considerably greater importance that do not appear in the Ortega *tasación* are Zinapécuaro and Charo (or Matalcingo, as the latter town is known almost universally in the documents of the early sixteenth century).

It would seem that Zinapécuaro was an important town as early as 1536, since by that time it had one of the three or four friaries of Franciscans in the province (Letters of Fr. Miguel de Boloña and Fr. Francisco de Boloña, 1537, AGN, Inquisición, vol. 2, exp. 2), but it must have been considered part of the encomienda of Araró. The *Libro de tasaciones de pueblos en Nueva España* (pp. 49-50), which dates from the midsixteenth century, treats them together and indicates that they had pertained to the crown since the death of Riobó in 1538. In *Suma de visitas* (pp. 77-78) and *Relación de los obispados* (pp. 44-45) it appears as a town belonging to the crown.

Matalcingo (Charo) was the object of a lawsuit between Juan Fernández Infante and Rodrigo de Albornoz; possibly for this reason Bachiller Ortega did not assess its tribute. The lawsuit involved both Matalcingo and Necotlan (Undameo), which were considered a single encomienda. The encomienda had originally been given to Contador Albornoz by Cortés on July 24, 1524, but on February 10, 1526, after Cortés' supporters regained power early in that year, they gave it to Comendador Juan Fernández Infante. Fernández Infante was a priest and a

member of the "Order of St. John or of the Holy Spirit . . . , perpetual *comendador* of the house of the Holy Spirit of the town of
Puerto de Santa Maria in the diocese of Seville." Previously he had
been a member of the Franciscan order, but in 1514 he had gone to
Rome and obtained bulls exempting him from the Franciscan jurisdiction. He arrived in Mexico while Cortés was away in Honduras.

He and Albornoz engaged in a lawsuit before Marcos de Aguilar,
beginning on August 1, 1526, which Aguilar decided in favor of Albornoz. Involved in the argumentation was the fact that Cortés, upon
his return from Honduras, had annulled all grants of encomienda made
by his lieutenants during his absence. Fernández Infante later accused
Albornoz of having suborned Aguilar to obtain a favorable judgment.
("El comendador Juan Fernández Infante con el contador Rodrigo de
Albornoz . . . sobre derecho a un pueblo de indios, 1531," AGI, Justicia,
leg. 113, no. 2.)

Cortés also possibly had his hand in Matalcingo during the period
after the Honduras expedition. In his letter to his father, written on
September 26, 1526, he mentioned "Matalcingo, where I have my livestock of cows, sheep, and pigs" (Cortés, *Cartas y otros documentos*, p.
33). And in January 1528, he made a contract with Pedro García to
be his overseer in Matalcingo ("Relación del descargo y data de García
de Llerena para en cuenta del cargo que le está hecho en esta cuenta,"
AGN, Hospital de Jesús, leg. 300, exp. 109). A problem with the name
Matalcingo, however, is that the Toluca Valley was also referred to as
the Valley of Matalcingo, and it is possible that Cortés' interests were
there (cf. Warren, *Vasco de Quiroga*, pp. 46, 73).

The lawsuit between Fernández Infante and Albornoz was reopened
before the audiencia on October 30, 1530. Fernández, who had accompanied Guzmán's army into New Galicia, presentd an interrogatory in
which he claimed that he had been in peaceful possession of the town
until Gonzalo Gómez, in agreement with Albornoz, sent miners into
the town, who used it to support gangs of Indians working in the
mines. He also asserted that servants of the *contador* had taken away
some *principales* and commoners of the town who had been living in
Mexico City and serving in the house of Fernández Infante. In spite
of Fernández' objections, however, on July 15, 1531, the Second Audiencia awarded the case to Albornoz.

Fernández Infante appealed the case to the Council of the Indies,
sending with it a judicial inquiry in which he claimed that Albornoz

had taken more than 2,000 Indians from the town as slaves and had sold them or killed them in the mines and that he had made the encomienda supply mines that were 60 or 70 leagues away or had taken Indians to Cempoal, more than 100 leagues distant. He also accused Albornoz of burning a cacique for not giving him gold and silver. But, since he presented very little testimony to support these accusations, it is hard to judge their veracity.

The appeal was not prosecuted for several years, perhaps because the king included Matalcingo among the towns of the Marquesado del Valle which he created for Cortés in 1529. The case was finally presented before the Council of the Indies in Valladolid, Spain, on September 14, 1543, but there is no decision with the record in the Archive of the Indies. ("Fernández Infante con Albornoz, 1531," AGI, Justicia, leg. 113, no. 2.)

In *Suma de visitas* (pp. 150, 163), Matalcingo and Necotlan are listed separately as towns belonging to the crown. Later, in 1560, King Philip II confirmed that Matalcingo would be one of the towns that composed the Marquesado del Valle, as Charles I had granted it to Cortés in 1529. (*The Harkness Collection*, pp. 215, 233, 241.) But, since Undameo (Necotlan) had been split off from it, Matalcingo's importance was considerably reduced.

Gonzalo Gómez had an encomienda named Istapa, according to *Suma de visitas* (p. 132), and the *Relación de las encomiendas, 1564* (pp. 33–34) indicates that he passed it on to his son Amador Gómez. We have seen above that Tarímbaro was also known as Istapa, but this was obviously not Gómez' encomienda, since the same sources show that Tarímbaro belonged to Cristóbal de Valderrama, who passed it on to his son-in-law Diego Arias de Sotelo (*Suma de visitas*, p. 251; *Relación de las encomiendas*, p. 27).

Suma de visitas indicated that Gómez' encomienda lay between Tiripetio, Necotlán, and Tuzantla, one of the most forbidding mountainous regions of Michoacán. There do not seem to have been any other encomiendas in this vast region, and perhaps Gómez, who lived at the site of present-day Morelia, just north of the region, carved out an encomienda there for himself, but there were surely very few Indian tributaries in it. (As noted in chapter 10, Gómez also had the estancias of Guayangareo and Itacaro, which seem to have foreshadowed the establishment of haciendas within the area of another Spaniard's encomienda.)

APPENDIX C

Chronology of the Cazonci's Last Days

December 22, 1529	Departure of Guzmán's expedition from Mexico City (the Cazonci had been sent on ahead)
December 25	Expedition in Jiquipilco
December 27	Expedition in Ixtlahuaca
Ca. January 4, 1530	Arrival of expedition in Tzintzuntzan
Ca. January 7	Cazonci imprisoned
Ca. January 22	Cazonci threatened with torture
January 26	Accusations brought against the Cazonci by Villegas
January 27	Interrogation of the Cazonci by Guzmán
January 28	Witnesses presented by both parties
January 29	Departure of expedition from Tzintzuntzan
January 30	Expedition reaches a town of Villaseñor (Puruándiro)
January 31	Expedition reaches another town of Villaseñor
February 2	Expedition arrives at the Río Lerma
February 5	Accusation of treason against the Cazonci; Interrogation of the Cazonci under torture
February 6	Interrogation of Don Pedro under torture
February 7	Guzmán takes possession of the land that lies ahead
February 8	Interrogation of Don Alonso under torture
February 11	Interrogation of Gonzalo Xuárez and Alonso de Ávalos (Indian interpreters) under torture; Don Pedro delivers skins of Christians
February 13	Trial concluded; Cazonci confronted with evidence
February 14	Cazonci condemned to death and executed

ABBREVIATIONS USED IN NOTES

ACM	*Actas de cabildo de la ciudad de México.* Edited by Ignacio Bejarano. 50 vols. México, 1889–1916.
AGI	Archivo General de Indias. Seville, Spain.
AGI, Justicia, leg. 130.	"Autos del obispo y la ciudad de Michoacán con Juan Infante, vecino de México, sobre que a éste la restituyeran los pueblos de Comanja y Naranja con las estancias a éllos sujetos que le habían sido encomendados, 1540."
AGN	Archivo General de la Nación. Mexico City.
BAGN	*Boletín del Archivo General de la Nación.* México.
DII	*Colección de documentos inéditos relativos al descubrimiento, conquista y organización de las antiguas posesiones españoles de América y Oceanía.* 42 vols. Madrid, 1864–84.
DIU	*Colección de documentos inéditos relativos al descubrimiento, conquista y organización de las antiguas posesiones españoles de Ultramar.* 25 vols. Madrid, 1885–1932.
IP	Agustín Millares Carlo and J. Ignacio Mantecón, eds. *Índice y extractos de los protocolos del Archivo de Notarías de México, D.F.* 2 vols. México, 1945–46.
RGM	*Relaciónes geográficas de la diócesis de Michoacán, 1579–1580.* Edited by José Corona Núñez. 2 vols. Guadalajara, 1958.
RM	*Relación de las ceremonias y ritos y población y gobierno de los indios de la provincia de Michoacán.* Edited by José Tudela. Madrid, 1956.
"Tasaciòn Ortega."	"Tasaciones de ciertos pueblos de la provincia de Michoacán por el Bachiller Ortega, 1528," AGI, Justicia, leg. 130, fols. 959–73.

Notes

Chapter 1

1. "Información de los méritos y servicios de D. Antonio Huitsimíngari y de su padre Cazonci, rey y señor natural que fue de toda la tierra y provincia de Tarasca confines de México hasta Culiacán en N. E., 1553" (pregunta 2), AGI, Patronato, leg. 60, no. 2, ramo 3; hereafter cited as "Información de D. Antonio Huitsimíngari."

2. *RGM*, 1:70. See also Howard F. Cline, ed., "The Relación Geográfica of Tuzantla, Michoacán, 1579," *Tlalocan* 5, no. 1 (1965):58-73. The terms Aztec and Mexican (or Mexico), when used in relation to the early sixteenth century, are rather inexact but have roughly equivalent meanings. If one uses Aztec in a very precise sense, it would apply only to the dominant residents of the city of Tenochtitlan. It may also be used of the area dominated by Tenochtitlan, in which case it is sometimes applied to the whole area of the empire or at others only to the cities of the Valley of Mexico. Aztec is the more commonly used term in modern English writings, but the sixteenth-century sources from Michoacán generally use the terms Mexico and Mexican, by which they sometimes mean the city of Tenochtitlan, sometimes the Basin of Mexico, sometimes the Aztec empire. It is not always possible to interpret which they mean in each case.

3. R. H. Barlow, *The Extent of the Empire of the Culhua Mexica*, p. 12.

4. "Relaciones de los Motines, 1580," Real Academia de Historia, Madrid, 12-18-3, no. 16, quoted in Carl O. Sauer, *Colima of New Spain in the Sixteenth Century*, p. 72.

5. "Relación de Quacomán, 1580," Real Academia de Historia, Madrid, 12-18-3, no. 16, quoted in ibid.

6. *RGM*, 2:102, 88, 94; "Relación de Amula, Tuxcacuesco y Cusalapa," 1579, in *Noticias varias de Nueva Galicia, intendencia de Guadalajara* (Guadalajara, 1878), cited in Sauer, *Colima*, pp. 78-79. An archaeological examination of this western extension of the empire is found in Otto Schöndube Baumbach, *Tamazula-Tuxpan-Zapotlan, pueblos de la frontera septentrional de la antigua Colima*.

7. "Tasación Ortega," fol. 972. The document is published in J. Benedict Warren, *La conquista de Michoacán, 1521-30*, pp. 411-25.

8. *RGM*, 2:68, 60, 59. An effort to gain a clearer understanding of the northeastern border by means of archaeological analysis is found in Shirley Gorenstein, ed., *The Tarascan Frontier: The Acámbaro Focus*.

9. *RGM*, 2:60. An attempt to delineate the Tarascan core area and the routes of imperial expansion is found in Dan Stanislawski, "Tarascan Political Geography," *American Anthropologist*, n.s., 49 (1947):46-55. Robert C. West made a very useful geographical study of the area in his *Cultural Geography of the Modern Tarascan Area*.

10. Pablo Beaumont, O.F.M., *Crónica de Michoacán*, 2:34-35, map facing p. 460. Cf. also Carolyn Miles Osborne, "An Ethnological Study of Michoacán in the Sixteenth, Seventeenth and Eighteenth Centuries" (master's thesis, University of New Mexico, 1941), pp. 18-19.

11. José Corona Núñez, *Mitología tarasca*, p. 7.

12. Maurice Swadish, *Términos de parentesco comunes entre Tarasco y Zuñi*.

13. Juan de Torquemada, O.F.M., *Monarquía indiana*, 3:332.

14. Commentary of Eduard Seler in Bernardino de Sahagún, O.F.M., *Historia general de las cosas de Nueva España*, 5:143.

15. Fernando Rojas González, "Los tarascos en la época precolonial," in Lucio Mendieta y Núñez, ed., *Los tarascos*, p. 5.

16. *RGM*, 2:110.

17. Juan Baptista de Lagunas, O.F.M., *Arte y dictionario: con otras obras en la lengua Michuacana*, p. 146.

18. Question 6 and answers to it by Suero Asturiano, Pedro Moreno, Juan Borallo, Alonso de Ávalos (Indian), and Don Francisco (Indian) in "Información hecha a pedimiento del obispo electo Quiroga para que conste del mal asiento y disposición del lugar donde estaba la iglesia primera y que conste de lo contrario en Pátzcuaro, 1538," AGI, Justicia, leg. 173, no. 1, ramo 2. The questions of this inquiry were published by Nicolás León in *El Ylmo. Señor Don Vasco de Quiroga, primer obispo de Michoacán*, pp. 210-15. The entire document appears in Warren, *Conquista*, pp. 439-57. All testimony in judicial acts in the Spanish system at this period was recorded by a notary and presented in the third person.

19. Helen Perlstein Pollard, "An Analysis of Urban Zoning and Planning at Prehispanic Tzintzuntzan," *Proceedings of the American Philosophical Society* 121 (1977):46-69; Helen Perlstein Pollard, "Prehispanic Urbanism at Tzintzuntzan, Michoacán." (Ph.D. diss., Columbia University, 1972).

20. "Información hecha a pedimiento del obispo electo Quiroga," in Warren, *Conquista*, p. 441.

21. Pollard, "An Analysis," p. 48.

22. Helen Perlstein Pollard and Shirley Gorenstein, "Agrarian Potential, Population, and the Tarascan State," *Science* 209 (1980):274-77.

23. *RM*, p. 247; "Relación de Pátzcuaro," 1581, *RGM*, 2:111.

24. Lagunas, *Arte*, p. 146; "Relación de Cuseo de la Laguna," 1579, *RGM*, 1:49.

25. Sahagún, *Historia*, 3:135.

26. The dictionary is subsequently cited as "Diccionario tarasco-español." It came from the collection of Nicolás León, who attributed it to Maturino Gilberti in "Fr. Maturino Gilberti y sus escritos inéditos," *Anales del Museo Michoacano* 2 (1889):133-34. He does not give any reason for considering Gilberti the author, admitting that the dictionary is entirely different from Gilberti's published *Vocabulario*. There is no indication of authorship in the work itself. The portion that is preserved consists of 148 folios, 28 of which have been nearly destroyed by the corrosive ink used in the writing.

It begins with *Pumbaçata* and continues through *Thzuril*. Words beginning with *Tz* (*Thz*) are placed after those beginning with X.

27. "Relación de Cuseo de la Laguna," p. 49. "Diccionario tarasco-español" gives the following definition: "*Purepecha*. Gente plebeya, villanos." Maturino Gilberti gives "*Purepecha*. Maceguales, la gente común." Maturino Gilberti, O.F.M., *Diccionario de la lengua tarasca o de Michoacán*, p. 94. Gilberti first published his dictionary in 1558.

28. Manuel Toussaint, *Pátzcuaro*, p. 5.

29. Juan de Tobar, S.J., "Historia de la venida de los indios a poblar México de las partes remotas de Occidente . . ." (MS, John Carter Brown Library), fols. 4v-5. For a more extended treatment of the theories of Tarascan origins, see Rojas González, "Los tarascos," pp. 7-12.

30. Corona Núñez, *Mitología*, p. 7.

31. "Carta del Contador Rodrigo de Albornoz a S. M.," 1525, DII, 13:63.

32. Rojas González, "Los tarascos," p. 23; RGM, 2:60.

33. "Los indios del barrio de San Andrés del pueblo de Zinzonza, provincia de Michoacán, con el gobernador de ella, D. Antonio Guizenméngari sobre pago de tributos . . . , 1557," AGI, Justicia, leg. 157, no. 1.

34. Testimony of Antón Tziguangua, Martín Inaguana, Francisco Yacota, Juan Tziquipu, and Fray Antonio de Beteta in "El monesterio y religiosos de San Francisco de la provincia de Michoacán con la iglesia catedral de la dicha provincia sobre la administración de la pila del bautismo," AGI, Justicia, leg. 178, no. 1, ramo 2.

35. F. Plancarte, "Los tecos," *Anales del Museo Michoacano* 2 (1889):16-26.

36. For those interested in a more extensive discussion of linguistic groups in the Tarascan empire, a still unsurpassed study is that of Donald D. Brand, "An Historical Sketch of Geography and Anthropology in the Tarascan Region: Part I," *New Mexico Anthropologist* 6-7 (1943):37-108. A careful study of the manuscript material from the sixteenth century would possibly give us a more precise idea of linguistic boundaries. For instance, Antón Yringua, native and lieutenant governor of Turicato, said that he was "de la lengua apenecha" ("of the Apenecan language"), "Diego Hernández Nieto, vecino de esta ciudad de México, contra Antonio de Oliver sobre el cumplimiento de la ejecutoria del Consejo de Indias," 1548; AGN, Hospital de Jesús, leg. 292, exp. 119. This would extend Apaneca considerably farther north than Brand indicates; "Historical Sketch," p. 52.

37. Agustín García Alcaraz has written an excellent analysis of Tarascan social organization at the time of the Conquest, based on the *Relación de Michoacán* and other published and manuscript sources. Those who desire a more detailed treatment of the material covered in the following paragraphs should consult it. Agustín García Alcaraz, "Estratificación social entre los tarascos prehispánicos," in Pedro Carrasco et al., *Estratificación social en la Mesoamérica prehispánica*, pp. 221-44.

38. RGM, 2:112.

39. RM, p. 238.

40. Alonso de la Rea, O.F.M., *Crónica de la Orden de N. S. Padre San Francisco, provincia de San Pedro y San Pablo de Mechuacán en la Nueva España*, p. 22.

41. Corona Núñez, *Mitología*, pp. 7-8.

42. Delfina E. López Sarrelangue, *La nobleza indígena de Pátzcuaro en la época virreinal*, pp. 31-32, 25n.

43. "Información de D. Antonio Huitsimíngari," pregunta 3, AGI, Patronato, leg. 60, no. 2, ramo 3.

44. *RM*, p. 245.

45. Ibid., pp. 219, 223-25.

46. Corona Núñez, *Mitología*, pp. 13, 18.

47. *RM*, p. 173. The first part of the *Relación*, to which the text refers here, has unfortunately been lost.

48. Ibid., p. 181; Corona Núñez, *Mitología*, p. 15.

49. Rojas González, "Los tarascos," pp. 22-24. Carlos Herrejón Peredo delineates the history of the conflicts between the Tarascans and the Aztecs in "La pugna entre mexicas y tarascos," *Cuadernos de Historia* 1 (1978):9-47.

50. La Rea, *Crónica*, p. 16.

51. *RM*, p. 171.

52. Ibid., p. 173.

53. Ibid., pp. 173-78.

54. Ibid., pp. 181-83.

55. Corona Núñez, *Mitología*, p. 13.

56. Ibid., pp. 14-16. Pollard notes the great numbers of pipes and pipe fragments found in sectors of Tzintzuntzan that appear to have been associated with religious activities; Pollard, "An Analysis," p. 54.

57. Testimony of Don Francisco Quirongari, in "Información de D. Antonio Huitsimíngari," AGI, Patronato, leg. 60, no. 2, ramo 3, fol. 77.

58. Corona Núñez, *Mitología*, pp. 55-57.

59. Osborne, "An Ethnological Study," p. 73.

60. *RM*, pp. 9-10.

61. Corona Núñez, *Mitología*, p. 71; Eduardo Noguera, "Xipe Totec" and "Tlaloc" in Alfonso Caso and Jorge A. Vivó, eds., *México prehispánico*, pp. 458-64.

62. Corona Núñez, *Mitología*, pp. 71-76.

63. Pollard, "An Analysis," pp. 57-60; Ignacio Marquina, *Arquitectura prehispánica*, pp. 254-59.

64. Corona Núñez, *Mitología*, p. 23.

65. La Rea, *Crónica*, p. 46.

66. *RM*, p. 181.

67. Ibid., pp. 179-82.

68. Bartolomé de las Casas, *Apologética historia*, in *Obras escogidas*, 4:286; Osborne, "An Ethnological Study," pp. 79-81.

69. Juan Focher, O.F.M., "Tractatus de baptismo et matrimonio noviter conversorum ad fidem" (MS, John Carter Brown Library), fol. 17v; cf. *RM*, pp. 217-18.

70. "El fiscal contra Don Pedro de Arellano sobre el oro que tomó a los indios de Michoacán y demás cosas de que fue acusado, 1532," AGI, Justicia, leg. 187, no. 1, ramo 2.

71. Osborne, "An Ethnological Study," pp. 26, 31; *RM*, p. 176.

72. Rosemary Mudd, "The Hallucinogens of Meso-America: An Ethnohistorical Survey" (Master's thesis, University of New Mexico, 1966), pp. 74-76, 109-17. Lagunas gives the following pertinent definitions: "Ezcani, mirar. Ezqua, los ojos, o la vista, o una yerba que hace ver visiones (Ezcani, to look. Ezqua, the eyes, or the sight, or an

herb that causes one to see visions)," Lagunas, *Arte,* p. 288.

73. José Tudela, "Prólogo," *RM,* p. v.

74. Ibid., pp. 171-78.

75. Las Casas, *Apologética historia,* 3:208.

76. Osborne, "An Ethnological Study," pp. 48-49, 53-54; "Testimonio de la cuenta que fue tomado a Julián de Alderete, primer tesorero de Nueva España desde 25 de septiembre de 1521, año de 1522," AGI, Contaduría, leg. 657, no. 1; see Warren, *Conquista,* app. 1, pp. 377-78.

77. Sauer, *Colima,* pp. 6-7, 84-85.

78. "Cierta información sobre lo del cobre de la Nueva España, Michoacán, 1533," AGI, Indiferente General, leg. 1204; published by J. Benedict Warren, ed., "Minas de cobre de Michoacán, 1533," *Anales del Museo Michoacano 2ª época,* no. 6 (1968):35-52. For a study of Tarascan metalworking see Daniel Rubín de la Borbolla, "Orfebrería tarasca," *Cuadernos americanos* 3 (1944):125-38.

Chapter 2

1. *RM,* pp. 231-36.

2. "Noticias para la historia del Antiguo Colegio de la Compañía de Jesús de Mechuacán," *BAGN* 10 (1939):28. This brief relation of the history of the Jesuit college in Pátzcuaro was apparently written in the early 1580s. The last dates and the most abundant detail refer to 1583.

3. Gerónimo de Mendieta, O.F.M., *Historia eclesiástica indiana,* ed. Joaquín García Icazbalceta, p. 376.

4. Beaumont, *Crónica,* 2:69-73.

5. Diego Muñoz, O.F.M., "Descripción de la Provincia de los Apóstoles San Pedro y San Pablo en las Indias de la Nueva España," in Atanasio López, "Misiones o doctrinas de Michoacán y Jalisco (Méjico) en el siglo XVI, 1525-1585," *Archivo Ibero-Americano* 18 (1922):392.

6. *RM,* p. 238.

7. Ibid.

8. Ibid., p. 240.

9. Ibid., p. 239.

10. Ibid.

11. "Información de D. Antonio Huitsimíngari," fol. 12.

12. *RM,* pp. 243-44.

13. Toribio de Motolinía, O.F.M., *Motolinía's History of the Indians of New Spain,* ed. and trans. Francis Borgia Steck, O.F.M., pp. 87-88. For a general treatment of the Narváez expedition and its effects, see Francisco López de Gómara, *Historia general de las Indias, "Hispania Vitriz," cuya segunda parte corresponde a la Conquista de Méjico,* ed. Pilar Guidebalde and Emiliano M. Aguilera, 2:181-212. Gómara gives July 10 as the date of the Noche Triste; ibid., 2:207. The same date is given by Bernal Díaz del Castillo, *Historia verdadera de la conquista de la Nueva España,* ed. Joaquín Ramírez Cabañas, 1:402. But information that Cortés gives in his "Second Letter of Relation," October 30, 1520, a much earlier source, indicates the date of June 30. Fernando Cortés,

Cartas de relación, ed. Manuel Alcalá, pp. 83-86.

14. *RM*, p. 245.

15. "Codex Plancarte," *Anales del Museo Michoacano* 1 (1888): 58.

16. *RM*, pp. 245-46.

17. Ibid., p. 245.

18. La Rea, *Crónica*, p. 32.

19. *RM*, p. 246.

20. Sauer, *Colima*, p. 5.

21. Francisco Cervantes de Salazar, *Crónica de la Nueva España*, ed. M. Magallón, p. 763; Antonio de Herrera y Tordesillas, *Historia general de los hechos de los castellanos en las islas y tierra firme del Mar Océano*, dec. 3, lib. 3, cap. iii. In his first chapter on the discovery of Michoacán, Herrera includes the story of Villadiego, a soldier whom Cortés sent out to reconnoiter new areas and who never returned. Herrera does not say that he went to Michoacán, but that has been inferred from the position of the story; ibid. An inspection of Herrera's source in Cervantes de Salazar shows that Villadiego's expedition was not connected with the discovery of Michoacán; Cervantes de Salazar, *Crónica*, p. 763.

22. *RGM*, 1:84 n. 11; Pedro Carrasco Pizana, *Los Otomíes: cultura e historia prehispánica de los pueblos mesoamericanos de habla otomiana*, p. 278.

23. Cervantes de Salazar, *Crónica*, pp. 764-65.

24. "Further [let them be asked] whether they know etc. that among many other services that the said Juan de Herrera did for His Majesty in the said conquest and pacification of the land, he did one that was outstanding, and it was that immediately after the conquest of this city [Tenochtitlan] was finished, the said Juan de Herrera with two other Spaniards, one of whom was named Porras and the other Juan Francés, was in Tacuba with Don Pedro de Alvarado, captain for Captain-General Don Fernando Cortés, who at the time was captain-general for His Majesty. Without knowing anything about the province of Michoacán, they went to the said province and they brought in peace many Indian *principales* of the towns of the said province, and the Indians gave obedience to the said captain-general in the name of His Majesty, and from this has followed and follows great profit for His Majesty and for many Spaniards."

Juan de Nájera "said that he knows and saw that the said Juan de Herrera and Juan Francés and a certain Porras, named in the said question, left from the town of Tlacuba where the camp of Don Pedro de Alvarado was at that time, and several days later they returned to the said camp and brought certain Indians and provisions and said that they were from the said province of Michoacán, which this witness knows was not conquered or pacified, because the abovesaid happened immediately after this city had been conquered, and he does not know about the other matters contained in the said question."

Andrés de Trozas said that "as soon as this said city of Mexico was conquered, while Don Pedro de Alvarado was in the town of Tlacuba with his men and camp, where this witness was also, he [this witness] saw that the said Juan de Herrera and the said Porras contained in the said question left the said camp, and after a number of days, when they [the men in camp] were already thinking that they were dead, they returned to it and they brought certain Indians and other things and it was said in the said camp that they brought it all from the said province of Michoacán, and this witness knows that the said province was not conquered or pacified at the time because it was conquered later, and he does not know about the other matters contained in the said question."

Diego Hernández said that "this witness was in the town of Tlacuba where the camp of the said Don Pedro de Alvarado was at the time, and he saw the said Juan de Herrera and the others named in the said question come with certain Indian *principales* from the said province of Michoacán, and he saw how they took them to Coyoacán where the said Don Fernando Cortés was and resided, who was captain-general at the time for His Majesty, and for this reason he knows it."

"Probanza de los méritos y servicios de Juan de Herrera y de Pedro Hernández su hermano de los primeros conquistadores de México con Hernán Cortés y descubridores de la tierra de Michoacán, México a 4 de junio de 1541," AGI, Patronato, leg. 56, no. 2, ramo 3.

25. Cortés, *Cartas*, p. 163.
26. "Información de D. Antonio Huitsimíngari," fol. 42v.
27. Cortés, *Cartas*, p. 163.
28. Ibid.
29. Ibid.; López de Gómara, *Historia general*, 2:277.
30. "A la quinta pregunta dijo que lo que de ella sabe es que antes que el dicho Cristóbal de Olí, capitán, fuese a poblar y conquistar la dicha provincia de Michoacán por mandado del dicho Marqués, fue Antón Caycedos y otros dos españoles con cierto mensaje del dicho Marqués al dicho Cazonci, el cual los recibió muy bien y les dio cierto presente de oro y de plata para el dicho Marqués, el cual vio este testigo que lo trajeron muchos principales indios de la provincia de Michoacán, estando el dicho Marqués en Cuyuacán, el cual dicho Cazonci le envió a decir que le enviaba aquel presente y le quería tener por amigo." ("To the fifth question he said that what he knows about it is that before the said Cristóbal de Olid went as captain to settle and conquer the said province of Michoacán by command of the said Marqués, Antón Caicedos and two other Spaniards went with a certain message of the said Marqués to the said Cazonci, who received them very well and gave them a certain present of gold and silver for the said Marqués, and this witness saw that many Indian *principales* of the province of Michoacán brought it while the Marqués was in Cuyuacán, and the said Cazonci sent a message to him that he was sending him that present and that he wanted to have him for a friend." "Información de D. Antonio Huitsimíngari," fols. 43v-44.
31. *RM*, p. 246. This source says nothing about ambassadors from the Cazonci to Cortés.
32. Ibid., pp. 246-47.
33. Gilberti, *Diccionario*, p. 50.
34. Cortés, *Cartas*, p. 166; López de Gómara, *Historia general*, pp. 277-78.
35. *RM*, p. 248.
36. Ibid., p. 258.
37. Ibid., p. 247.
38. Cortés, *Cartas*, p. 166.
39. "Testimonio de la cuenta que fue tomada a Julián de Alderete, primer tesorero de Nueva España desde 25 de septiembre de 1521, año de 1522," AGI, Contaduría,

leg. 657, no. 1; see Warren, *Conquista*, app. I, pp. 377–78. Perhaps the articles that I have called diadems here were the metallic "garlands" with which the Spanish soldiers were crowned; *RM*, p. 246.

40. "Relación del oro, plata e joyas y otras cosas que los procuradores de Nueva España llevan a su Majestad," 1522, *DII*, 12:358–59.

41. Cortés, *Cartas*, p. 166.

42. *RM*, p. 247.

43. Ibid.

44. "Probanza de los méritos y servicios de Francisco Montaño, uno de los primeros descubridores, conquistadores y pobladores de N. E. con Pánfilo de Narváez y en socorro de D. Pedro de Alvarado, 11 agosto 1531," AGI, Patronato, leg. 54, no. 7, ramo 1.

45. Ibid.

46. Ibid.

47. "Petición de Francisco Montaño," sin fecha, AGI, México, leg. 3171.

48. Cervantes de Salazar, *Crónica*, pp. 765–802.

49. Cortés, *Cartas*, pp. 166, 176.

50. "Carta de Don Luis de Cárdenas a su Majestad, Sevilla, 30 agosto 1527," AGI, Patronato, leg. 16, no. 2, ramo 6.

51. "Como Cortés envió a la mar del Sur a hacer dos bergantines, y como envió a Juan Rodríguez de Villafuerte, e Sandoval fue a Ypilcingo e a Zacatula y de lo que más pasó"; Cervantes de Salazar, *Crónica*, p. 809 (lib. 6, cap. xxxiii).

52. Herrera y Tordesillas, *Historia general*, dec. 3, lib. 3, caps. iii–viii.

Chapter 3

1. Díaz del Castillo, *Historia*, 2:74–75.

2. Cortés, *Cartas*, p. 176.

3. Díaz del Castillo, *Historia*, passim.

4. Cortés, *Cartas*, p. 176.

5. López de Gómara, *Historia general*, 2:278; Herrera y Tordesillas, *Historia general*, dec. 3, lib. 3, cap. xi; Fernando de Alva Ixtlilxochitl, *Obras históricas*, ed. Alfredo Chavero, 1:383.

6. *RM*, p. 248.

7. Ixtlilxochitl, *Obras*, 1:383.

8. RM, pp. 249, 254, 256.

9. "Relación de la plata que se hubo de la provincia de Michoacán blanca y dorada al tiempo que a ella fue por capitán Cristóbal de Olid y Juan Rodríguez de Villafuerte por mandado del magnífico señor Hernando Cortés, capitán general y gobernador de esta Nueva España por sus Majestades," AGI, Justicia, leg. 223. The judgment of residencia was a judicial review to which many Spanish officeholders were subject at the end of their tenure of office. The judge was to seek out evidence and testimony regarding malfeasance in office; the officeholder could present evidence and testimony in his own support.

10. Testimony of Pedro de Vargas, 1544, in "Probanza de méritos y servicios de Cristóbal de Maeda . . . ," AGI, Patronato, leg. 63, ramo 18.

11. *RM*, p. 247.

12. "Códex Plancarte," p. 56.

13. *RM*, p. 237.

14. In the following pages we follow the story as it is given in ibid., pp. 248–56. In this and later instances in which long passages from the *Relación* are utilized, the conversational parts are translated more or less literally; greater liberty is often taken with the narrative sections.

15. "Probanza de méritos y servicios de Cristóbal de Maeda, 1544," AGI, Patronato, leg. 63, ramo 18.

16. "Información de D. Antonio Huitzimíngari," fol. 38r–v.

17. "Noticias para la historia del antiguo colegio," p. 28.

18. "Información de D. Antonio Huitsimíngari," fols. 38v, 44, 69v, 76r–v.

19. "Información hecha a pedimiento del obispo electo Quiroga . . . , 1538," AGI, Justicia, leg. 173, no. 1, ramo 2.

20. *RM*, p. 256.

21. "Información de D. Antonio Huitsimíngari," fol. 39.

22. Unless otherwise noted, the next several pages follow the narrative of *RM*, pp. 256–62.

23. Lagunas, *Arte*, pp. 221–22, gives the following series of definitions that show the relationship between being a valiant man and wearing a lip plug: "Angandaqua, pillar, or post. . . . Angamecha, those who had lip plugs between the beard and the lip. Angameni, to be with one's feet in the water, or to put in those lip plugs, which the King put in for the lords and men who were valliant in war, marking them with this nobility, as though for the support, pillar, favor, and protection of the other plebeian people, and thus such men could also intercede, persuade, importune, and stand up for them, as: Angandahpeni, to do the abovementioned, and to be the pillar and general support for everyone. Angandarhunstani, to favor, and Angandarhupenstani, to favor generally, that is, to return to lift up, or sustain, or protect the needy, etc."

24. "El fiscal contra Don Pedro de Arellano sobre el oro que tomó a los indios de Michoacán . . . , 1532," AGI, Justicia, leg. 187, no. 1, ramo 2.

25. José Tudela interprets this statement as scatological humor by the Cazonci, referring to Aztec codices that depict some gods eating the golden droppings of other deities. *RM*, p. 260n.

26. *Patol*, or patolli, was a game of chance played widely in Mesoamerica. The players used beans with marks on them, after the manner of dice, and moved counters along positions on a cross-shaped board. The winner was the one who could first get back to his starting point. The Indians gambled heavily on its outcome. George C. Vaillant, *Aztecs of Mexico*, p. 207; *Codex Mendoza, Aztec Manuscript*, Commentaries by Kurt Ross, p. 113.

27. Díaz del Castillo, *Historia*, 2:80.

28. "El fiscal contra Don Pedro de Arellano . . . ," AGI, Justicia, leg. 187, no. 1, ramo 2.

29. "Testimonio del cuaderno de cuenta original de Diego de Soto, tesorero de Nueva España por ausencia de Julián de Alderete, tomada en 12 de mayo de 1524," AGI, Contaduría, leg. 657, no. 2 (see Warren, *Conquista*, app. 2, p. 379).

30. *RM*, p. 262; Cortés, *Cartas*, p. 176.

31. *RGM*, passim.

32. "Relación de la plata . . . ," AGI, Justicia, leg. 223.

33. Francisco Fernández del Castillo, ed., *Tres conquistadores y pobladores de la Nueva España: Cristóbal Martín Millán de Gamboa, Andrés de Tapia, Jerónimo López*, pp. 18, 61, 209.

34. Testimony of Domingo Niño, AGI, Justicia, leg. 220, fol. 239.

35. Cortés, *Cartas*, p. 176. Bernal Díaz suggests that Olid returned to Mexico at this time because his beautiful young Portuguese wife, Doña Felipa de Arauz, who had arrived in Mexico shortly before his departure, had more attraction for him than the rigors of the conquest. Díaz del Castillo, *Historia*, 2:99.

36. "Probanza de méritos y servicios de Juan Rodríguez de Villafuerte, Zacatula, 1525," AGI, México, leg. 203.

37. *RM*, p. 256.

38. Testimony of Jerónimo Flores, in "Probanza de méritos y servicios de Juan de Vera, 1560," AGI, México, leg. 206.

39. *RM*, p. 262.

40. Testimony of Alonso Ortiz de Zúñiga (fol. 246), Jerónimo de Aguilar (fol. 263), and Andrés de Monjaraz (fol. 207), AGI, Justicia, leg. 220.

41. Testimony of Ruy González, ibid., fols. 142v-43.

42. "Probanza de . . . Juan Rodríguez de Villafuerte, 1525," AGI, México, leg. 203; testimony of Diego Ruiz, in "Probanza de méritos y servicios de Diego Garrido, 1557," AGI, Patronato, leg. 61, no. 1, ramo 1.

43. Herrera y Tordesillas, *Historia general*, dec. 3, lib. 3, cap. xvii.

44. Cortés, *Cartas*, pp. 176-77.

45. López de Gómara, *Historia general*, 2:281.

46. Díaz del Castillo, *Historia*, p. 99.

47. Ibid., 2:92-97.

48. Probanza de . . . Juan Rodríguez de Villafuerte, 1525," AGI, México, leg. 203; testimony of Diego Ruiz, in "Probanza de . . . Diego Garrido, 1557," AGI, Patronato, leg. 61, no. 1, ramo 1; "Probanza de . . . Juan Fernández, Colima, 1535," with witnesses Alonso del Río, Antonio del Castillo, Alonso de Arévalo, Martín Monje, Pero Gómez, Juan Bautista, and Bartolomé Thavaran, all *vecinos* of Colima, who stated that they had arrived there with Sandoval after having served with Olid in Michoacán, AGI, Patronato, leg. 64, ramo 9.

49. Cortés, *Cartas*, p. 183; "Probanza de méritos y servicios de Jerónimo Flores, México, 1536," AGI, México, leg. 203.

50. Cortés, *Cartas*, p. 183.

51. *RM*, pp. 263-64.

52. Cortés, *Cartas*, pp. 183-84.

53. Besides those mentioned in note 47 above, we find the names Diego Garrido, Fernando de la Peña, Jorge Carrillo, Antón López, Gonzalo de Talavera, Alonso Lorenzo, Juan Pérez, Martín Jiménez, Diego de Chávez, Rodrigo Manrique, Pedro de Santana, and Jerónimo Flores; "Vecinos y pueblos de Colima en 1532," *BAGN*, 10:7-23.

54. Cortés, *Cartas*, p. 176.

55. López de Gómara, *Historia general*, 2:278.

56. "Carta de Luis de Cárdenas a Su Majestad, 1527," AGI, Patronato, leg. 16, no. 2, ramo 6.

57. "Testimonio del cuaderno de cuenta original de Diego de Soto, 1524," AGI, Contaduría, leg. 657, no. 2 (see Warren, *Conquista*, app. 2, p. 379).

58. "Relación de la plata . . . ," AGI, Justicia, leg. 223 (see Warren, *Conquista*, app. 3, pp. 380-85).

59. Díaz del Castillo, *Historia*, 2:91; López de Gómara, *Historia general*, 2:308.

60. "Información de D. Antonio Huitsimíngari, fols. 29v-30.

61. Cortés, *Cartas*, p. 202.

62. "Juan Velázquez de Salazar, vecino y regidor de la Ciudad de México, con Pedro Bazán y Antonio Anguiano, de la propia vecindad, sobre el derecho a los pueblos de Pungarabato y Charcharando, 1537," AGI, Justicia, leg. 126, no. 5.

63. "Aquesta nació sin par; / Yo en serviros sin segundo; / Vos sin igual en el mundo." López de Gómara, *Historia general*, p. 308.

64. *RM*, pp. 262-63.

65. Cortés, *Cartas*, pp. 184-85, 192-93.

66. Ibid., pp. 191-92; López de Gómara, *Historia general*, 2:290-91; Díaz del Castillo, *Historia*, 2:113-18.

67. Fernández del Castillo, *Tres conquistadores*, pp. 18, 209.

68. *RM*, p. 264.

69. Cortés, *Cartas*, p. 193.

70. *RM*, p. 264.

71. Cortés, *Cartas*, p. 202; López de Gómara, *Historia general*, 2:310-12; Díaz del Castillo, *Historia*, 2:184-87.

72. *RM*, p. 264.

Chapter 4

1. Much of the material in the first part of this chapter appeared previously in Fintan [J. Benedict] Warren, "The Caravajal Visitation: First Spanish Survey of Michoacán," *The Americas* 19 (April, 1963):404-12.

2. Fernando Cortés, *Cartas y otras documentos de Hernán Cortés*, ed. Mariano Cuevas, S.J., p. 33.

3. France V. Scholes and Eleanor B. Adams, eds., *Proceso contra Tzintzicha Tangaxoan, el Caltzontzin, formado por Nuño de Guzmán, año de 1530*, p. 20.

4. The visitation of Turicato is found in "Hernández Nieto contra Oliver, 1548," AGN, Hospital de Jesús, leg. 292, exp. 119, fols. 432-34. The visitation of Uruapan is in "Francisco de Villegas, vecino de la ciudad de México, con Juan Infante, de la misma vecindad, sobre el pueblo de Capacuero, 1541," AGI, Justicia, leg. 138. Another copy of the visitation of Uruapan and the visitations of Comanja, Huaniqueo, and Erongarícuaro are contained in "Autos del obispo y la ciudad de Michoacán con Juan Infante, vecino de México, sobre que a éste le restituyeran los pueblos de Comanja y Naranja con las estancias a éllas sujetas que la habían sido encomendados, 1540," AGI, Justicia, leg. 130, fols. 1636-38, 952v-59, 1984-85v, 1177-84, 1856v-63, 1145-52 (hereafter cited as AGI, Justicia, leg. 130). Published versions of all five fragments appear in Warren, *Conquista*, app. 4, pp. 386-408.

5. This is supported by the introduction of the notary to one of the copies of the

visitation of Huaniqueo: ". . . it is in a book of visitations which appears to have been made in the province of Michoacán of the town of Guaniqueo and of the others subject to it, which it appears was made by Francisco Morcillo, who was notary of the said visitation, on the twenty-second day of the month of March of the year 1524, as it is all apparent from the said original visitation, which is signed at the end of the said book by the said Francisco Morcillo." AGI, Justicia, leg. 130, fol. 1856r–v.

6. "Probanza de los méritos y servicios de Antonio de Caravajal, México, 1559," AGI, Patronato, leg. 62, no. 1.

7. *RGM*, 2:40.

8. "Probanza de Caravajal," AGI, Patronato, leg. 62, no. 1.

9. "To the eighth question he said that this witness knows about what is contained in the said question. Asked how he knows it, he said that it was because before the said Marqués divided up the said province of Michoacán, in order to divide it he sent a certain Francisco [sic] de Caravajal to visit it and to know the towns with their subjects which are distinct one from another in it, and this witness also went as interpreter by command of the said Marqués in order to know and ascertain the abovesaid in the said province." Testimony of Tomás de Rijoles, August 18, 1540, AGI, Justicia, leg. 130, fol. 1274v.

10. AGI, Justicia, leg. 130, fol. 1152.

11. See n. 4 above.

12. "Hernández Nieto contra Oliver, 1548," AGN, Hospital de Jesús, leg. 292, exp. 119, fol. 317v.

13. *RGM*, 2:40.

14. The earliest cedulas that have come to light for Michoacán are dated July 24, 1524, for Matalcingo (Charo) and Taxinda (Taximaroa). "El Comendador Juan Fernández Infante con el Contador Rodrigo de Albornoz . . . sobre derecho a un pueblo de indios, 1531," AGI, Justicia, leg. 113, no. 2; "El fiscal con Gonzalo de Salazar y Pedro Almíndez Cherino . . . sobre . . . Taximaroa, 1529," AGI, Justicia, leg. 185, ramo 1.

15. *RM*, pp. 173–74.

16. "Hernández Nieto contra Oliver," AGN, Hospital de Jesús, leg. 292, exp. 119, fol. 294.

17. Scholes and Adams, eds., *Proceso contra Tzintzicha Tangaxoan*, p. 14.

18. "Probanza de Caravajal," AGI, Patronato, leg. 62, no. 1.

19. AGI, Justicia, leg. 130, fol. 1145v; Warren, *Conquista*, p. 404.

20. AGI, Justicia, leg. 130, fol. 1178; Warren, *Conquista*, p. 397.

21. Gilberti, *Diccionario*, pp. 381, 469.

22. AGI, Justicia, leg. 130, fols. 952-59; Warren, *Conquista*, pp. 386-92.

23. AGI, Justicia, leg. 130, fol. 953; Warren, *Conquista*, p. 386.

24. "Hernández Nieto contra Oliver," AGN, Hospital de Jesús, leg. 292, exp. 119, fol. 272r–v; "Autos de Diego Hernández Nieto, vecino de México, con Antonio de Oliver, de la propia vecindad, sobre derecho a la mitad del pueblo de Turicato y sus sujetos, 1547," AGI, Justicia, leg. 145.

25. "El Comendador Juan Fernández Infante con el Contador Rodrigo de Albornoz . . . sobre derecho a un pueblo de indios, 1531," AGI, Justicia, leg. 113, no. 2.

26. "El fiscal con Gonzalo de Salazar y Pedro Almíndez Chirino, factor y veedor en México, sobre el derecho a un pueblo de indios llamado Taximaroa, 1529," AGI, Justi-

cia, leg. 185, ramo 1 (see also "Gonzalo de Salazar contra Fernando Cortés sobre Taji-maroa," AGN, Hospital de Jesús, leg. 265, exp. 12); "El fiscal de su Majestad con Diego Enríquez de Medina y Doña Luisa de Velázquez sobre el pueblo de indios de Tancítaro, 1573," AGI, Escribanía de Cámara, leg. 160, fol. 21; "Juan de Albornoz, vecino de la ciudad de México, con el Veedor Pedro Almíndez Chirino, sobre derecho a la mitad del pueblo de Xacona, 1536," AGI, Justicia, leg. 123, no. 1; "Francisco de Villegas, vecino de la ciudad de México con Juan Infante de la misma vecindad sobre el pueblo de Capaquero, 1541," AGI, Justicia, leg. 138.

27. "Juan Velázquez de Salazar . . . con Pedro Bazán y Antonio Anguiano . . . sobre derecho a los pueblos de Pungarabato y Charcharando, 1537," AGI, Justicia, leg. 126, no. 5.

28. López de Gómara, *Historia general*, 2:308-309.

29. "Información sobre los pueblos que Fernando Cortés tenía al tiempo que fue a la conquista de Honduras así como lo que rentaban, Fernando Cortés contra Peralmíndez Chirino, sobre los pueblos de Tuspa, Amula, y Zapotlán, 1531," AGN, Hospital de Jesús, leg. 265, exp. 5.

30. "Residencia de Fernando Cortés," AGI, Justicia, leg. 220, fols. 55r–v, 217–18.

31. "Probanza de méritos y servicios de Jorge Carrillo," AGI, Patronato, leg. 61, no. 2, ramo 5.

Chapter 5

1. "Ordenanzas de Fernando Cortés, Tascaltecal, 22 diciembre 1520," AGN, Hospital de Jesús, leg. 271, exp. 11. There are some small tears in the manuscript, and a few words are missing. I have filled out the sentences, supplying the missing words in brackets.

2. "Relación de la plata . . . ," AGI, Justicia, leg. 223.

3. Interrogatory of Gonzalo Gómez, July 17, 1537, in "Proceso del Santo Oficio de la Inquisición y el doctor Rafael de Cervanes, fiscal, en su nombre, contra Gonzalo Gómez," AGN, Inquisición, vol. 2, exp. 2.

4. *IP*, 1:66, no. 178; Certificación del R. P. Francisco Martínez, México, 4 septiembre 1537, in "Proceso contra Gonzalo Gómez," AGN, Inquisición, vol. 2, exp. 2.

5. "Relación de la plata . . . ," AGI, Justicia, leg. 223.

6. *RM*, p. 264.

7. Ibid.

8. See chap. 6.

9. *RM*, p. 264.

10. José Bravo Ugarte, S.J., *Historia de México*, vol. 2, *La Nueva España*, p. 98.

11. Díaz del Castillo, *Historia*, 2:189.

12. Pedro Oroz, O.F.M., *The Oroz Codex*, tr. and ed. Angelico Chavez, O.F.M., pp. 57-60, 80-85, 205-206, 279-81, with special attention to the very ample footnotes.

13. Edmundo O'Gorman, "Introducción," in Toribio Motolinía, *Memoriales, o libro de las cosas de la Nueva España y de los naturales de ella*, pp. ci-cii.

14. Oroz, *The Oroz Codex*, p. 82; Robert Ricard, *The Spiritual Conquest of Mexico: An Essay on the Apostolate and the Evangelizing Methods of the Mendicant Orders in New*

Spain, 1523-1572, p. 208.

15. Mendieta, *Historia eclesiástica,* p. 376.

16. See chap. 6.

17. Mendieta, *Historia eclesiástica,* p. 376.

18. *RM,* p. 267; Cervantes de Salazar, *Crónica,* p. 801.

19. Mendieta, *Historia eclesiástica,* p. 376.

20. Oroz, *The Oroz Codex,* p. 282.

21. *RM,* p. 264, line 17 and n.

22. *Cartas de Indias,* facsimile F.

23. Oroz, *The Oroz Codex,* pp. 281-83; Torquemada, *Monarquía indiana,* 3:435-36.

24. Francisco Gonzaga, O.F.M., *De origine Seraphicae Religionis,* p. 1281.

25. Torquemada, *Monarquía indiana,* 3:332.

26. Muñoz, "Descripción," p. 393.

27. "Alonso de Mata, vecino de la Ciudad de los Ángeles, con el Bachiller Juan Ortega y Francisco de Santa Cruz . . . sobre derecho a una encomienda de indios, 1541," AGI, Justicia, leg. 135, no. 3.

28. "Información de D. Antonio Huitsimíngari," fol. 28v.

29. Mendieta, *Historia eclesiástica,* p. 249.

30. "Mata con Ortega y Santa Cruz, 1541," AGI, Justicia, leg. 135, no. 3; Joaquín García Icazbalceta, *Don Fray Juan de Zumárraga,* ed. Rafael Aguayo Spencer and Antonio Castro Leal, 1:60-62.

31. García Icazbalceta, *Zumárraga,* 2:271; Mariano Cuevas, S.J., *Historia de la Iglesia en México,* 1:427.

32. Oroz, *The Oroz Codex,* p. 292 and nn.

33. Antonio Tello, O.F.M., *Crónica miscelánea de la Sancta Provincia de Xalisco,* Libro 3, p. 7; Oroz, *The Oroz Codex,* p. 288.

34. "Mata con Ortega y Santa Cruz, 1541," AGI, Justicia, leg. 135, no. 3.

35. Testimony of Diego de Soria, 1531, AGI, Justicia, leg. 226.

36. "El fiscal contra Don Pedro de Arellano, 1532," AGI, Justicia, leg. 187, no. 1, ramo 2.

37. Mendieta, *Historia eclesiástica,* p. 249; see also Oroz, *The Oroz Codex,* p. 133.

38. Beaumont, *Crónica,* 2:136.

39. "Proceso contra Gonzalo Gómez," AGN, Inquisición, vol. 2, exp. 2.

40. Beaumont, *Crónica,* 2:110.

41. Ibid., and p. 106.

42. Bravo Ugarte, *Historia de México,* 2:98.

43. Motolinía, *Memoriales,* p. cii.

44. Mendieta, *Historia eclesiástica,* p. 376.

45. Isidro Félix de Espinosa, O.F.M., *Crónica de la Provincia Franciscana de los Apóstoles San Pedro y San Pablo de Michoacán,* ed. Nicolás León and José Ignacio Dávila Garibi, p. 83.

46. Muñoz, "Descripción," p. 393.

47. Espinosa, *Crónica,* p. 83.

48. Beaumont, *Crónica,* vol. 3, picture facing p. 218, compared with a manuscript copy in Beaumont's rough draft, in John Carter Brown Library, Providence, R.I. I am indebted to Agustín García Alcaraz for the translation of the Tarascan text.

49. "Información hecha a pedimiento del obispo electo Quiroga, 1538," AGI, Justicia, leg. 173, no. 1, ramo 2.

50. Ibid.

51. AGI, México, leg. 1088, Tomo de 1529-30.

52. "Información hecha a pedimiento del obispo electo Quiroga, 1538," AGI, Justicia, leg. 173, no. 1, ramo 1.

53. Beaumont, *Crónica*, vol. 3, picture facing p. 218; Toussaint, *Pátzcuaro*, pp. 204-13.

54. *RM*, p. 264.

55. Torquemada, *Monarquía indiana*, 3:436.

56. La Rea, *Crónica*, p. 45.

57. Espinosa, *Crónica*, pp. 86-87.

58. Beaumont, *Crónica*, 2:125.

59. Diego Valadés, *Rhetorica Christiana ad concionandi et orandi usum accommodata utriusque facultatis exemplis suo loco insertis que quidem ex indorum maxime deprompta sunt historiis inde praeter doctrinam suam quoque delectatio comparabitur*, p. 211.

60. "Proceso contra Gonzalo Gómez," AGN, Inquisición, vol. 2, exp. 2.

61. Espinosa, *Crónica*, pp. 83-84.

62. Ibid., p. 84.

63. *RM*, p. 264.

64. Mendieta, *Historia eclesiástica*, p. 306.

65. *RM*, p. 265.

66. Ibid., p. 264.

67. Ibid.

68. "Testimonio del proceso de residencia," in Rafael Aguayo Spencer, ed., *Don Vasco de Quiroga: documentos*, p. 443.

69. Tello, *Crónica*, lib. 3, p. 7.

70. *RM*, p. 264.

71. Espinosa, *Crónica*, pp. 89-90.

72. Ibid., pp. 87-89.

73. *RM*, p. 264.

74. Testimony of Diego de Soria, 1531, AGI, Justicia, leg. 226.

75. Muñoz, "Descripción," p. 393-94.

76. The following material on the continuation of idolatry, unless otherwise indicated, is taken from "El fiscal contra Don Pedro de Arellano sobre el oro que tomó a los indios de Michoacán y demás cosas de que fue acusado, 1532," AGI, Justicia, leg. 187, no. 1, ramo 2.

77. *RM*, p. 179.

78. Fintan B. [J. Benedict] Warren, *Vasco de Quiroga and His Pueblo-Hospitals of Santa Fe*, p. 82.

79. Interrogatory of Gonzalo Gómez, July 17, 1537; testimony of Gonzalo López, July 18, 1537, in "Proceso contra Gonzalo Gómez," AGI, Inquisición, vol. 2, exp. 2.

80. Espinosa, *Crónica*, pp. 98-99.

81. "Información de D. Antonio Huitsimíngari," question 9 and supporting testimony.

82. Testimony of Andrés Suárez, AGI, Justicia, leg. 232, fol. 492.

83. Testimony of Don Francisco, ibid., fol. 432v.

84. Testimony of Don Ramiro, ibid., fol. 430v.

85. *RM*, pp. 265–66.

86. Beaumont includes in his chronicle certain paintings of Tarascan origin which, he writes, were given to him by Cuini, an Indian *principal*. They appear to be authentic, even depicting the native judges carrying bows and arrows as insignia of office and smoking long-stemmed pipes. The main judge carries a spear in his hand and has a calabash on his back, as was the custom (Beaumont, *Crónica*, vol. 3, facing p. 122). The styles of clothing seem to be somewhat influenced by the styles introduced by the Spaniards. It is impossible to give a date to the items of mission history that they portray. Fray Martín de Jesús and Fray Ángel are shown receiving the obedience of Axayatl, or Ayacatl, and Ziguangua, lords of Tzirosco and Iguatzio, with their wives Cuinierángari and Zintzun (ibid.). In another picture the same two friars are shown catechizing, with the assistance of a faithful and fervent Indian general named Nanuma (ibid., facing p. 314). Jesús Romero Flores is probably correct in taking the title of the first picture to indicate the conversion of four lords, Ayacatl, Ziguangua, Cuinierángari, and Tzintzun, with their wives. Cf. Jesús Romero Flores, *Historia de Michoacán*, 1:126. Cuinierángari was Don Pedro's Tarascan name, and Zintzun, or Tzintzun, would be the Tarascan equivalent of this brother's name, Huitzitziltzi, which is Nahuatl. Nevertheless, the person in the painting could not be Don Pedro's brother, since he had gone to Honduras before the arrival of the friars.

Chapter 6

1. *RM*, p. 261.

2. Scholes and Adams, eds., *Proceso contra Tzintzicha Tangaxoan*, pp. 14, 22.

3. A good general survey, from which I have drawn much of the following material on this troubled period in the Spanish colony, is found in Manuel Orozco y Berra, *Historia de la dominación española en México*, 1:113–17, 163–89. A survey in English can be found in: Hubert Howe Bancroft, *History of Mexico*, 2:203–39. For precise dating, the best documentary source is *ACM*, 1:20–90.

4. The date October 12, 1524, is given as the date of departure in Cortés' Fifth Letter of Relation and in an interrogatory presented in a legal case by Bachiller Juan de Ortega, *alcalde mayor* of Mexico, in February 1526, before Cortés' return. Cortés, *Cartas*, p. 221. "Acusación del Bachiller Juan de Ortega, alcalde mayor, contra Gonzalo de Salazar y Peralmíndez Chirino, 13 febrero 1526," AGI, Justicia, leg. 225. This indicates that Cortés' Fourth Letter of Relation, which is dated in Tenochtitlan, October 15, 1524, was either postdated or completed after Cortés had actually left the city, perhaps while he was still within its jurisdiction. Cortés, *Cartas*, p. 218.

5. "Proceso entre Juan Bello y el fiscal sobre Tlacintla y Izquimilpa," AGN, Hospital de Jesús, leg. 285, exp. 92. See published version by Robert S. Chamberlain, "Two unpublished documents of Hernán Cortés and New Spain, 1519 and 1524," *Hispanic American Historical Review* 18 (1938): 523–25.

6. *ACM*, 1:23.

7. Ibid., pp. 30–31.

8. "Carta a su Majestad del electo obispo de Méjico, D. Juan de Zumárraga . . . (27 de agosto de 1529)," *DII*, 13:112, 119.

9. ACM, 1:35-36.
10. Ibid., p. 41.
11. Gonzalo Fernández de Oviedo y Valdés, *Historia general y natural de las Indias,* lib. L, cap. X, pars. 32-36 (5:350-55).
12. ACM, 1:51-55.
13. G. Micheal Riley, *Fernando Cortés and the Marquesado in Morelos, 1522-1547,* p. 23.
14. *IP,* 1:47-48, no. 93; ibid., p. 56, no. 130.
15. "El promotor fiscal contra Rodrigo de Paz, 1525," AGI, Justicia, leg. 111.
16. ACM, 1:59-60.
17. Ibid., pp. 60-63.
18. "Carta del contador Rodrigo de Albornoz a S. M., 1525," *DII,* 13:45-84.
19. ACM, 1:65-67.
20. The judicial records of this incident are published in *DII,* 26:198-223.
21. ACM, 1:75-76.
22. Ibid., p. 76.
23. "Ortega contra Salazar y Chirinos, 1526," AGI, Justicia, leg. 225.
24. "Albornoz a su Magesdad, 1525," *DII,* 13:72.
25. "Ortega contra Salazar y Chirinos, 1526," AGI, Justicia, leg. 225.
26. Ibid.
27. AGI, Contaduría, leg. 657.
28. Ibid.
29. "Ortega contra Salazar y Chirinos, 1526," AGI, Justicia, leg. 111.
30. AGI, Contaduría, leg. 657.
31. ACM, 1:37.
32. "Tasación Ortega," fols. 962, 967, 971.
33. "Probanza de méritos y servicios de Alonso de Ávila, 1531," AGI, Patronato, leg. 54, no. 7, ramo 6.
34. "Probanza de méritos y servicios de Alonso de Ávila, hijo de Gil González de Ávila, 1550," AGI, Patronato, leg. 59, no. 2, ramo 2.
35. "Probanza de méritos y servicios de Alonso de Ávila, 1526," AGI, Patronato, leg. 54, no. 3, ramo 3.
36. Ibid.
37. "El fiscal contra don Pedro de Arellano, 1532," AGI, Justicia, leg. 187, no. 1, ramo 1.
38. Testimony of Juan Tirado, AGI, Justicia, leg. 220, fol. 201.
39. Testimony of Hernando de Sosa, AGI, Justicia, leg. 226, fol. 188v.
40. "El Marqués con los herederos de Hernán López de Ávila," AGN, Hospital de Jesús, leg. 264, exp. 2, cuaderno 2.
41. *IP,* 1:86-87, no. 276.
42. "El fiscal contra Jorge Carrillo," AGI, Justicia, leg. 198, no. 3.
43. *RM,* pp. 264-65.

Chapter 7

1. ACM, 1:85.

2. Ibid., p. 87.

3. Ibid., pp. 90-94.

4. Ibid., p. 98.

5. Ibid., pp. 95, 98.

6. "Petición de los procuradores de las villas, y respuesta de Fernando Cortés, México, 20 julio 1526," AGN, Hospital de Jesús, leg. 271, exp. 14, fols. 39-42.

7. "Requerimiento del señor gobernador al señor Lic. Marcos de Aguilar, 1526," AGN, Hospital de Jesús, leg. 271, exp. 9.

8. ACM, 1:97-101.

9. Ibid., pp. 101-23.

10. Ibid., pp. 140-41, 123-24.

11. Ibid., pp. 139-42.

12. Ibid., pp. 142-86.

13. "Instrucciones dadas al Licenciado Luis Ponce de León," Toledo, 4 noviembre 1525, DIU, 9:218.

14. "Información hecha contra la comisión de Cristóbal de Tapia, México, 1522," AGN, Hospital de Jesús, leg. 271, exp. 13.

15. AGN, Hospital de Jesús, leg. 203, fol. 74.

16. Ibid., fol. 65.

17. "Carta de Fernando Cortés a Francisco Cortés, 1524," AGN, Hospital de Jesús, leg. 271, exp. 11, cuad. 4.

18. "Albornoz a S.M., México, 15 diciembre 1525," DII, 13:53, 63.

19. AGN, Hospital de Jesús, leg. 203, exp. 1.

20. "Conocimiento de Pedro Tiscareno de cosas que llevó para la armada del Sur, Uchichila, 11 marzo 1527," AGN, Hospital de Jesús, leg. 203, fol. 69. For the complete list see Warren, Conquista, p. 159.

21. AGN, Hospital de Jesús, leg. 203, fol. 76.

22. "El Estado y Marquesado del Valle sobre la satisfacción de lo que erogó Don Fernando Cortés en la expedición del descubrimiento de las islas de Maluco y otras, 1769," AGN, Hospital de Jesús, leg. 438, exp. 1. For a general history of the voyage see Ione Stuessy Wright, Voyages of Álvaro de Saavedra Cerón, 1527-1529.

23. AGI, Patronato, leg. 199, ramo 2.

24. "Pedro de Bazán con Antonio Anguiano, vecino de México, sobre derecho al pueblo de Pungarabato, 1541," AGI, Justicia, leg. 135, no. 2.

25. "Probanza de méritos y servicios de Alonso Álvarez de Espinosa, México, 1558," AGI, Patronato, leg. 61, no. 2, ramo 9. For a discussion of the changing definition of the area known as Los Motines, see Donald D. Brand et al., Coalcomán and Motines del Oro, an Ex-Distrito of Michoacán, Mexico, pp. 60-63.

26. Sauer, Colima, pp. 14-15. Brand et al., Coalcomán, p. 60.

27. "Probanza de méritos y servicios de Francisco de Torres, México, 1545," AGI, México, leg. 204, no. 17; "Probanza de méritos y servicios de Francisco de Torres, México, 1558," AGI, Patronato, leg. 61, no. 2, ramo 1; "Probanza de méritos y servicios de Alonso Álvarez de Espinosa, México, 1558," AGI, Patronato, leg. 61, no. 2, ramo 9.

28. ACM, 1:126-36, 149-66.

29. "Probanza . . . Torres, 1558," AGI, Patronato, leg. 61, no. 2, ramo 1.

30. "Probanza de méritos y servicios de Antón Caicedo, México, 1566," AGI, Patro-

nato, leg. 67, ramo 7.

31. "Tasación Ortega," 1528, AGI, Justicia, leg. 130, fol. 962.

32. "Probanza . . . Torres, 1545," AGI, México, leg. 204, no. 17; "Probanza . . . Álvarez de Espinosa, 1558," AGI, Patronato, leg. 61, no. 2, ramo 9.

33. "Probanza . . . Torres, 1558," AGI, Patronato, leg. 61, no. 2, ramo 1.

34. "Probanza . . . Torres, 1545," AGI, México, leg. 204, no. 17.

35. *IP*, 1:149, no. 572.

36. "Probanza . . . Torres, 1558," AGI, Patronato, leg. 61, no. 2, ramo 1.

37. "Probanza . . . Torres, 1545," AGI, México, leg. 204, no. 17.

38. *IP*, 1:129, no. 469.

39. *IP*, vol. 1, nos. 531, 558, 600, 612, 618, 642, 692, 697, 702, 718, 755.

40. Ibid., p. 173, no. 697.

41. Ibid., p. 234, no. 1030.

42. Ibid., p. 184, no. 755.

43. "Probanza . . . Torres, 1558," AGI, Patronato, leg. 61, no. 2, ramo 1.

44. Testimony of Álvarez de Espinosa, ibid.

45. Ibid.

46. Testimony of Torres in "Probanza . . . Álvarez de Espinosa, 1558," AGI, Patronato, leg. 61, no. 2, ramo 9. The fact that the *probanzas* of Torres and Álvarez de Espinosa were made within two weeks of one another and that each conqueror was the best witness for the other regarding the activities in Michoacán leaves the researcher with some suspicion of collusion. Be that as it may, they do give us the clearest statements available regarding the military action in southwestern Michoacán.

47. "El fiscal contra Arellano, 1532," AGI, Justicia, leg. 187, no. 1, ramo 2.

48. Scholes and Adams, eds., *Proceso contra Tzintzicha Tangaxoan*, p. 14.

49. Ibid., p. 35.

50. AGI, Contaduría, leg. 657. Unfortunately, in relation to determining the chronology of Sánchez Farfán's activities in Michoacán, this bit of information is not dated.

51. *IP*, 1:68-69, no. 184.

52. "Mata con Ortega y Santa Cruz, 1541," AGI, Justicia, leg. 135, no. 3.

53. AGI, Justicia, leg. 130, fol. 1813.

54. Ibid., fol. 728.

55. Scholes and Adams, eds., *Proceso contra Tzintzicha Tangaxoan*, p. 18.

56. Ibid., p. 15.

57. Ibid., pp. 32-33.

58. Francisco de Santa Cruz claimed Tuzantla as his encomienda. "Mata con Ortega y Santa Cruz, 1541," AGI, Justicia, leg. 135, no. 3.

59. Scholes and Adams, eds., *Proceso contra Tzintzicha Tangaxoan*, p. 33.

60. The letters bear the dates of March (sic—May) 27, July 12, and July 28, 1528. Ortega presented them as evidence in his lawsuit with Mata over Tuzantla. AGI, Justicia, leg. 135, no. 3. See Warren, *Conquista*, app. 7, pp. 425-32.

61. ACM, 1:141.

62. *IP*, 1:271, no. 1242.

63. "Tasación Ortega," fol. 960; *IP*, 1:271-72, no. 1247.

64. "Mata con Ortega y Santa Cruz, 1541," AGI, Justicia, leg. 135, no. 3; *IP*, 1:271, no. 1245.

65. As noted above, the letters from Estrada to Ortega are found in "Mata con Ortega y Santa Cruz, 1541," AGI, Justicia, leg. 135, no. 3. The folios of the trial record are not numbered. In references to the letters through the rest of this chapter, the date of the letter cited is given in the text without a corresponding footnote.

66. "Mata con Ortega y Santa Cruz, 1541," AGI, Justicia, leg. 135, no. 3.

67. The record of the assessment is given in "Tasación Ortega," AGI, Justicia, leg. 130, fols. 959-73. Another copy is in the Archivo Histórico del Instituto Nacional de Antropología e Historia (Mexico), Col. Gómez de Orozco, MS 171; see Warren, *Conquista*, app. 6, pp. 411-25.

68. See n. 65 above.

69. Díaz del Castillo, *Historia*, 1:397.

70. Ibid., 2:247.

71. Ibid., p. 192.

72. AGI, Justicia, leg. 130, fols. 966v, 967v, 970v, 965v, 966, 970, 1242.

73. Interrogatory of Alonso de Mata, AGI, Justicia, leg. 135, no. 3.

74. "Mata con Ortega y Santa Cruz, 1541," AGI, Justicia, leg. 135, no. 3.

75. AGI, Patronato, leg. 199, ramo 3.

76. Interrogatory of Bachiller Juan de Ortega, January 18, 1541, AGI, Justicia, leg. 135, no. 3.

77. "El fiscal contra Arellano, 1532," AGI, Justicia, leg. 187, no. 1, ramo 2.

78. Scholes and Adams, eds., *Proceso contra Tzintzicha Tangaxoan*, pp. 33, 35.

79. *RM*, p. 267. The transcription reads "aporreó aquellos principales" but the manuscript has "aperreó aquellos principales." The change in one letter makes the difference between using clubs on them and setting dogs on them.

80. Scholes and Adams, eds., *Proceso contra Tzintzicha Tangaxoan*, p. 21.

81. *RM*, p. 267.

82. "Tasación Ortega," fols. 964, 968; Scholes and Adams, eds., *Proceso contra Tzintzicha Tangaxoan*, p. 14.

83. The witnesses mentioned that the town was also called Chuina or Juina. AGI, Justicia, leg. 130, fols. 2099, 1797, 2101, 2128.

84. Testimony of Alonso de Mata, AGI, Justicia, leg. 135, no. 3.

85. "Relación de la plata . . . ," AGI, Justicia, leg. 223.

86. AGI, Justicia, leg. 130, fol. 962v.

87. Ibid., fols. 1284v-85.

88. Scholes and Adams, eds., *Proceso contra Tzintzicha Tangaxoan*, p. 16.

89. Ibid., p. 29.

90. AGI, Justicia, leg. 135, no. 3.

91. Ibid.

92. Ibid.

93. "El fiscal contra Arellano, 1532," AGI, Justicia, leg. 187, no. 1, ramo 2.

94. Scholes and Adams, eds., *Proceso contra Tzintzicha Tangaxoan*, pp. 16-17, 29.

95. AGI, Justicia, leg. 130, fols. 1787bis verso, 1788, 1993, 1995v.

96. Ibid., fols. 251v-252, 1993r-v.

97. AGI, Justicia, leg. 220, fols. 78, 143.

98. "Probanza de méritos y servicios de Juan Gallego, México, 15 mayo 1551," AGI,

México, leg. 204, no. 33; "Probanza de . . . Alonso Álvarez de Espinosa," AGI, Patronato, leg. 61, no. 2, ramo 9.

Chapter 8

1. Donald E. Chipman, *Nuño de Guzmán and the Province of Pánuco in New Spain, 1518-1533*, pp. 221-22.

2. The background of Nuño de Guzmán and his career in Pánuco is best covered in ibid.; and Donald E. Chipmán, "New Light on the Career of Nuño de Guzmán," *The Americas* 19 (April 1963):341-46.

3. Nuño de Guzmán, *Memoria de los servicios que había hecho Nuño de Guzmán, desde que fue nombrado gobernador de Pánuco en 1525*, ed. Manuel Carrera Stampa, pp. 40-50 (hereafter cited as Guzmán, *Memoria*). See also Chipman, *Nuño de Guzmán*, pp. 141-72; Chipman, "New Light," p. 346; Silvio Zavala, "Nuño de Guzmán y la esclavitud de los indios," *Historia Mexicana* 1 (en.-mar. 1952):410-28.

4. ACM, 1:134.

5. Ibid., pp. 152-53.

6. Ibid., p. 160.

7. Ibid., pp. 167-68.

8. Letters of Fernando Cortés to García de Llerena, México, June 12, 1527, June 22, 1527, August 11, 1527; AGN, Hospital de Jesús, leg. 265, exp. 1.

9. Royal cedula to Fernando Cortés, Toledo, November 24, 1525, AGN, Hospital de Jesús, leg. 123.

10. *RM*, pp. 267-68.

11. Petition of Diego de Osorio, attorney for Cortés, México, November 15, 1525, in "Domingo Niño contra Fernando Cortés sobre Oztuma y Alavystlan, 1527," AGN, Hospital de Jesús, leg. 264, exp. 5.

12. Testimony of Andrés de Tapia, ibid.

13. AGI, Patronato, leg. 199, ramo 2.

14. A decree was issued on August 22, 1527, commanding them to mark off the boundaries of the towns and cities of New Spain. *DII*, 29:436. Another, dated the next day, August 23, ordered them to investigate the reported depopulation of the town of Segura de la Frontera. *The Harkness Collection in the Library of Congress, Manuscripts Concerning Mexico: a Guide*, with selected transcriptions and translations by J. Benedict Warren, pp. 137-43.

15. Chipman, *Nuño de Guzmán*, p. 221.

16. The king gave Cortés the title of Marqués on July 6, 1529. Riley, *Fernando Cortés*, p. 29.

17. Ibid., p. 26.

18. Vasco de Puga, *Provisiones, cédulas, instrucciones de su Magestad . . .* , 1:70-71.

19. Ibid., p. 82.

20. ACM, 1:186.

21. Ibid.

22. Ibid., p. 187.

23. *The Harkness Collection*, pp. 137-43.

24. Chipman, *Nuño de Guzmán*, p. 221.

25. ACM, 1:193.

26. Bravo Ugarte, *Historia de México,* 2:297.

27. Juan de Zumárraga, "Carta a su Magestad del electo obispo de México," (27 agosto 1529), in Joaquín García Icazbalceta, *Don Fray Juan de Zumárraga, primer obispo y arzobispo de México,* ed. Rafael Aguayo Spencer and Antonio Castro Leal, 2:190.

28. "Información contra Salazar y Chirinos, 1525," AGI, Justicia, leg. 225.

29. AGI, Justicia, leg. 224, fol. 181v.

30. "Probanza de méritos y servicios de García del Pilar, México, 12 agosto 1529," AGI, México, leg. 203.

31. Zumárraga, "Carta a Su Magestad," 1529, p. 189.

32. "Probanza sobre lo que dicen y dijeron los indios de Michoacán y contra el dicho de Pilar, 1532," AGI, Justicia, leg. 229; hereafter cited as "Probanza contra Pilar, 1532."

33. Zumárraga, "Carta a Su Magestad," 1529, p. 190.

34. Don Pedro calls this interpreter Coynze. "Probanza contra Pilar, 1532," AGI, Justicia, leg. 229. Pilar uses the name Coyulihi. "Averiguación de la plata del Cazonci: el dicho de García del Pilar y otros testigos, 1532," AGI, Justicia, leg. 226; hereafter cited as Pilar, "El dicho, 1532." There was a powerful *principal* in Tzintzuntzan whose name is given as Coyuze in the published records of the trial of the Cazonci and who died before June 25, 1529 (Scholes and Adams, eds., *Proceso contra Tzintzicha Tangaxoan,* p. 37), and it may have been he who brought this first tribute to Guzmán. In the handwriting of the epoch Coyuze and Coynze are very similar. Cf. "Proceso contra Tzintzticha Tangaxoan, 1530," AGI, Justicia, leg. 108, no. 6.

35. "Probanza contra Pilar, 1532," AGI, Justicia, leg. 229.

36. Pilar, "El dicho, 1532," AGI, Justicia, leg. 226.

37. AGI, Justicia, leg. 130, fol. 1993.

38. Zumárraga, "Carta a Su Magestad," 1529, pp. 195–96.

39. "Dicho de Antonio de Godoy," AGI, Justicia, leg. 226. Also in "El gobernador Nuño de Guzmán con el fiscal sobre cantidad de 6,000 pesos en que fue condenado por el presidente y oidores de México por otros tantos que sin orden de S.M., había o suponía haber gastado en la conquista de los Teules Chichimecas," AGI, Justicia, leg. 186, no. 4.

40. *RM,* p. 268.

41. "Tasación Ortega," fols. 966, 970.

42. "Dicho de Antonio de Godoy," AGI, Justicia, leg. 226.

43. A problem with the narrative of the *Relación* is that it treats the imprisonment of the Cazonci under Guzmán as though it happened only once, while in reality, as we shall see, he was imprisoned twice. As a result the *Relación* lumps together conversations that must have occurred at different times.

44. *RM,* pp. 268–69.

45. "Dicho de Godoy," AGI, Justicia, leg. 226.

46. Zumárraga, "Carta a Su Magestad," 1529, p. 196.

47. "Información de D. Antonio Huitzimíngari," fol. 76v.

48. "Juicio seguido por Hernán Cortés contra los Lics. Matienzo y Delgadillo, año 1531," *BAGN* 9 (1938):361; hereafter cited as "Cortés contra Matienzo y Delgadillo."

49. "Ceinos toma información, 1531," AGI, Justicia, leg. 226.

50. AGI, Justicia, leg. 130, fols. 1502–1503.

51. Zumárraga, "Carta a Su Magestad," 1529, pp. 196, 243–45.

52. "Acuerdo para hacer la guerra donde fue Nuño de Guzmán, México, 15 mayo 1529," AGI, Justicia, leg. 227.

53. ACM, 2:8.

54. "Ceinos toma información, 1531," AGI, Justicia, leg. 226.

55. Ibid.; "Cortés contra Matienzo y Delgadillo," p. 364. In the documents this interpreter and principal is referred to as either Alonso de Ávila or Alonso de Ávalos. He is not, however, to be confused with Don Alonso, one of the major Tarascan *principales* and a son-in-law of the Cazonci, since both were subjected to torture in the trial of the Cazonci. Scholes and Adams, eds., *Proceso contra Tzintzicha Tangaxoan*, pp. 55, 61.

56. "Cortés contra Matienzo y Delgadillo," p. 384.

57. Letter of Nuño de Guzmán to Antonio de Godoy, August 20, 1529, AGI, México, leg. 3177.

58. Letter of Antonio de Godoy to Gonzalo López, undated, AGI, México, leg. 3177.

59. AGI, Contaduría, leg. 657, no. 3, fols. 49-52.

60. *RM*, pp. 268-69.

61. Ibid., pp. 269-70; Pilar, "El dicho, 1532," AGI, Justicia, leg. 226; "Ceinos toma información," AGI, Justicia, leg. 226.

62. *RM*, pp. 270-71.

63. The other statements regarding the amount of treasure that the Tarascans brought to Guzmán treat of the Cazonci's imprisonment as something that happened only once. The earliest of the statements was made by García del Pilar on February 24, 1532. He said that when the Cazonci came he brought about 200 marks of silver in ingots and plates; about 1,000 pesos of gold in ingots, plates, and purses for the arm, and in two large plates. (Presumably the "purses for the arm," *alforjas del brazo*, contained gold dust or nuggets.) Later the Indians brought treasure on three or four occasions, and it amounted to about 800 marks of silver; 3,000-4,000 pesos of gold. Pilar, "El dicho, 1532," AGI, Justicia, leg. 226. Later in 1532, Guzmán had testimony taken to counteract Pilar's statement. Don Pedro made a deposition in which he spoke of two shipments of treasure to Guzmán. On the first occasion the Indians brought 100 plates of silver; 5 small shields of gold; 1 large shield of gold. On the second occasion they brought 400 pieces of gold and silver; among the gold pieces there were bracelets, ear plugs, mitres, small vessels, and shields. Don Pedro said that Pilar took all of both shipments and that Guzmán never knew about it, but at this time Don Pedro was still a virtual prisoner of Guzmán in New Galicia, with a vivid memory of the torture that he had suffered during the Cazonci's trial. "Probanza contra Pilar, 1532," AGI, Justicia, leg. 229. About 1540, Don Pedro told the author of the *Relación* that there had been three shipments of treasure. The first consisted of 600 shields of gold; 600 shields of silver. (Pilar took 100 shields of gold and 100 shields of silver.) The second shipment consisted of 400 shields of gold; 400 shields of silver. (Again Pilar took 100 of each.) The third shipment consisted of 200 shields of gold; 200 shields of silver; also crescents of gold, ear plugs, and bracelets. (Pilar took 100 of the jewels.) *RM*, pp. 269-71.

64. Zumárraga, "Carta a Su Magestad," 1529, pp. 196-97.

65. Pilar, "El dicho, 1532," AGI, Justicia, leg. 226.

66. Cf. n. 63 above and "Cortés contra Matienzo y Delgadillo," pp. 361, 368. The. interpreter Alonso de Ávalos, in his statement of February 14, 1531, spoke of three

deliveries of treasure. In the first the Indians brought 80 medium-sized silver plates and 20 shields; Pilar took the 20 shields. The second time they brought 80 silver plates, 80 silver bracelets, and 40 silver shields; Pilar took the 40 shields. On the third occasion they brought 140 silver plates, 140 silver bracelets, 120 silver shields, 3 gold shields, and 5 gold bracelets; Pilar took 100 of the pieces of silver. "Ceinos toma información, 1531," AGI, Justicia, leg. 226.

67. *RM*, p. 270.
68. "Residencia de Nuño de Guzmán y de la Audiencia de la Nueva España, 1531," AGI, Justicia, leg. 226.
69. "Ceinos toma información, 1531," AGI, Justicia, leg. 226.
70. "Nuño de Guzmán con el fiscal," AGI, Justicia, leg. 186, no. 4.
71. "Carta de Godoy a López," AGI, México, leg. 3177.
72. Answers to question 14, "Cortés contra Matienzo y Delgadillo," pp. 364, 367, 370.
73. Ibid., p. 372.
74. Ibid., p. 376. The reputation of this muleteer, turned alcalde and grave robber, apparently did not improve with age. Twenty years later Diego Hernández Nieto attacked him as "a man who secretly took other people's livestock and changed their brands into his brand and sign, and he did this to many livestock of Juan Borallo and of other citizens of Michoacán." "Hernández Nieto Oliver," AGN, Hospital de Jesús, leg. 292, exp. 119, fol. 382.
75. "Escrituras presentadas por Nuño de Guzmán para los descargos de su residencia," AGI, Justicia, leg. 229.
76. AGI, Patronato, leg. 199, ramo 4.

Chapter 9

1. Silvio Zavala, *La encomienda indiana;* Lesley Byrd Simpson, *The Encomienda in New Spain: The Beginning of Spanish Mexico.*
2. "El fiscal con Jorge Carrillo," AGI, Justicia, leg. 198, no. 3; "Juan Velázquez de Salazar con Pedro de Bazán," AGI, Justicia, leg. 126, no. 5.
3. Testimony of Diego de Coria, in "Gonzalo de Salazar contra Fernando Cortés," AGN, Hospital de Jesús, leg. 265, exp. 12; "Información del Marqués del Valle para que se mande arraigar de fianzas al veedor Peralmíndez Chirino, 1532," AGN, Hospital de Jesús, leg. 265, exp. 5; "Fernando Cortés con Pedro Almíndez Cherino . . . sobre abono de los perjuicios que recibió en el tiempo que le tuvo despojado de los pueblos de Tuspa, Amula y Zapotlan, 1532," AGI, Justicia, leg. 118, no. 4.
4. "Fernández Infante con Albornoz, 1531," AGI, Justicia, leg. 113, no. 2. For the text of the cedula, see Warren, *Conquista*, pp. 264-65.
5. "Mata con Ortega y Santa Cruz, 1541," AGI, Justicia, leg. 135, no. 3; Hernández Nieto contra Oliver, 1545," AGI, Justicia, leg. 145.
6. "Instrucciones dadas al Licenciado Luis Ponce de León, Toledo, 4 noviembre 1525," *DIU*, 9:221.
7. See below, the discussion of the legal cases involving Pungarabato and Turicato.
8. AGI, Justicia, leg. 130, fols. 2058v-59.

9. Testimony of Antonio de Oliver, AGI, Justicia, leg. 130, fol. 1296v; letter of Estrada to Ortega, March [i.e., May] 27, 1528, AGI, Justicia, leg. 135, no. 3.

10. See chapter 6, n. 6 and appendix B, under the names of the specific towns mentioned.

11. Puga, *Provisiones*, 1:82.

12. "Cortés contra Matienzo y Delgadillo," pp. 391-92; *The Harkness Collection*, pp. 140-42.

13. *The Harkness Collection*, p. 142.

14. AGI, Justicia, leg. 130, fols. 1502-1504v (see Warren, *Conquista*, app. 8, pp. 433-35).

15. "El Marqués contra los licenciados Matienzo y Delgadillo sobre Tuxpan y Amula," AGN, Hospital de Jesús, leg. 276, exp. 86 (see Warren, *Conquista*, app. 8, p. 435).

16. "Cortés contra Matienzo y Delgadillo," p. 361.

17. AGI, Justicia, leg. 130, fols. 1504v-1505 (see Warren, *Conquista*, app. 9, p. 436).

18. See appendix B, under Tajimaroa and Tiripetío, and below in this chapter in the discussion of Juan Infante.

19. *The Harkness Collection*, pp. 144-51.

20. AGI, Justicia, leg. 130, fols. 1852r-v, 1864-78, 1898-1904.

21. "Cortés contra Matienzo y Delgadillo," AGN, Hospital de Jesús, leg. 264, exp. 3; "El Marqués del Valle con Nuño de Guzmán sobre las frutas e intereses de la Ciudad de Uchichila, 1542," AGI, Justicia, leg. 139, no. 1; "El Marqués contra los licenciados Matienzo y Delgadillo sobre 160 pesos, 1531," AGN, Hospital de Jesús, leg. 264, exp. 12.

22. *The Harkness Collection*, pp. 212-33.

23. Testimony of Cristóbal de Ojeda and Luis de Berrio, AGI, Justicia, leg. 226.

24. "El fiscal con Antonio de Godoy, sobre el derecho del pueblo de Cinagua que le había sido encomendado, 1542," AGI, Justicia, leg. 197, no. 4.

25. "Pedro de Bazán . . . con los licenciados Matienzo y Delgadillo, oidores que fueron . . . sobre que éstos le satisficieren los perjuicios que le habían ocasionado en el tiempo que estuvo deprivado de un pueblo de indios, 1532," AGI, Justicia, leg. 116, no. 5.

26. "Juan Velázquez de Salazar, vecino y regidor de la ciudad de México, con Pedro Bazán y Antonio Anguiano, de la propia vecindad, sobre el derecho a los pueblos de Pungarabato y Charcharando, 1537," AGI, Justicia, leg. 126, no. 5.

27. "Pedro de Bazán con Antonio de Anguiano, vecino de México, sobre derecho al pueblo de Pungarabato, 1541," AGI, Justicia, leg. 135, no. 2.

28. Luis Sánchez con Hernando Bazán, vecinos de México, sobre derecho a la mitad del pueblo de indios de Pungarabato, 1550," AGI, Justicia, leg. 148, no. 2, ramo 1.

29. *Relación de los obispados de Tlaxcala, Michoacán, Oaxaca y otros lugares en el siglo XVI*, ed. Luis García Pimentel, pp. 49, 173; Francisco del Paso y Troncoso, ed., *Papeles de Nueva España*, vol. 1, *Suma de visitas de pueblos*, pp. 181-82.

30. "Probanza de méritos y servicios de Diego Hernández, México, 13 febrero 1539," AGI, México, leg. 204; "Autos de Diego Hernández Nieto, vecino de México, con Antonio Oliver, de la propia vecindad, sobre derecho a la mitad del pueblo de Turicato y sus sujetos, 1547," AGI, Justicia, leg. 145; "Diego Hernández Nieto . . . contra Antonio de Oliver sobre el cumplimiento de la ejecutoria del Consejo de Indias,

1548," AGN, Hospital de Jesús, leg. 292, exp. 119; "El fiscal con Antonio de Oliver . . . sobre derecho a la mitad del pueblo de Turicato, 1549," AGI, Justicia, leg. 201, no. 1; "Autos de Diego Hernández Nieto . . . con Antonio de Oliver sobre derecho de un pueblo de indios, 1552," AGI, Justicia, leg. 150; "Diego Hernández Nieto con Antonio Oliver . . . sobre ajuste de cuentas de los tributos de un pueblo que tenían en encomienda, 1564," AGI, Justicia, leg. 166, no. 2, ramo 1.

31. Testimony of Antonio de Oliver, Antonio de Godoy, and Rodrigo de Baeza, AGI, Justicia, leg. 130, fols. 1299r–v, 1387, 1808.

32. Interrogatory of Licenciado Cristóbal de Benavente, ibid., fol. 1215.

33. Testimony of Juan de Burgos, AGI, Justicia, leg. 220, fol. 69v.

34. AGI, Patronato, leg. 199, ramo 1.

35. *IP,* 1:105, no. 357; ibid., 1:141, nos. 532, 531; ibid., 1:218, no. 928.

36. Testimony of Francisco Morcillo and Hernando Jerez, AGI, Justicia, leg. 130, fols. 1929r–v, 1958r–v.

37. "Tasación Ortega," AGI, Justicia, leg. 130, fols. 965v, 970.

38. Various testimonies of Bachiller Ortega, ibid., fols. 1930v–31v (year 1531), 1979r–v (year 1533), 1813v–14 (year 1536), 1284r–v, 1285v–86 (year 1540).

39. Interrogatory of Juan Infante, ibid., fols. 1787r–v.

40. Testimony of Bachiller Ortega, ibid., fol. 1979v.

41. Testimony of Cristóbal de Cáceres, 1534, ibid., fol. 1843r–v.

42. Testimony of Antonio de Oliver, 1536, ibid., fol. 1798r–v.

43. Testimony of Alonso Lucas, 1540, ibid., fol. 1261v.

44. "Cédula de encomienda, Tenochtitlan, 20 octubre 1528." There are several copies of the cedula (ibid., fols. 1508-1509, 1701r–v, 1779v–80v) with the usual number of copyists' variations in the spellings of the names of the towns. Carlos Salvador Paredes Martínez, "El tributo indígena en la región del Lago de Pátzcuaro, siglo xvi" (Tesis de licenciatura, Universidad Nacional Autónoma de México, 1976), pp. 70–77, discusses the location of Infante's towns and includes a helpful map of them.

45. Regarding Ruiz' death see Testimony of Alonso de Orduña, AGI, Justicia, leg. 130, fol. 1963.

46. Testimony of Cristóbal de Cáceres, 1534, ibid., fol. 1843.

47. Interrogatory of Juan Infante, ibid., fol. 1788r–v.

48. Testimony of Antonio de Oliver, 1540, ibid., fol. 251v.

49. Testimony of Cristóbal de Cáceres, 1534, ibid., fol. 1844r–v.

50. Ibid., fols. 1508-1509, 1701r–v, 1779v–80v.

51. Ibid., fols. 1765v, 1295v.

52. "Mandamiento de Antonio de Godoy," ibid., fols. 1618v–19; Interrogatory of Juan Infante and replies of Antonio de Godoy, ibid., fols. 1993-97.

53. Testimony of Alonso de Veas, 1534, ibid., fols. 1825v–26.

54. Ibid., fols. 1620v–21.

55. Testimony of Rodrigo de Baeza and Miguel López de Legaspi, ibid., fols. 1808r–v, 1531v–33.

56. "Francisco de Villegas con Juan Infante sobre el pueblo de Capaquero, 1535-1541," AGI, Justicia, leg. 138 (not catalogued).

57. "Cortés contra Matienzo y Delgadillo," p. 357.

58. "Proceso contra Gonzalo Gómez, 1537," AGN, Inquisición, vol. 2, exp. 2.

59. Warren, *Vasco de Quiroga*, pp. 88-103. Paredes Martínez, *El tributo indígena*, and Marcela Irais Piñón Flores, *La tenencia de la tierra en la región de Tlazazalca-Zacapu-Huaniqueo en el siglo xvi* (Tesis de licenciatura, Universidad Nacional Autónoma de México, 1976), also discuss various aspects of the career of this very important figure of sixteenth-century Michoacán.

Chapter 10

1. ACM, 1:12.
2. AGI, Justicia, leg. 130, fols. 2130-32.
3. "Relación de la probanza de tachas," AGI, Justicia, leg. 112, no. 4.
4. *IP*, 1:359, no. 1726; "Cortés contra Matienzo y Delgadillo," p. 383.
5. *IP*, 1:129, no. 470.
6. Ibid., p. 197, no. 822.
7. "Cortés contra Matienzo y Delgadillo," p. 356; AGI, Justicia, leg. 130, fols. 1503-1504v, 1952-54v.
8. *IP*, 1:32, no. 31.
9. Ibid., pp. 243-44, nos. 1080, 1086.
10. Ibid., p. 209, no. 894.
11. AGI, Justicia, leg. 130, fols. 1529-31v.
12. It has not been possible to identify this Villafuerte as an encomendero in Michoacán. Perhaps the name should be Villaseñor.
13. "Proceso contra Gonzalo Gómez," AGN, Inquisición, vol. 2, exp. 2.
14. Scholes and Adams, eds., *Proceso contra Tzintzicha Tangaxoan*, passim.
15. Ibid., pp. 33, 35; *RM*, p. 267; Testimony of Antón Caicedo, AGI, Justicia, leg. 187, no. 1, ramo 2.
16. "Tasación Ortega," fols. 959v-61, 963v, 965v.
17. AGI, Justicia, leg. 130, fol. 1928.
18. See chap. 9, n. 19.
19. *RM*, p. 267.
20. AGI, Justicia, leg. 135, no. 3; AGI, Justicia, leg. 130, fols. 1502-1504v; AGN, Hospital de Jesús, leg. 276, exp. 86.
21. AGI, Justicia, leg. 130, fol. 962.
22. *IP*, 1:273, no. 1254; ibid., p. 284, no. 1314.
23. Ibid., p. 214, no. 907; ibid., p. 243, no. 1080; ibid., p. 234, no. 1030.
24. Cf. "Tasación Ortega," passim; "Villegas con Infante," AGI, Justicia, leg. 138, fol. 98.
25. Sauer, *Colima*, p. 90.
26. "Carta de Luis de Cárdenas, 1527," AGI, Patronato, leg. 16, no. 2, ramo 6.
27. Ibid.
28. Testimony of Domingo Niño, AGI, Justicia, leg. 220, fol. 239.
29. Testimony of Hernando de Sosa, AGI, Justicia, leg. 226, fol. 188v.
30. "Proceso de Domingo Niño contra Fernando Cortés, sobre Oztuma y Alavistlan, 1527," AGN, Hospital de Jesús, leg. 264, exp. 5.
31. The account is incorporated in "El Marqués contra los licenciados Matienzo y

Delgadillo sobre 160 pesos, 1531," AGN, Hospital de Jesús, leg. 264, exp. 12.

32. Torquemada, *Monarquía*, 1:575.

33. López de Gómara, *Historia*, 2:278; Herrera, *Historia general*, dec. 3, lib. 8, cap. 15; *Relación breve y verdadera de algunas cosas de las muchas que sucedieron al Padre Fray Alonso Ponce en las provincias de la Nueva España, escrita por dos religiosos sus compañeros*, 2:114-15.

34. Herrera, *Historia general*, dec. 3, lib. 8, cap. 15.

35. The only volumes for the 1520s preserved in the notary archive cover the periods from August 9 to December 9, 1525; January 29 to November 15, 1527; and December 27, 1527, to December 1, 1528. Cf. *IP*, 1:23, 95, 211. These records were produced by notaries in Mexico City and do not ordinarily indicate the activities of the citizens of Colima and Zacatula, who were carrying on extensive mining operations along the edges of Michoacán.

36. *IP*, 1:78, no. 233; ibid., p. 88, no. 280.

37. Herrera, *Historia general*, dec. 3, lib. 8, cap. 15.

38. ACM, 1:48; Testimony of Cristóbal de Ojeda, AGI, Justicia, leg. 220, fol. 53.

39. ACM, 1:107.

40. "Albornoz a Su Magestad," 1525, *DII*, 13:71-72.

41. *IP*, 1:129, no. 469.

42. Ibid., p. 141, no. 531.

43. Ibid., p. 146, no. 558.

44. Ibid., pp. 154-55, no. 600.

45. Ibid., p. 157, no. 612.

46. Ibid., p. 158, no. 618.

47. Ibid., p. 164, no. 647.

48. Ibid., p. 172, no. 692.

49. Ibid., p. 173, no. 697.

50. Ibid., p. 174, no. 702.

51. Ibid., p. 177, no. 718.

52. Ibid., p. 184, no. 755.

53. Ibid., no. 756.

54. Ibid., p. 214, no. 904.

55. Ibid., p. 234, no. 1030.

56. Ibid., p. 239, no. 1058.

57. Ibid., p. 243, no. 1080; ibid., p. 262, no. 1189; ibid., p. 266, no. 1212.

58. Ibid., p. 247, no. 1259; see under "Alonso, Fernando" in appendix B.

59. *IP*, 1:303, no. 1421; ibid., p. 306, no. 1436; ibid., p. 312, no. 1467; ibid., p. 316, no. 1488; ibid., p. 326, no. 1548.

60. Ibid., p. 359, no. 1726.

61. "Mata con Ortega y Santa Cruz, 1541," AGI, Justicia, leg. 135, no. 3.

62. For a general treatment of Indian slavery in the colonial period, see Silvio Zavala, *Los esclavos indios en Nueva España*.

63. "Cortés contra Matienzo y Delgadillo," p. 354.

64. *IP*, 1:164, no. 647; ibid., p. 262, no. 1189; ibid., p. 266, no. 1212.

65. Ibid., p. 214, no. 907.

66. Ibid., p. 273, no. 1254; ibid., p. 284, no. 1314.

67. Ibid., pp. 262–63, nos. 1191–93.
68. Ibid., p. 120, no. 431; ibid., p. 157, no. 612.
69. Testimony of Alonso de Ávalos, interpreter, "Cortés contra Matienzo y Delgadillo," p. 366.
70. *IP,* 1:184, nos. 755–56.
71. Ibid., p. 141, no. 531; ibid., p. 274, no. 1259.
72. Ibid., p. 177, no. 718; ibid., p. 184, no. 756; ibid., p. 326, no. 1548.
73. "Bazán con Matienzo y Delgadillo, 1532," AGI, Justicia, leg. 116, no. 5.
74. *IP,* 1:194, no. 803; ibid., p. 251, no. 1126.
75. AGI, Justicia, leg. 220, fols. 52v–53.
76. *IP,* 1:154–55, no. 600.
77. "Hernández Nieto contra Oliver sobre Turicato," AGN, Hospital de Jesús, leg. 292, exp. 119.
78. "Información sobre los pueblos que Fernando Cortés tenía, 1531," AGN, Hospital de Jesús, leg. 265, exp. 5.
79. *IP,* 1:32, no. 31.
80. "Mata con Ortega y Santa Cruz, 1541," AGI, Justicia, leg. 135, no. 3.
81. AGI, Justicia, leg. 130, fols. 1493r–v.
82. Ibid., fols. 1483r–v.
83. "Villegas con Infante," AGI, Justicia, leg. 138, fols. 84v, 93v.
84. "Pedro de Meneses con los hijos de Guillén de la Loa, 1543," AGI, Justicia, leg. 141.
85. "Tasación Ortega," fols. 959v–72v.
86. AGI, Justicia, leg. 130, fols. 1491r–v.
87. "Villegas con Infante," AGI, Justicia, leg. 138, fol. 103v.
88. "Tasación Ortega," fols. 960r–v, 963–64.
89. "Mata con Ortega y Santa Cruz, 1541," AGI, Justicia, leg. 135, no. 3.
90. "Tasación Ortega," fols. 966v–67.
91. "Mata con Ortega y Santa Cruz, 1541," AGI, Justicia, leg. 135, no. 3.
92. Ibid.
93. *IP,* 1:343, no. 1645.
94. The following material regarding Tuzantla, unless otherwise noted, is taken from "Mata con Ortega y Santa Cruz, 1541," AGI, Justicia, leg 135, no. 3.
95. *IP,* 1:129, no. 470.
96. See Warren, *Conquista,* app. 7D, pp. 431–32.
97. "Petición de Alonso de Mata a Su Magesdad, 26 febrero 1552," AGI, México, leg. 168.
98. *The Harkness Collection,* pp. 218–31.
99. "Cortés contra Matienzo y Delgadillo," p. 354.
100. Testimony of Gonzalo Gómez, February 25, 1531, AGI, Justicia, leg. 226.
101. "Dicho de Antonio de Godoy," ibid.
102. "Cortés contra Matienzo y Delgadillo," p. 361.
103. "El licenciado Ceinos toma cierta información acerca de la verdad de qué plata y oro había dado en la provincia de Michoacán a Nuño de Guzmán, 1531," AGI, Justicia, leg. 226; hereafter cited as "Ceinos toma información, 1531."
104. "Tasación Ortega," AGI, Justicia, fol. 971.
105. "Carta de Nuño de Guzmán a Antonio de Godoy, 20 agosto 1529," AGI, México,

leg. 3177.

106. AGI, Justicia, leg. 226.

107. "Dicho de Godoy," ibid.

108. AGI, Justicia, leg. 226.

109. Testimony of Serván Bejarano, 1531, ibid.

110. AGI, Justicia, leg. 226.

111. "Proceso del Marqués del Valle contra el Lic. Diego Delgadillo sobre lo que llevó como cesionario de Juan Ruiz Martínez, 1531," AGN, Hospital de Jesús, leg. 293, exp. 134.

112. "Cortés contra Matienzo y Delgadillo," p. 352; Testimony of Francisco de Santa Cruz, AGI, Justicia, leg. 226.

113. Testimony of Francisco de Herrera, AGI, Justicia, leg. 226.

114. Ibid.; "Cortés contra Matienzo y Delgadillo," p. 383.

115. "Descargas por parte de Fernando Cortés en la residencia de los licenciados Matienzo y Delgadillo," AGI, Justicia, leg. 222.

116. Testimony of Gonzalo de Riobó de Sotomayor, 1531, AGI, Justicia, leg. 226.

117. "Información manda[da] recibir por el Illmo. Señor obispo Zumárraga como protector de los indios, sobre los malos tratamientos que reciben de los españoles, y tributos que les cargan por la Real Audiencia, 1531," Bernardo Mendel Collection, Indiana University Library, Bloomington.

118. AGI, Justicia, leg. 130, fol. 1456.

119. Ibid., fol. 1466.

120. Ibid., fol. 1843v.

121. Ibid., fol. 1492v.

122. Ibid., fols. 1480, 1495.

123. Ibid., fol. 1494.

124. "Acusación de Cristóbal de Valderrama, 19 septiembre 1536," in "Proceso contra Gonzalo Gómez," AGN, Inquisición, vol. 2, exp. 2.

125. "Interrogatorio de tachas," ibid.

126. "Interrogatorio de defensa," ibid.

127. Testimony of Gonzalo Gómez, 1532, AGI, Justicia, leg. 130, fols. 1495r-v.

128. "Hernández Nieto contra Oliver sobre Turicato," AGN, Hospital de Jesús, leg. 292, exp. 119.

129. RM, p. 174.

130. Ibid., p. 267.

131. "Mata con Ortega y Santa Cruz," AGI, Justicia, leg. 135, no. 3.

132. Testimony of Juan de Burgos, 1531, AGI, Justicia, leg. 130, fol. 1933.

133. Testimony of Martín Gómez, 1531, ibid., fol. 1928v.

134. "Tasación Ortega," fols. 966, 972r-v.

135. RM, p. 173.

136. Testimony of Diego Rodríguez de Soria, 1531, AGI, Justicia, leg. 130, fol. 1935.

137. Scholes and Adams, eds., Proceso contra Tzintzicha Tangaxoan, pp. 14-15.

138. Ibid., p. 34.

139. Ibid., p. 15.

140. Ibid., pp. 20-21.

141. Ibid., pp. 36-42.

Chapter 11

1. Testimony of Francisco López, AGI, Justicia, leg. 226.
2. "Acuerdo para hacer la guerra donde fue Nuño de Guzmán, 1529," AGI, Justicia, leg. 227.
3. AGI, Contaduría, leg. 657, no. 3, fols. 49-52v.
4. Zumárraga, "Carta a Su Magesdad," 1529, pp. 196, 243-45.
5. Testimonies of Alonso de Ávila, Cristóbal Hernández, Francisco Morcillo, Hernando de Sosa, and Francisco de Herrera, AGI, Justicia, leg. 226.
6. "Luis Sánchez con Hernando Bazán, 1550," AGI, Justicia, leg. 148, no. 2, ramo 2.
7. "Pedro de Bazán con Matienzo y Delgadillo, 1532," AGI, Justicia, leg. 116, no. 5.
8. The Harkness Collection, pp. 62-65, 106-11, 116-21.
9. Guzmán, Memoria, pp. 64-65.
10. "Información sobre los acaecimientos de la guerra que hace el Gobernador Nuño de Guzmán a los indios, para con los pareceres de las personas examinadas, tomar resolución, año de 1531," DII, 16:363. For other estimates of the size of the expedition see Guzmán, Memoria, p.64 n. 59.
11. RM, p. 268.
12. Testimony of Alonso de Ávila, AGI, Justicia, leg. 226.
13. "Carta de Guzmán a Godoy, 20 de agosto de 1529," AGI, México, leg. 3177.
14. Testimonies of Juan de Salcedo and Gonzalo Ruiz, 1531, AGI, Justicia, leg. 226.
15. Because of the varied and contradictory nature of the documentation, printed and manuscript, that must be used here, some introduction to sources is in order. The primary source, giving the clearest dates and most definite information for this chapter, is the record of the Cazonci's trial by Guzmán, to which extensive reference has been made previously: Scholes and Adams, eds., Proceso contra Tzintzicha Tangaxoan. There are two documents directly from the pen of Nuño de Guzmán. On July 8, 1530, he wrote a letter to the king from Omitlán, in New Galicia, reporting what his expedition had accomplished up to that time: "Carta a Su Magestad del Presidente de la Audiencia de México, Nuño de Guzmán, en que refiere la jornada que hizo a Mechuacán, a conquistar la provincia de los Tebles-Chichimecas que confinan con Nueva España," July 8, 1530 (DII, 13:356-93). Later he also wrote a memorial of his activities from the time of his appointment as governor of Pánuco in 1525 until the end of his career in Mexico in 1538: Guzmán, Memoria. A number of narratives of the expedition were presented to the Audiencia of New Spain by men who had gone with Guzmán. The narratives that interest us here are Pedro de Carranza, "Relación hecha por Pedro de Carranza sobre la jornada que hizo Nuño de Guzmán, de la entrada y sucesos en la Nueva Galicia, 1531" (DII, 14:347-73); "Cuarta relación anónima de la jornada que hizo Nuño de Guzmán a la Nueva Galicia" (the "Fourth Anonymous Relation"), in Guzmán, Memoria, pp. 93-128; and Pilar, "Relación de la entrada de Nuño de Guzmán que dio García del Pilar su intérprete" (cited as Pilar, "Relación"), in Guzmán, Relación, pp. 177-93. The last of these relations was written after Pilar broke with Guzmán and is highly critical of him. There is also a fairly evident literary dependence between Pilar's "Relation" and the "Fourth Anonymous Relation." In 1532 the audiencia asked Pilar to expand on his report in regard to the Cazonci. This he did on January 24, 1532, again giving a very damning description of Guzmán's activities. Pilar's deposition is incomplete; he died be-

fore being able to return to finish it. Included with this later statement by Pilar is a deposition by Álvaro de Ribera concerning gold and silver that he had brought to Mexico City for Guzmán. These two unpublished depositions are found in "Averiguación de la plata del Cazonci: el dicho de García del Pilar y otros testigos, 1532," AGI, Justicia, leg. 226. In the same *legajo*, the first *legajo* of the residencia of Guzmán as president of the Audiencia of Mexico, there is also found much testimony from other eyewitnesses, who supplied many major and minor pieces of information. Note especially the statements by Juan de Burgos and Antonio de Godoy. Also found there are an inquiry that the *oidor* Ceinos made in February, 1531, in which he took testimony from several Tarascan witnesses ("El Licenciado Ceinos toma cierta información acerca de la verdad de qué plata y oro había dado en la provincia de Michoacán a Nuño de Guzmán, 1531," cited hereafter as "Ceinos toma información"); and another inquiry of the same nature that Don Pedro de Arellano, *corregidor* of the city of Michoacán, made in June, 1531 ("Información de Don Pedro de Arellano, 1531"). Also in June, 1531, Cortés was having testimony taken in Michoacán for his lawsuit against Matienzo and Delgadillo over the income from the towns of Tzintzuntzan and Tamazula, which netted some information on Guzmán's activities: "Cortés contra Matienzo y Delgadillo."

Guzmán did not let the accusations against him go unanswered. In 1532 he brought forward witnesses in reply to the accusations of Pilar and the Indian witnesses: "Probanza contra Pilar, 1532," AGI, Justicia, leg. 229. Again in 1539 an agent of Guzmán had testimony taken in Michoacán regarding Guzmán's treatment of the Cazonci: "Probanza de Nuño de Guzmán hecha en grado de suplicación por carta receptoria sobre lo que toca al Cazonci, 1539," AGI, Justicia, leg. 227.

Finally, we must not neglect to mention the last section of the *Relación de Michoacán*, which was written down in 1540-41 and contains Don Pedro's final statement regarding the last days of the Cazonci.

These, then, are the principal documents upon which the present chapter relies. Our attempt will be to find some unity in their diversity.

16. "Cuarta relación anónima," p. 94.

17. Pilar, "Relación," p. 177; AGI, Patronato, leg. 199, ramo 4.

18. "Cuarta relación anónima," pp. 95-96. Regarding Muñoz' encomienda, see *Relación de las encomiendas, 1564*, p. 20.

19. "Instrucciones que envió el gobernador al Licenciado Mondragón, su alcalde mayor, Ixtlahuaca, 27 de diciembre de 1529," AGI, Justicia, leg. 230, fols. 520v-23.

20. Testimony of Juan de la Torre, 1531, AGI, Justicia, leg. 226.

21. Pilar, "Relación," pp. 177-78. In his later testimony before the audiencia Pilar distributed the number of days differently, but the sum is approximately the same. The "Fourth Anonymous Relation" makes the stay even longer, stating that the Cazonci was imprisoned after three or four days, was kept in prison for fifteen days before being threatened with torture, and remained in prison for another ten days before the expedition left Tzintzuntzan. "Cuarta relación anónima," pp. 96-97.

22. *RM*, p. 272.

23. Pilar, "Relación," p. 177.

24. Pilar, "El dicho, 1532," AGI, Justicia, leg. 226; Guzmán, *Memoria*, p. 65; *RM*, p. 272.

25. "Cuarta relación anónima," p. 96.

26. Testimony of Juan de Burgos, AGI, Justicia, leg. 226.

27. *RM*, p. 272.

28. Ibid. I have interpreted the expression "que cómo me ha de ver aquí" ("how can he see me here?") as being faultily transcribed for "que cómo me ha[n] de ver aquí," ("how can they see me here") since there is no singular noun in the context to serve as the subject of the verb *ha*.

29. Ibid.

30. "Dicho de Godoy," AGI, Justicia, leg. 226 and leg. 186, no. 4.

31. Pilar, "El dicho, 1532," AGI, Justicia, leg. 226.

32. "Probanza contra Pilar, 1532," AGI, Justicia, leg. 229; "Probanza de Nuño de Guzmán hecha en grado de suplicación, 1539," AGI, Justicia, leg. 227.

33. Testimony of Juan Pascual in "Probanza contra Pilar, 1532," AGI, Justicia, leg. 229.

34. Testimony of Juan Pascual in "Relación de los descargos que dieron al señor Nuño de Guzmán del cargo que tuvo de gobernador de [Nueva] Galicia," AGI, Justicia, leg. 338.

35. "Información de Don Pedro de Arellano, 1531," AGI, Justicia, leg. 226.

36. "Ceinos toma información, 1531," ibid.

37. "Dicho de Godoy," ibid.

38. Testimony of Alonso de Ávila, 1531, ibid.

39. AGI, Patronato, leg. 199, ramo 4.

40. Carranza, "Relación," p. 350; Pilar, "Relación," p. 180; Pilar, "El dicho, 1532," AGI, Justicia, leg. 226; "Cuarta relación anónima," p. 100.

41. *RM*, p. 275. Cf. the testimonies of Alonso de Ávila and Gonzalo Xuárez in "Ceinos toma información, 1531," AGI, Justicia, leg. 226.

42. "Cortés contra Matienzo y Delgadillo," p. 365.

43. "Cuarta relación anónima," p. 101.

44. "Información de Don Pedro de Arellano, 1531," AGI, Justicia, leg. 226.

45. "Cortés contra Matienzo y Delgadillo," p. 405. The "Fourth Anonymous Relation" refers to women of the Cazonci having been brought but places the incident before the death of the Cazonci.

46. "Averiguación de la plata del Cazonci: el dicho de García del Pilar y otros testigos, 1532," AGI, Justicia, leg. 226.

47. Scholes and Adams, eds., *Proceso contra Tzintzicha Tangaxoan*, pp. 8, 68. In the published text the name of the town is given as Comitlan.

48. Guzmán, "Carta a Su Magestad," July 8, 1530, p. 393.

49. AGI, Patronato, leg. 199, ramo 5.

50. "Información de las joyas . . . ," AGI, Justicia, leg. 226.

51. Guzmán, *Memoria*, p. 65.

52. "Cuarta relación anónima," p. 96; Pilar, "Relación," p. 177.

53. Pilar, "Relación," p. 177; "Cuarta relación anónima," p. 96. In his "Dicho," Pilar said that it occurred seven or eight days after their arrival, but this seems less trustworthy.

54. Carranza, "Relación," p. 348; Pilar, "El dicho, 1532," AGI, Justicia, leg. 229. López-Portillo comments that the word *retrete* meant the room which we now designate by the letters W.C. José López-Portillo y Weber, *La conquista de la Nueva Galicia*, p. 152. As the architectural historian Manuel Toussaint notes, however, such little rooms were kept at a considerable distance from the dwellings before water was introduced to them, so it is unlikely that the room where the Cazonci was imprisoned was such a place. Toussaint,

Pátzcuaro, p. 16 n. 5. A sixteenth-century usage of the word *retrete* is shown in the following definition from the "Diccionario Tarasco-español" in the John Carter Brown Library: "Quahta ononandeni. Ser casa de muchas vueltas, o retretes, o muchos aposentos o celdas" ("To be a house of many vaults or private rooms [possibly alcoves] or many apartments or cells"). All the witnesses give the impression that it was a small and unpleasant room.

55. Carranza, "Relación," p. 348.

56. Pilar, "El dicho, 1532," AGI, Justicia, leg. 226.

57. All the major accounts except those of Guzmán contain some references to this incident. Pilar, "Relación," p. 178; Pilar, "El dicho, 1532," AGI, Justicia, leg. 226; "Cuarta relación anónima," p. 97; Carranza, "Relación," p. 348; RM, p. 273; "Cortés contra Matienzo y Delgadillo," pp. 262-65.

58. Pilar, "El dicho, 1532," AGI, Justicia, leg. 226.

59. RM, p. 273. The two interpreters Alonso de Ávalos and Gonzalo Xuárez, testifying for Cortés in 1531, asserted that on one occasion in Tzintzuntzan, possibly at this time, the Cazonci was subjected to the same torture at Guzmán's command: ". . . he commanded the Indians [of Mexico] that they should tie his arms and testicles up, and they hit him on the testicles with a rod, . . . and an alguacil jumped with his feet on the chest of the said Cazonci." "Cortés contra Matienzo y Delgadillo," pp. 362, 365. There is no confirmation of this incident in any of the many sources that we have for this period, and the fact that the testimony of the two interpreters is verbatim identical makes it suspicious, suggesting that they were coached in their testimony.

60. RM, p. 273.

61. Pilar, "El dicho, 1532," AGI, Justicia, leg. 226.

62. RM, p. 273.

63. Pilar, "El dicho, 1532," AGI, Justicia, leg. 226.

64. Pilar, "Relación," p. 178.

65. Puga, *Provisiones, cédulas, etc.*, 1:289-90.

66. Tello, *Crónica miscelánea*, lib. 2, pp. 69-70.

67. Scholes and Adams, eds., *Proceso contra Tzintzicha Tangaxoan*, pp. 11, 68. The published edition is made from the copy of January 25, 1532, preserved in AGI, Justicia, leg. 108, no. 6. I differ with Scholes and Adams regarding the date of the presentation of the copy in the Council of the Indies. They read the script roman numerals of the date as 1533, but I think that they must be interpreted as 1534.

68. It is difficult to determine how much confidence can be placed in the statements of Pilar. He was a conniving scoundrel, as was recognized by both Zumárraga and Guzmán, and his principal concern was to keep himself on the winning side. He and Guzmán disagreed over something during the Jalisco campaign. (Guzmán claimed that it was because he had had Pilar arrested and punished for trying to kill Bartolomé López; "Probanza contra Pilar, 1532," AGI, Justicia, leg. 229.) He and Pilar proved the saying that there is no honor among thieves. Pilar went to the Second Audiencia and made two seriously incriminating depositions against Guzmán, in which, of course, he painted himself as the softhearted interpreter who was deeply moved by the trials of the poor Cazonci. Unfortunately for Pilar, he died soon after he made these declarations and was unable to take advantage of any prestige that he might have gained with the Second

Audiencia. Cf. Pilar, "El dicho, 1532," AGI, Justicia, leg. 226.

69. Scholes and Adams, eds., *Proceso contra Tzintzicha Tangaxoan*, p. 50.

70. Ibid., pp. 11-13.

71. AGI, Contaduría, leg. 657; AGN, Hospital de Jesús, leg. 249, exp. 2.

72. ACM, 1:178-79; *IP*, 1:336, no. 1607.

73. ACM, 2:1.

74. AGI, Hospital de Jesús, leg. 265, exp. 12.

75. Testimony of Diego de Soria, AGI, Justicia, leg. 226.

76. Scholes and Adams, eds., *Proceso contra Tzintzicha Tangaxoan*, pp. 13-20.

77. Testimony of Juan de Burgos, AGI, Justicia, leg. 226.

78. Scholes and Adams, eds., *Proceso contra Tzintzicha Tangaxoan*, pp. 20-22.

79. Ibid., pp. 22-24.

80. Ibid., pp. 26-36.

81. Ibid., pp. 36-42.

82. Ibid., pp. 42-44.

83. Ibid., p. 44.

84. *RM*, p. 273. Pilar, in his "Relación" (p. 177), also says that Guzmán asked for 8,000 men; the "Fourth Anonymous Relation" (p. 96) says 8,000 to 10,000.

85. *RM*, p. 274.

86. Pilar, "Relación," p. 178; Pilar, "El dicho, 1532," AGI, Justicia, leg. 226.

87. "Cuarta relación anónima," p. 97; *RM*, p. 274.

88. *RM*, p. 272.

89. Ibid., p. 274.

90. Carranza, "Relación," p. 349.

91. "Cortés contra Matienzo y Delgadillo," p. 365; AGI, Justicia, leg. 226, fol. 226.

92. Guzmán, "Carta a Su Magestad," July 8, 1530, p. 357. Antonio Tello, O.F.M., dated the arrival of Guzmán at the river as December 8. The error arose from the fact that he knew that the river was named for a feast of the Virgin Mary, but he associated it with the Feast of the Immaculate Conception, December 8, rather than the Feast of the Purification, February 2. Tello does not even have Guzmán pass through Tzintzuntzan but writes that Chirinos went through Tzintzuntzan and later caught up with the army at the river, bringing the Cazonci with him. Tello, *Crónica miscelánea*, Libro segundo, pp. 65-66.

93. Scholes and Adams, eds., *Proceso contra Tzintzicha Tangaxoan*, pp. 44-48.

94. "Cuarta relación anónima," p. 99.

95. *RM*, p. 274.

96. Scholes and Adams, eds., *Proceso contra Tzintzicha Tangaxoan*, pp. 48-50.

97. Ibid., pp. 50-55.

98. Guzmán, "Carta a Su Magestad," July 8, 1530, p. 358.

99. "Cuarta relación anónima," p. 98; Carranza, "Relación," p. 349.

100. "Cuarta relación anónima," p. 98.

101. Scholes and Adams, eds., *Proceso contra Tzintzicha Tangaxoan*, pp. 55-58.

102. Ibid., pp. 59-61.

103. Ibid., pp. 61-63.

104. *RM*, p. 274; Carranza, "Relación," p. 349; testimony of Martín Gómez, "Cortés

contra Matienzo y Delgadillo," p. 384. Carranza puts Ávalos before Xuárez, but since both were tortured the same day, this is not a significant change.

105. Pilar, "Relación," pp. 179-80; Pilar, "El dicho," AGI, Justicia, leg. 226; "Cuarta relación anónima," pp. 99-100.

106. RM, p. 274.

107. "Ceinos toma información, 1531," AGI, Justicia, leg. 226.

108. "Cortés contra Matienzo y Delgadillo," p. 365.

109. "Ceinos toma información, 1531," AGI, Justicia, leg. 226.

110. RM, p. 275.

111. Scholes and Adams, eds., Proceso contra Tzintzicha Tangaxoan, pp. 63-65.

112. Pilar, "Relación," p. 180; Pilar, "El dicho, 1532," AGI, Justicia, leg. 226.

113. Scholes and Adams, eds., Proceso contra Tzintzicha Tangaxoan, p. 66.

114. "Averiguación de la plata del Cazonci: el dicho de García de Pilar y otros testigos, 1532," AGI, Justicia, leg. 226.

115. Scholes and Adams, eds., Proceso contra Tzintzicha Tangaxoan, p. 8.

116. Ibid., pp. 66-67.

117. Carranza, "Relación," p. 350. The term tetuan is apparently a hispanization of tlatoani, the term for a high lord among the Aztecs.

118. Scholes and Adams, eds., Proceso contra Tzintzicha Tangaxoan, pp. 67-68.

119. Pilar, "El dicho, 1532," AGI, Justicia, leg. 226. Pascual later contradicted Pilar's statement, saying that the Cazonci "said to certain principales that they should regard how they [the Spaniards] were killing him because he had killed certain Christians and had conducted himself badly in other ways and had not served the Christians well, that they should consider that they should be good and not kill any Christians and that they should serve them well; otherwise they [the Spaniards] would do to them as they were doing to him" ("Probanza contra Pilar, 1532," AGI, Justicia, leg. 229). At the time of this statement, however, Pascual was still under the control of Guzmán, who took the testimony specifically to contradict Pilar's statement. Pascual later flatly contradicted some of the testimony that he had given on this occasion, e.g., regarding Guzmán's demands for gold and silver (see above, nn. 33-34).

120. Scholes and Adams, eds., Proceso contra Tzintzicha Tangaxoan, p. 68.

121. Tello, Crónica miscelánea, Libro segundo, pp. 68-69.

122. Pilar, "Relación," p. 181; Pilar, "El dicho, 1532," AGI, Justicia, leg. 226; "Cuarta relación anónima," p. 100.

123. RM, p. 275; "Ceinos toma información, 1531," AGI, Justicia, leg. 226.

124. López de Gómara, Historia general, 2:363-64.

125. "Probanza de Nuño de Guzmán hecha en grado de suplicación, 1539," AGI, Justicia, leg. 227.

126. RM, pp. 275-76.

127. Ibid., pp. 276-77.

128. Scholes and Adams, eds., Proceso contra Tzintzicha Tangaxoan, p. 68. The published version of the trial record interprets the name of the town as Acuaro, but my reading of the manuscript is Acucio, and I judge that it refers to Cuitzeo, on the Río Santiago north of Lake Chapala, a town where Guzmán's force had a major battle with the Indians. See López-Portilla y Weber, Conquista, pp. 183-92; Guzmán, Memoria, p. 101 n. 32.

Chapter 12

1. Scholes and Adams, eds., *Proceso contra Tzintzicha Tangaxoan*, p. 22.
2. Charles Gibson, "Conquest, Capitulation, and Indian Treaties," *American Historical Review* 83 (February 1978):1-15.
3. "Probanza contra Pilar, 1532," AGI, Justicia, leg. 229.
4. Scholes and Adams, eds., *Proceso contra Tzintzicha Tangaxoan*, p. 36.
5. Ibid., p. 35.
6. Bancroft, *History of Mexico*, 2:346-47.
7. "El fiscal contra Arellano, 1532," AGI, Justicia, leg. 187, no. 1, ramo 2.
8. Guzmán, *Memoria*, p. 861.
9. Chipman, *Nuño de Guzmán*, pp. 277-78; Chipman, "New Light," pp. 347-48.
10. Nuño de Guzmán, *Testamento de Nuño Beltrán de Guzmán*. Reproducción facsimilar y transcripción paleográfica con una nota introductoria por Jorge Palomino y Cañedo y un apéndice documental. See also Nuño de Guzmán, "The Will of Nuño de Guzmán; President, Governor and Captain General of New Spain and the Province of Pánuco, 1558," trans. and ed. Donald E. Chipman, *The Americas*, 35 (October 1978):238-48.
11. "El fiscal contra Arellano, 1532," AGI, Justicia, leg. 187, no. 1, ramo 2.
12. Delfina Esmeralda López Sarrelangue, *La nobleza indígena de Pátzcuaro en el época virreinal*, pp. 167-228; RGM, 2:112-13.
13. The expression of the New Laws which seems to prohibit the exaction of personal service as a form of tribute is ". . . ni se sirvan de ellos por vía de naboría ni en otra manera alguna en poca ni en mucha cantidad, ni hayan mas de gozar de su tributo, conforme a la orden que la audiencia o gobernador diere, que la cobranza de él." (". . . nor shall they make use of them by way of an allotment of free Indian servants nor in any other manner in small or large quantity, nor are they to partake of their tribute more than the collection of it, in accord with the order which the audiencia or governor shall establish.") See "Códice de leyes y ordenanzas nueuamente hechas por su Magestad." *DII*, 16:395. A much more specific and detailed statement of the prohibition is found in a royal decree of February 22, 1549. Puga, *Provisiones*, 2:14-18.

Bibliography

Manuscript Sources

I shall not here repeat the individual citations of manuscript sources that have been used in the preparation of this work and are cited fully in the notes, but a few general words about the location and nature of these materials may be helpful.

The most important depository of documentary sources for this work is the Archivo General de Indias (AGI), Seville, Spain. Of particular value was the section of Justicia, in which are found the many lawsuits over encomiendas that have supplied much information concerning the early development of the system of encomiendas in Michoacán. Of special importance was the accumulation of lawsuits incorporated into the mammoth volume of Justicia, leg. 130. The judgments of residencia of Fernando Cortés (Justicia, legs. 220-25) and of Nuño de Guzmán as president of the First Audiencia of New Spain (Justicia, legs. 226-29) also supplied data of primary importance concerning relations between Michoacán and Mexico. For the activities of individual conquerors, the bundles of relations of merits and services in the sections of Patronato and México were particularly enlightening. The section of Contaduría also supplied some important data from the royal treasury records.

In the Archivo General de la Nación (AGN), Mexico City, the most important section for this work was Hospital de Jesús. Because it consists of the archive of the Marquesado del Valle, it includes important documentation on Cortés' interests in Michoacán during the 1520s. The trial of Gonzalo Gómez in the section of Inquisición contributed insights into the social and religious history of the period.

The version of Juan de Ortega's tribute assessment from the Colección Gómez de Orozco of the Archivo Histórico of the Instituto Nacional de Antropología e Historia helped to clarify passages in that important document.

The John Carter Brown Library in Providence, Rhode Island, was especially helpful for linguistic materials, notably the sixteenth-century manuscript Tarascan dictionary and the rare sixteenth-century edition of Lagunas's grammar and dictionary.

Published Materials

Among published materials a few items must be singled out as being of primary importance. For the native side of the story we have the *Relación de las ceremonias y ritos y población y gobierno de los indios de la provincia de Michoacán*, compiled in 1540-41, probably by Fray Jerónimo de Alcalá, from narratives of the native priests and nobles. Fray Jerónimo, a Franciscan priest, was active between 1538 and 1541 in the region of Tzintzuntzan and Pátzcuaro. He is referred to by the Franciscan chronicler Muñoz as "the first who wrote and knew the language of Michoacán," and the Tarascan nobleman Don Pedro Guaca spoke of him as a "religious . . . who composed the Tarascan language." These qualifications lend considerable probability to the judgment that he was the one who compiled the *Relación* (see my article on Fray Jerónimo, listed below). The first two parts of the *Relación* record the Tarascan priestly tradition regarding their pre-Spanish culture and history (only one folio of the first part is extant); the third part describes the events of the Spanish conquest and the immediate post-Conquest period as seen through the eyes of the Tarascan nobleman Don Pedro Cuinierángari, a close associate and adoptive brother of the Cazonci, who also served as native governor of Michoacán during the 1530s. The *Relación* was first published in 1869 by Florencio Janer in *Colección de documentos inéditos para la historia de España*, series 1a, 113 vols. (Madrid, 1842-95), vol. 53, and was reprinted in 1875. A second edition appeared in Morelia in 1903, with an introduction by Manuel Martínez Solórzano. It was based on a comparison of the Madrid edition with the nineteenth-century manuscript copy of the *Relación* in the Peter Force Collection of the Library of Congress, Washington, D.C. Neither of these editions was completely adequate, but the defect was remedied in 1956 with the publication of a monumental edition in Madrid, which incorporated a facsimile reproduction of the manuscript from the Library of the Escorial. A reprint of the facsimile reproduction and transcription of the edition of 1956 appeared in Morelia in 1977. The latest edition, issued in Morelia in 1980, contains a new transcription of the text, introduction, and notes by Francisco Miranda Godínez. The paintings of the original are reproduced in colored prints made from photographs of the manuscript. An English translation, by Eugene R. Craine and Reginald C. Reindorp, appeared in 1970. It was based on the Morelia edition of 1903, even though the much better Madrid edition of 1956 had been available for more than a decade.

Published materials for the Spanish side of the story of the first contacts and the Conquest are limited mainly to the scanty information afforded by Cortés's "Third Letter of Relation," dated May 15, 1522, and "Fourth Letter of Relation," October 15, 1524, and to the somewhat fanciful narrative preserved in Antonio de Herrera y Tordesillas's *Historia general de los hechos de los castellanos en las islas y tierra firme del mar océano*, dec. 3, lib. 3, caps. 3-8, 9, 17. It is now evident that chapters 3-8 of this narrative are merely a slightly edited version of Francisco Cervantes de Salazar's *Crónica de la Nueva España*, lib. 6, caps. 13-27, written in the 1550s. It is remarkable that, although Cervantes de Salazar's *Crónica* has been in print since 1914, little attention has been given to it as Herrera's source. Manuel Toussaint, writing his work on Pátzcuaro in 1942, was still speculating on the copious documentation that Herrera must have had before him regarding Michoacán.

For the founding of the Franciscan missions in Michoacán, the source most frequently cited is the *Crónica de Michoacán*, by Fray Pablo Beaumont. His work, written in the early eighteenth century, drew together that of his Franciscan predecessors, Gonzaga, Mendieta, Torquemada, La Rea, and Espinosa, and also utilized certain unpublished sources of both Spanish and native origin.

Of greatest importance for the closing period of the Cazonci's life is the *Proceso contra Tzintzicha Tangaxoan, el Caltzontzin, formado por Nuño de Guzmán, año de 1530*, published in 1952 by France V. Scholes and Eleanor B. Adams. With this publication nearly all of what had been previously written about the death of the Cazonci became out of date.

Aguayo Spencer, Rafael, ed. *Vasco de Quiroga: documentos*. México, 1939.
Bancroft, Hubert Howe. *History of Mexico*. 6 vols. San Francisco, 1883-88.
Barlow, Robert H. *The Extent of the Empire of the Culhua Mexica*. Berkeley, Calif., 1949.
Beaumont, Pablo, O.F.M. *Crónica de Michoacán*. 3 vols. México, 1932.
Brand, Donald D. "An Historical Sketch of Geography and Anthropology in the Tarascan Region: Part I." *New Mexico Anthropologist* 6-7 (1943):37-108.
——— et al. *Coalcomán and Motines del Oro, an Ex-Distrito of Michoacán, Mexico*. The Hague, 1960.
Bravo Ugarte, José, S.J. *Historia de México*. Vol. 2: *La Nueva España*. 3d ed., rev. México, 1952.
———. *Historia sucinta de Michoacán*. 3 vols. México, 1962-64.
Carrasco Pizana, Pedro. *Los Otomíes: cultura e historia prehispánica de los pueblos mesoamericanos de habla otomiana*. México, 1950.
Casas, Bartolomé de las. *Apologética Historia*. In *Obras escogidas*, vol. 4. Madrid, 1958.

Caso, Alfonso, and Jorge A. Vivó, eds. *México prehispánico*. México, 1946.
Cervantes de Salazar, Francisco. *Crónica de la Nueva España*. Ed. M. Magallón. Madrid, 1914.
———. *Crónica de la Nueva España*. Ed. Francisco del Paso y Troncoso. Vol. 1, Madrid, 1914; Vols. 2–3, México, 1936.
Chamberlain, Robert S. *The Conquest and Colonization of Honduras*. Washington, 1953.
———. "Two Unpublished Documents of Hernán Cortés and New Spain, 1519 and 1524." *Hispanic American Historical Review* 18 (1938):514–25.
Chipman, Donald E. "New Light on the Career of Nuño de Guzmán." *The Americas* 19 (1963):341–48.
———. *Nuño de Guzmán and the Province of Pánuco in New Spain, 1518–1533*. Glendale, Calif., 1967.
The Chronicles of Michoacán. Trans. and ed. Eugene R. Craine and Reginald C. Reindorp. Norman, Okla., 1970.
Codex Mendoza. Ed. Kurt Ross. Fribourg, 1978.
Colección de documentos inéditos relativos al descubrimiento, conquista y organización de las antiguas posesiones españoles de América y Oceania. 42 vols. Madrid, 1864–84.
Colección de documentos inéditos relativos al descubrimiento, conquista y organización de las antiguas posesiones españoles de Ultramar. 25 vols. Madrid, 1885–1932.
Colección de documentos para la historia de España. 112 vols. Madrid, 1842–95.
Corona Núñez, José. *Mitologia tarasca*. México, 1957.
Cortés, Fernando. *Cartas y otros documentos de Hernán Cortés*. Ed. Mariano Cuevas, S. J. Seville, 1915.
———. *Cartas y relaciones de Hernán Cortés al Emperador Carlos V*. Ed. Pascual de Gayangos. Paris, 1866.
———. *Cartas de relación*. Ed. Manuel Alcalá. México, 1975.
Cuevas, Mariano, S. J. *Historia de la Iglesia en México*. 5 vols. Tlalpam, D. F., and El Paso, Texas, 1921–28.
Díaz del Castillo, Bernal. *Historia verdadera de la conquista de la Nueva España*. Ed. Joaquín Ramírez Cabañas. 2 vols. México, 1968.
Espinosa, Isidro Félix de. *Crónica de la Provincia Franciscana de los Apóstoles San Pedro y San Pablo de Michoacán*. Ed. Nicolás León and José Ignacio Dávila Garibi. México, 1945.
Fernández del Castillo, Francisco, ed. *Tres conquistadores y pobladores de la Nueva España, Cristóbal Millán de Gamboa, Andrés Tapia, Jerónimo López*. México, 1927.
García Alcaraz, Agustín. "Estratificación social entre los tarascos prehispánicos," in: Pedro Carrasco et al. *Estratificación social en la Mesoamérica prehispánica*. México, 1976. Pp. 221–44.

García Icazbalceta, Joaquín. *Don Fray Juan de Zumárraga.* Ed. Rafael Aguayo Spencer and Antonio Castro Leal. México, 1947.
Gibson, Charles. "Conquest, Capitulation, and Indian Treaties." *American Historical Review* 83 (1978):1–15.
Gilberti, Maturino, O.F.M. *Diccionario de la lengua tarasca o de Michoacán.* Nota preliminar de José Corona Núñez. Morelia, 1975 (facsimile of the edition of México, 1902).
Gonzaga, Francisco, O.F.M. *De origine Seraphicae Religionis.* Rome, 1587.
Gorenstein, Shirley, ed. *The Tarascan Frontier: The Acámbaro Focus.* Troy, N.Y., 1976.
————, and Helen Perlstein Pollard. *The Development of the Protohistoric Tarascan State: Report to the National Science Foundation and the National Endowment for the Humanities.* Troy, N.Y., 1980.
————, and ————. *The Tarascan Civilization: A Late Prehispanic Cultural System.* Vanderbilt University Publications in Anthropology, no. 28. Nashville, Tenn., 1983.
Guzmán, Nuño de. *Memoria de los servicios que había hecho Nuño de Guzmán desde que fue nombrado gobernador de Pánuco en 1525.* Ed. Manuel Carrera Stampa. México, 1955.
————. *Testamento de Nuño Beltrán de Guzmán.* Ed. Jorge Palomino y Cañedo. México, 1973.
————. "The Will of Nuño de Guzmán; President, Governor and Captain General of New Spain and the Province of Pánuco, 1558." Trans. and ed. Donald E. Chipman. *The Americas* 35 (1978):238–48.
The Harkness Collection in the Library of Congress, Manuscripts Concerning Mexico: A Guide. With selected transcriptions and translations by J. Benedict Warren. Washington, D. C., 1974.
Herrejón Peredo, Carlos. "La pugna entre mexicas y tarascos." *Cuadernos de Historia* (Universidad Autónoma del Estado de México) 1 (1978):9–47.
Herrera y Tordesillas, Antonio de. *Historia general de los hechos de los castellanos en las islas y tierra firme del Mar Océano.* 4 vols. Madrid, 1730.
Ixtlilxochitl, Fernando de Alva. *Obras históricas de Don Fernando de Alva Ixtlilxochitl.* Ed. Alfredo Chavero. 2 vols. México, 1891–92.
"Juicio seguido por Hernán Cortés con los Lics. Matienzo y Delgadillo, año 1531." *Boletin del Archivo General de la Nación* 9 (1938):339–407.
Lagunas, Juan Baptista de, O.F.M. *Arte y dictionario: con otras obras en lengua michuacana.* Introduction by J. Benedict Warren. Morelia, 1983 (facsimile of the edition of México, 1574, with an added sequential pagination throughout).
León, Nicolás. "Fr. Maturino Gilberti y sus escritos inéditos." *Anales del Museo Michoacano* 2 (1889):133–34.
————. *El Ylmo Señor Don Vasco de Quiroga, primer obispo de Michoacán.*

México, 1903.

Libro de las tasaciones de pueblos en Nueva España, siglo xvi. México, 1952.

López de Gómara, Francisco. *Historia de la conquista de México.* Ed. Joaquín Ramírez Cabañas. 2 vols. México, 1943.

——. *Historia general de las Indias "Hispania Vitrix" cuva segunda parte corresponde a la Conquista de Méjico.* Ed. Pilar Guibelalde and Emiliano M. Aguilera. 2 vols. Barcelona, 1965.

López Portillo y Weber, José. *La conquista de la Nueva Galicia.* México, 1936.

López Sarrelangue, Delfina E. *La nobleza indigena de Pátzcuaro en la época virreinal.* México, 1965.

Marquina, Ignacio. *Arquitectura prehispánica.* México, 1964.

Mendieta, Jerónimo de, O.F.M. *Historia eclesiástica indiana.* México, 1876.

Mexico (City) Cabildo. *Actas de cabildo de la ciudad de México.* Ed. Ignacio Bejarano. 50 vols. México, 1889–1916.

Millares Carlo, Agustín, and J. Ignacio Mantecón, eds. *Indice y extractos de los protocolos del Archivo de Notarias de México, D.F.* 2 vols. México, 1945–1946.

Motolinía, Toribio, O.F.M. *Memoriales, o libro de las cosas de Nueva España y de los naturales de ella.* Ed. Edmundo O'Gorman. México, 1971.

——. *Motolinia's History of the Indians of New Spain.* Trans. and ed. Francis Borgia Steck, O.F.M. Washington, D.C., 1951.

Mudd, Rosemary. "The Hallucinogens of Meso-America: An Ethnohistorical Survey." Master's Thesis, University of New Mexico, 1966.

Muñoz, Diego, O.F.M. "Descripción de la Provincia de los Apóstoles San Pedro y San Pablo en las Indias de la Nueva España," pp. 384–424. In: Anastasio López, "Misiones o doctrinas de Michoacán y Jalisco (Méjico) en el siglo XVI, 1525-1585." *Archivo Ibero-Americano* 18 (1922):341-425.

"Noticias para la historia del Antiguo Colegio de la Compañía de Jesús de Michoacán." *Boletin del Archivo General de la Nación* 10 (1939):24-106, 411.

Oroz, Pedro, O.F.M. *The Oroz Codex.* Trans. and ed. Angelico Chavez, O.F.M. Washington, D.C., 1972.

Orozco y Berra, Manuel. *Historia de la dominación española en México.* 4 vols. México, 1938.

Osborne, Carolyn Miles. "An Ethnohistorical Study of Michoacán in the Sixteenth, Seventeenth and Eighteenth Centuries." Master's thesis, University of New Mexico, 1941.

Oviedo y Valdés, Gonzalo Fernández de. *Historia general y natural de las Indias.* 5 vols. Madrid, 1959.

Paredes Martínez, Carlos Salvador. "El tributo indígena en la región del Lago de Pátzcuaro, siglo XVI." Tesis de licenciatura, Universidad Nacional Autónoma de México, 1976.

Paso y Troncoso, Francisco del, ed. *Epistolario de Nueva España.* 16 vols. México, 1939-42.

——, ed. *Papeles de Nueva España.* 2d ser. 7 vols. Madrid, 1905-1906.

Piñón Flores, Marcela Irais. "La tenencia de la tierra en la región de Tlazazalca-Zacapu-Huaniqueo en el siglo XVI." Tesis de licenciatura, Universidad Nacional Autónoma de México, 1976.

Plancarte, F. "Los tecos." *Anales del Museo Michoacano* 2 (1889):16-26.

Pollard, Helen Perlstein. "An Analysis of Urban Zoning and Planning at Prehispanic Tzintzuntzan." *Proceedings of the American Philosophical Society* 121 (1977):46-69.

——. "Central Places and Cities: A Consideration of the Protohistoric Tarascan State." *American Antiquity* 45 (1980):677-96.

——. "Ecological Variation and Economic Exchange in the Tarascan State." *American Ethnologist* 9 (1982):250-68.

——. "Prehispanic Urbanism at Tzintzuntzan, Michoacán." Ph.D. dissertation, Columbia University, 1972 (available through University Microfilms, Ann Arobr, Mich.).

——, and Shirley Gorenstein. "Agrarian Potential, Population, and the Tarascan State." *Science* 209 (1980):274-77.

Puga, Vasco de. *Provisiones, cédulas, instrucciones de su Magestad.* 2 vols. México, 1878.

Rea, Alonso de la. *Crónica de la Orden de N.S. Padre San Francisco, provincia de San Pedro y San Pablo de Mechoacán en la Nueva España.* Querétaro, 1945.

Relación breve y verdadera de algunas cosas de las muchas que sucedieron al Padre Fray Alonso Ponce en las provincias de la Nueva España, escrita por dos religiosos sus compañeros. 2 vols. Madrid, 1873.

Relación de las ceremonias y ritos y población y gobierno de los indios de la provincia de Michoacán. [RM.] Spanish editions: Madrid, 1869; Morelia, 1903; Madrid, 1956; Morelia, 1977; Morelia, 1980. The Madrid edition of 1956, edited by José Tudela, has been used for citations in this book. (English translation: *The Chronicles of Michoacán.* Trans. and ed., Eugene R. Craine and Reginald C. Reindorp. Norman, Okla., 1970.)

Relación de los obispados de Tlaxcala, Michoacán, Oaxaca y otros lugares en el siglo XVI. Ed. Luis García Pimentel. México, 1904.

Relaciones goegráficas de la diócesis de Michoacán, 1579-1580. Ed. José Corona Núñez. Guadalajara, 1958.

Ricard, Robert. *The Spiritual Conquest of Mexico: An Essay on the Apostolate and the Evangelizing Methods of the Mendicant Orders in New Spain: 1523-1572.* Berkeley,Calif., 1966.

Riley, G. Micheal. *Fernando Cortés and the Marquesado in Morelos, 1522-1547.* Albuquerque, N.Mex., 1973.

Rojas González, Fernando. "Los tarascos en la época precolonial," In: Lucio Mendieta y Núñez, ed. *Los tarascos*. México, 1940.

Romero Flores, Jesús. *Historia de Michoacán*. 2 vols. México, 1946.

Rubín de la Borbolla, Daniel. "Orfebrería tarasca." *Cuadernos Americanos* 3 (1944):125-38.

Sahagún, Bernardino de, O.F.M. *Historia general de las cosas de Nueva España*. 5 vols. México, 1938.

Sauer, Carl O. *Colima of New Spain in the Sixteenth Century*. Berkeley, Calif., 1948.

Scholes, France V., and Eleanor B. Adams, eds. *Proceso contra Tzintzicha Tangaxoan el Caltzontzin, formado por Nuño de Guzmán, año de 1530*. México, 1952.

————, eds. *Relación de las encomiendas de indios hechas en Nueva España a los conquistadores y pobladores de ella, año de 1564*. México, 1955.

Schöndube Baumbach, Otto. *Tamazula-Tuxpan-Zapotlan, pueblos de la frontera septentrional de la antigua Colima: Tesis*. 2 vols. México, 1973-74.

Simpson, Lesley Byrd. *The Encomienda in New Spain: The Beginning of Spanish Mexico*. Berkeley, Calif., 1952.

Stanislawski, Dan. "Tarascan Political Geography." *American Anthropologist* 49 (1947):46-55.

Swadish, Maurice. *Términos de parentesco comunes entre tarasco y zuñi*. México, 1957.

Tello, Antonio, O.F.M. *Libro segundo de la crónica miscelánea*. Ed. José López Portillo y Rojas. Guadalajara, 1942.

————. *Crónica miscelánea de la Sancta Provincia de Xalisco*. Libro 3. Ed. José Cornejo Franco. Guadalajara, 1942.

Torquemada, Juan de. *Monarquía indiana*. 3 vols. México, 1943-44.

Toussaint, Manuel. *La conquista de Pánuco*. México, 1948.

————. *Pátzcuaro*. México, 1952.

Vaillant, George C. *Aztecs of Mexico: Origin, Rise, and Fall of the Aztec Nation*. Rev. by Suzannah B. Vaillant. Baltimore, Md., 1965.

Valadés, Diego. *Rhetorica Christiana ad concionandi et orandi usum accommodata utriusque facultatis exemplis suo loco insertisque quidam ex indorum maxime deprompta sunt historiis inde praeter doctrinam suam quoque delectatio comparabitur*. Perusia, 1579.

Wagner, Henry R. *The Rise of Fernando Cortés*. [Los Angeles], 1944.

Warren, Fintan B. [i.e., J. Benedict]. "The Caravajal Visitation: First Spanish Survey of Michoacán." *The Americas* 19 (1962-63):404-12.

Warren, J. Benedict. *La conquista de Michoacán, 1521-1530*. Morelia, 1977.

————. "Fray Jerónimo de Alcalá: Author of the *Relación de Michoacán?*" *The Americas* 27 (1970-71):306-27.

———— [Fintan B. Warren]. *Vasco de Quiroga and His Pueblo-Hospitals of Santa*

Fe. Washington, D.C., 1963. (Spanish version, with some revision and a documentary appendix: *Vasco de Quiroga y sus hospitales-pueblo de Santa Fe.* Morelia, 1977.)

————, ed. "Minas de cobre de Michoacán." *Anales del Museo Michoacano.* 2a época, 6 (1968):35–52.

West, Robert C. *Cultural Geography of the Modern Tarascan Area.* Washington, D.C., 1948. Reprint: Westport, Conn., 1973.

Wright, Ione Stuessy. *Voyages of Alvaro de Saavedra Cerón, 1527–1529.* Coral Gables, Fla., 1951.

Zavala, Silvio. *La encomienda indiana.* Madrid, 1955.

————. *Los esclavos indios en Nueva España.* México, 1967.

————. "Nuño de Guzmán y la esclavitud de los indios." *Historia Mexicana* 1 (1952):410–28.

Index

The place names from Appendix A are not included in the index except for the names of the five principal towns.

337

Norman Oklahoma :-

1-405-555 1212 .-